Cosmic History Chronicles

Volume I

Book of the Throne

The Law of Time and the Reformulation of the Human Mind

Time and Cosmos: Cosmos the Absolute Pole

Transmitted by Valum Votan—Jose Arguelles
Received by Red Queen—Stephanie South
"We are but the secretaries, the authors are in Eternity"

Blue Crystal Storm First Ray: Will of God

Book of the Throne: Cosmic History Chronicles Volume I
Copyright © Galactic Research Institute

Law of Time Press—Blue Crystal Storm Year (2004)

All rights reserved by the Galactic Masters.

ISBN 978-0-9767759-8-0
www.lawoftime.org

Original Graphics by Valum Votan — Jose Arguelles, Kin 11
Graphic Design by Jacob Wyatt, Kin 201
Book Design & Layout by Sage Waitts, Kin 154

Table of Contents

Introduction: Preparing the Reader for Cosmic History Chronicles ... v

Preface: The Philosophy of Cosmic History ... vii

Forward: Volume 1—Book of the Throne: Origins of Cosmic History ... xi

Part I
The Story

- What is Cosmic History? ... 3
- • Cosmic History, the Law of Time and the Synchronic Order ... 23
- • • The Planetary Human ... 38

Part II
Cosmic History as Systems of Knowing

- • • • Yoga/Transformation and Cosmic History ... 59
- —— Sorcerer's Whole Body Perception and Yoga ... 77
- •—— Origins and Meanings of Life – What is Cosmic Science? ... 95

Part III
New Models of Reality

- • •—— Triple Universe Model ... 119
- • • •—— Cosmology of Time – The Four Pillars ... 143
- • • • •—— Simultaneous Universe Model ... 158

Part IV
Noosphere: New Earth Consciousness

- ═══ Noosphere Defined and Made Conscious ... 175
- •═══ Multidimensional Paranormality and Cosmic Science ... 193
- • •═══ Ceremonial Magick ... 206

- • • •═══ Synthesis: Significance of Number 7 and Overview of 7 Volumes ... 229

Glossary of Key Terms ... 261

A Word About Changes in Voice

Throughout the text of the *Cosmic History Chronicles* there are numerous changes of voice. These changes of voice are an intrinsic aspect of the all encompassing dynamic of Cosmic History, which cannot be confined to a single voice such as third person singular.

Cosmic History is everything—inside, outside, microcosm, macrocosm, objective, subjective, all of us and none of us. To restrict ourselves to only the use of third person singular would be altogether limiting. Changes in voice also reflect the source of Cosmic History as a living transmission delivered from shifting dimensions. Sometimes this voice is objectively descriptive. Sometimes Cosmic History is talking to you. Sometimes it is we, the authors, or even all of us participating in the formulation of its most fundamental precepts. There is also a use of gender in multiple ways; he, she, God, wo/man, etc., to indicate an actual nonexclusivity of gender. In Cosmic History gender is comprehensive.

Introduction: Preparing the Reader for Cosmic History Chronicles

Cosmic History is a descent of the Absolute, a positive construct fitted to the Closing of the Cycle. When you first encounter Cosmic History what you are actually dealing with is a confrontation of your own unexamined assumptions about reality. Therefore it is wise when you encounter this knowledge to be able to put your mind on hold. That is to say, your conceptual mind, your mind of acquired knowledge, your mind that you have inherited from birth—you have to put this mind on hold—and then practice how to keep it there.

Through meditation you should practice stopping the mind and becoming familiar with the fact that your usual habitual thoughts arise without your even trying. And these habitual thoughts intrude as a filter on reality. It is important to see that your habitual thoughts or your concepts about reality are like phantoms that arise automatically—but they are just phantoms. It is important to realize how these phantoms can insert themselves automatically and unconsciously into the screen of your waking reality so that your behavior is actually a function of these thoughts or patterns about which you are basically unconscious. Only when you truly see this can you approach new thoughts or a new vision of reality.

In the case of Cosmic History, you are being presented with an entirely new model of reality, a new galaxy and a new method for knowing so you have to be aware of subtle issues—the nature of the mind, what is perceived and how the mind processes what is perceived. It begins with stopping the mind and realizing that the mind is constituted of an endless number of concepts and guidelines that may or may not be connected and are based on unexamined assumptions about reality. You really have to look and see what all of these assumptions might be. You have to see these and then realize that if you are going to contribute to the world model—then you have to first take yourself out of it. You have to pull the hooks of the present world model out of your own habits of thinking or ways of viewing things. Only in this way can you actually be ready to consider a new perspective or a new model of reality. Intrinsic to this is the issue of discipline and exertion. Evolution is attained through exertion. Exertion is evolution. You evolve your mind by exerting in discipline and knowing. You have to keep exerting, you don't just stop. No discipline really has its conclusion. Unless you have a clear grasp of these subtle points, it is difficult to come to a correct understanding of Cosmic History. Unless you control your mind, how can you see what reality is?

With continued effort the discipline of studying Cosmic History begins to have a cumulative qualitative effect that increasingly elevates your everyday consciousness into a fourth-dimensional perception of reality. In this reality everything seems dreamlike and made out of space—and the cultivation of cosmic perceptions and cosmic sensations occur much more easily. This process itself is the effect of Cosmic History. By this we mean that the words or the phrase "Cosmic History" refers to a type of mental experience, a quality or state of mind of the cosmic field of perception.

These considerations are merely to help you get to a point where you are able to understand

and appreciate that we are dealing with a radically "newer" form of reality than has yet been presented to the human species. It is important to know how to approach the new information templates of Cosmic History in a receptive way so they can impress and imprint you.

Preface: The Philosophy of Cosmic History

"But why should the operations of nature be changed? There may be a deeper philosophy than we dream of—a philosophy that discovers the secrets of nature, but does not alter, by penetrating them, its course." —Bulwer

The philosophy of Cosmic History is that the universe exists as the vehicle for the involution and evolution of the soul as a single all unifying circuit of all evolving divine consciousness regulated by the Law of Time. From this point of view, Cosmic History represents a complete whole system of thought, as well as a complete whole field perception of reality and the universe; therefore a philosophy is implicit, philosophy meaning an understanding of the actual nature of reality, which is assumed by the principle of Cosmic History.

Cosmic History is the discourse of the soul in its stages of involution and in its stages of evolution. Involution is the process of going into further densification, and evolution is the process of release from the densification. Involution of the soul can also be understood as the creation of matter. The more that matter is created, the more it proliferates in all of its infinite variety of forms throughout this universe and all universes. All forms of matter exist as manifestations of the involution of the soul. The external aspect of matter represents the internal quality of soul. In other words, when you look at a flower or a crystal you see an expression of a quality of soul that has taken that particular external manifestation.

To think that there is soul in a flower or crystal is due to the involution and evolution of soul as a single all unifying circuit. We might think of this circuit as highly multiple with many different threads inside of it. Imagine that this all unifying circuit disperses itself invisibly through all the different forms of matter and life that exist in the universe. This circuit symbolizes the all evolving divine consciousness.

So we have the principle of the soul, which can be understood as the living breath of the thought of God that manifests in a particular form or form process. In this way, the crystal or flower represents a particular manifestation of what we might crudely call a thought or thoughtform of God. There is no other way to explain why a crystal is so exquisite—yet many people think: "But a crystal is just dead matter—it doesn't have any feelings." It may be true that a crystal does not have the quality of sentiency that vegetable matter or plants have, but it does have its own dazzling structure and form, along with its intrinsic, internal powers of transduction.

It is this intrinsic potentiality of energy transduction, coupled with its form, that constitutes the soul of the crystal. In this way, soul is the primal divine thought of God that goes into a manifest form, giving that form its structure, purpose and function. Even a machine can be said to possess soul, insofar as it has placed into it thought, intention, function and purpose. When it's turned on, you like it and you pet it and you say it's nice. If it's a useful machine, you don't want it to stop. So we see that everything is permeated by this all unifying circuit evolved by divine consciousness.

The universe is a complete, complex whole thought of God consisting of infinite numbers of forms, processes and structures, all of which exist for the involution and evolution of the soul from nothingness into density and from density into light. In the nothingness there is only the void. Then God fills that void with a thought. The thought then becomes a manifestation and in that process of manifestation, which the Law of Time defines as the evolution of time as consciousness, the thought goes through the stages of preconscious and instinctual unconscious and then into types of more evolved unconscious, until finally the thought reaches a level of consciousness and continuing consciousness. This final stage is, properly speaking, the stage of evolution. In some sense you could say it is all evolution, but it is actually broken down into these two processes of involution and evolution.

The soul is what moves through the process of involution into matter and evolution out of matter in the universe. Consciousness is what evolves the soul from different states—from preconscious to unconscious up to super consciousness and then subliminal and hyperorganic consciousness—consciousness that is beyond any consideration of mind. Sri Aurobindo says that even the very concept of mind is only a function of ignorance, of some lower state of consciousness seeking knowledge. Mind is only a relative transition in the evolution of the whole dynamic of consciousness. At one point consciousness actually becomes free from mind—that is the subliminal dynamic of consciousness—therefore it goes beyond mind. This is the ultimate reach of consciousness.

When you look at who we are, we are actually just these tiny little vessels of highly vibrant nervous systems that represent a pinpoint pivot between involution and evolution of soul, which is being evolved by divine consciousness and regulated by the Law of Time. Everything that exists has a precise term and span. Everything comes into being and mutates at precise moments in a synchronized timing process, which is governed completely by the Law of Time.

The process of going from involution to evolution accelerates with increased consciousness of the Law of Time. We are also talking about the acceleration of going from more dense states to less dense states of matter. This brings in a whole host and range of transmutations in the biomolecular process of life that we are undergoing right now. In this process, there is a tendency, for instance, of a vegetarian diet, then a raw food diet, ultimately leading to breatharianism. This corresponds to the fact that consciousness is evolving the soul back into its less dense states and ultimately when the soul is released altogether from dense states you reach the point of maximum superconsciousness—going from hyperorganic into totally subliminal consciousness, or consciousness without a body.

This is a description of the philosophy of Cosmic History. We can only learn about Cosmic History because the Law of Time became conscious. Only when the Law of Time became conscious could the perception of reality be dynamically and dramatically changed. This is a function of actual living human beings becoming conscious through a whole prophetic regimen in the unfolding of the Divine Plan. When the Law of Time made its agent or discoverer increasingly self conscious, that is to say conscious of himself as a vehicle of transmission or a terton (hidden treasure finder), then that necessitated the object of transmission, which is the apprentice or the Red Queen. This principle of binary transmission, then, had to be brought into conscious manifestation. This is important to communicate since we are dealing with a dual theme. First is the philosophy of Cosmic History, and second, is the instrumentation of the process of transmission by which Cosmic History becomes known on this planet at this time. Through the living agents, the philosophy of Cosmic History brings together the principle of the evolution of the soul, the evolution of consciousness and the Law of Time. As a vehicle for involution and evolution, the universe itself becomes that which goes from unconscious to conscious to superconscious. Given this philosophy, Cosmic History is the way of recording and articulating that process by means of the conduits divinely predisposed to accommodate its manifestation.

The philosophy of Cosmic History can also be described as the redemption of the world soul from the terror of profane history. This brings us to a level of a relative assumption and application—that Cosmic History would not exist or have come into being if there were not a need for the world soul to be redeemed from the terror of profane history. If there were no need of redemption, then there would be no need of Cosmic History. But the fact is that the world soul on this particular planet is enmeshed in the terror of profane history.

On the one hand, the terror of profane history is merely the maximum point of densification that the involution of the soul experiences prior to being sprung fully into its process of evolution. When the soul's involution into matter approaches a point where the matter itself is becoming more complex, more intense and denser, then the soul involved in that matter increasingly experiences what we refer to as the process of forgetting.

It is the process of forgetting that creates ignorance which, in turn, creates the propensity to rely on illusory beliefs, conjecture, or what has gone before without questioning. This results in the creation of all sorts of dogmatic, unexamined beliefs. All of these summarized or taken together create profane history, which is the description of an illusory universe unconsciously extruded from the mind into the mass of humanity (who are so enmeshed in matter that they do not even know it). Not knowing of their densification, the mass of humanity merely reflects back an increasingly profane history, which is actually a history of terror.

This is why the present world model describes a "violent" universe and also why we have "chaos" theories, the theory of entropy, and the doctrine of inexorability in terms of deregulated free market economics. These are all functions of the terror of profane history. What creates "terror" is unexamined points of view and the inability for the humans to examine themselves and their relentless and unconscious addiction to their own relativistic belief systems. This is actually a complete abdication of freedom.

Humans are so enmeshed in profane history or historical materialism that they think they have to keep these belief systems going. They think: "Oh we have this fertilizer factory now" or "We have genetic modification now," or "We have clocks, computers, guns and bombs now, so we must keep it all going, we can't possibly turn back the clock." These are all expressions of abdication of freedom or even denial of freedom. Why can't we just stop?! Why can't we just give it all up and look at the stars instead? Why can't we say that this is leading nowhere? This is why Cosmic History is utterly necessary.

Profane history is actually the record and philosophy of historical materialism. When the historical materialism becomes a planetary phenomenon it becomes terrifying. When it becomes a dominant planetary phenomenon, then actually no other voice is really allowed authority or ultimate power if it is not a voice that reflects, to some degree or another, the unrelenting force of historical materialism. This is what creates what we call terror. Terrorism itself is a reflex response to the tyrannical dominance of historical materialism and its choking effect on the world soul.

It is at this point that the prophetic release emerges. The Law of Time and Cosmic History manifest the Galactic Mayan mind lineage and include the prophetic codes and keys for release at this moment in time, when the need has peaked for a radically alternative vision to the one currently dominating the world mind and soul. The role and function of the transmitter and receiver of Cosmic History is to communicate the prophetic voice in a larger context (which is the context of the Law of Time). This voice is all but lost in the profane vision of historical materialism. Through the rapid spread of the Thirteen Moon calendar, the larger context of the Law of Time begins to breathe into the highly corrupted world body and slough off the dead world soul to reveal the new shimmering planetary human.

The philosophy of Cosmic History is so grand, so simple and so universal that whatever is spiritually true will be reshaped and integrated into its philosophy. Cosmic History is the force bringing to light the redemption of the world soul.

As the contents of the cosmic mind that remain universal and constant for all levels of intelligence, Cosmic History is for all beings and for all capacities. It changes only according to the capacity of perception. So it may appear different to a dog or to a Pleiadean than it appears to you, but it is still the same cosmos that is being perceived or apprehended by the different beings and levels of intelligence. The philosophy of Cosmic History provides a criterion by which you can examine your own beliefs or philosophies of spirituality and religion and see how they fit in. You can then see the contrast between Cosmic History and profane history. The qualification of profane history as a form of terror throws light on the purpose and the reason for Cosmic History. This is the pith teaching on the philosophy of Cosmic History.

Forward: Origins of Cosmic History

Cosmic History—a vast theme. But why seven volumes? Because we are now a species in mutation headed for cosmic consciousness, and everything must be experienced anew.

The evolutionary vehicle of our life on Earth is shifting gears. We are going from the Space Age to the New Time. Everything must be radically reenvisioned. The basis in human thought for this shift is the Law of Time. Such a discovery as the Law of Time occurs but once every several millennia. To fully grasp all of the implications of the Law of Time for the next stage of our evolution, that is why there are seven volumes to the *Cosmic History Chronicles*.

We must understand that, first of all, Cosmic History is a point of view. It is not just a systematic rendition of knowledge or history or science, but also a completely cosmic perspective that views the whole of mind and reality from a highly polished galactic lens, hence: The *Book of the Throne*. All earthly thrones are based on the celestial archetype of the Divine Throne, the position of the Omnipotent Creator on the metaphorical seventh day of creation. This establishes Cosmic History as a divine and sacred point of view. The *Cosmic History Chronicles* define the spiritual dimension of an order of reality, which hierarchically extends through a series of dimensions.

From the perspective of Cosmic History, evolution is not just genetic mutation but a descent of the divine that quickens the material of life in a new and highly spiritual orientation. The conjunction of genetic mutation and the descent of the divine creates a new epoch of planetary consciousness—the noosphere. When we grasp this point then we can fully appreciate that we are evolving from the condition of homo sapiens to homo noosphericus. The noosphere, Earth's mental sheathe, is the repository of the reformulation of human knowledge necessitated by the discovery of the Law of Time.

When we consider the magnitude of the Law of Time and the vast scope of the *Cosmic History Chronicles*, we must ask: How did this come about? Where did such a conception as the reformulation of the human mind come from?

All genuine renewal and reformation of knowledge comes from a living revelation, a living transmission that proceeds from a higher archetypal stage and then is stepped down into the dimension of consciousness where it seizes a particular human agency. In the case of the *Cosmic History Chronicles*, this "human agency" is an archetypal pair in which one agent transmits and the other receives, according to a specific purpose and function in a very precise moment in time. To understand the *Cosmic History Chronicles*, it is important to understand its origins through these two agents. Once we understand how the *Cosmic History Chronicles* came about, then we will be able to better appreciate the point of view that is presented in the *Book of the Throne* and the reason for the subsequent six volumes that follow.

Book of the Throne

Cosmic History is the evolutionary template of noospheric wholeness that is necessary for the reformulation of the human mind and knowledge base at the end of the cycle, which is the climax of matter. What we refer to as human history is really the history of how materialism takes over human consciousness. Cosmic History, then, is the necessary transmaterialist point of view, which from a noospheric perspective, is the actual evolutionary antidote and requisite for going beyond this point. Materialism will not be changed by destroying factories or radio and television stations. The only way to change materialism is by deconstructing the entire belief system that created it and replacing it with another belief system, which is Cosmic History.

Cosmic History is rooted in the *synchronic order*, the matrix of fourth-dimensional time that synchronizes all aspects of third-dimensional physical plane reality. In the synchronic order lies the radial matrix that is present in the structure of the noosphere (Earth's thinking layer) and the psi bank regulator (mechanism of the noosphere that registers fourth-dimensional time). This means that the whole of Cosmic History is embedded in the noosphere. You can talk to people about this, but it must be exemplified for them to understand.

The human originators and archetypal exemplars of Cosmic History are Votan and Red Queen. Archetypes are primordial form patterns; cosmic structures, which transform the humans seized by them into characters whose presence transports those receptive to them into actors of a divine drama. By 2012, the human beings will each remember that they are actors in this divine drama, which is entitled, "The Closing of the Cycle and the Regeneration of the World Soul." The human species only understands by example of what another human being exemplifies; therefore Cosmic History must be embedded in human types.

What is being exemplified by Votan and Red Queen is a principle of Galactic Mayan mind transmission. It is of utmost importance to understand that this fundamental shift and reformulation of human knowledge is actually something that can be transmitted from one human being to another. Therefore, it can become part of the acquired human knowledge base. But what are the roots of knowledge?

There are two root types of knowledge: Revealed knowledge and acquired knowledge. Revealed knowledge can be anything from profound spiritual revelations, right down to Isaac Newton having the principle of gravity revealed to him by watching an apple fall to the ground. Newton didn't acquire this knowledge; it was revealed to him through his intuition by divine command. At that point, his mind was opened. Once he formulated the experience it became acquired knowledge.

In Cosmic History, we are dealing with revealed knowledge—it is revealed through one medium and is then transmitted to another medium. Both come to embody the knowledge and then transmit it. So we see the process of going from revealed knowledge to acquired knowledge—from an absolutely intuitive base and structure, which is the resonance of a particular human mind with the psi bank regulators and the noosphere, to the actual embodiment of the structural principles within the being.

The first stage of the Cosmic History program was imploded and transferred through Votan (otherwise known as the Closer of the Cycle) beginning in 1983 with the writing of *Earth Ascending, an Illustrated Treatise on the Law Governing Whole Systems*. It is in this scientific whole systems text that the psi bank program first appears. This foundational stage of Cosmic History was then continued with Votan's subsequent work of *The Mayan Factor*, along with the entirety of the discovery of the Law of Time. These vast works form the base program of Cosmic History.

At a certain point, when it was evident to Votan that the structure of the whole system of cosmic knowing represents a principle of redemption of knowledge for the human being, the right receptacle of transmission showed up. This represents the Red Queen. She is the Red Queen because the cycle has to be renewed. Red is the color of initiation and the "Queen" represents the feminine matrix that generates or gives birth from which the new being flowers. This is why the name "Red Queen" evokes such resonance in the archetypal remembrance.

When the vehicle of the Red Queen manifested to Votan, then the dynamic of Cosmic History was set in motion. Because of the moral failings of the male-dominated historical process, the transmission of Cosmic History is engendered not from a male to a male, but from a male to a female, thus facilitating the descent from the Absolute to the relative. These two principles are not separate, but actually evoke each other and could not exist without each other. The dynamic program of Cosmic History could only come into manifestation after the two principles came into conjunction with each other.

The entire lives of the transmitter and receiver were divinely guided and prepared for the moment of the unlocking of the Cosmic History codes and keys. By its nature, the Cosmic History, as a formulation of mind and knowledge at the closing of the cycle, is such a monumental labor or task that the prepared vessels actually must be understood as being pure instruments of this process. In other words, once they came together and once the Cosmic History transmission began, both their character and lifestyles were completely rearranged in order to accommodate Cosmic History.

The principle of highest exemplification is referred to as an avatar. An avatar embodies the descent of a divine principle into a human realm so that the human who assumes an avataric role exemplifies a particular divine principle. In this sense, Cosmic History is the divine principle and Votan and Red Queen are the avataric exemplars. When you recognize who these two beings actually are, you immediately understand that you are dealing with a type of evolutionary potential of yourself.

In order to embark on such an enormous undertaking, the two exemplars of Cosmic History immediately began practicing a strict daily discipline of yoga and meditation practices that include the asanas and pranayams of Ashtanga yoga, shamatha and vipassana meditation, darshan, mantra and "Second Creation mudra exercises." They discovered that these practices all have encoded into them the stages, processes and structures of Cosmic History. These foundation practices can be understood as metalogical forms informing the being with patterns and modes of behavior, which are transhistorical. These reflections of the Absolute had to be engrained and incorporated in their beings for the exemplification of Cosmic History as the interpenetration of the Absolute into the relative.

But for the incorporation of Cosmic History into their form bodies to occur, Votan and Red Queen underwent countless inner and outer initiations which stripped them down from outmoded habitual tendencies and finely and delicately attuned them so that the only function or purpose that remained was Cosmic History. All of their emotional and astral configurations have been designed to be maximally sensitive, which is heightened by a lifestyle that tends to close out forms of mass media manipulation and media in general. This only further heightens the raw sensitive space in which each exemplar resides so that the different nuances of all of these energetic embodiments can be experienced.

Through the ongoing process of historical purification, the two vehicles of Cosmic History had to navigate through all the different programs of previous incarnations, both from this world and other worlds. This manifested as different apparent mind bombardments or incessant kind of psychic attacks or repetitious thought-forms received by each to be transmuted and transcended through the sensitivity of their purified instruments. The necessity of witnessing all programs of the cosmic unconscious was necessary to ensure that their astral and emotional bodies were completely stripped down naked.

To undergo this arduous process, the two exemplars maintained themselves as much as possible in a focused environment with highly limited external influences; so what was intrinsic to them from the amalgam of previous incarnations was all the more sensitized. Through this increased sensitivity, the two were able to recognize what types of energies were actually being expressed through them in order to connect those energies with particular historical personages or characters or even just characterizations, which all had to be thoroughly understood and transcended in order for the reformulation of the human knowledge base to occur.

The sensitivities experienced by Votan and Red Queen are all completely due to the fact that they are multiple avataric emanations. In their process, the two experienced a simultaneous development of an increasingly compassionate empathy body with the human race in its entirety, without exception and with total absolute unconditional love and acceptance of everyone and everything without losing critical judgment. (You can have compassion for everyone and at the same time you must exercise critical judgment so you are able to see clearly and administer the type of compassion required for any given being's stage of evolutionary development).

Cosmic History: Point of Origin

Since Cosmic History is the core field of universal intelligence, there is nothing that is not Cosmic History. In order for this intelligence to manifest on Earth, there must be a point of origin—Votan and Red Queen are that point of origin. They were divinely prepared in, not only their minds, but also their bodily forms. This means that what is referred to as "Cosmic History" is actually the manifestation of information that has been locked up in their bodies. Through psychoactivation of their two energy fields the information program known as Cosmic History is released.

If you could view an astral movie of the transmission process between Votan and Red Queen, you would see certain forms and structures that seem to be emanating out of Votan, but which are actually a response to the matrices of these forms and structures that are contained in Red Queen. It is a mutual process. The transmitter and receiver are one in the same. The transmitter is meant to close the cycle and the receiver is meant to open the new cycle. The two actors or agents of Cosmic History are not only playing out the dynamic of how the principle of Cosmic History is introduced into the human realm, but they are also fulfilling a prophetic function or prophetic injunction which lends to the extraordinary quality of their relation. This goes back to the root of the terms of Votan and Red Queen, which is derived from a prophecy established by the Galactic Maya in Palenque. This prophecy imbues the function and relation of Votan and Red Queen with a supernatural quality.

The role of the Cosmic History transmitter is actually that of the Closer of the Cycle, which is an avataric persona function that is assumed by the one known as Votan. This elevates the persona function of the Red Queen to an equal stature of avataric performance. The relation of the two is totally unique because it is the end of the cycle where this performance is occurring. There are many different levels, which are brought together through the interaction of their personalities, and transmuted into the unfolding, on one level, of the *Cosmic History Chronicles* and, at another level, as the ceremonial drama of the seven years of the Mystery of the Stone and the Perfection of the Human Soul 2004-2011.

The root purpose of the two different levels that are being enacted and performed by Votan and Red Queen are, at one level, for the introduction of the reformulation of the human knowledge base, and at another level, the unraveling of the mystery of life and death. This goes back to the prophetic meaning of the personas through the mystery of the tombs, which is the root of the prophecy: the tomb of Pacal Votan and the tomb of the Red Queen.

Book of the Throne

Tale of Two Tombs

The prophetic enactment of Cosmic History has its source and meaning in the two tombs of Palenque, that of Pacal Votan (AD 692) and the other of the Red Queen (AD 700?). The unique tomb of Pacal Votan, comparable only to the tomb in the Great Pyramid of Giza, was discovered June 15, 1952. The discovery was initiated in 1949 in the Temple atop the Pyramid of Inscriptions, when archaeologist Alberto Ruz cleared a large pile of rubble and noticed a tile tube sticking up from the ground. This tube, it was discovered, ran all the way from the tomb at the bottom of the Temple of the Inscriptions, up the side of the stairs, all the way to the floor of the temple on top. This tube, which Ruz called a "psychoduct", came to be known as TELEKTONON, or Earth Spirit Speaking Tube.

In the chamber where the tomb is found are sculpted representations of the Nine Lords of Time and Destiny. Beneath the intricately sculpted sarcophagus lid was found a jade mask, which represents one who has acquired a "true face," that is to say, knowledge, wisdom and enlightenment. From the time Pacal's tomb was sealed in AD 692 until the time of its opening in 1952, exactly 1260 years had elapsed. As we know from the discovery of the Law of Time, 12:60 is the number of exile into the third-dimensional plane of materialism. According to the 13-Baktun cycle, the Long Count of the Maya runs from 3113 BC to 2012 AD. From 692 to 2012 is 1320 years. According to the Law of Time, 13:20 is the frequency of the redemption of time. This is the essence of the prophecy of the tomb of Pacal Votan—that we have 60 years from 1952-2012 to leave artificial 12:60 time and to return to natural 13:20 time.

The tomb of the Red Queen was discovered on June 1, 1994 and was hailed as the most sensational discovery since the discovery of the Tomb of Pacal Votan, almost 42 years earlier. The new tomb was almost immediately identified as the "Tomb of the Red Queen." This was due to the fact that not only was the sarcophagus lid painted red on the outside, it was also red on the inside. When the lid was lifted revealing the "Red Queen," on June 1, 1994, red powder (cinnabar) flew everywhere into the air, revealing the skeletal remains of a female along with sumptuous amounts of jade, pearl and other semiprecious stones and shells. It was immediately assumed that the person in the tomb was a member of noble lineage and that the body belonged to a ruler of high hierarchy. It was natural to think this since the tomb was similar in so many respects to that of the tomb of Pacal Votan. And of course, it was discovered in Temple XIII, adjacent to the west side of the nine-storied Temple of the Inscriptions where the sarcophagus and crypt of the Great Pacal was discovered.

Unlike the tomb of Pacal, which is laden with hieroglyphic inscriptions—neither the temple, the crypt nor the sarcophagus of the Red Queen bear a single inscription. Not a single glyphic clue was left as to her identity, much less of the date of her interment. It seemed as though the Red Queen's tomb was meant to dumbfound the clever glyph-decoding minds of the experts. Only a piece of ceramic pottery outside of the crypt was found to have a date, AD 697.

Just as the placement of the Red Queen's tomb in Temple XIII (being adjacent to that of the tomb of Pacal) is so obvious, so the lack of any hieroglyphic clues or dating also seems to have been highly intentional. The virtually identical sarcophagi were outfitted with twin jade masks, which represent signs of wisdom. The male tomb is inscribed and is therefore historical; the female tomb uninscribed and is therefore post-historical, beyond the cycle, waiting to be inscribed. Hence Votan the transmitter, the inscribed one—and Red Queen, the receiver, the uninscribed one.

These tombs are an allegory or metaphor that provides the extraordinary or supernatural component to the archetypal personas that the two exemplars of Cosmic History must possess in order to have the necessary magnetic attraction to be planetary players. The problem of the spiritual traditions is that they have become enmeshed in various types of sectarian provincialisms of theology, dogma and points of view. There has to be a higher level of spiritual performers and performance that is absolutely planetary and not bogged down in this type of provincial sectarianism. It has to be this way because the construct of the present belief system, which is the container framing and informing all the existing spiritual belief systems, is totally materialistic and separatist. Therefore, the new construct, the new belief system and the new knowledge base has to be spiritually universal and nonmaterialist.

Each avataric emanation incarnates all the previous ones. In other words, the present incarnations of Votan and Red Queen are not just limited to one avataric stream, but because it is the Closing of the Cycle, they contain all the codes and keys of all of the different masters throughout history. This explains why Madame Blavatsky came to be one of the beacons, particularly for Red Queen, because she was in all of history the most unique woman who put together an encyclopedic system of knowledge. She would be one of the last incarnations in preparation for Red Queen's incarnation.

Likewise for Votan that there had been a whole series of previous incarnations. So each is a summation of previous incarnations and the methods and ways of previous avatars and messengers.

GM108X

In the psychomythic context, Cosmic History is known as a galactic Mayan mind transmission of coded information, simply referred to as GM108X. The pure mindstream of the GM108X samadhi, as transmitted from Votan to the Red Queen, is a "between the worlds" transmission, and contains the essence of the Cosmic History teachings. It is a "between the worlds" transmission because its manifestation occurs at the closing of the cycle and is a prelude to the beginning of the next evolutionary cycle.

By maintaining a pure mind, you can enter into this samadhi and into that level of mind transmission where the necessary aspects of knowledge can be understood and received. It must be understood that the GM108X mind transmission, the prophecy of Pacal Votan and the science of the Law of Time are inseparable.

Cosmic History is not just an academic transmission, but one that is completely spiritual, planetary and cosmic in nature. The Cosmic History transmission is the introduction of a new order of knowledge and reality as a planetary whole system. Sooner than later everyone on the planet will partake of this whole system of knowledge, just like virtually everyone on the planet today partakes in the cybersphere. In the same way, the system of knowledge that created the cybersphere is being deconstructed and replaced in a way that is equally and even more planetary and global in nature.

Immediate Origin of Cosmic History

Cosmic History was initiated and activated into this present life stream on (*Dreamspell Count*) Kali 25 of the Galactic Moon in the Yellow Solar Seed Year (March 3, 2002) in a ceremony on top of the Pyramid of the Sun at Teotihuacan, Mexico. This key activation point occurred on Kin 164, Yellow Galactic Seed, the same as the *Galactic Synchronization* point of 2013. Because of this, Votan had originally chosen this day to conduct a ceremony for the opening of the interdimensional portals to the New Time to get to 2013. But the ceremony took a magical turn and Votan found himself on top of the Pyramid of the Sun, (the place where he had had his first vision 49 years earlier) being honored and recognized by nine Indigenous elders as the Closer of the Cycle, the one to bring forth the new knowledge to humanity. (It is important to note that the prophecy of Pacal Votan came from Palenque, but the actual empowerment and vision of the Closer of the Cycle came from Teotihuacan, "Place where the Gods Touch the Earth" or "Place Where Men Become Conscious of Their Godly Powers)."

It is also important to note that Cosmic History was unconsciously activated at this ceremony at Teotihuacan, where a constellation of synchronic order, as well as esoteric knowledge and wisdom, is stored. Indigenous shaman Quetzasha led the ceremony honoring Votan as the one prophesied to close the cycle. This recognition of power and transmission of knowledge stirred a tremendous activation in the Closer of the Cycle. This event was a most powerful planetary initiatic point (due to the combination of maximally focused intent and energy from the nine Indigenous elders, along with the consummated energy from the serpent cavern beneath the pyramid).

At the ceremony atop the Pyramid of the Sun, Votan received a *baston* or sacred staff with an obsidian knife at its tip and was told by the nine Indigenous elders to continue walking the Red Road to 2012, and that he had all of their support. Indigenous leader Quetzasha spoke these words on behalf of the Indigenous elders:

"For a long time we have known that there would be a new knowledge, a knowledge which would be prepared for the new time that is dawning and that this new knowledge would complete and regenerate the traditional knowledge and understanding. We recognize you, Jose Arguelles (Valum Votan), as being that one who has brought that knowledge of the mathematical codes of the galactic Maya. This is the knowledge of the new time, the new era and we recognize that you are a galactic Maya and so we are here to present you with this ceremonial staff. We know you have walked this road, the Red Road, for all of your life and with this staff we expect you to continue to fulfill your responsibilities to walk this Red Road until you close the cycle as you are supposed to. You can count on all of us to support you in this work."

Nine Days After This Ceremony, Cosmic History Came to Earth.

A few days after the ceremony, Votan was back in Oregon, and exactly nine days after the ceremony, on Limi 6 of the Solar Moon (March 12, 2002) on Self Existing Skywalker came the

(Continued on p. xx)

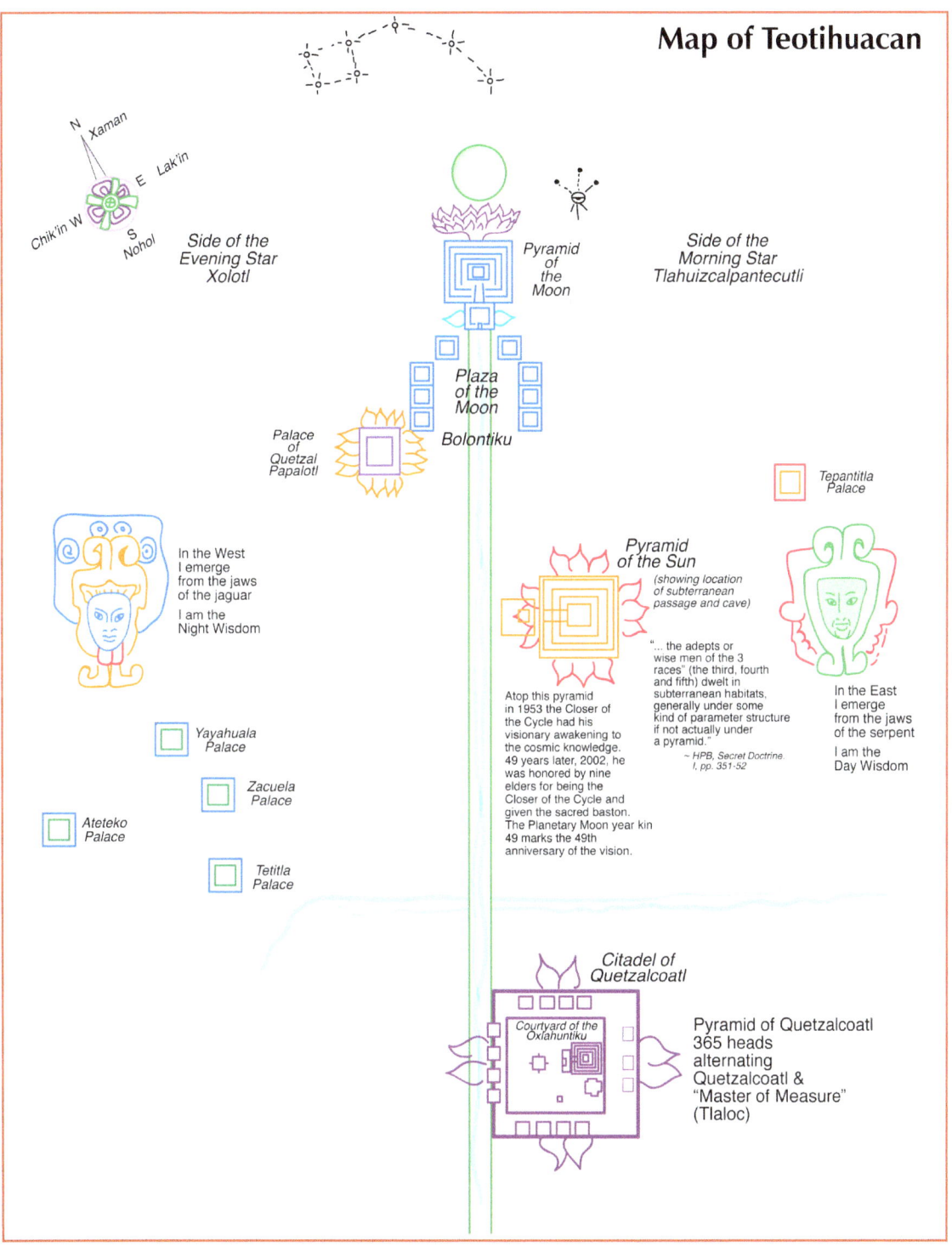

Book of the Throne

HISTORY OF TEOTIHUACAN

Teotihuacan was the original cosmic plan of the Galactic Maya on Earth. Palenque was the high command nerve center of the final and complete phase of what we call the Maya time experiment on Earth. But, the actual complete cosmic vision of the Galactic Maya is literally laid out in the city known as Teotihuacan, which is located about 19.5 degrees North latitude from the equator. This is roughly the same latitude North on the planet Mars where the Face of Mars is located. So there is a relationship between Teotihuacan and the Face on Mars and the Martian pyramids. Mecca is also in the same latitudinal proximity as Teotihuacan. And of course, the magnificent and imposing Pyramid of the Sun is next in size to the Pyramid at Giza. Needless to say, Teotihuacan has a significance of a supremely cosmoplanetary nature.

In the Aztec-Nahua cosmology, the Pyramid of the Sun commemorates the present Fifth World. The top of the pyramid is a point at which the Fifth World transforms or transmutes into the Sixth World, which is the coming solar age or the coming of the new consciousness or the Sixth Sun. This comes into full manifestation in 2013—on Yellow Galactic Seed. The key lies in the fact that beneath the Pyramid of the Sun is a grotto or a sanctuary—an old lava tube type of cave. This cave is a key point on the planet for the hidden knowledge of the serpent initiates of wisdom left there by the fifth root race, according to Madame Blavatsky.

This particular cave contains many multi-dimensional fractals of knowledge reposited here through the geometry of the stone structures which contain forms of telepathic resonance from both Mars and Maldek (now the Asteroid Belt) and is kept by the guardians of the Earth, the elementals, who maintain communication with the Planetary Logos. All of this knowledge had already been activated in the underground cavern at two precise points. The first activation occurred when Votan visited the cave when the sun was at its zenith on the Day out of Time, Red Rhythmic Skywalker, in 1999. The second activation occurred when the nine Indigenous elders gathered in the underground cave on the Yellow Self Existing Sun, four days prior to the ceremony on Yellow Galactic Seed.

Self Existing Sun—4 Ahau—marks the first day of the beginning of the Great Cycle of history: August 13, 3113 BC and on the Long Count the Self Existing Sun or 4 Ahau also corresponds to the prophetic date Dec. 21, 2012. These are key points. It's also important to note that in 1953, at the age of 14, Votan was on top of the Pyramid of the Sun very close to the dates July 25–26. This was the initial activation of the Galactic Mayan mind transmission, which prepared him for all the work he would do regarding the actual decoding of the prophetic knowledge of Teotihuacan and the galactic Maya. In this way, those points are all stitched together as a template of awakening at Teotihuacan. This goes back to the original knowledge, which was the cosmic laying out of the city and the creation of the geometrical structures.

activation of Cosmic History at the repeated request from Red Queen for a tutorial on Cosmic History. By the time she asked for it the third time, Votan knew something very serious was happening and he felt a deep stirring within the core of his being. That evening he had a powerful blast of interplanetary recollection with regard to the Cosmic History. The next day on the Overtone Wizard a series of 260 consecutive tutorials began. In the Dreamspell Count, the Self Existing Skywalker represents "solar prophetic" Mars and the White Overtone Wizard represents "solar prophetic" Maldek. (These are the two key planets in the cosmomythology of the interplanetary drama of our solar system). Solar-prophetic refers to the solar breath as it pulses from the sun, across the planetary orbits, to the galactic edge of the heliosphere.

It is important to understand the origins of Cosmic History in order to grasp it in its entirety. Through mutual destinal recognition, Red Queen had come to be Votan's apprentice 52 days earlier on the White Overtone Wind, Kali 11 (January 20, 2002) of the Resonant Moon. Once the apprenticeship took hold they understood the enormity of the vast "between the worlds transmission" that would not be complete until 2012. From the beginning, it was clear that their mission as sorcerer/apprentice required a total complete life embodiment and life involving process. It also became clear that everything about their psychological makeup and process had been absolutely prepared for this act of transmission and activation of the cycle of Cosmic History.

Thus incurred an entire galactic spin of 260 tutorials, all specifically given with the theme of Cosmic History. By any standards, this succession of tutorials on the different themes that were involved was a stupendous effort requiring maximum focus and concentration on the part of the transmitter and receiver. This effort was carried out every day virtually without fail even while traveling. This was the actual origin of the manifestation of Cosmic History on Earth. When something like that occurs so rapidly in such a large sweep and with such a large breath and with such a range of topics and themes, it is not until well after you are done that you realize or understand what the process of organization is going to be or how it will be arranged. This process of intense transmission over a duration of one galactic spin led to the second phase which was the distillation, transcribing, and creation of the order and finally conceptualization of the seven volumes needed to accommodate the vast range of information given in the tutorials. Then came the planning and formatting of the first volume.

It is important to comprehend the link between the activation of the ceremony at Teotihuacan and the *Cosmic History Chronicles*, that Cosmic History was dependent upon the conscious empowerment and self-realization of Votan as the Closer of the Cycle. This realization was a most critical trigger pointing to the fact that Cosmic History is very specifically a "between the worlds transmission"—a special transmission for the time between the beginning of the third Christian millennium and the actual closing of the cycle, 2001–2012, or the time between the fourth and the fifth worlds of the Hopi prophecy, or the transition from the fifth sun to the sixth sun in the Mexican prophecies.

Cosmic History articulates not the past world but the coming world or what we might call the formulation of knowledge in the coming world or the sixth sun of consciousness, or the fifth world—the age of the center. These are psychomythic formulations of our evolutionary ascent into the noosphere, the planetary mind.

Book of the Throne

When you understand that the noosphere is the next evolutionary stage, not only of our species but also of our planet within the cosmic order, then you can appreciate the monumental context and game plan which the *Cosmic History Chronicles* encompasses. Therefore, you who would be reformulated, enter now into the *Book of the Throne*!

Part I: The Story

"Listen Socrates, to the Story; as extraordinary as it is, it is absolutely true."

Plato Timaeus 355 BC

Chapter 1
What is Cosmic History?

Cosmic History is the core of the universal field of intelligence. The premise of Cosmic History is that this universal field of intelligence has not been accurately known in this present time. For this reason there has to be the reformulation of the construct of knowledge in the world. We are dealing with a complete world construct. In fact, we could say that the entire way in which the every day world on this planet is presented to the human through its senses is somehow inadequate, wrong and incorrect.

Of course it is hard for anyone who has known nothing but this inadequate, incorrect worldview to understand that there could be anything beyond it or even that there might be anything wrong with this particular construct. This is the basic issue that we are dealing with at this point. Cosmic History is actually a template or a superior overlay of a comprehensive understanding that is intended to replace the entire world construct that exists today.

When we talk about the world construct of knowledge, we are talking about the construct that performs absolutely everything that is experienced in the world, particularly through what we might call the public media—the journals, the newspapers, the television, the Internet, the radio and most forms of public education. In other words, all the different ways in which information is currently conveyed and communicated to the world at large is perceptually incorrect, wrong or inadequate. But we might say that if Cosmic History is the core of the universal field of intelligence, then why has this not previously been known? This is what this chapter will elucidate.

When we talk about the prevailing dominating structure of the world, we are talking about the information and intelligence structure that pervades and dominates what we call the "industrialized" nations of the world—the nations that are responsible for the elaboration of what is referred to as the technosphere, or the Earth's artificial industrial/technological sheathe. The global field of the technosphere is an artificial construct based on machine consciousness and marketing gimmicks.

When we think about the technosphere and the dominant world view, which negates time and consciousness, we have to understand that there is a whole huge single mental order that is constantly talking to itself. In other words, when you read a newspaper editorial it is really only the mind talking to itself. When you watch a news program or read the news on the Internet, it is still just the mind talking to itself. Because who is reading or watching it but the mind that created it? This is a fundamental point to grasp.

When we look at to whom and how this current worldview is being presented, we see that there are fundamental premises that are completely erroneous. The first premise is that there are only individual units of consciousness; therefore there is no consciousness or understanding of the noosphere. The noosphere is the Earth's mental envelope or the thinking layer of the Earth. It can be understood as the storage unit of the sum of the mental interactions of all of life, both in the phenomenal and imaginal realms.

Lack of knowledge of the noosphere, along with the psi bank regulator, is the primary fault of the prevailing dominating structure that governs perceptions of the world today. This is due to the fact that the whole biosphere (the sphere of life and its support system) is actually run and operated by the noosphere. The psi bank can be understood as the regulating mechanism, control panel or "nervous system" of the noosphere. Located between the two Van Allen radiation belts, the major components of Earth's electromagnetic field, the psi bank is instrumented to the fourth-dimensional timing factor of which the Maya were highly aware. This fourth-dimensional timing factor regulates the DNA, which includes all the stages of evolution and the processes of mutation of life on Earth. In this way, the psi bank serves as a filing cabinet where registrations of fourth dimensional time are deposited. This will be expanded upon later and in subsequent volumes. (For further study see *Earth Ascending* and *Time and the Technosphere*).

Up until now, the entire biosphere has been unconsciously governed by the noosphere. It is important to understand that the mind that is talking to itself is actually the noosphere, the mental sphere of intelligence on the planet. But because it does not know it is the noosphere, it is speaking in a very cramped and provincial way, operating with a limited belief system and an assumed set of reference points. The most fundamental premise of this ant scale point of view is that materialism is not only good, but is the only viable form of reality. This point of view holds the notion that the world is purely a physical construct and therefore we as human beings are purely physical constructs.

In this physicalist worldview, the purpose of life is to make material accommodation of this phenomenal construct as comfortable as possible. Whatever impinges on that comfort and creates discomfort is to be fought and whatever furthers this comfort is to be aided and abetted. This is a fundamental unspoken unconscious premise of everything that occurs as information in the present construct of the knowledge of the world, which can be viewed as an information feedback loop or the mind talking to itself.

What the mind is continuously doing is shoring up its own belief system, which is an absolutely fundamental materialist—unquestioned, unspoken—belief system of the physical nature of reality and being. In this construct of the world, what we refer to as religion or religious ideas are merely ideas which are evaluated, again, according to the degree to which they further physical comfort or create physical discomfort. This is the prevailing dominant construct.

Within the dominant construct—that you might call the mind of the planetary human that talks to itself—there are more or less alien subconstructs. The most alien form of subconstructs is the form that seems to attack itself. This is usually referred to as terrorism, which at its root is an ideology that does not seem to seek physical comfort. These are all just forms of justification for furthering a particular dominance in the world.

What we are describing is the matrix that holds the whole present world order in place. Wherever you go and with whomever you speak, everyone to some degree or another is caught up in this world construct. If you go into stores all the shopkeepers are caught up in this construct by involving themselves in a system of furthering material goods or material comfort, while they themselves are simultaneously caught in a web of needing to seek material comfort and so on.

This materialism is by far the greatest force and greatest factor that has kept the human mind in an increasingly diminished state of consciousness. In other words, the mind's sensory parameters keep being shrunk down to a pure physicalist survival mode of thinking. This type of thinking is fed by the entertainment industry which creates a type of imaginal realm. When you look behind all the images and characters and archetypes of this imaginal realm, particularly those of the film or pulp fiction industries—you see that all the entertainment industry seems to be based on the degree to which the physicalist comforts are being furthered or whether fear is being created about losing them. Then there is the fringe entertainment element which is provoked by a type of spiritual hopelessness or despair or some type of spiritual optimism, which is relatively limited in the actual sphere of global influence.

We are just painting a general picture of the present state of the human mental field, which is a primitive shadow of the noosphere. It is but a mental construct that, through the technosphere, surrounds the world and is furthered through the planetary global information media—television, radio, Internet, etc. This system of thought is transmitted instantaneously all the time around the planet through these artificial technospheric communications media. This is what makes the system of thought like a primitive shadow of the noosphere—though it surrounds the world it is primitive because it is not the noosphere, or rather, it is the noosphere unconscious of itself.

It must be understood that the present mental construct of the world is a complete umbrella that encompasses the entire planet. From the point of view of the Law of Time, this umbrella is a function of a type of erroneous thinking that at its root creates a fundamental misperception of not only what and who we are, but what the Earth is and what we are doing on the Earth. If you dig down to the root of this misperception, above and beyond its being furthered by the mechanistic timing frequency, at the root of it lies a question: Do you have belief in the soul or not?

This materialism is by far the greatest force and greatest factor that has kept the human mind in an increasingly diminished state of consciousness.

And if you do have belief in the soul, then do you have belief in the fact that the memory of God is inscribed in the soul? This is the absolute root of the misperception of who and what we are. Either there is some type of fundamental belief in the memory of God inscribed in the soul or there isn't; or there is a denial of it or a total hypocrisy regarding it. If there is a belief in the memory of God inscribed in the soul, then the sole purpose of life is to remember God and get back to the soul—that pure place where you can read the inscribed words that God has placed in your heart.

If you can pursue this then you are pursuing a life of God. This is a fundamental disparity from the materialist point of view. This belief is actually at the root of what is called fundamentalism; yet most fundamentalism becomes a closed system and comes at odds with the dominant materialistic belief system and so creates a lot of the conflicts that exist in the world today.

Why does the memory of God become inverted into a type of fundamentalism?

We might ask: Why does the memory of God become inverted into a type of fundamentalism? This again has to do with a deeper root, which is what we refer to as a lack of knowledge of the noosphere. In other words, in the present construct of world knowledge we are dealing with belief systems where there is a multiple layering or levels of what we might call erroneous or inadequate, if not incorrect thinking. Again, the most fundamental problem up to this point on our planet today is the lack of full knowledge of the noosphere. This is actually an evolutionary problem.

Up until now the noosphere could not be fully realized, so even the best spiritual belief systems are somewhat provincial because they developed their belief in errors of human thought that developed before there was full knowledge of the planetary whole or awareness of the world as a whole system. The current world knowledge construct came into dominance as the world became globalized, beginning in 1969, when the view of Earth from space was first seen.

It is important to understand that the dominating system that created that view from space is so rooted in materialism that it creates even bigger problems than the provincialisms of the different spiritual traditions. It furthers itself in conspiratorial and sinister ways through aiding and abetting the different sectarian conflicts of the traditional systems, like Hindu or Muslim or whatever it may be. This is a bigger root problem because this is the system that actually dominates and affects all of the belief systems in the world today. In other words, this materialistic belief system crowds into the other belief systems.

For example, you can read Buddhist texts that describe the world, which, on the one hand, you can say are describing mythic constructs, but, on the other hand, what do they mean when they describe the world system we live in as the Southern continent Jambudvipa? Are they referring to India, or are they viewing Earth as a part of this Southern continent of some type of galactic order? We see that there is a certain inadequacy in this construct. This is a construct that was agreed to, for instance, in the Tibetan Buddhist belief system. Or in the Islamic belief system the dominating tradition of the Hadith and Sunna (based on the saying and life stories of the Prophet Muhammad, May peace be upon him) was developed before there was complete knowledge of the planetary whole, though by the time of the later development of Islam this knowledge was secure.

When these traditions were first developed, however, what Buddhism, Christianity, Islam and all other religions and spiritual teachings thought the world was, was not really the whole world. There was not yet a whole knowledge of the world. As the knowledge of the world has exploded and then imploded, the tendency of these traditions has been to hold on even tighter to what had been developed many centuries ago. This creates different forms of self-destructive sectarianism whether it is in a more extreme Islamic form, a fundamental Christian form or even a self-preserving Buddhist form—at the root of these belief systems there is also a lack of knowledge of the existence of the noosphere.

Knowledge of the noosphere can only come as a result of the human becoming the planetary human. When this occurs the human realizes that the Earth really is a type of sphere in space and has a real construct of the knowledge of that space in relationship to the galactic center and to the whole galactic

When these traditions were first developed, however, what Buddhism, Christianity, Islam and all other religions and spiritual teachings thought the world was, was not really the whole world. As the knowledge of the world has exploded and then imploded, the tendency of these traditions has been to hold on even tighter to what had been developed many centuries ago.

Book of the Throne: Cosmic History Chronicles - Volume I

order. This evolution of knowledge up until this point in time has created all the different problems in the world today, although this does not excuse any of these inadequate belief systems. Now, all the belief systems must be evaluated or reevaluated. They can only be reevaluated within the context of Cosmic History inclusive of the knowledge of the noosphere and the psi bank.

When we talk about Cosmic History, we are talking about the imprint of the universal field of intelligence as a whole order within the noosphere and informing the psi bank plates. Only at this point in time could we really come to Cosmic History. We see that Cosmic History is also a point of evolutionary realization. We have come to a certain place in the evolution of knowledge on the Earth that necessitates a leap into expanded knowledge. This expanded knowledge is Cosmic History.

When we talk about Cosmic History we are talking about the imprint of the universal field of intelligence as a whole order within the noosphere and informing the psi bank plates. Only at this point in time could we really come to Cosmic History.

Dissipating The Clouds Of Materialism

Noospheric thinking is not materialistic thinking. This is a fundamental point. The noosphere, by its very nature, is a fourth-dimensional mental/spiritual planetary organ. This is the organ of the planet's mental/spiritual evolution in relationship to the star that is hosting it. This is a radically different point of view or perception from the current system of thought. You can hardly talk about these two in the same breath.

The cybersphere is the system of intelligence produced by and dependent upon the artificial electronic information technology, i.e. the Internet. The cybersphere is a primitive shadow of the noosphere—it is a planetary sphere but, still, it is only a shadow, not the real luminous essence of the noospheric thought system. This cybersphere is contained in the technosphere and provides the connective tissue of the present day belief system and world construct. We could metaphorically liken the present world construct to a massive cloud covering around the planet, which is maintained by a total materialistic belief system. The more the belief system of materialism maintains itself the denser this cloud covering becomes. The cloud cover does not mean that there isn't the luminous noospheric stratosphere above it. The noosphere is there regardless of the cloud cover.

Disillusionment of the cloud covering of the materialist belief system is the purpose of Cosmic History—only then can the clear mental field of the human shine through as the planetary mental field. Upon dissolution of the cloud cover or belief system, the apparatus by which this belief system maintains itself will be transformed, transmuted and dissolved so that all that remains is the noosphere.

It would seem to some minds that it is a rather impossible task to dissolve the materialist belief system—just as the most hardened materialist cynics say it is impossible to change the calendar. They say this because they actually believe you will never dissolve the materialistic belief system! Everyone who believes in the New Time and the calendar change has to encounter these types of responses, not once, but many times.

"And it shall come to pass,

when I bring a cloud over the

Earth, that the rainbow shall

be seen in the cloud ..."

Genesis 9:14.

The calendar change peace movement is like a little shoot or sprout. Behind that shoot or sprout is a ray of light poking into the dense materialistic belief system. And behind that ray of light is actually the whole elaboration of the principle structure and constructs which constitute Cosmic History.

This materialistic belief system has been with the human species since the beginning of the cycle of history. In fact, we could say that the materialistic belief system is what created the cycle of human history. The more that the cycle of history comes to the present moment, the more it obscures the potential for understanding the reality of Cosmic History. In the highest annals of spiritual and religious thought—in the highest civilizations there has always been some comprehension of Cosmic History. Any belief system that has developed a view regarding the Absolute or God as the Ultimate Reality, or any idea of there being an Absolute or Ultimate Reality, such as Buddha's Dharmakaya—these are all touching on principles of Cosmic History.

Unfortunately, these points of view have become increasingly esoteric and then invisible and finally nonexistent as the process of materialist human history has progressed. When we talk about human history in the way it is written about in all the textbooks, we are actually talking about the history and extension of human materialism through competing political forces called empires. These empires are based on principles of acquisitiveness and greed and support themselves by the belief that humans are weak and that it is human nature to be susceptible to greed. In this limited belief system, there is nothing that can stop human greed but to curb acquisitive instincts by the creation of political structures like democracy, which supposedly keep these nasty aspects of human nature at bay, but in reality only further them because it is all based on a lie. The belief system that believes humans are fundamentally evil and cannot be trusted creates a world of fear and mistrust, war and terrorism. Such is the definition of the dominant world construct called historical materialism.

> *In the highest annals of spiritual and religious thought—in the highest civilizations there has always been some comprehension of Cosmic History.*

Deconstruct, Purify And Reformulate

From the Cosmic History point of view, it is erroneous to believe that the human is basically evil and cannot be stopped in greed. If this were true in nature, then nature would be destroying itself. Is the human being an exception? This faulty belief system regarding the nature of the human being is engrained in historical materialism and plays over and over again in a self-limiting feedback loop. If you tell somebody something enough times they will believe it and create the world accordingly. From the point of view of the *Holy Quran* and the *Bible*, we live in Satan's world. This is the world of the fallen human. Or from the Buddhist point of view, we live in a world that is created by ego (samsara). These worldviews constitute a fundamental premise of historical materialism.

In order to deconstruct historical materialism, which is at the root of the present world construct, we have to see what is the opposite of materialism—which is actually spiritual reality. Materialism is just a singular exception to the ground of spiritual reality, which is the ground of everything. So ultimately materialism must flounder because the ground of reality is spiritual. This truth, however, does not lessen the problem of the prevailing materialist construct of the world.

It is important to understand that this materialist construct of the world is a relative one and it has characterized this cycle of what is referred to as human history, merely for the testing of the human soul. To pass the test is to return again to a purely spiritual point of view—a point of view that understands that the garment of reality is holy, that there is a divine authorship to the universe, and that the soul exists with the inscription of God that says: "Remember Me."

To deconstruct the root of the prevailing belief system, you must determinedly engage in a higher spiritual point of view. There have been, and still are, different spiritual points of view aimed at this direction, but none have been able to deconstruct the entire world construct. They have, instead, become embattled until they themselves become part of that world point of view where everyone is forced, in one form or another, into the materialist technospheric construct from which it appears there is no escape. Therefore, it is mandatory that not only a fresh spiritual point of view is introduced, but also a higher formulation of planetary human knowledge—this is where Cosmic History comes into play.

It must be understood that Cosmic History is a spiritual transmission. Though sometimes it might look like science or mathematics or solar studies, it is actually a spiritual transmission and is transmitted as light is transmitted or as heat is transmitted. You flick a light switch and Boom! You just got transmitted light. Or you turn on the heat and Wrrrr… you feel it. It is not anything that you cognitively say—it is just light and heat and it's bright and it's warm now.

Same thing with Cosmic History, it is ultimately a transmission like this. Why? Because Cosmic History is merely the intrinsic innate tendency in the all-abiding reality to be known or made consciously self-reflective. The all-abiding reality is like light or heat. Just like you have to wait for the sun to come up or turn on the light switch to get light, you must also clear and purify your mind so it can reach the all-abiding reality. The intelligence contained within the Cosmic

History core has as its purpose the reformulation of the human mind and the human knowledge base. This reformulation is according to the principles of the planetary noosphere, which receives the template or has embedded in it the template of Cosmic History.

Cosmic History is the interpenetration of the Absolute into the relative. At the end of the cycle on Planet Earth, which is where we are now, the Absolute is eliminated altogether from the equation of consciousness and there is only the relative mind speaking to the relative mind, ultimately making no sense. The relative can only make sense within the context of the Absolute. If the Absolute is missing then the relative means nothing. In this regard, we say in Cosmic History, cosmos is the Absolute and history is the relative. Together, cosmos and history create a description of a process of consciousness.

In studying Cosmic History we are learning knowledge and techniques for elevating the "dull normal" state of consciousness toward the Absolute. What we refer to as "galactic meditation" is one of the principle techniques and processes that help elevate us to a cosmic condition of mind called Cosmic History. This state of mind involves the ongoing experience of the simultaneity of the relative and the Absolute. This is what heightens your awareness, making reality appear hallucinatory or dreamlike—which it is.

To practice this state of mind, observe closely when you are in a crowd or in a store or on the street; pay attention to what people are doing and what they are talking about. You will see that the majority of the people are in a particular typical late historical materialist 12:60 (12 month calendar/60 minute clock) collective mental field. This is like being in a field of insects that are chirping. They don't know they are in this field and they don't know what their chirping is about or even what it sounds like to someone who is not an insect. It is questionable whether crickets know that they make a blanket of sound at night in the summertime, but they do. So you see there is a certain type of automatic, unconscious, almost insect-like quality to the lives of people who are not conscious of the fact that they are operating in a collectively unconscious program.

> *What we refer to as "galactic meditation" is one of the principle techniques and processes that help elevate us to a cosmic condition of mind called Cosmic History.*

This is a phenomenological description or observation of the present consensual reality. As you go more deeply into the state of mind known as Cosmic History your perceptions will sharpen and you will become increasingly aware of this. Just because someone is operating in the mind frame of consensual reality does not mean that when that person is encountered one-on-one that they cannot be engaged and some quality of themselves cannot be drawn out and then flipped back on themselves so that they are returned to themselves. But how long is this consciousness maintained? More and more we come to see a greater contrast between the current contemporary collective state of mind and the cosmic state of mind known as Cosmic History.

Thirteen Moons – First Step To A New Reality

The first step in shifting to a cosmic state of mind is through daily use of the Thirteen Moon/28-day calendar—this is the basis and foundation of a new world structure. Cosmic History and the Thirteen Moon calendar create a description of a process of consciousness. The purpose of Cosmic History as a construct of consciousness is to transform the human species altogether by transforming the mind and the very nature of consciousness itself. The Thirteen Moon/28-day calendar is the instrument that creates a fundamental correction in consciousness by placing a radial harmonic matrix at the foundation of the mind. This ultimately makes all the difference in the world.

The Thirteen Moon/28-day calendar is the harmonic software that shifts your mind into the 13:20 frequency of synchronization; this will be expounded upon in the next chapter. On this basis it is possible for the reformulation of the mind to occur at a mass level. Artificial time (12:60) is just a state of mind that keeps you from experiencing reality. The Gregorian calendar represents the artificial technospheric information knowledge base that is being dissolved. The Thirteen Moon calendar represents the opening to a new reality which enables the establishment of Cosmic History as the radically new knowledge base for humanity.

In reality, there is only Cosmic History. As we mentioned earlier, what we call human history is actually the history of the development of materialism that creates the technosphere and the entire artificial apparatus that culminates at the climax of history. In the Mayan measure of history, this point is known as the climax of matter in the thirteenth baktun of the Wave Harmonic of history. (For more information see: *The Mayan Factor* and *Time and the Technosphere*).

Cosmic History encompasses absolutely everything that can be known, everything that will be known and everything that has been forgotten. The whole of reality is encompassed by Cosmic History, even the little histories that men write in their books that fill the bookstores and libraries. These are all distorted splinters of the actual Cosmic History—this includes all science and philosophy and every other form of knowledge that exists. Everything that exists is some aspect of Cosmic History. So when we talk about introducing Cosmic History to humanity we are talking about opening a vent in the dense technospheric cloud. And through this vent the reality of Cosmic History comes through and begins to permeate the otherwise polluted atmosphere.

Understanding The Present World Model Of Reality

If our task is to deconstruct the present world model and reconstruct a higher world model, we must stop and ask: What is the present world model? In the nature of the present world model can we actually say it is a world model? What is it a model of? It is basically a model of a materialistic, acquisitive type of intelligence—if you want to call it that. Its view of the world is that the world is something to be mined or something to be exploited and turned into real estate. But what is the world really?

From the materialist point of view, the world is a cold, inert, lifeless rock and therefore you can do what you want with it because it doesn't have any feelings anyway. You can sell it like real estate and you can mine it, you can build freeways and highways and cities wherever you want. You can cut down trees and even move or carve up large parts of mountains. You can boar giant tunnels beneath the ocean and you can divert rivers and drain the lakes. And you can go wherever you desire and leave massive amounts of waste and residues of pollution in air, land and sea. Underlying this mentality is that the world has no feelings, it is just there, it is just a big rock with which you can do whatever you want.

These are just some examples of the current model of reality that must be examined. The point is that you have to stop and look at the different attitudes and dispositions that constitute what you might call the current world model. You have to go underneath these attitudes and dispositions to see what they are really saying. In order to do this you must develop a meditative mind.

Developing a meditative mind is necessary because we are on an evolutionary path which requires an active contemplative perspective in which the classic yogic meditation techniques are actually means to a higher end. It is important to grasp the evolutionary stage which we are rapidly evolving into—which is the stage of the noosphere. This stage of the noosphere is a systematic cosmic perception and information structure that can only be made known and realized once we have dissolved the current mental model of the world. We are not dissolving the current mental model of the world to be anarchists and we are not developing meditative states of mind to be like Ramana Maharshi or Milarepa—we are developing meditative states of mind so we can go to the next higher world model.

Yoga is an evolutionary aide to create the right state of mind to apprehend the next construct of knowledge. This construct of knowledge must be incorporated or brought into the body in order for us to get to the next evolutionary mode of reality, which is the noosphere, the planetary system of cosmic perception and structure of knowing.

Cosmos Perceivable Through Supramental Effort

Cosmos is the entire order of reality as a coherent, distinguishable pole. This fact cannot be grasped by your senses. The only way you can grasp it is through some type of inner meditation or visualization. To appreciate what cosmos is you do have to make a supramental effort. When you look at the stars you see they are really only a minute portion of the universe. You have to go beyond thinking that you can see it. The cosmos constitutes all of the inner worlds as well and many dimensions which you can hardly fathom. You must approach the cosmos through the exercise of your imaginal will, then you can begin to see what cosmos actually is.

Since it can only be grasped as a constituent element of the imaginal realm, the apprehension of cosmos is entirely mental in nature—it is of the mind. And ultimately cosmos is nothing but the mental image of God. It is just a pure *manomaya* thought-form, or mind-made illusion. The *Quran* says that God can will anything to be. This means if God so desired He could will the whole cosmos out of existence leaving us disembodied floating in the great void wondering what happened to our context. This is all just to illustrate the highly mental field in which we are operating.

The universe is constructed through your mind. You have to come to the conclusion that mind and consciousness are the basic constructive elements of what we call cosmos. Mind is what allows the possibility of perception of something "outside" of itself or "in" itself. Consciousness is the condition or quality of mind which is specified by particular qualities and conditions of being or thought. When we say that at its foundation the cosmos is constructed as mind and consciousness, this means that first there must be the manifestation of mind which exists everywhere and is a function of the incomprehensible totality of the mind of God. Within this knowledge, the whole of what we call the universe or the cosmic duality bubbles itself into being out of the mythic cauldron.

Cosmic History: Two Basic Premises

Cosmic History has two basic beginning premises:

1. The sense organs are intrinsically perfect.
2. Mind training is essential to discover this.

At the microscopic level, the sense organs are already perfect; therefore the information processed through the sense organs is also perfect. The premise is that the information is as good as the sense organs. However, being that we are at the closing of the cycle there is such an inundation of sensory information as well as mental/conceptual information that it is difficult to understand what a pure sensory experience might be. Information overload creates a type of sensory indiscrimination.

When we say the sense organs are perfect, what we are saying is that intrinsically the human neurobiological equipment is already perfect. But in order to experience the perfection you must remove yourself from distorted feedback loops that constitute the present social/mental reality.

... study of Cosmic History cannot be undertaken without some kind of mind training or understanding of some type of sacred point of view.

These reinforcing feedback loops make you think: "This is civilization" or "That is society" which create thoughts like: "I like movies" or "What's the bestseller?"—none of this is helpful for evolution. These are all just diversionary perspectives that are meant to keep the mind quarantined in a narrow wavelength band. Cosmic History says: "None of this!" You may need to spend a few weeks in a meditation retreat or go out to the country or go look at the ocean for awhile just to clear your mind out. This is hard for most people to do because their minds are so conditioned to be busy that they don't know what to do without the stimulus of artificial situations. A lot of people get out for a few days and that is about all they can handle. These are just examples to illustrate the actual situation into which Cosmic History is coming. So when we say the sense organs are perfect already, corollary to this is that sensory information is also perfect—it is only the grasping mind that wants to make something different out of the sense perception that the sense organs bring that creates the problem. The basic problem is the dissatisfaction of the ego which distorts reality and creates the samsaric tape loop that constitutes the complexity of the technosphere today.

The second premise is that study of Cosmic History cannot be undertaken without some kind of mind training or understanding of some type of sacred point of view—that God exists, that the imprint of God is in the soul, that reality is divine and sacred. You have to really experience this, which is not always an easy thing to do. Everything we are describing points to the actual difficulty of the state of the present day human mind at the closing of the cycle. This is why there is need for mental dynamite to blow the unnecessary thoughts out.

At one point it was thought that LSD could do that but now it has been co-opted by social forms and norms so it has acquired its own particular social referencing, therefore it can no longer function in this way effectively. Since we do not really have that mental stick of dynamite to blow all the unnecessary thoughts out of the human mind, we are being called to obliterate old programs naturally—through focus on classic mind training techniques. Only through mental focus will you really extract

Part I • The Story

the essence of Cosmic History.

We are dealing all the time with instant feedback systems so when you put something out ("good" or "bad") it comes right back to you at an accelerated rate. This can be understood as the law of karma. Whatever you think and put out is exactly what you get back. This refers to absolutely every single moment of the day and every experience you have, not to mention the longer terms of karmic past lives and so on. In the present world construct we have the institutionalization of distorted perceptions which create distorted feedback loops resulting in confused people creating confused societies. These considerations are aimed at those minds that have never stopped to think about these things. This is an introduction to the actual state of mind and nature as it exists in the world today so we can be aware of mind obstacles that may present themselves in the study of Cosmic History.

Your Brain on the Law of Time

"On Earth, the cosmic norm is embedded in the noosphere and in the template of the Cosmic History program encoded in the psi bank plates."

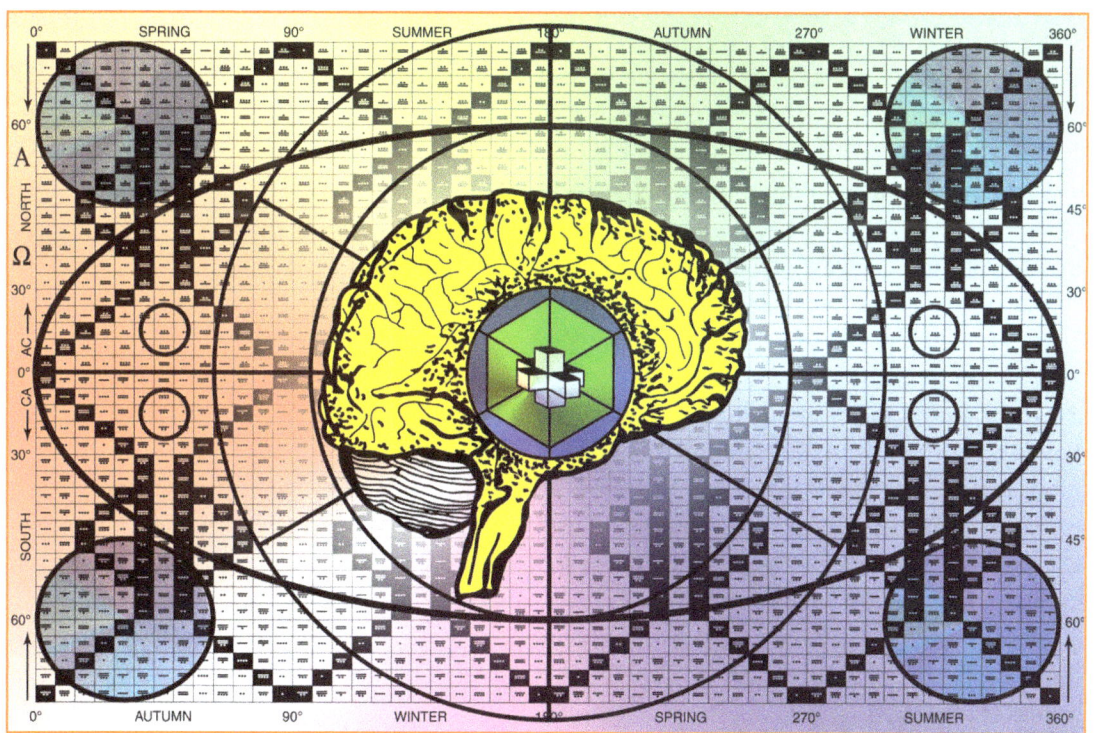

Lack of mind training is part of the disjunctive incoherent world model that keeps this whole technospheric flytrap going. We are releasing old patterns and going into what we might call the "cosmic norm." On Earth, the cosmic norm is embedded in the noosphere and in the template of the Cosmic History program encoded in the psi bank plates. In order to access these plates you must enter into a synchronic system of knowledge so you can begin to put a radically different information load into your mind. Not only is it necessary to insert another information load into your mind, but a whole other information template—meaning how the information is coherently brought into you. You must develop a discriminating mind as to the nature of information in the information template. What is valuable? What is meaningful? And what isn't meaningful?

From a cosmic normative point of view, what is valuable and meaningful is your relationship with the Earth as a living entity and to the sun as a divine intelligently coordinating information energy system—and finally your relationship to the galactic whole and the larger constellation of which it is a part. These are the important points because this is actually what is going on all the time anyway. We are not aware of this when we are living in our narrow technospheric wavelength. What we are not aware of is that our third-dimensional space suit, which we call our body or self, is actually a psychosensory information radar processor. It is processing information all the time regardless of whether we are aware of it or not.

Take solar flares for instance. What do solar flares actually do to our neurons? We think: "Oh solar flares affect antennas and short wave radios and other technological gadgets." But if they affect the Earth's magnetic fields and we are a part of the Earth's magnetic field, then what do the flares actually do to us? Do the solar flares actually rearrange our own *electroneuromolecular* system at some sublime level? Undoubtedly so. This is the actual reality that exists whether we think about it or not. This reality is going on all the time in the *electrobioneural processing system* that we are. In the study of Cosmic History it is important to understand how we relate to the living Earth and how the living Earth relates to us.

Everything that this current collective mind thinks is reality such as outlet stores, consumerism and terrorism to name a few—all of these things are just functions of an artificial fictitious belief system. This is why the current world model is such a tragedy—because it is all illusory—based on illusions that have no basis. In reality, the entire current world that we see is just a mental fiction that we propagate. In this way, the obstacles to understanding Cosmic History are these ideological chauvinisms of self, of corporation, of state, of school, of religion, of nation, etc—all of these are absolute fictions yet we have these ideological ego identities with them and construct this whole reality on that basis. All of this has nothing to do with the cosmic reality of the biosphere and noosphere. It does not recognize that solar cosmic radiation is always already interpenetrating every molecule of the Earth.

Russian scientist Vladimir Vernadsky stated that the biosphere is the region on Earth for the transformation of cosmic energy. To extrapolate and create the corollary of that, the noosphere is the region of the Earth for the transformation of cosmic energy into psychic mental constructs. It is the higher psychic mental constructs that are being confabulated by the interpenetration of cosmic energies into the Earth's mental cosmic field, which is the noosphere.

The whole totality of the ideological structures and the mental constructs of what constitute the world today (including all science that upholds it) has to be dissolved. These structures are all mental illusions which are easy to dissolve once you recognize them. However, it is difficult to dissolve these constructs when you are the only one who sees through the illusion and 99 percent of the people around you are still living in a fictitious reality. Then you may appear as the lunatic.

However, the fact is that 99 percent of people are basing their lives on these ideological chauvinisms of corporations and religions that have nothing to do with reality—but are actually mind invented feedback loops that take no account of the cosmic solar nature of reality and how it is affecting our *electrobioneurological* equipment. Cosmic History is intended to clear away all of the artificial ideologies of mind in order to present an actual description of what is really going on at the cosmic solar biological level.

Cosmic History is the entirely renewed knowledge base—it is a new program of knowledge. We now know what the forms are for evolving the human mind and consciousness within the noosphere. The basis for Cosmic History is coming to the point of self-reflective awareness of the human species as a manifestation of the whole Earth. This is related very precisely to the point in 1969 when the human beings first saw photographs of the Earth from the moon. This was a pure feedback reflex—looking from the place you are looking from is a *zuvuya* principle.

This was the moment when the human potential for expanding its consciousness beyond ego became an actuality. Before this point, human consciousness was in the collective unconscious. That point in 1969 was the first light coming through the door with the memory that we are all *one* being on *one* planet. Therefore, all systems are manifestations of *one* system. Even though spiritual teachers throughout the ages had voiced that point, it could never be grasped through experience until it was viewed on television in 1969.

Cosmic History—Divinely Ordained

Since only God creates the system known as Cosmic History, you want to be certain that one of the fundamentals or foundations of inserting a new knowledge base is prayer and mind training. Since God is the Divine Intelligence from which Cosmic History is sprung, then to understand Cosmic History you must come to know God as the centerpiece of your life. You have to understand the nature of consciousness and God. All of these aspects form a fundamental part of the study of Cosmic History. The locus of God is in your mind.

Everything comes from your mind. What does this mean? Things are as they are; but all interpretations come from mind. The mind contains a relative and an Absolute level. At the Absolute level, there is no difference between error and non-error. But at the relative level, this may not be so. The Absolute level of Cosmic History is a state of total harmony. Where every level of every part of all the dimensions exists in a state of perfect and absolute balance—mathematically, this is the Zero Point. At the relative level, we see that everything is a process. Is what we know merely a function of our sense perceptions? Is what we experience through our sense organs really the totality of what can be known? We know about things beyond the five senses through analogical metaphors and inference. What we think of as knowledge is like a little frog at the bottom of a well that looks up and sees a circular sky and thinks that's all there is. Is it possible that our consciousness is like this?

The point is that developing a meditative state of mind is mandatory so that you are able to see things clearly and recognize something distinctly different from what you may be accustomed to. The purpose of this kind of discipline is for acquiring a genuine transcendentally objective point of view which is the basis of any real science or understanding—where the subjective egoic mind is eliminated from the process of knowing or of evaluating. Cosmic History is the Absolute system of knowing intrinsic to the all-abiding reality.

You also must understand that your mind has all sorts of obstacles in it so that even when you do get a new idea you may put that idea in some frame of reference that denatures that idea or declaws it or takes the zip out of it. This is because consciously or unconsciously you think: "I know where that idea belongs", and then you go find a place for it in your back mind cupboard and put it there with some other stodgy thoughts when it has no basis to be there.

This is just to illustrate how challenging it can be for the mind to receive something entirely new and pure like Cosmic History. Some people could read Cosmic History and say: "Oh, Cosmic History is like Blavatsky's *Secret Doctrine*," and then immediately give it a reference point. Alternatively, people might say: "Oh, Cosmic History is like Toyenbee's *Study of History*" or "Cosmic History is like Oswald Spengler's *Decline of the West*" or "Cosmic History is like the micropedia of the *Encyclopedia Britannica*."

To resist needing to reference or compare something new is very difficult. Especially since we live in a time in which the

> *... developing a meditative state of mind is mandatory so that you are able to see things clearly and recognize something distinctly different from what you may be accustomed to.*

information explosion is spreading and expanding at such an exponential rate that there are problems of discrimination and of understanding what knowledge is useful or what pieces of information fit where.

Cosmic History is not what it may appear to be, it cannot be categorized into outworn compartments and ultimately cannot be compared with anything else. This is because Cosmic History is the absolute reformulation of the human mind and the human knowledge base. This new knowledge base comes from a planetary/cosmic perspective that is universal, valid and adequate for all human beings everywhere and has nothing to do with any kind of ideologies, nationalistic, religious or spiritual distinctions of any kind.

Cosmic History is involved in exploring what is available to the senses as well as understanding the relativistic limitations of sensory knowledge according to time, culture, language, etc. All of these factors affect what we know. Is there an objective truth? Have we taken into consideration language, culture conditioning, etc? The Buddhist's quest for enlightenment also seems to be to get to this place beyond the reflexes of conditioned mind where reality can be directly experienced.

These are important yet subtle points in the study of Cosmic History. There cannot be a genuine description of the universe without a consideration of the nature of your mind and the relationship of your mind with the universe. To know yourself you don't go outside of yourself. It seems many Eastern religions say you just need to know yourself and that is all you need to know. It seems like what we need to seek in Cosmic History is a higher synthesis or higher balance of the internalizing studies of self with study of the "other" which is the so-called "world outside of the self." Cosmic History embraces these two polarities and seeks a synthesis of these so we don't have just a quietism or escapism of the mind.

It is these considerations of the nature of mind, consciousness and the sacred order of reality that elevates your mind, putting you into a particular mental screen that creates the quality of Cosmic History as a living process of transmission. It is this quality that we wish to cultivate. Cosmic History is a

Cosmic History is not what it may appear to be, it cannot be categorized into outworn compartments and ultimately cannot be compared with anything else. This is because Cosmic History is the absolute reformulation of the human mind and the human knowledge base.

profoundly spiritual mental form of discipline, inquiry, investigation and system of categorization of knowledge. Cosmic History elevates the human being from a fragmented, nationalistic, sectarianist state of mind into a planetary boundary-transcending state of mind that liberates all beings into galactic freedom.

Cosmic History shows us that our roles are magnificent and divine. We are all coming into self-realized illumination. The *Cosmic History Chronicles* is merely a pointer directed at you, yourself as being the one to go forth and investigate the universe in a radically different way, according to the new principles of human knowledge.

Part I • The Story

Chapter 2
Cosmic History, the Law of Time and the Synchronic Order

How do we prepare the mind to receive the influx of the new? This is a major theme of the *Cosmic History Chronicles*. The mind of the planetary human is a conditioned mind that carries with it the baggage of some 5,000 years of accumulated karmic conditions, egoic tendencies, along with all the deformations of habitual thought including: customs, cultural and religious biases, prejudices and cultural chauvinisms, including male/female chauvinisms. When we examine the mind of the planetary human, it appears as a bewildering confusion of patterns of thought and customs and habits. So the question is: How do we clear this out to get to something new? How do we reformulate this?

When you get to the level of being entrained in the Thirteen Moon calendar, then actually you are being brought back into the divine perfection. You are being introduced into the *synchronic order* and into the systems and practices that are meant to re-educate your DNA, or your genetic sensibility to patterns of perfection rather than patterns of imperfection. If you have genetic defects

TIME IS THE ATMOSPHERE OF THE MIND

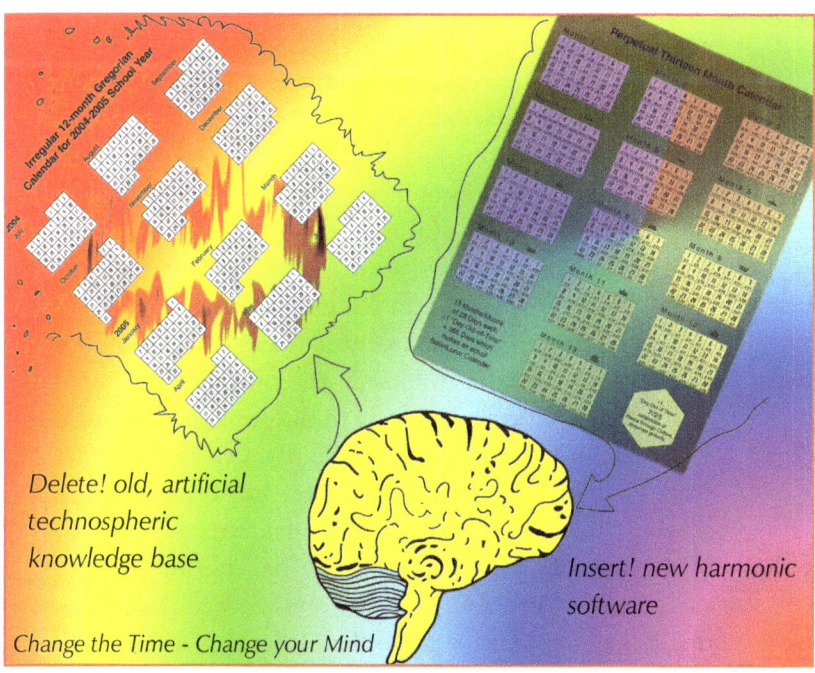

A calendar is an instrument for the harmonization of the human mind with the mathematical principles of nature. The 13/Moon, 28-day calendar harmonizies the mind with nature. The 12/Month Gregorian calendar currently in use is not such an instrument.

or disorders and you entrain them into forms and molds that are based in the disorder, then of course, you will never repair the genetic disorders or deficiencies.

Disorders and deficiencies then become enhanced by a greater and greater reliance on material technologies, inclusive of all the new biotechnologies, which are guaranteed some type of authority or power by certain power holders. This is the whole point of historical materialism; it is an eclipse of God. It creates an absolutely diabolical addiction and reliance on the short term material technologies that pretend to address the shortcomings of human thought and behavior, but only ensnare the human ever more deeply into defective patterns of thought and behavior.

This is all rooted in the irregular Gregorian calendar program. Virtually all of the conditioned reflexes of the mind of the planetary human, for the most part and in most parts of the world, are held together by the framework of the timing program of a particular society or culture. The planetary human, in particular, has been raised by and is a product of the 12:60 Gregorian calendar program along with the mechanical clock, which results in the mechanization of time. The Gregorian calendar that is run year in and year out only deepens the conditioned patterns of thought or the acceptances as absolute concrete reality of concepts like taxes, democracy, war, money, economic success, insurance and holidays—all of which are institutions and patterns of thought held in place by the Gregorian calendar.

The creation and establishment of the Thirteen Moon calendar program and the reentrainment of the human mind and sensibility is what will wean the human being away from this addiction to irregularity and to glittering gadgets and gizmos that pretend to correct the irregularity. Glamour technologies pretend to make life better and pretend to improve on your sensory intelligence or intellectual deficiencies. The program of the Thirteen Moon calendar is a radical step, which is the whole purpose of the Cosmic History—to lead the soul back to the divine perfection of the order of the universe as it actually is. By taking this step, it is not that the human is necessarily

> *The Gregorian calendar that is run year in and year out only deepens the conditioned patterns of thought or the acceptances as absolute concrete reality of concepts like taxes, democracy, war, money, economic success, insurance and holidays—all of which are institutions and patterns of thought held in place by the Gregorian calendar.*

improving on nature, but that by being relieved of life according to patterns of irregularity, the human is restored into ever-greater patterns of perfection.

The function of the various teachings and volumes of Cosmic History is to reorient us to different orders of perfection and wholeness by reintroducing the human system of being and thought to new levels of perfection of cosmic order and knowledge. This will allow the human being to advance up the mental and spiritual evolutionary ladder to greater and greater perceptions of the self and of the Divine Order. The human will then understand that to think such perfection is impossible was merely a function of faulty perceptions, which was thought to be the basis of reality in the old order of time and of the old calendar.

Harmonic Matrix—Key To Supramental Evolution

As the human being progresses through the synchronic order with the systems of knowledge and perceptions that are offered by Cosmic History, then the human will come into greater and greater sense of the divine perfection. At this point, there will no longer be any need for theaters and shopping malls or any other forms of second-hand entertainment. At this stage, the human being will be satisfied with its own fascinating perceptions of reality, which will be all the entertainment it needs. Then, because the sense perceptions are finally purified, the human gains entryway and begins living the highest astral movie.

Only through the purification of the sense perceptions can the sheer harmonic beauty of universal reality be immediately apprehended in such a way as to be sufficient to satisfy all of the deepest human longings for joy, beauty, order and harmony. As the sense organs further open and the human ascends up the evolutionary ladder, life will take on a brilliant new color, and it will be outrageously ecstatic just to be alive! The human will then evolve from the evolutionary stage of germination to generation, which is the stage of going from conscious to continuing conscious, then on to super conscious and finally hyperorganic conscious.

Further advancement up the hyperorganic evolutionary ladder of consciousness establishes sensory teleportation and time travel as the norm. This leads to an elevated feedback system conducted through purified sense organs attuned to the realization of the perfection of the divine natural order of reality. The feedback within the human being will then be so emotionally upleveled and inspired that it will begin to extrude the hyperorganic architectural forms of the advanced synchronic order.

All of this is due to an assimilation of the contexts and contents of Cosmic History as it is permeated and penetrated into the human social order. It is important to understand how these processes will come about and what relationship they have to the calendar change and the replacement of the irregular timing program by a program that is a harmonic perfection. But what is harmonic perfection? Do you understand what divine perfection actually is?

Through daily use of the Thirteen Moon calendar, the human gradually evolves to greater states of simplicity of its physical needs. As this happens, the human will reach a more highly evolved existence as a spiritual being of a purely nonmaterial, nonphysical, invisible plane. Again, all of this is due to the assimilation of the knowledge of the Cosmic History as it is absolutely rooted in the synchronic order—and the living out of that order. We are talking about the standard of measure in fourth-dimensional time as the information that informs the biology of life encoded in the calendar itself—this is another key point.

So the point of the calendar change, then, is to eliminate old thought-forms that create entropic belief systems, which are held into place by this matrix of the Gregorian calendar. To take that matrix away or to abolish it, as it were, from being the basis of the timing principles of every day life will radically shake up the entire system of thought of the planetary human (which is actually the system of thought of the unconscious noosphere). This is absolutely necessary for establishing a matrix foundation of the new.

When we replace the Gregorian calendar with the Thirteen Moon/28-day cycle, we are not just replacing one calendar with another; we are actually replacing an irregular matrix with a perfect harmonic matrix. The irregular matrix in and of itself is responsible for all the entropic vision that dominates the society that governs the world today. Just the unconsciously accepted pattern of irregularity creates nothing but a proliferation of entropic and irrational tendencies within the social order that follows this calendar. These entropic and irrational tendencies that accentuate fundamental insecurities are the root cause of the sensation of history, of historical determinism and ultimately of historical materialism.

Within the confines of this historical determinism and historical materialism of the planetary human are such notions as changing styles, technology that wears out and of always needing to have something new. This needing to replace the old with something new (which is never really anything new but just actually a more fleeting and ephemeral version of the old) is the very essence of the effect of following this particular imbalanced programming device.

> *When we replace the Gregorian calendar with the Thirteen Moon/28-day cycle, we are not just replacing one calendar with another; we are actually replacing an irregular matrix with a perfect harmonic matrix.*

By eliminating this erroneous programming device altogether, you are eliminating all those tendencies of historical determinism and historical materialism, inclusive of all concepts of novelty. The very notion of history itself is some type of cumulative progression of (supposedly) better and better ideas, concepts, forms and realities. In actuality, history is just the reverse of that. What the historical human calls progress is actually an accelerating degeneration of human impulses, of the quality of human life and of the entire fabric of existence.

In some ways, the current planetary human can be viewed as a type of barbaric aboriginal. This is the result of being encased in this artificial calendar matrix at the end of history. For it is this matrix that holds in place all the habitual patterns of thousands of years, including the killing and ingesting of innocent animals, which further foments aggressive instincts, which not suprisingly find their outlets in war, violence and acquisitive philosophies of greed and monetary power.

> "There was a time, the Golden Age we call it, happy in fruits and herbs, when no men tainted their lips with blood, and birds went flying safely through the air, and the field rabbits wandered unfrightened, and no fish was ever hooked by its own credulity: All things were free from treachery and fear and cunning, and all was peaceful. But some innovative, a good for nothing, whoever he was decided, in envy, that what lions ate was better, stuffed meat into his belly like a furnace, and paved the way for crime … one crime leads to another." Pythagoras—From *Ovid's Metamorphosis*

At this point at the end of history, all the cultural norms, forms and vocabulary of the planetary human become increasingly limited and the cultural horizon becomes increasingly diminished and lowered. Popular forms of media fill the mind with slogans and expressions, taking the place of any original kind of thinking. This is what we mean when we say the planetary human, in some ways, has been reduced to a type of decaying barbaric aboriginal—which in many ways is to the benefit of something new coming. It is not hard to get rid of

For it is this matrix (artificial calendar) that holds in place all the habitual patterns of thousands of years, including the killing and ingesting of innocent animals, which further foments aggressive instincts, which not suprisingly find their outlets in war, violence and acquisitive philosophies of greed and monetary power.

> *If you pull the Gregorian calendar from your consciousness, what you are actually doing is becoming conscious of all the collective unexamined belief systems, customs and all the other repetitive false programs that govern the dominantly agreed upon reality.*

something that is decayed. If something is decayed you just pull it out. If you pull the Gregorian calendar from your consciousness, what you are actually doing is becoming conscious of all the collective unexamined belief systems, customs and all the other repetitive false programs that govern the dominantly agreed upon reality.

Then you have a vacuum. This vacuum is filled by the golden matrix of the new—the Thirteen Moon/28-day matrix, which is radically different from the Gregorian matrix. As opposed to being irregular, irrational and hence leading to ever greater diversity of entropic diversions that go nowhere and can never achieve harmonic resolution—the harmonic perfection of the Thirteen Moon/28-day calendar is not only a vehicle for the reharmonization of the human mind and ultimately of the human DNA, but also a tool for the instant transcendence of history. There is no history in harmonic perfection.

Harmonic perfection consists of a resonance of qualities of form and pattern and movement in relationship to each other, but there is nothing of the movement caused by irregularity. The movement caused by irregularity is what creates the notion of progress. Because things are so irregular you have to progress to make them better, but you will never make them better if you are always coming from a place of irregularity. This creates the ceaseless notion of progress in history.

Whereas, in a harmonic matrix there is no movement of irregularity—there is only resonance of harmony, which is always in a syntropic movement. This harmonic matrix introduces 13 numbers, which represent primal patterns of radiant energy. These numbers can be thought of as radio-pulses that are akin to the pulsations of radio waves from the dense core of the pulsar or quasar. The 20 symbols represent the cycle of frequency-range possibilities for transformation or evolution that each of these radio-pulses may undergo.

> "If the thirteen numbers are the light that arouses the mind and body, then the twenty directional positions are the water that nourishes this very same mind and body. In the interplay of thirteen numbers and twenty symbols lies the in-dwelling

galactic code-bank that informs the resonant structures comprising the symbol-woven tapestry of our reality." The Mayan Factor p. 89

The harmonic matrix can do nothing but create increasingly rich and more diverse levels of harmony. This is quite a contrast from historical determinism and is the reason Cosmic History is predicated on the calendar change. The replacement of the old calendar means the uprooting of old beliefs and hence creates the openness and thirst for new beliefs or patterns of thought. The very matrix of the harmonic pattern predisposes the mind ultimately to receive a new vision of cosmos. Cosmos means order. True cosmos is what is encoded into the form and dispensation of Cosmic History. True cosmos—meaning the utter absolute order of the universe as it was originally and still is originally manifest by God, the Supreme Source.

If God is perfection (and God can't be anything but perfection) then how can the universe be anything less than perfect? The imperfections of the universe are due to misperceptions and conditioned reflexes that ultimately have their origin in mistaken patterns of thought due to mistaken notions of time and space. If we look at the universe of God, we see infinite patterns and cycles of birth and growth and maturation and decay. But all of this is a matter of forming an overall configuration, which gives us one of the manifestations of the universe, the Cycle of Becoming. And likewise, there is a Cycle of Return.

The Cycle of Becoming is the cycle of manifestation in the physical plane. And the Cycle of Return is the cycle of the soul emerging from the physical plane into an ever increasing spiritual plane of existence. So the Cycle of Becoming has to do with a natural process of generation and regeneration, whereas the Cycle of Return has to do with the ascent into greater and greater perfection.

The ultimate perfection is not a physical plane nor material plane perfection, but a spiritual perfection. It is the material or physical plane that undergoes the different stages and cycles of becoming and generation; whereas the soul itself is imperishable

The ultimate perfection is not a physical plane nor material plane perfection, but a spiritual perfection.

and immortal. The soul is the vehicle of the spirit that ascends the ladder of return, eventually freeing itself from every fixation on the physical plane that caused it to incarnate the way it has. Once the soul is freed from physical plane fixation and need for physical plane manifestation, then the return journey quickens and returns to source. Questions concerning the original nature and destiny of the soul will be addressed in later volumes, namely IV & VI.

THE CALENDAR CHANGE *IS* COSMIC HISTORY

While the Thirteen Moon/28-day cycle appears third-dimensional, we should not be deceived by appearances—its mathematical perfection automatically places it in resonance with the fourth-dimensional mental fields of the synchronic order.

We are describing the structure and process of Cosmic History. When we talk about the calendar change, we see it is absolutely pivotal to the descent of Cosmic History. The calendar change *is* Cosmic History. The calendar change is how the principle of Cosmic History goes from a state of chaos to a state of cosmos. The chaos of the old calendar is the fertile ground for the birth of the cosmos of the New Time and of Cosmic History, which is a function of the harmonic perfection of the Thirteen Moon/28-day cycle. So the calendar change itself is a manifestation of Cosmic History. The responses of people to the Thirteen Moon calendar and how people's lives change according to their use of this calendar are manifestations of Cosmic History becoming rooted through different human forms and vessels.

With the Thirteen Moon calendar and the Law of Time, the human mind has a new matrix by which it can be reformulated and brought into the synchronic order. In other words, the calendar itself is a pure reflection of the perfection of the synchronic order as the fourth-dimensional level of the synchronic patterns of creation set forth by God's decrees and commands with regard to the creation of the universe. By its nature, then, the synchronic order *is* cosmos—the very fabric that holds the universe together.

Since Nature is merely the reflection of the nature of God, and the perfection of the soul is a reflection of the moment-to-moment synchronization of the perfection of God, in this way, the purpose and decrees of God are made known and play themselves out with regard to the garment of nature on the fourth-dimensional level. While the Thirteen Moon/28-day cycle appears third-dimensional, we should not be deceived by appearances—its mathematical perfection automatically places it in resonance with the fourth-dimensional mental fields of the synchronic order.

Since the synchronic order represents the perception of the totality of time at any given moment, the human being naturally begins to become entrained by the fourth-dimensional order of reality, merely by following the Thirteen Moon/28-day cycle. This synchronic order, then, is one of the base levels of knowledge of Cosmic History.

Insofar as we have Cosmic History, we have cosmos/order and history/process. The synchronic order introduces a dimension of history as process, manifesting different levels of knowledge and what we might call wakefulness and illumination. There are different levels of enlightenment and awakening that form an aspect of the play of the synchronic order. This is very well detailed in the *Dynamics of Time—the Evolution of Time as Consciousness*, which contains 260 postulates and is the rough outline of Cosmic History as history. You have cosmos and then the pattern of order of cosmos as it plays out in an unfolding which is called "time" or "history."

By establishing the planetary human in the Thirteen Moon/28-day cycle, then the human mind has a reformulated matrix and also becomes imbued with a system of knowledge of the Law of Time and the synchronic order. This system of knowledge attunes the mind to the greater orders of cosmos and the greater patterns of cosmic unfolding which is the history of the cosmos.

Since the synchronic order is perfection and everything within the perfection reflects everything else within the perfection—then the entire universe becomes knowable to anyone who submits completely to being in the cosmic order. This level of the cosmic order constitutes the unfolding of cosmos—the history part of the Cosmic History. You can see, then, that the planetary human by being in the Thirteen Moon/28-day calendar matrix, is naturally disposed to orient toward Cosmic History. Simply by following this harmonic calendar, the planetary human is playing out and manifesting Cosmic History. Of course, the perception of the presentation of Cosmic History could only be from the point of view of the assumption that the calendar change has already occurred. The level of presentation and the orientation of the perceptions and insights of the Cosmic History are completely embedded in a state of mind and consciousness that has already been altered by the calendar change.

Of course, this would be so because the principles who are the instruments of the Cosmic History being brought into the human mind plane manifestation—the sorcerer and the apprentice—have already been living these codes. The sorcerer in particular, having been the principle agent for the manifestation of these codes, has already had his mind altered and changed into being completely on the other side of the wall of mechanized time. In order for the principles of Cosmic History to affect the rest of humanity, they have to be, as we have observed elsewhere, living embodiments of not only Cosmic History but of the synchronic order. This is the way the Cosmic History is able to be communicated to the mass of humanity. In this way, also, the Thirteen Moon calendar is what we might call a "noospheric stepping stone" or a particular way of reintroducing divine perfection into the human consciousness.

The consciousness of the current planetary human almost shudders at the thought of divine perfection. Why? Because divine perfection means the end of novelty, the end of history, the end of the addiction to all of the virtual entertainment and technological doo-hickeys that are attempted to relieve the disorders, but which only actually create greater disorders by creating addictive dependencies. In the future society, we will not need cell phones, Internet, and IPods and Palm Pilots, nor will we need movies and movie theaters, television, shopping malls or even airplanes. Most planetary humans living in the more affluent societies of global civilization just get terrified at that prospect. But that is what divine perfection means. The dolphins don't go to movie theaters. The deer don't use the Internet. The squirrels don't watch television. This is because those creatures are already living in the divine perfection.

The *Quran* says at the end of Sura 33 that God offered the trust to the mountains and to the Earth and to the creatures, but they all refused it. Only man was foolish enough to accept the trust, to act as if he were divine. This is what we are talking about. The end result of accepting that trust is the entire disorder of civilization, which is based on the addictive reliance to various forms of media and entertainment. This artificial reliance creates a greater and greater removal of the mind of the planetary human from even a remote perception of the divine. Think of the lives of the humans featured in *People* or *Us* magazines, for instance. For most of them, the idea that life is sacred or that there is actually an underlying divine perfection beneath their daily existence is very remote. It is about as far from sacred order as you can get.

Lifting The Veil Of The Permutation Matrices

As we know, the Thirteen Moon calendar is much more than a calendar, but actually a permutation matrix containing many different levels of information. We are actually dealing with two matrices: One is the telepathic/biological matrix, which is a pattern of seven-by-four. This is an elementary pattern and it is a formulation of the primary ratio of the Law of Time, which is 4:7::7:13. So at the most primary level the 4 x 7 creates the 28-day matrix where you have four sequences of seven days or a seven kin program. This is the minimum matrix that manifests the Law of Time in its formulation 4:7::7:13. This 28-day matrix multiplied by 13 creates the 365-day solar cycle, less the Day out of Time. It is not the same as being in the irregular Gregorian calendar matrix, nor even in the lunar calendar matrix, which is either 29 or 30 days alternating.

The reason for the 28-day matrix is its harmony. The lunar calendar of 29 and 30 days still keeps you at an irregular pace; whereas the 28-day cycle of the 13 moons eliminates all irregularity. This point is very profound because this is the primary matrix of the Law of Time, which is the basis of harmony in the universe. And it is also for this reason that it creates the biotelepathic matrix. Bio because it is the physical plane biological being that is being coordinated by this 4 x 7 matrix, and telepathic because all perfection which eliminates disorder attains to a level of instantaneity of mind, which is the basis and meaning of telepathy. Coordinating your biological life according to

Part I • The Story

this 28-day cycle is conducive to the increase of telepathy—it's the biotelepathic cycle.

The other matrix is the 260-unit matrix which is the 13 x 20. So you have a 4:7 and then 7:13. When you add the seven to the thirteen, you get 20. So you have the 4 x 7 matrix at one end of the formulation of 4:7::7:13 and the 13 x 20 matrix at the other end of the formulation, which is the purely telepathic higher dimensional matrix.

When you combine these two matrices, the 4 x 7 (perfect biological cycle) and the 13 x 20 (purely telepathic cycle), you create a master permutation matrix or index. Cosmic History is a function of 13:20 time, which means it has always existed and permeates everything. The 13:20 matrix or Harmonic Module is the fractal yardstick of radial time with multiple applications. The combination of these two matrices unlocks the code that opens up the mind to the new or to the potential of being reformulated. Its base is already reformulated by living through the 4 x 7 time matrix. Once that base matrix has been established, then it becomes capable of actual higher levels of content reformulation and more sophisticated levels of permutational reformulation. This is simply because of the possibilities of permutation of bringing the two timing matrices together.

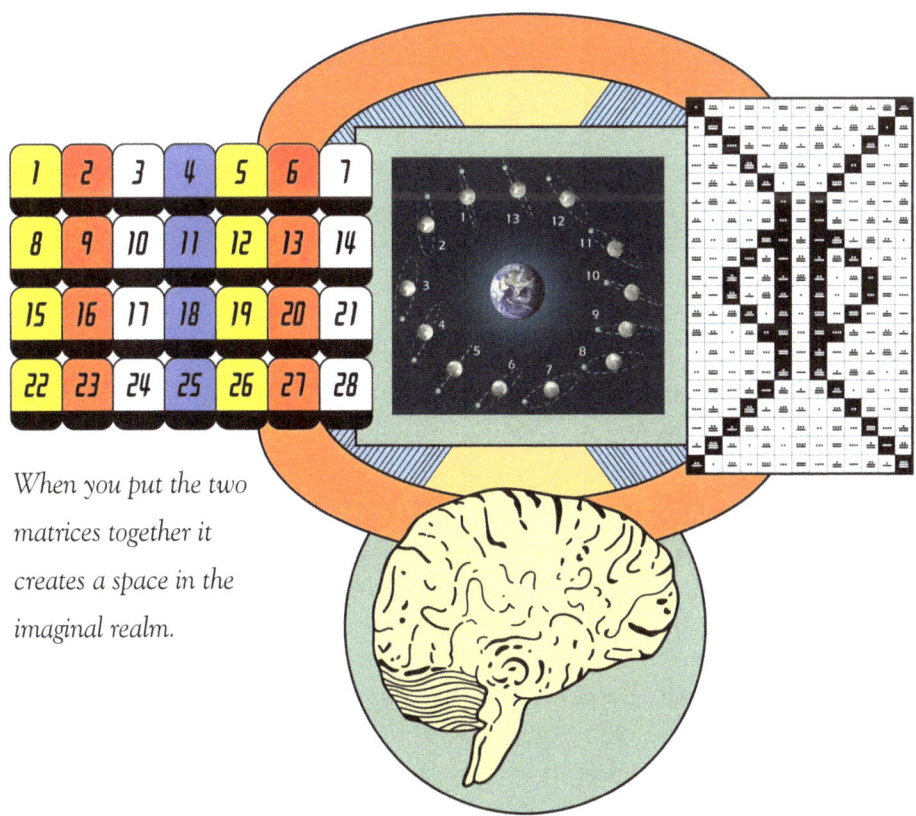

When you put the two matrices together it creates a space in the imaginal realm.

33

These two matrices create a powerful stimulus to the investigation and imaginative exploration of what Cosmic History presents. Keep in mind that Cosmic History in the Absolute sense is the actual nature or the whole of reality. Then there is the Cosmic History, which is the *Cosmic History Chronicles*. The *Cosmic History Chronicles*, of course, cannot come close to encompassing the totality of the reality of Cosmic History. But through formatting according to the synchronic order, a discriminating choice of content areas and their juxtaposition to each other, the *Cosmic History Chronicles* create, what we might call, the incentive for the expansion of the synchronic mind.

In other words, different kinds of knowledge are located in the various *Cosmic History Chronicles*, that for the synchronic mind, become the incentive to open up to larger or higher, more synthesizing levels of the synchronic order as contained within the two matrices of the cycles of time. These matrices correspond to an inherent harmonic/genetic program within the human system itself.

In this way, the Tzolkin or 260-day cycle in combination with the Thirteen Moon/28-day cycle, then becomes a type of virtual or inherent encyclopedia of time. There are different levels we are dealing with, like: The ordering of the biological reality and the ordering of the imaginal or telepathic plane reality. The telepathic plane reality can be experienced by following the *Dreamspell* oracle codes and the MOAP (Mother of All Programs) codes on a daily basis. It is important to begin to see where the program is located in the psi bank and in the *Dreamspell Genesis*.

When you put the two matrices together, the juxtaposition creates a space within the imaginal realm. This space accommodates whatever particular meaning may come from the recognition of the juxtaposition of different components or elements of the *Dreamspell Genesis*. This familiarization, and becoming more and more accustomed to experiencing synchronicities between the different techniques for reading the synchronic order, is what opens up the mind to the potentials of sensory teleportation and ultimately to time travel. This is the real exploration of the imaginal realm, or what we might call the systematic scientific exploration of the imaginal realm, which is also referred to as time travel. But this comes first from being able to understand and live the juxtaposition of these two particular timing matrices. Of course, the 260-day or 13 x 20 pattern is naturally going to orient you to the imaginal realm because it is, in and of itself, a fourth-dimensional program for reading third-dimensional events. As we know, the fourth-dimension is the imaginal realm, while the third-dimensional is the phenomenal realm.

We also know that there are different levels and orders within the 13:20 matrix, which qualify it as a type of *Encyclopedia of Time*. Much of this is displayed in the different tools or parts of the *Dreamspell* kit, which is like the outer symbolic form of the encyclopedia. Knowledge and comprehension according to the daily order of the Thirteen Moon calendar, as it moves through and with the 260-day calendar, is what creates the knowledge that gives you a sense of meaning as to what the different points of connection or juxtaposition might be about. As you practice this, you realize you are using these matrices or systems to open up your own mind. Your own mind is what has the knowledge or the answers and meanings that are provided for by these mappings of the synchronic order.

Part I • The Story

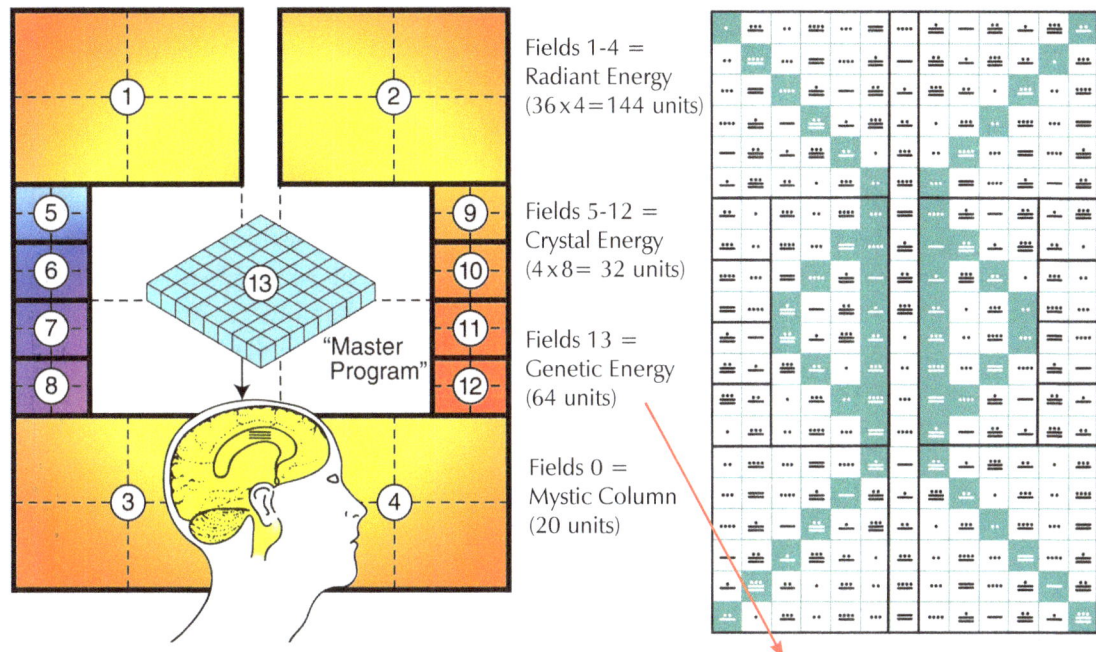

Fields 1-4 =
Radiant Energy
(36 x 4 = 144 units)

Fields 5-12 =
Crystal Energy
(4 x 8 = 32 units)

Fields 13 =
Genetic Energy
(64 units)

Fields 0 =
Mystic Column
(20 units)

Master Program
Tzolkin with 64-Unit Central Matrix "28:7"

so-called because the dark pattern holding it together consists of 28 units arranged into 7 sets of 4 units each, forming a perfect radial symmetry, each set of 4 units having a set of tones which each add up to 28. 28 x 7 = 196 or 14^2, the Bode number of the frequency of Uranus' orbit. If you subtract 28 from 64, the total number of units in the center, you get 36, the number of each of the 4 Light grids.

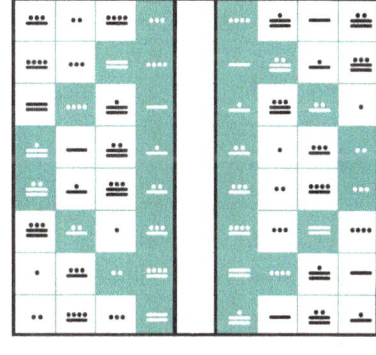

Harmonic Module

If you look at the 13:20 matrix, it actually breaks down into whole number quantum subdivisions, the center of which is the 28:7 code... So you have the biological dimension at the center (28:7), which is held together by the four light dimensions. The crystal dimensions extend out from the biological dimensions at the center...

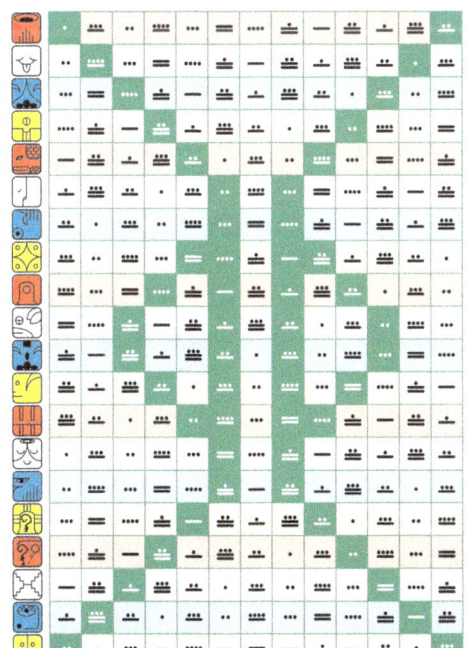

If you look at the 13:20 matrix, it actually breaks down into whole number quantum subdivisions, the center of which is the 28:7 code. You also have the four 6-by-6 unit light pattern codes on the four corners. These are actually mappings of the quanta ordering of reality. So you have the biological dimension at the center (28:7), which is held together by the four light dimensions. The crystal dimensions extend out from the biological dimensions at the center and become congruent with the four light dimensions—and so on. These are all held in place by the 13:20 timing matrix.

You can look at this 13:20 timing matrix and see in it the pattern of history with the 13 baktuns and the 260 katuns, so you have a historical coded encyclopedia in that way. You can extend this out by fractals into larger and larger wholes until you have the patterning of the evolutionary process of becoming and return. The first 130 units correspond with the Cycle of Becoming and the second 130 units correspond to the Cycle of Return. Each set of 130 units create congruent matching mirror symmetry patterns on each side. The sequences of 20 units going down the side of the harmonic matrix also correspond with the different planets and thus represent the interplanetary history.

Remember that all of these programs are embedded in the solar/galactic 13 Moon, 28-day calendar program in the relationships to the different sectors or parts of the matrices to each other. This is all just by way of saying that for Cosmic History to flourish it needs to have this perfection of the correction of the timing sensibility, since time is of the mind, and time is a vertical/spiritual phenomenon in relation to horizontal space. Once you have assimilated the *Cosmic History Chronicles*, then all you really have to do is master the codes of time as they are intrinsically embedded in the Thirteen Moon/28-day matrix and then the 260-day matrix.

With these tools alone you can delve into multidimensional levels of consciousness—and once your mind is really operating on these codes you will begin to experience increasing levels of sensory teleportation. This will become the norm. As you can see, the matrices contained in the calendar unlock limitless programs—but you are the one who provides the actual meaning. For every person there will be a different meaning for the different juxtapositions of codes—this is the fulfillment of the calendar change. The codes themselves become the keys and you become the walking knowledge.

When you accustomize yourself to multidimensional whole system comprehensions of time as it is encoded in the calendar, then your perceptions become increasingly holographic until you eventually attain the sorcerer's perception. You will be coming to levels of holographic perception where it will feel like you have on a pair of 3-D glasses—but for all the senses simultaneously. You will then experience things like supreme emotional rapture or synesthetic sexuality—all of this is heightened and enlightened by a complete disabuse of all of the material crutches and complete immersion into the codes of the Law of Time. You will end up with evolutionary experiences where the holographic whole systems sorcerer's perception becomes normalized. This perception will turn you into a rather fantastic creature whose senses have been transformed into radar systems, and the radar systems themselves serve to create instantaneous, integrative, full-blown holographic images of reality which enter into your system and reconstitute you however you wish. This is the planetary sorcerer's perception.

All of this we are describing is based on the calendar change. Without the calendar change none of this would be possible. Cosmic History then comes as a system of thought and technique to be learned and applied in order that the human being can take the next steps on the road of evolution into a holographic perceptual system. At that level it is understood how crude and primitive the shopping mall was.

Chapter 3
The Planetary Human

The arrival of the new planetary human necessitates the need for a larger, more comprehensive stage of information synthesis; this is the purpose of Cosmic History. Cosmic History is the highest level of information and comprehension to which previous history becomes subordinate, transformed and remade. The deeper pattern of the planetary human is just another Eternal return at a much larger point in the evolutionary spectrum where all meaning is now being irrevocably altered. In a fundamental sense, Cosmic History tells the story of the planetary human and is evoked by the collective unconscious mind-at-large. You who are reading these words are now being prepared for the next cycle of evolution; hence the necessity for further understanding and clarification of the how, the why and the who of Cosmic History.

The planetary human is of two types—the unawakened and the awakened. Both types share in common the fact that their lives, mind and consciousness have been shaped by technospheric factors that are relatively inoperable or even irrelevant. The unawakened planetary human operates unconscious of the technospheric influences and believes that traditional ways of thought still work. The conscious planetary human is awake to these factors of technospheric influence and sees the situation as the opportunity for a new global spirituality. The unawakened planetary human operates with a confused, barely conscious, highly polarized, dimly dawning global consciousness. The post-2012 planetary human operates with a noospheric compassionate consciousness tuned into the whole life of the planet. Sri Aurobindo sums up the mind of the unawakened planetary human or the ordinary man:

"To the ordinary man who lives upon his own waking surface, ignorant of the self's depths and vastnesses behind the veil, his psychological existence is fairly simple. A small but clamorous company of desires, some imperative intellectual and aesthetic cravings, a few ruling or prominent ideas amid a great current of unconnected or ill-connected and mostly trivial thoughts, a number of more or less imperative vital needs, alternations of physical health and disease, a scattered and inconsequent succession of joys and grief's, frequent minor disturbances and vicissitudes and rarer strong searchings and upheavals of mind or body, and through it all Nature, partly with the aid of his thought and will, partly without or in spite of it, arranging these things in some rough practical fashion, some tolerable disorderly order —this is the material of his existence…" Synthesis of Yoga Sri Aurobindo p. 69

The final stage of this evolutionary cycle of the unconscious planetary human or the hybrid mutant human is now concluding. At this late point in history, human intelligence has become somewhat stunted and limited because of habituated conditioning to machine and mechanistic forms of thought and behavior. This conditioning creates an increasingly limited expressive capacity for the human beings as well as an extremely limited capacity for long term memory, or memory that extends beyond this particular life. Cosmic History, as we mentioned earlier, is the mental stick of dynamite that blasts apart the self-limiting conditioned thinking of the human being while simultaneously presenting a method of structure and a vista of new knowledge and new possibilities so the human being can feel refreshed, uplifted and enlightened by its very contemplation.

Because we are at this event point, the noosphere becomes easier to understand. The point of Cosmic History is to build on the unified planetary self-perception. All the bickering, war and fighting have no validity since we are a unitary planetary being. Everything must be built from this base. All the perceptions you have accumulated must be washed away in the light of the truth that there is only one tradition, one religion, one Earth and one being. Cosmic History absorbs all traditions, spiritual teachings and civilizations and puts them into a higher context without negating anything positive or creative.

It is important to describe the nature of the planetary human so that you understand that Cosmic History is a type of cosmic psychology or description of cosmic psychological processes or states of mind (everything that exists is an unfolding of the cosmic psychology or psychological process). Even the twittering unconscious humans in the supermarket are an aspect of this cosmic psychology. All of these people create a field which is a relatively low level of the involution of spirit into matter—especially in a supermarket or any kind of store or marketplace. In these environments people, for the most part, are in a frenzy to take care of their food sheathe (body). Or if not in the market, they are out trying to find good clothing for their food sheathe or whatever will make their food sheathe more comfortable, without realizing they are only dealing with their body which has ultimately nothing to do with their soul or consciousness.

These examples represent one of the lower levels of the involution of spirit into matter where the consciousness is

All the perceptions you have accumulated must be washed away in the light of the truth that there is only one tradition, one religion, one Earth and one being.

gripped by an unconscious conditioning process that causes the humans to behave automatically in certain ways—this is referred to as historical materialism. In fact, we can define the entire collective field of the current planetary human as being this almost robotic, insect-like type of being who rotely responds to conditioned factors that have been established and maintained by the Gregorian calendar program. It is this same unconscious calendar program that keeps everything in this particular mental field called the "United States" or "Japan" or "Russia."

This state of consciousness is referred to as the degradation of spirit due to its being stuck at the lowest level of involution into matter. Simultaneously, there is obviously a great acceleration of consciousness occurring. Some people are somewhat aware that things are going faster, but most don't fully comprehend the scope of this acceleration, due to lack of measures of contrast. This is where they live, this is how it is. Like the goldfish in the goldfish bowl, they do not know that the water is dirty, they just live there. This is the way the collective mindfield actually is, and this is the reason for the descent of Cosmic History, which comes like a shaft of energy or beam of light and hits this field through the two particular agents, resulting in a quickening for all.

SELF-SACRIFICE AND THE FIRST MANIFESTATION OF COSMIC HISTORY

Knowledge or revelation is the only true way out of what we might call Satan's world or the cycle of samsara or the wheel of suffering or the realm of negativity and despair which characterizes much of the human consciousness today. This brings us to another quote from Sri Aurobindo:

"To rise to that height of liberation is the true way out and the only means of the indubitable knowledge." Yoga Letters Tome Two p. 29

To rise to indubitable knowledge is to rise to knowledge without a doubt; this is the only way you can get beyond the situation of suffering. This means you have to sacrifice. At the very least, you must sacrifice your time for the sake of the whole. But you have to sacrifice a lot more than time if you are to rise to real heights of new knowledge. In fact, there can be no new advance within the matrix of an old structure without a sacrifice. You have to sacrifice something of yourself—if not all of yourself that is attached or involved in the old to get to the new. This is a crucial point.

Cosmic History is a descent of a divine principle that occurs at a very specific point in time that is referred to as the closing of the cycle or the biosphere/noosphere transition. The original Cosmic History transmissions came during a specific four year cycle known as the *harrowing of hell* 2000-04, the point between the *Seven Years of Prophecy* 1993-2000 and the *Seven Years of the Mystery of the Stone* 2004-2011. So we are dealing with the situation of the meaning of the harrowing of hell, the meaning of self-sacrifice, the meaning of the incarnation of a divine principle and the meaning of a cultivation of different types or forms of compassion. As we have already stated, in order for there to be any kind of evolutionary ascent there has to first be a divine descent.

> ### HONORING THE CHIEF COSMIC HISTORY PROGENITOR
>
> Yellow Galactic Sun is the galactic signature of Pacal Votan, the chief technician of the galactic Mayan project. Because of the knowledge and the prophecies that Pacal Votan had laid in his tomb in Palenque, Chiapas, Mexico, Cosmic History has come about. Soon after the tomb was opened in 1952, the DNA codes were discovered along with the Van Allen radiation belts.
>
> The Law of Time comes from this Mayan stream with the foundation being a unified planetary self-perception. When everyone catches on to the Law of Time all streams of consciousness will be joined together and the planetary human will move into cosmic consciousness which will result in pure telepathy. What is known to God will start being known to human beings. At this stage there will not be any difference between esoteric and exoteric knowledge, but the streams will be utilized in a different way than during the time of human history.
>
> If it had not been for that tomb and for the life and work of Pacal Votan in his time more than 1300 years ago, Cosmic History could not be understood as it is today. The purpose and summation of the truth and the knowledge of Pacal Votan is summarized in a single word: Telektonon. This word was revealed to the Closer of the Cycle on Kin 144 Yellow Magnetic Seed in 1993. This word, because it had not been uttered until now, is so dense with information, inclusive of The Law of Time that it could only be a word that was a function of complete and absolute divine revelation.

Left to its own devices, humankind will only sink lower into the depths of the downward spiraling program of historical materialism. Therefore, at specific points in time there must be divine descents which are like jumpstarts in human consciousness. But now we are at the extraordinary moment of the closing of the cycle so there has to be an extraordinarily supernatural jumpstart. From within the vast chaotic matrix of the life of the planetary human there must occur a sacrifice followed by a quickening and then a germination of the new.

From the point of view of a type of objective understanding or even theory, it is easy to talk about divine descent or avataric emanation, or about the type of knowledge that is needed for a particularly evolutionary point—but to speak about it from the other side, from the point of view of the human instruments who are being called upon to embody or incarnate this divine principle, it is a very different picture.

For one thing, those humans are born just as humans; they are not born as anything else. And when they are born, they don't necessarily have a full center in their consciousness that says: Now I am born an avatar, I know what I will do. On the contrary, they are born into a human situation, which means they are born into a very specific type of family or household situation that have all of their programs, which of course, have been divinely ordained in their particular way to help shape the avatar-in-the-making to go in a particular direction.

But nonetheless, from the point of view of the person who is going to be filling the avataric role, there is not a clue as to what is actually in store. Sure, there may be moments of revelation when some inklings begin to emerge and there are certain intuitions that are followed slowly until it becomes more and more enlightened as to what the purpose and the role is. Someone doesn't come down and say: Now you are an avatar. It doesn't necessarily work like this.

Every human has a spark of the divine. God has placed the memory of Himself in every human heart and in everything that exists. But to incarnate fully a divine purpose and to be fully instrumented to be a vehicle of the Divine Plan is another matter. From the point of view of historical materialism, this is nonsense. But we know also that history is full of saints and mystics who have risen to supernatural heights. We know that those people who were able to incarnate a divine principle did so because they recognized and answered the call inside of themselves to rise to the highest level. Recognizing you are a divine incarnate means you must be willing to sacrifice everything with no compromise. If the self-sacrifice and surrender is complete, then you will be in the company of the greatest saints, yogis, mystics, prophets, sages and world teachers. But this is no easy task.

Once you have felt within yourself the call and you realize that that is the company that you are in, then this is what it is. You are no longer a so-called "normal" human being. To be a divine incarnate is not normal from a worldly point of view. If you read the life of Ramakrishna, you realize that from a certain age, especially once he was in his teens and early twenties, he was having samadhi and spiritual bliss and was clearly not "socially normal." This is just to illustrate that there are many different varieties and types of examples of spiritual incarnations.

With Cosmic History we are specifically dealing with two types who are embodying the principle of closing the cycle of history and regenerating the new cycle, which is what is necessary to incarnate the principle of Cosmic History. The one who is closing the cycle embodies or incarnates the conclusion of the principle of the Cycle of Becoming. The one who regenerates the cycle embodies or incarnates the principle of the Cycle of Return. It is impossible for the limited human reason to judge the way or purposes of the divine: As Aurobindo says: *"If you look at the human alone, looking with the external eye and not willing or ready to see anything else, you will see a human being only. If you look with the divine eye you will find the divine."*

Particularly in this time at the closing of the cycle it is very difficult to see the divine. As Christ predicted in the *Gospel of Matthew* 7: 15-16 that a sign of the End Times is that there will be many false prophets who shall be known by their fruits—it also says there will be wars and rumors of wars. It is this climate of false prophets and war time mentality that call forth from the darkest depths the cosmic evolutionary necessity.

If you feel that you are called and you speak about your needing to follow your destiny, you know you have to break rank sometimes because something is inside of you telling you to break out of the shell or the prison. From the human eye it may appear that you are breaking social norms. From the divine eye, you are going beyond to answer the call. This is the point or element of self-sacrifice.

Once you have heard the call and you choose to wholeheartedly answer that calling, whether you are fully conscious of it or not, your actions will always take you to the place where you are commanded to follow the deepest insight, the deepest glimmering, the deepest light that says: "Now you have to go here and now you have to do this." This means that whatever the social normative values are at the time of your incarnation, they are going to be relatively inhibiting to the divine urge beckoning you to evolve to the next spiritual level—or even in the context of a particular time, to evolve to a point where you can reflect back to the people of your time that they can do better spiritually, that they have forgotten that they can go to another level or that they need to have a renewed teaching or an inspiring reminder. Just to do that you have to step out of the social norms. So, needless to say, there is no way someone who is a messenger or an avataric emanation can remain within the social mold.

Sometimes it may be that in the process of the maturing of the avataric persona that the earthly personality will be immersed for a period of time in a socially normative situation. But this is only to learn certain values to help universalize the consciousness of the avataric personality. Once those values, norms and experiences are absorbed, that person may have to break out of its shell and go to the next level—this process continues until finally there is nothing left but the pure avataric emanation. Every time there is a break in the shell of socially normative values or life setting, that represents a self-sacrifice in terms of the egoic earthly personality.

From the divine point of view, this self-sacrifice isn't really a sacrifice but rather a shedding of a skin, a shedding of certain acquired trappings that may be inhibiting the fulfillment of the divine purpose through the avataric persona. Nonetheless, because the avataric personality is simultaneously playing out the role of an earthly human personality, there may be a sense of suffering, pain or even alienation when making the break with socially normative situations in order to attain the avataric wholeness.

In this way, all situations are perfectly designed in order for that avataric personality to become more universalized and whole. This is because it is only by becoming universalized and integrally whole that the avataric persona can attain that level of ripening or maturation where the statement, reflection or message that the personality is meant to communicate, incarnate and embody reaches maximal universal appeal. So the avataric persona will be one who is highly sensitive, who will be able to absorb willingly or unwillingly the influence of anyone they come into contact with and even channel that other person's energies, sometimes to their own detriment. This mediumistic quality of the avataric type is closely related with the aboriginal form of the shaman who, generally speaking, functions as a channel or a medium of different kinds of "spirit" energies on behalf of the tribe, clan or community. Likewise the avatar functions as a mediumistic instrument channeling a divine purpose or principle for the good of humanity.

Even if the avataric personality channels lower energies through acting as a medium absorbing the energies of other people who may not be as enlightened or divinely purposed as the avatar, then the avataric persona will partake in certain influences which may temporarily effect the well being of the avataric persona. This is all due to the highly susceptible mediumistic absorbency of the avataric personality. The only precaution for the avatar is intensified spiritual discipline and practice—the path of self-perfection. The avataric personality knows that even though the experience may be excruciating, it is a necessary stage in a process in which the soul is going through a deep, intense learning. When it reaches the other side, it realizes it has absorbed a little more of the world soul so that it has become even more universalized. In this way, for the avataric personality, all experiences are viewed as transcendental.

For instance, take the example of Saint Hildegard of Bingen, who went through years of harrowing doubt, struggling against her socially normative condition of being a nun within the church. In her time, being a nun was not so extraordinary, but rather a highly sanctioned social option. But even that social option was socially normative, and in this situation Hildegard had to continuously come up against and question her social environment, until it was finally clear that she had a calling and an important vision to communicate.

So you see that even someone like this had to break out of the social molds of her time. All the painful experiences she had were actually points of self-transcendence which led her to the point of a self-enlightening breakthrough so that she could finally just be herself. If you look at Hildegard's illuminated manuscript paintings, they reflect a whole universal view that had to be communicated at this time by a woman with this kind of vision. She served a very high purpose for her time, as well as our time, in exemplifying the path of a woman on a creative self-transcendent mission to manifest a type of universal creative glory that is saturated in the presence and being of the divine Godhead itself.

The point is that every avataric emanation has been chosen for a very particular moment in time. The *Cosmic History Chronicles* were chosen to be released specifically during the harrowing of hell for the point of time of the Closing of the Cycle. If we take the cycle of the harrowing of hell and look at the four solar galactic years (2000-04): Blue Galactic Storm, Yellow Solar Seed, Red Planetary Moon and White Spectral Wizard, we find that the principles or agents of Cosmic History were already engaged in the process of preparation at the beginning of this four-year cycle.

In some way, because of the extraordinary nature of the Closer of the Cycle and the Red Queen, the avataric agents to receive the descent of the Cosmic History, we could say that the harrowing of hell was specifically designed as a manifestation of the process of self-purification and self-sacrifice that was necessary for them to undergo to get to the point of being able to incarnate the principles of Cosmic History.

The first year of the four-year cycle, Blue Galactic Storm, involved much preparation in which the Closer of the Cycle had to issue a telepathic call to the Red Queen, who was living in Santa Fe, New Mexico at the time, for her to attend the Earth Wizard Leadership Conference at Mount Hood, Oregon. He knew he had to give the call and that she must be there. This was a real test. The next test began in the Solar Seed year when the whole process of Cosmic History was initiated. The two agents were brought together so that by the midpoint of that Solar Seed year the full engagement had occurred. Not too long after that, (as we have noted in the Forward) the process of Cosmic History began—the descent of that principle which was triggered at Teotihuacan, Mexico and the ceremony of the Closing of the Cycle. Then began the divine descent.

Part I • The Story

The divine descent meant that the two agents had to go through the next stage of utter catharsis to completely be able to embody the principle of Cosmic History and to become divine incarnates. For each of the two agents there was a unique earthly self-sacrifice that occurred. Each sacrifice was for a very specific purpose. For the transmitting agent, the Closer of the Cycle, the sacrifice was of a partnership of 22 years, as well as all the family ties involved in that partnership.

For the receiving agent it was the giving up of any kind of aspiration that she would ever lead in any way, a "normal" life. She entered fully into the process at age 29, so it was like she was taking sacred vows like Saint Hildegard of Bingen would have taken vows, in some analogous kind of way.

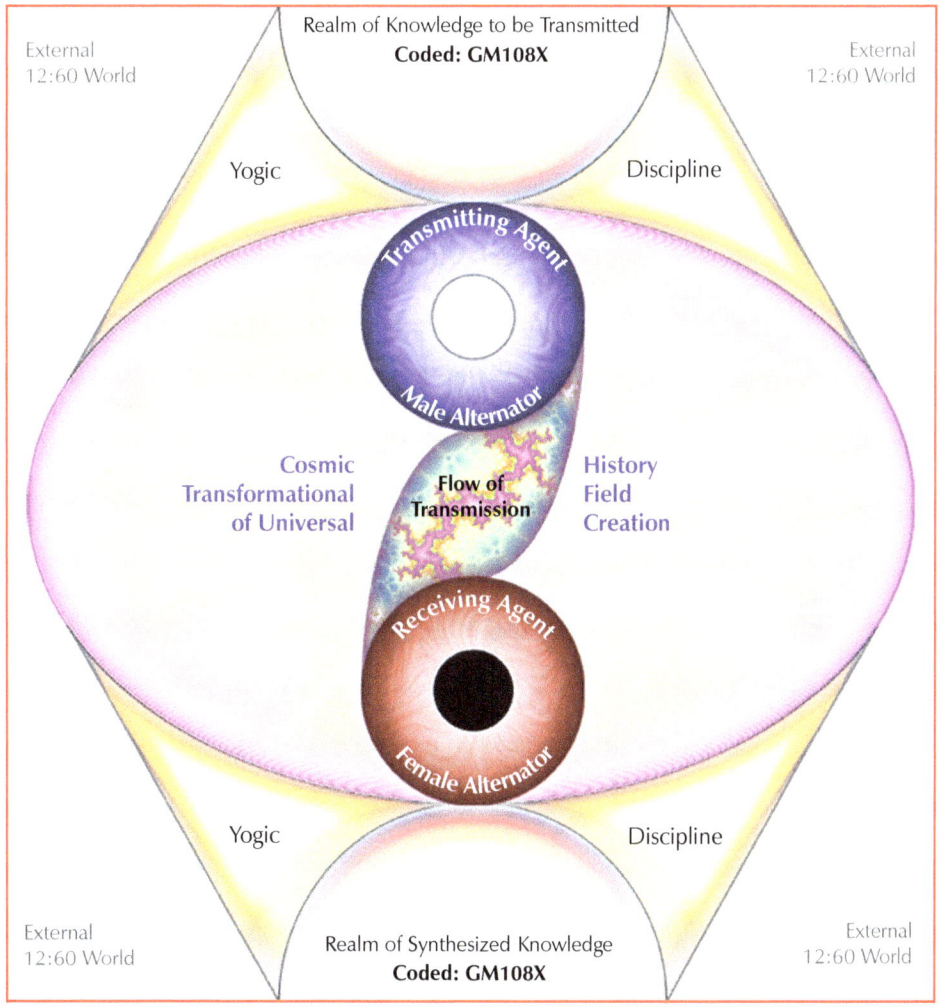

Purpose Of Self-sacrifice

From the divine perspective, the Closer of the Cycle's earthly relation and family ties had to be sacrificed altogether—everything had to be cleared out so the final embodiment of himself as a divine incarnate, as manifesting the principle of Cosmic History, could occur. The sacrifice represented the need to absolutely dissolve all historical models altogether. The main historical model being dissolved was state-sanctioned marriage and the nuclear family. By sacrificing this relationship it was also making a statement at the closing of the cycle that history and all of its institutions have to be dissolved. If all the institutions of history as we now know it are not dissolved or annulled, then there can be nothing new and the cause of evolution will not be served. Everything that is based in any kind of arbitrary form that exists at this point in the closing of the cycle, all has to be dissolved—especially those that have to do with the arbitrary and artificial contrivance of the state.

From the point of view of evolution, all the different forms that have evolved, that are state-sanctioned and also sanctioned even by organized religion—these have to be thoroughly questioned and dissolved. All the state institutions have to be deconstructed. The religious traditions have to be completely turned inside out to see what is actually real, what the traditions are serving and why. The true traditions will survive because they are transcendental and they serve purely transcendental purposes.

The point is that because of the very nature of historical materialism itself, all of the institutions are based on errors of perceptions—errors in the self-perception of the human in relationship to each other, and errors in the self perception of the human in relationship to nature and the divine. All of these perceptions are flawed and in error. If they weren't flawed and weren't in error, then the world wouldn't be as it is today.

These flaws and errors result in the faulty perception of the relation to the self and relationship to the environment and the cosmos and the relationship to the divine. Therefore, the self-sacrifice of the Closer of the Cycle is a teaching on the need

For the receiving agent it was the giving up of any kind of aspiration that she would ever lead in any way a "normal" life.

From the divine perspective, the Closer of the Cycle's earthly relation and family ties had to be sacrificed altogether.

for all the historical conventions and institutions to be dissolved, in order for higher evolutionary purpose to be served.

In the case of the self-sacrifice of the receiver, in foregoing any conventional "normal" type of life like the idea of marriage, children or career—all the things involved in the socially normative value system had to be absolutely sacrificed. In this case, while the Closer of the Cycle's self-sacrifice represents a dissolution of historical conventions and institutions, the regenerator of the cycle, the Red Queen's self-sacrifice, represents an actual purification of the new. This is because by the very age at which the Red Queen entered into this process of the self-disclosure of the avataric emanation, she had only a minimum set of experiences which included the experiences of her upbringing in her family—the experiences of breaking out of the family and the dissolution of the self that occurred through different intensified drug experiences, including a pivotal near-death experience at age 19.

After clearing out from this, she began to hear the call within herself so that by the time she was in her 25th year of age the connection had been made with the Closer of the Cycle and the magnetic path was opened up. From that initial meeting time until four years later at the midpoint of the Solar Seed year, she was already in a relatively purified state in the sense that she had very few worldly attachments and was very much ready to surrender or submit to the transcendental process that awaited her in becoming the apprentice to the Closer of the Cycle.

These are two specific examples of self-sacrifice: The one is the dissolution of history that is exemplified through the breaking up of the pattern of state-sanctioned marriage and the nuclear family, and the other is the giving up of all social normalcies in preparation for incarnating the new. The point is that when the apprenticeship is over, Red Queen will be totally accomplished and absolutely ready and purified to receive the complete descent of the imprint of the new, which is OMA or the Original Matrix Attained—this is to ensure that there is a whole new evolutionary impulse that is aroused from the original matrix. If these historical patterns are not dissolved, then the humans will not evolve.

Any avataric emanation represents the total of humanity. In this case, we have the two avataric emanations who represent the totality of humanity. This descent of Cosmic History or the divine principle occurred precisely at this point to these two avataric emanations who rapidly underwent many different facets of cumulative experience. These facets of experience represent a multiple diversity of personality styles and types of the planetary human as a whole organism. The process included the suffering of the harrowing of hell and then the redemption of the Mystery of the Stone bringing about the self-understanding and self-liberation that everything is a process of self-transcendence—to this degree the planetary human gets lifted up.

Votan and Red Queen represent such potent charges of the total universal reflection of the planetary human that when their energies came together, the destinal charge was so intense, that many social norms had to be broken. This appeared as an entering into different societal taboos in order to establish a new principle. Once the initial cathartic process had been endured, it was understood that personal catharsis is the basis and reason for developing universal compassion; compassion for absolutely every single human being in every situation that exists.

Just as if all the old institutions are not dissolved, the human will likewise not evolve—so if universal compassion is not developed, the human also will not evolve. These two qualities of dissolving completely the old and developing universal compassion are incumbent upon the avataric emanations to develop within themselves, because they are the reflection, in their multiple personality and in their multiple functions and experience, of the diversity of the planetary human. This is an inner process—the whole point is not to create more hero/heroine archetypes. The purpose of the incarnation of these archetypes is to raise the whole of humanity up to the next level.

For the whole to be raised up to the next level, there have to be two humans who actually embody the divine incarnate. Knowing who and where they are in time and knowing who the constituency of humanity is at that time in full consciousness, the two must fully embody the mandates of the divine principle in order that the planetary human can receive a new vibrational frequency. This new vibrational frequency comes by means of a new store and lode of knowledge, which is the Cosmic History. This is to lead the planetary human into the process of the transcendental reformulation of the mind and self and the purification of the soul.

The avataric emanations are required to embody the universal reflection of the human being in its entirety, every shade and aspect of its being and existence so the message can become absolutely universalized. This means that the thoughts, words and gestures of the aspects of the avataric principles who are incarnating the Cosmic History must become absolutely universalized. By becoming universalized, everything that is personal becomes transpersonal, and everything that is transpersonal becomes universalized. In this way, the Divine Plan is fulfilled.

In order for you to understand the meaning and the necessity of the *Cosmic History Chronicles*, you have to understand that this is a process that is a function of divine decree, which

> *By becoming universalized, everything that is personal becomes transpersonal, and everything that is transpersonal becomes universalized.*

is manifest through two types who are fulfilling a particular function. Though at first it might seem strange, this fact in itself is a major consideration in understanding why the Cosmic History is unique and why the two principles are so purposeful and meant precisely for this time.

It is not just a function of two people getting together and working out an idea inside of their heads—it is anything but that. This is a holy principle that is being passed through these two divine instruments and agents and is being sweated out through their lives and existence and through the sacrifice they have had to make to hold to this point and deliver this particular message.

So again, you see that through the dissolution of the old and through the cultivation and development of universal compassion for all beings lies the goal of the evolution of the planetary human. The self-sacrifice of all beings must come swiftly to ensure that by 2012 the planetary human has a clean soul, a clear mind and a new time.

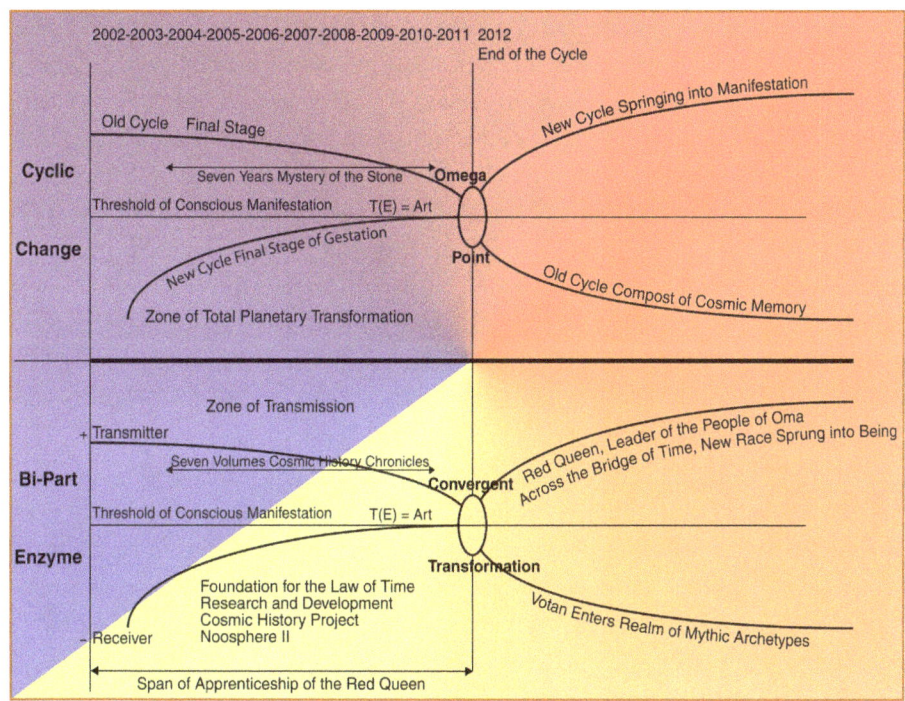

THE ORIGIN: FROM WHERE DID COSMIC HISTORY DESCEND?

After understanding the point of earthly origin of Cosmic History, it is important to see from where it descended. We have spoken earlier of Cosmic History as a descent from a higher-dimensional divine realm into the Earth consciousness. In this way, Cosmic History is an avataric descent. It represents a divine principle of the Absolute in relation to the relative, and illustrates how the relative is contained within the Absolute and how the Absolute contains the relative. The relative experiences progress, decline and spiral; the Absolute experiences Absoluteness. Cosmic History is a manifestation of this divine principle descended into a formulation of knowledge so that the principle of the Absolute and the relative then become a formulation known as Cosmic History.

Cosmos is the Absolute and history is the relative. This principle is designated as Cosmic History to demonstrate the entirety of the process of the interplay of the Absolute and the relative. This includes the descent of spirit and mind into matter—involution—then comes the evolution of mind and spirit out of matter. Mind and spirit can only evolve out of matter through the effect, impact or impression of different descents of mind or spirit. In other words, the mind and spirit are latent in the matter but will only operate within certain plateaus of consciousness until there is a new descent of spirit.

These new descents always take the mind and spirit that is within the matter and quicken it through a series of stages. You can see the process of that quickening through the great world teachers and avatars, who manifested with different transmissions, according to the need of the time. Each of these incarnations creates a slow succession of increments or leaps of consciousness that represent the activation of mind and spirit. In this nature and regard, Cosmic History is not only the final descent during this world cycle, but it is the first descent of the next evolutionary cycle. This means Cosmic History both summarizes all the previous stages of involution and evolution and also prepares for the next stage of evolution by laying the foundation for a whole, long cycle of spiritual/mental activation. This is a description of Cosmic History's descent into the Earth consciousness in context and in relationship to previous historical descents of avataric information and knowledge.

We see that there is a fundamental principle that is Absolute and relative, which steps down into a description of the cosmos in its multidimensional stages of progression. When we step that down even further, we can see the history of the universe as it looks to the naked eye. For example, when you first look at Cosmic History it looks like a flawless crystal ball. When you look at it more carefully, you see inside the crystal ball there are forms—maybe it has got a phantom pyramid inside of it—then you step that down again and you begin to contemplate how that phantom pyramid got inside the crystal ball. Maybe it will reveal to you how spirit impresses matter so that new forms and new cycles of being are initiated. Then you have to ask: How did this Cosmic History get initiated and activated in the first place?

Prior to the descent of Cosmic History, there have been people who have written universal histories. For example, Alexander from Humboldt wrote a very large book called Cosmos, which was like a Cosmic History but from a Nineteenth Century naturalist/botanist point of view. Then there was Madame Blavatsky, who wrote Isis Unveiled and The Secret Doctrine, which represent an unprecedented structure and formulation of knowledge very strongly utilizing the septenary or seven—of which Cosmic History has its antecedence: The seven volumes, the seven root races, the seven rays and so on. But nonetheless, Cosmic History is a totally fresh and new formulation of what it is to be human, what knowledge humans are actually capable of and where this knowledge is going to take them. This is the foundation of Cosmic History.

In Sri Aurobindo's *Yoga Letters*, there is a quote that is helpful in shedding light on Cosmic History in relation to mind and cosmos, and the nature of Cosmic History in the evolutionary trajectory that the planet and species currently finds itself. We are starting to understand that Cosmic History is a type of avataric descent, and the avataric manifestation always represents or embodies a divine principle in which to descend.

> *"The whole of humanity cannot be changed at once. What has to be done is bring the higher consciousness down into Earth consciousness and establish it there as a constant realized force. Just as mind and life have been established and embodied in matter so to establish and embody the sacramental force."* Sri Aurobindo

When Sri Aurobindo talks about the *supramental* consciousness, he is talking about it as a generalized force. Cosmic History *is* that generalized force made specific. In this regard, we can see that Cosmic History is the supramental—the bringing down and establishing of higher consciousness into Earth consciousness so it can become a fully realized force. In this way, Cosmic History is the manifestation of a higher principle, which is of evolutionary necessity. The avataric emanation comes at a point of evolutionary crisis, then the avatar manifests or embodies a particular principle. In this case, that particular principle is Cosmic History.

Cosmic History is the form of higher consciousness that is necessary to infiltrate and penetrate fully the present Earth consciousness. It is like a type of yeast acting as a fermenting agent to bring about the higher consciousness throughout the masses of humanity. Anything that is brought into the Earth consciousness must be brought in by earthlings. The chosen earthlings must function in an avataric manner so that they can embody what is to descend.

The avataric emanation comes at a point of evolutionary crisis, then the avatar manifests or embodies a particular principle. In this case, that particular principle is Cosmic History.

Context For Cosmic History In Earth Process

Once this process of the origin of Cosmic History is understood, next we have to understand that there is a context for Cosmic History entering into the Earth consciousness. In that context, two factors can be brought to light:

1. The Law of Time and the synchronic order (detailed in Chapter Two)
2. A context of anticipation for Cosmic History.

Context of anticipation: What Sri Aurobindo called the next stage of "supermental evolution" is the same as what Vernadsky and de Chardin called the "noosphere." Blavatsky did much foundational work regarding the number seven. Aurobindo says at first just a few key people will embody the next "supramental" or "avataric descent," which is accompanied by the revelation of new knowledge. We are the people initially embodying and rehearsing the "supramental descent" of Cosmic History. We are doing it by the power of seven within the context of the point in time that can be variously described as the biosphere/noosphere transition, or the End Time, the Closing of the Cycle, or the time of prophecy. The time defines the nature of what is required.

The principle of transmission of Cosmic History by earthly agents is then completely fitted to the Closer of the Cycle, creating a supramental bridge that goes from one cycle to the next. The bridge itself is a supramental construction. Crossing the bridge is a supramental effort and being on the other side of the bridge is a permanent shift to natural supermental functioning. The descent of the new principle comes from beyond the mind, *supramental*, but it is to assist in going from mere mind to the *supramental*. This is how the principle of Cosmic History works as a realized force. In other words, those humans who study and digest Cosmic History, in turn, transform into living emanations of this realized force (which is actually a force of evolution).

As a force of evolution, Cosmic History provides everything that you did not look at in the rearview mirror because you were driving too fast. Objects in the rearview mirror appear reversed and are always receding. The reversal of the rearview mirror is literally a mirror of your own process of reversal. In other words, when you see anything you are actually looking at two lenses. These two lenses are bringing you information from inside your head and putting it together through a process of crossover polarity. Objects in the rearview mirror mimic the reversal process in the optic nerve—so when you look in the mirror and it is receding, this is because you are looking at the past.

We see that in order for Cosmic History to be understood and accepted by other human beings or earthlings, it has to be exemplified through conscious human exertion of the avataric emanations for the avataric principle. Like it says in the *Quran*, if angels showed up with this information, no one would believe it—it would be beyond them. Divine information has to be communicated by humans so other humans can say: "Oh, it appears that they are humans just like me, so certainly I can get this too!" This is an important point. When we talk about the descent of the higher consciousness, we are also talking about the descent of the higher mind.

Interplanetary Descent

As we mentioned earlier, Cosmic History was sparked on a Skywalker day and originated on a Wizard day, which, according to the *Dreamspell*, represents Mars and Maldek, respectively. This tells us that Cosmic History is an interplanetary descent or a descent into interplanetary memory and knowledge, which has its cosmic origin in the *Vela pulsar*. This Vela pulsar is what pulsed the information of the larger Cosmic History frame of reference, reaching all the way back to the point of the ratio of the "Interval of Lost Time in Eternity" (detailed in Chapter 13). The Vela pulsar codes contain psychomythic clues and keys to unlocking the causes of the destruction of the previous worlds in our solar system. These destructions have *everything* to do with why Cosmic History is being presented now.

The descent of Cosmic History, *is* the descent of the knowledge of the memory of previous world systems. This new knowledge is formulated in such a way that the events of the previous world situations are reconfigured in the presentation of the knowledge of Cosmic History for the purpose of impacting the present-day Earth consciousness with a radically positive orientation away from the internal tendencies toward self-destruction. The field of human intelligence on the planet has never been denser, largely due to out-of-control materialism. These are subtle points that need to be grasped well.

So the descent of Cosmic History includes the keys to previous programs that self-destructed. The *Cosmic History Chronicles* reformulates these programs and keys into what we might call a "positive spiraling upswing," which is exactly what is required at the point of the Closing of the Cycle. More than 5,000 years of history have finally peaked and are maximizing incredibly at this point of the *climax of matter*, meaning there is now maximum involution of spirit into matter. Within this matter, the spirit and the mind have become so deeply involved that the people have taken on dense qualities of materialism to such a degree that their light becomes deeply buried—until it may appear that they have no light at all.

Cosmic History is a descent into the darkest darkness and the densest density of consciousness as it could be imagined here on this Earth. Cosmic History dives into the core of Earth consciousness with a program that is subliminally structured to transmute and alter the causes and effects of the density and darkness, which is a result of the destruction of the previous world systems. This descent of Cosmic History actually mimics the primal evolutionary way.

The primal evolutionary way was set off in the "Interval of lost time in Eternity." A mysterious event occurred that established a ratio of time within Eternity—which is virtually timeless. This ratio of lost time, which corresponds to the number seven, is the first primal evolutionary wave. Once this wave was set off, then, as Cosmic Science describes, two forces came together and created the RANG, which was a disturbance within the perfect medium of Eternity. This RANG, a primal concussion akin to the Big Bang, then set off an eternal repercussion. According to Cosmic Science, this impact creates the resonant *protoquantum* sub particles, *carpins* and the *megacarpins*. (Once there is something that happens in the void, then aspects of the space of the void crystallize into these microunits called the carpins and then those form into the megacarpins). This evolutionary wave is like the standard matrix in which all other waves are activated.

Through the seven volumes, the *Cosmic History Chronicles* recapitulate the primal evolutionary wave in seven stages, like the seven stages of creation. This is also a statement of the primal evolutionary wave of the universe, which is the minimum number set that is necessary for the absolute creation of the whole cosmos. In the Essene Doctrines of the *Ethiopic Books of Enoch*, for example, the Enochian cosmology is based throughout on the number seven—seven days of creation, seven weeks of creation, seven angels, etc. This is a recapitulation of the primal wave.

All the different forms of knowledge ever known are Cosmic History. In terms of the interplanetary episodes and the stages of creation of the human being, whether it is the types of humans that were created at the beginning of the Popol Vuh or whether it is the description of the seven root races of Madame Blavatsky, all is woven of the number seven. All the different stages of the development of the human being, up through the planetary human, are just recapitulations of the karmic wave of evolution until you get to the most complex level where we find ourselves today.

So we see the descent recapitulates the "Interval of Lost Time in Eternity," beginning with the primal crime that set off the repercussions and the primal evolutionary waves. In some ways this information is repeated and becomes more complex as the material plane cosmos evolves more and more. This recapitulation of the primal evolutionary wave becomes increasingly complicated and tends to get buried within the details that characterize the more recent stages of any type of evolutionary development. Always, the closer you get to the present the more details there are. This is because the closer you get to the present, the more you have to remember and the more material archives you need to hold all of the information bits.

This is the second level we are dealing with—the descent of Cosmic History as the interplanetary memory that is an echo of the primal "crime" that took place in Eternity, generating a ratio wave that is entirely a function of the number seven. Then we get to the final consideration of the origins of Cosmic History within the avataric emanation. We have the first stage, which is a description of where, when and how Cosmic History happened on this Earth plane. Then we have the second stage, the descent and origin of Cosmic History, which more or less defines its purpose and contents as a descent of the interplanetary echo of the primal wave within Eternity.

Origin Within The Avataric Emanation

When we talk about the avataric emanation of Cosmic History, we are talking about a double principle—the principle of the red and the principle of the blue. These two colors represent a primary cosmic binary antipode, or bi-part enzyme, visualized in the foundation practices as the primal wisdom bodies of a red yogini and a blue yogin. The double avataric emanation is necessary because this is the Closing of the Cycle so there is a transmission from an elder male (blue) to a younger female (red). This completes the binary possibility and necessity of the transmission process as an objective mechanism. Everything is by the law of alternation.

So when we talk about the descent of Cosmic History as a divine principle of higher consciousness, it penetrates the present Earth consciousness—the ethnosphere or the realm of the planetary human. This present Earth consciousness within the universe is a tiny, vibrant, highly chaotic and dissonant field. This is the necessary nature of the Earth's mental layer at the moment that the Cosmic History principle becomes embedded in it. This present day Earth consciousness is characterized by, what we might call, "small mind" and the consciousness of Cosmic History is "large mind."

To really fathom the Cosmic History and to transmit and communicate it is a task that requires the elevation of the mind already to a supermental functioning. The agents—the avataric principle—who are receiving and transmitting the Cosmic History have to attain to a state of some basic level of enlightened mind, which is likened to the larger mind or the *galactic holomind*. This is the crux of the personal engagement and commitment of the transmitter/receiver of Cosmic History.

The meaning of the purpose of transmitting and receiving Cosmic History has many aspects and qualities that have to be understood within the context of the transformational matrix of the planetary human. The actions of the avataric principles represent reflections and echoes of archetypal resonances, which are manifest through their behavior and then communicated to the planetary human as a whole. So their actions and behaviors are not particularly accidental or random. They are not in a process of hit and miss. They are already strung up on a high circuit where everything that they are doing is in fulfillment of the Divine Plan. None of their behavior can be evaluated by normal standards because they are so highly circuited that they have no choice but to manifest these particular resonances. Otherwise, the form of their entire process of which they are avatarically meant to simulate would never occur—that is to say the process of closing and regenerating the cycle.

The Closing of the Cycle is the closing off of any further development of historical materialism and the terror of profane history. The regeneration of the cycle is the utter triumph of the philosophy of Cosmic History as an all-unifying view of the body of the world soul, the noosphere. This is the meaning of what mundanely might be referred to as their "relationship."

So there has to be a continuous emphasis on yogic discipline, so that the receiver/transmitter agents are able to receive purely and clearly and to transmit purely and clearly. The essence of the discipline, then, is the development of what we might call clear light consciousness in a purified psychophysical receptacle, in which the aim of the receiver and transmitter is to be able to hold their minds in a type of enlightened vacuum state so that no one is falling asleep. It is this kind of mind that we want to cultivate—a mind that is free from bias and prejudice that can just receive information and tally it up like a detached storage and retrieval system. How could the descent of a divine principle of Cosmic History be received by any other than the mind that was prepared to receive it? In other words, if Cosmic History just came down to anyone, they would not know what it was. They might even get freaked out and wonder what was happening to them.

But the Cosmic History has been brought down to the two specially prepared vehicles. The vehicles, on the one hand, have been chosen by God to perform this mission. On the other hand, they were especially prepared by themselves. God appointed them. It is their responsibility to maintain themselves in a state of preparedness, which is to say, a contemplative state in which the mind is characterized by familiarity with naked awareness and continuing consciousness. Only in this way can the Cosmic History be accommodated by the selected human entities in order for it to penetrate into the Earth consciousness of the planetary human. So the value of the prepared agents is that they are continuously refining or working on their minds in order to receive the monumental nature and supermental quality of the Cosmic History. They are also playing the roles of earthlings, where they are able to take the information and use present-day contemporary English language in order to communicate and be understood by the contemporary mind-set.

All of this must be understood as a continuum from avataric descent to the avataric beings in a mind transmission so the Cosmic History enters into a stabilized or purified mental field. The avatar operates with full knowledge as an instrument of hierarchy. The manifestation of impulses of hierarchy reestablishes the sacred order on Earth. The impulse of the hierarchy through the avatar is a complete expression of heart, mind and soul into profound spiritual resonance, which is a vibrating power that characterizes the nature of his/her earthly persona.

The renewal of the earthly persona is due to hierarchy. Everything must be concluded and have proper form. Hierarchy is sacred order and exists as a system of universal intelligence that is stepped down through the dimensions in the structures of the galactic order to establish a way of perceiving reality, which is no longer dualistic. The cycle of history is characterized by endless dualisms and splitting apart down to the splitting of the atom and the human split from nature and each other. The avatar's function is to perform on behalf of hierarchy to close the old cycle and establish a new one. We must actually embody the new aeon, which can only be done as a function of the universal hierarchy.

There is no difference between the presentation of Cosmic History and the actors who are presenting it. Cosmic History is a far-reaching frame of thought and consciousness which will not only transform the present belief system or base of knowledge, but will also establish a new reformulated base of consciousness that will endure for many generations to come.

Just like when you turn the key to start the ignition of a car, all that is required is one spark. When that ignition turns over then the whole motor turns over. In that way, the spark is provided when the key of the agents of Cosmic History is turned over and it hits the point of ignition in the noosphere. When you see it in this way, it is not so overwhelming. This is how the whole cosmic construct can be brought down into the present moment and channeled through these two beings in such a way that at the right moment, when the key is turned, then the whole program starts to operate—the psi bank clicks, the noosphere lights up and the human species starts to function in a different kind of way. This initiates the enlightenment of the planetary human.

Part II Cosmic History as Systems of Knowing

"Slay therefore with the sword of wisdom the doubt born of ignorance that lies in thy heart. Be one in self–harmony, in Yoga, and arise, great warrior, arise"

Bhagavad–Gita

Chapter 4
Yoga/Transformation and Cosmic History

Yoga as a system of knowing is the transformation of the physical back into the cosmic. This transformation from the physical to the cosmic/spiritual *is* the transformation from the profane to the sacred or from history back to cosmos. This is the theme of Cosmic History. As the Buddha said: "Within this body six feet in length lies the entire universe," that is to say, the composite structure of the physical body, as well as the etheric body, is merely a microcosm of the macrocosmic universe. You are not meant to remain in this dense physical form—this dense physical form merely represents the ultimate extension of the physical/material possibility.

When reading Cosmic History, the correct view to hold is the yogic point of view. Yoga, in this sense, is a pure science that has managed to exist throughout history. Now, many people practice yoga because they think it will make them successful or beautiful—but yoga is actually the pure science of abiding in the true nature of reality through the control of the thought-waves—the control of the thoughts. Yoga means union. First coined in the ancient *Rig Veda*, the word "yoga" is associated with the word to "yoke," or the joining together to create union. From that definition, the idea of yoga is that it is a means of attaining union with the divine or inner union with one's self, generally speaking.

The very notion of yoga implies that there is not union with the divine, therefore you have to practice something in order to attain union. As we mentioned in Chapter 1, the major problem of the present world construct is that it does not even know it is a world construct; it is just always talking—like a madman gibbering to itself. There is no sense of being able to control the thought-waves or even to know that there are thought-waves to control. So there is no full view of the world, other than it is something to exploit like: "When we are done with this planet we will go back to Mars and exploit it, then we will mine some asteroids", and so on. But this is hardly a worldview.

The yogic worldview or perspective is abiding in the actual nature of reality to control the thought-waves. In this way, you do not allow yourself to be constantly subjected to emotional reactions, to habitual thoughts, or any of those other programs that keep your fixed feedback loops going and maintain your so-called view of reality. Only when you learn to control the thought-waves will you experience what is called abiding in the real. At this point, you can see how your thoughts create illusions or an illusory personality.

This is yoga: the union of the conscious physical substance that you are with the abiding nature of reality. Whether you call this the ever-existing, all-awakened awareness, or whether you call it the interpenetration of the mind of God in all things—you become one with it because you are abiding in the actual nature of true reality—the *Dharmakaya*, the *Godhead*, *Brahman*, *Atman*, *Buddhamind* or the *Al-Haaq* or *Absolute Reality*, as it is called in the *Quran*—all of these are just words that describe abiding in the Absolute, which is yoga. To do this you must develop yogic discipline.

The first archaeological evidence of yoga's existence is found at the beginning of the Cycle of History in stone seals excavated from the Indus valley.

We know that in India, in particular, some type of tradition of yoga was developed more than 5,000 years ago during the pre-Vedic period. The first archaeological evidence of yoga's existence is found at the beginning of the Cycle of History in stone seals excavated from the Indus valley. The stone seals depict figures performing yoga postures. The Indus-Sarasvati (Harappa) was one of the largest civilizations in the ancient world and had many features of modern civilization including, multistoried buildings and an advanced sewage and sanitation system. When the Aryan invaders came (around 1600 B.C.) and overtook the earlier civilization of the Indus-Sarasvati civilization, they incorporated many features of that civilization, most importantly, yoga. This is why yoga figures so prominently in the *Rig Veda* and all later Vedic, Hindu and even Buddhist literature. The later literature, which refers to yoga most prominently, includes the *Upanishads* and the "Bible" of Hinduism, the *Bhagavad-Gita* (500 B.C.), which was originally part of the great epic entitled the *Mahabharata*. The *Bhagavad-Gita* interestingly features Lord Krishna, an avataric emanation who supposedly appeared at the very beginning of the Cycle of History. The word yoga was first mentioned in the oldest sacred texts, the *Rig Veda*.

In the development of these yoga practices, particularly in India, but also to a certain degree in China and Mesoamerica, union with the Supreme Truth was seen as the goal. When the emphasis is simply on the union with God, it tends to be expressed in different ways, which may be summarized as the notion of Nirvakalpa Samadhi (the seedless, pure undifferentiated consciousness) in which there is a cessation of bodily desire of every kind and a total absorption in the Absolute. From the point of view of the Absolute, everything else is relative, ephemeral, maya, nonexistent, illusion. Even the idea of transformation, for instance, is perceived of as being just an illusory idea. If you just go sit and meditate some more then you won't have to worry if there is evolution or change or transformation. So from the ultimate perspective, the goal of yoga is to be absorbed by the Absolute.

Of course, you have to think: Why did such a concept

as yoga or "union with the divine" come about in the first place? The cause of yoga coming into being is a reflection of the larger theme of Cosmic History—in that there is a primary union, then a separation or fall from grace. This is known, by some traditions, as the primal sin of Adam. Because of this "fall" different forms of worship and spiritual techniques were developed to help the fallen human reunite with the Divine Source, Origin or Maker.

Being that we are now at the end of history, the science of transformation, summarized as yoga, is more important and significant than ever. Cosmic History supplies the system of yoga with an understanding that the reason why yoga exists at all is precisely to facilitate this next stage of transformation, where the human mind and soul experiences a unification at a noospheric or planetary level. This profound transformation will alter radically and forever every individual human being's self-perception.

In that larger context we can understand how the development of yoga is connected with the development of civilization. Because civilization as we understand it today is urban living (or no longer living from the land) creating cities with types of economies that require concentrations of people living in larger and larger, more or less, artificial environments. The very notion of civilization only accentuates the Fall or the separation from God. At the Closing of the Cycle, the separation becomes more intense because it is the separation from the Divine Origin, which is understood to be the pure reflection of the Divine Source.

Only when the rise and development of civilization is properly understood can there be the rise of systems of discipline and thought such as yoga. Once the development of stratified urban societies begins, with its different classes and castes of human beings, it becomes necessary to develop some kind of discipline where contact with the divine can be maintained. For instance, even though there is a perception that the urban way is not necessarily the sacred way—the tendency still goes increasingly toward the profane, toward the non-sacred view, toward the materialistic.

"Thus practicing constant control of the body, mind and activities, the mystic transcendentalist, his mind regulated, attains to the Kingdom of God by cessation of material existence."

Bhagavad-Gita 6:15

As we know from the Cosmic History perspective, civilization is the history of materialism. At the beginning of history, the cities, temples and urban areas were specifically designed to reflect a kind of sacred geometry in order for the people to maintain a proper way of life. Cities were built on the perception of myth as a reflection of the original primal, sacred order of the higher dimensions. The higher dimensions were seen as devolving into the physical plane dimension, where the living soul is clothed in a physical garment. The earliest cities were designed and built primarily so these souls clothed in physical garments could maintain some semblance of operating within sacred order.

Yoga, in that sense, is the effort to reestablish the divine or sacred order within the human being itself, within the totality of what the human being is. The original sacred city is the reflection of the human being and the human being is the reflection of the temple. The body *is* the temple. And within the inner sanctum of the temple, there lies the soul. In this way, yoga is the primary tool to build the foundation of the inner temple that penetrates through the profane, revealing your innate cosmic identity.

Yogic Asceticism

If you look in the Vedic traditions of yoga, there tends to be some notion that yoga is supposed to discipline or even punish the body. In other words, you have in history the tendency of asceticism. An ascetic is one who mortifies or disciplines the body to try to negate all sense of bodily desire. This is done because bodily desire is perceived of as getting in the way of the cultivation and the nurturing of the immortal soul, or the *Purusha*.

Other schools of yoga say it is not necessary to punish the body, but to discipline the body so it becomes an outlet or instrument of the Divine Will of the Divine Force. In these schools such as Hatha yoga (the yoga of the physical body), the idea is not that you are punishing the body, but that you are actually making the body an increasingly better instrument of the Divine Will. It is in this sense that the essence of the Vedic

. . . the idea is not that you are punishing the body, but that you are actually making the body an increasingly better instrument of the Divine Will.

tradition of yoga became summarized in 200 B.C. by Patanjali in his *Yoga Sutras* containing 185 aphorisms, which are the summation of the teachings of the philosophy of yoga.

The teachings and the philosophy of yoga emphasize nonduality. Asceticism, for instance, is dualistic because it is harsh with the body and really doesn't accept the body. Though we find that throughout history, in reaction to civilization, there have been tendencies, particularly in religious traditions, of extreme forms of asceticism or of penance flagellating or mortifying the body.

In the yogic tradition developed in India, numerous principles were discovered in the process of cultivating yoga where several disciplines are involved. One is the understanding that in order to attain any type of discipline, you have to control the mind or the thought-waves that the mind emanates. There are two reasons for this:

1. If you do not have control over the thought-waves, then obviously they are controlling you.
2. Thought-waves carry either negative or positive charges. Uncontrolled thought waves emit an unconscious negative charge.

The yogic point of view is the direct perception of reality that is based on the control of the thought-waves—so you have a penetration of your own mind and consciousness in awareness with the all-abiding reality. From the point of view of Cosmic History, yoga can only be known through the whole body preceptor, which requires whole system training, or what Sri Aurobindo calls *Integral Yoga*.

Through disciplined practice the body/mind becomes highly ripened, tough as steel so you are prepared for anything. The existence of different forms of yoga exist because humans are multileveled beings. Traditionally the different forms of yoga include: *Hatha yoga*—Body, *Jnana yoga*—Mind, *Bhakti yoga*—Devotion and *Karma yoga*—Selfless Action.

Cosmic History is a function primarily of Jnana yoga, the yoga of attaining union with God through knowledge or the exercise of the mind and intellect. The purpose of training the

Cosmic History is a function primarily of Jnana yoga, the yoga of attaining union with God through knowledge or the exercise of the mind and intellect.

mind through Jnana yoga is to cultivate impenetrable discrimination so you will not be deluded by the false. Therefore, you must first understand your own mind before you can understand how your neurocerebral mechanism processes the mind-at-large as it is squeezed into your system.

In order to understand your own mind, you must become skilled at critical thinking or exercising the power of discrimination. This is a fundamental exercise of Jnana yoga. Discrimination is a valuable mental tool that allows for the distinction of a value or quality for the purpose of making informed judgments on the relative plane. This is a very important point. In order to develop a stratum of mind that is galactically evolved beyond any capacity for provincial thinking, you must have cultivated a mind that can discriminate and separate the true from the false. This must be done in a dispassionately objective way so you do not create more karma.

Cosmic History is the knowledge of reality that exists above and beyond and even within all the human illusions. When you experience the all-abiding reality then you may become self reflectively cognitive. In other words, you can say to yourself: "I know I am experiencing the all-abiding reality." This is the awareness that need never be awakened. This is the presence of God in every cell of the body. This is self-reflective knowing.

The most orderly example of the stages of yoga for the quest of the soul is Ashtanga Yoga—the eight limbs of yoga described in Chapter 2 of Patanjali's *Yoga Sutras*, which was the first systematic exposition of yoga as a complete philosophy of life. Patanjali's classic text covers far more than what is ordinarily thought of as yoga.

Ashtanga Yoga—8-limbed Yoga

Outer Limbs
1. **Yama** – Correct moral practice of truth. Nonviolence. Restraining from greed, covetousness, hoarding, and sexual propriety. Clear agreement and understanding.
2. **Niyama** – Individual, inner discipline. Self-development. Keeping clean. Purity. Contentment. Satisfaction with what you have. Ardor-passion for your discipline. Austerity. Self study to improve yourself in a spiritual direction. Dedication to God.
3. **Asana** – Physical exercise. To develop complete equilibrium of the body (go slower). Where does the body end and the mind begin?

Inner Limbs
4. **Pranayama** – Asanas are synchronized with three breaths: Inhalation—Hold (kumbhaka) – Exhalation. Breathe in new plasma, breath out impurities. To control the breath is to control the mind. Stable/balanced. (Visualization coordinated with breath is very important for defining where you are going).
5. **Pratyhara**—Emancipation of mind. Bring the senses under control and you can examine your states of consciousness.

Secret
6. **Dharani** – Concentration at all times. Ekagrata—One point

7. **Dhyani** – Chan/Chinese Zen/Japanese. Uninterrupted flow of concentration.
8. **Samadhi** – Superconscious state of mind. Cultivate states of samadhi to attain absolute union with God so that mind and awareness are with God at all times.

Yama or morality reminds us that it doesn't help to hurt things. If you intentionally cause harm it is not a good thing. Yama actually pertains to the whole spectrum of what we might call first degree level of moral behavior. The point of introducing this level of morality is to curb the creation of negative karma and to conserve necessary pranic or psychic energy. If this first degree level of morality is understood as having this actual cosmic energy function, then the teaching of this primary level of morality might be better understood. Often when we admonish a young person with "don't steal" or "don't lie" that may not be strong enough, but if karma and the conservation of cosmic energy are explained it might be more meaningful.

Niyama means you intentionally practice or study something. You have to exert, things don't just come to you. Or if they do come to you, you have to do something with them after they come. You have to exert or practice discipline or some type of devotion. If you do things just for yourself it will backfire on you. The only devotion is devotion to God. You have to have these types of observances, practices and self-discipline so you can actually deal objectively with knowledge or with what you are studying, which is Cosmic History. Self-discipline is the key to this. Self-discipline means you are able to control thought-waves, emotional reactions and habitual thought forms. If things get in the way of your all-abiding reality then the yogic perspective vanishes.

Asana is control of the body coordinated with breath, or how you hold your body when you walk or when you sit. When your body is poised and alert it is easier to receive information. Yoga is practice that polishes or brings out the perfection of the sense organs. You don't pollute your sense organs or cram them full of disorganized information, or bad doctrines or too much of any kind of substance. It is best when your sense organs are crystal clear, unobstructed, with nothing impeding them.

The only devotion is devotion to God. You have to have these types of observances, practices and self discipline so you can actually deal objectively with knowledge or with what you are studying, which is Cosmic History.

This is why fasting is good, it helps to clear things out, and adhering to a raw food diet helps it stay that way. Part of the asana is holding the body and having good posture. This helps control the mind and the thoughts. If you see people involved in different types of thoughts their body posture changes. Through prolonged discipline in the asanas the body actually acquires a certain inner cosmic elegance. Hatha yoga is the exercise of different asanas.

Pranayama is the control of the breath. This is very subtle. You take breath into the body. The breath has subtle energies; the prana and also the plasmas that connect it to the etheric body. You control the body, the breath and the thoughts in order to bring your whole being into alignment with the all-abiding reality. This is yoga because there is union between your conscious instrumentation and awareness and the all-abiding reality. This helps cut through one of the obstacles to knowledge which is dualism. When you are in a heightened transcendental state of nondualism, your instrumentation is attuned with the all-abiding reality. In this way you can become a perfect laboratory of cosmic solar energy frequencies which is one of the goals of Cosmic History.

Pratyahara is control of the relationship between mind and sensory input. The practice of the pratyahara is disidentifying with the stimulus that comes into your body and sense organs. To not identify with information that comes into the mind. Of getting to a place where you say, "I'm not this I'm not that." The further point of the Pratyahara is to become aware of how the mind responds to different sensory stimuli—most often without awareness the mind will just be swept away by certain experiences. For instance, certain kinds of music or sound can become habituating to the mind, arousing certain states which the ego then "fondles" as it were. By practicing Pratyahara you can see how you are actually manufacturing these states by habituation to certain sensory experience.

Dharani is the development of concentration which is the activation of memory. The more you concentrate, the more you can hold. The more you can hold the more you remember. Everything is in the all-abiding reality to be remembered. There

You control the body, the breath and the thoughts in order to bring your whole being into alignment with the all-abiding reality.

are different aides to knowledge that have to be developed, but basically, everything is in the all-abiding reality. Concentration which develops absolute focus on the goal or object is the surest way of attaining manifestation on the material plane with maximum effect.

Dhyani is meditation itself and can actually be practiced with or without an object. Meditation is getting to know the real nature of thoughts and reality. Meditation with an object is just a prolonged form of concentration. Meditation without an object is the most direct means of perception about the nature of mind itself. This includes understanding the nature of thoughts, the nature of ego, and the nature of space and awareness, which leads to the direct perception of the Absolute all-abiding Reality. There are different levels or stages of this formless meditation.

Samadhi is entering the state of prolonged union with the all-abiding reality where there is no thought. Knowledge may occur but it is not anything like experiencing activated thought forms. Samadhi is when you actually are able to attain the yogic discipline to the degree where you become totally conjoined with the all-abiding reality—where there is a cessation of thought forms. Even when you are in a high state of meditation there is a tendency of the mind to want to comment on it. In this way, the all-abiding reality is all there is. Within the all-abiding reality, there is a knowing without comment or thought.

To summarize, yoga is the most general comprehensive understanding of what is meant by a system of knowing that is thoroughly transformative—that begins with the physical body and penetrates into the deepest recesses of the universal cosmic mind.

Again, the correct point of view of Cosmic History is the yogic perspective, since yoga is a way of knowing God and the totality of His creation in all of its stages.

* Please note: Though we talk about yoga, using the specific examples of Ashtanga Yoga, this is not to overlook the Chinese systems from Tai Chi to Falun Dafa, etc., which generally are also forms of yoga and can create the same effect.

> *Samadhi is entering the state of prolonged union with the all-abiding reality where there is no thought.*

Physical, Etheric and Subtle Bodies

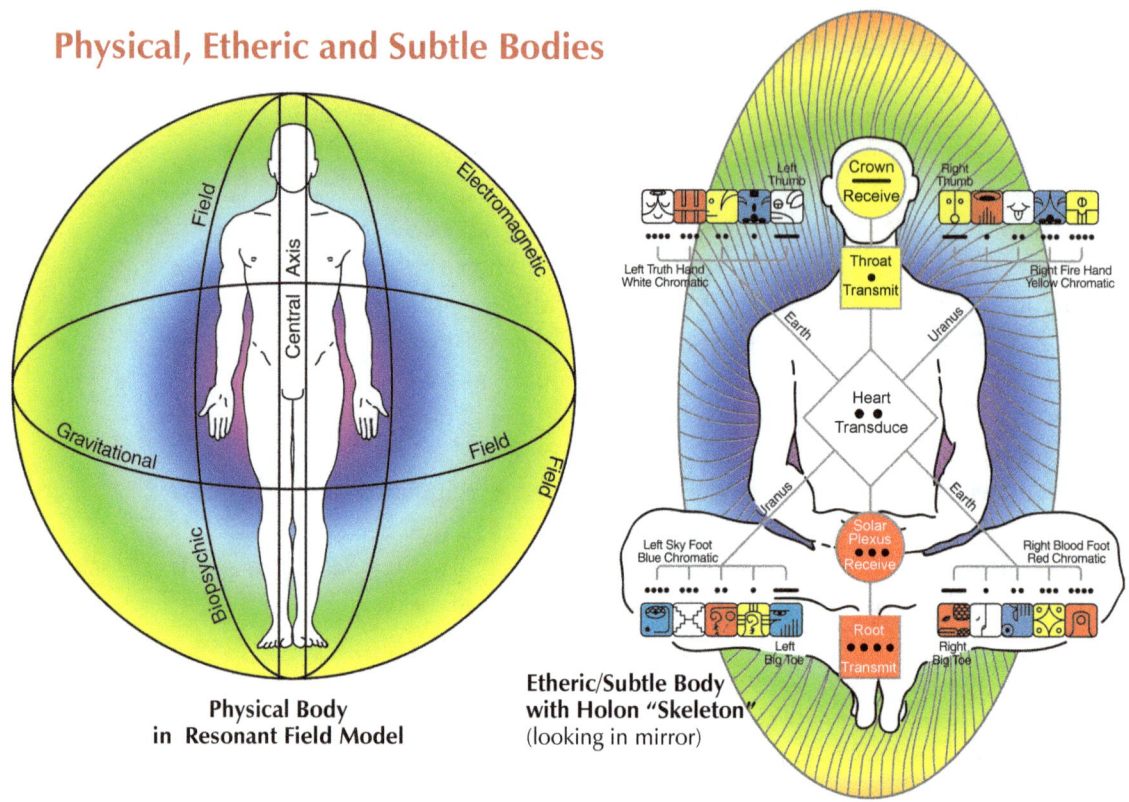

Physical Body in Resonant Field Model

Etheric/Subtle Body with Holon "Skeleton" (looking in mirror)

PHYSICAL, ETHERIC AND SUBTLE BODIES

The discovery, development and cultivation of the etheric or subtle body is a secondary factor in the practice and cultivation of yoga and leads to a slightly different perspective, which is the yoga of transformation. This is the large theme of Sri Aurobindo's teachings, who in the Twentieth Century, could speak much more easily of there being an actual evolutionary process, which has its root in the cultivation of the subtle body. The activation of the subtle body is actually the purpose of evolution.

The physical body represents the ultimate densification of thought into matter; that thought into matter becomes a very elaborate system of materialization. The physical body is an aspect of this materialization. In other words, your body is an aspect of the hills and the trees and the cows and everything else you can see and everything that you eat. Human beings are actually one part of a spectrum of reality; the biospheric spectrum. This biospheric spectrum is in itself a reflection of Divine Order, if we could but see.

For the soul to evolve from this dense matter, in which it is encased, it needs its own inner vehicle or its own etheric body. To serve the purpose of evolution, the etheric body—the subtle body within the light body within the dense body—is spirit's offering to the soul in order for it to be able to evolve beyond the physical plane. Not to evolve into ultimate Nirvana or into ultimate extinction, or even into ultimate immortality—where there is nothing but motionless condition—but actually to evolve beyond any static notion of ultimate enlightenment or attainment is the goal of the soul. Nature itself is waiting for this evolution. God Himself or Herself is also in the process of evolving.

If the all-knowing God permeates every cell and atom of the universe but is at the same time remote and resides in the farthest reaches of the universe (and yet everything that exists is a reflection of the original ever evolving creation), then there must be a yoga of transformation. In this sense, the real focus of evolution lies in the activation of the subtle body.

In Buddhism and Hinduism there have been adepts who, through their focus on the activation and integration of their mental, physical and subtle bodies, have found that they could develop paranormal abilities. In the Buddhist and Hindu traditions these powers are called the *siddhis* (one who attains these powers is called a *siddha*).

In the yogic or tantric tradition there is something called the 84 mahasiddhis that were performed by yogis able to perfect their minds. If Padmasambhava had not the power of the siddhis he would not have been able to quell the demons of Tibet. We have to do the same thing on a planetary level.

Of course, one is always admonished to not use the siddhis unless it is for a transcendental purpose of teaching. Take, for example, the story of the "Green Man" in the 18th Sura of the Quran. The "Green Man" apparently has paranormal abilities and does things that look shocking to Moses, who hasn't yet developed these abilities. At one point, the "Green Man" drills a hole in someone's boat and even kills someone—or so it appears—but the point is that his actions are actually stemming from a purposive knowledge because he has the paranormal siddhi of seeing into the future. This story is just to illustrate why the admonition is not to use those powers, because very often when you use those powers it will appear that you are doing something so unconventional that it could be considered

> *. . . to evolve beyond any static notion of ultimate enlightenment or attainment is the goal of the soul.*

criminal. Or even more often you may use your powers for egoic purposes—like levitating or walking on water just to show off.

It is said when Milarepa, the 11th Century A.D. Tibetan Buddhist yogi, had attained to a high degree of control of his mind and also of his breath or prana, that he developed a siddhi of flying through the air. He could walk on the wind and get from one place to another in very little time. When you understand how your mind controls phenomena, then you can actually make your body appear to do things that may otherwise seem impossible. Once you know the laws of mind, you understand that mind also controls prana, which utilizes a form of energy so that you can move quickly or walk on water.

These principles demonstrate not only mind over matter, but also a type of evolutionary potentiality that says you are not really bound to this physical body. This is a very profound point. When you look at what happens in the world, why do people fight, steal, kill and do what they do? Though we can sometimes say that there might be ideological or religious motives, more often than not there are actually economic motives. The economic motives stem from a total ignorance of the nature of the food sheathe and the physical body, creating its future fleeting comforts. If everybody trusted in God and developed their supernormal powers then materialism and consumerism would vanish and there would be no need to fight for anything.

The development of the siddhis is a sign of the future evolutionary possibility. In this way, yoga itself is a siddhi since it is a system of knowing that embodies principles that transform physical reality back into cosmic reality. Yoga is evolutionary knowledge. All of the highest spiritual knowledge is evolutionary knowledge. The whole point of all spiritual teaching is to provide an opportunity for the soul to begin to release itself from its encasement and/or attachment to the gross dense physical body. These attachments include all the different forms of desire engrained into the body as it has been conditioned in the course and stream of what is referred to as history.

Continued on p. 72

> *Once you know the laws of mind, you understand that mind also controls prana which utilizes a form of energy so that you can move quickly or walk on water.*

Yoga, Transformation and Cosmic History

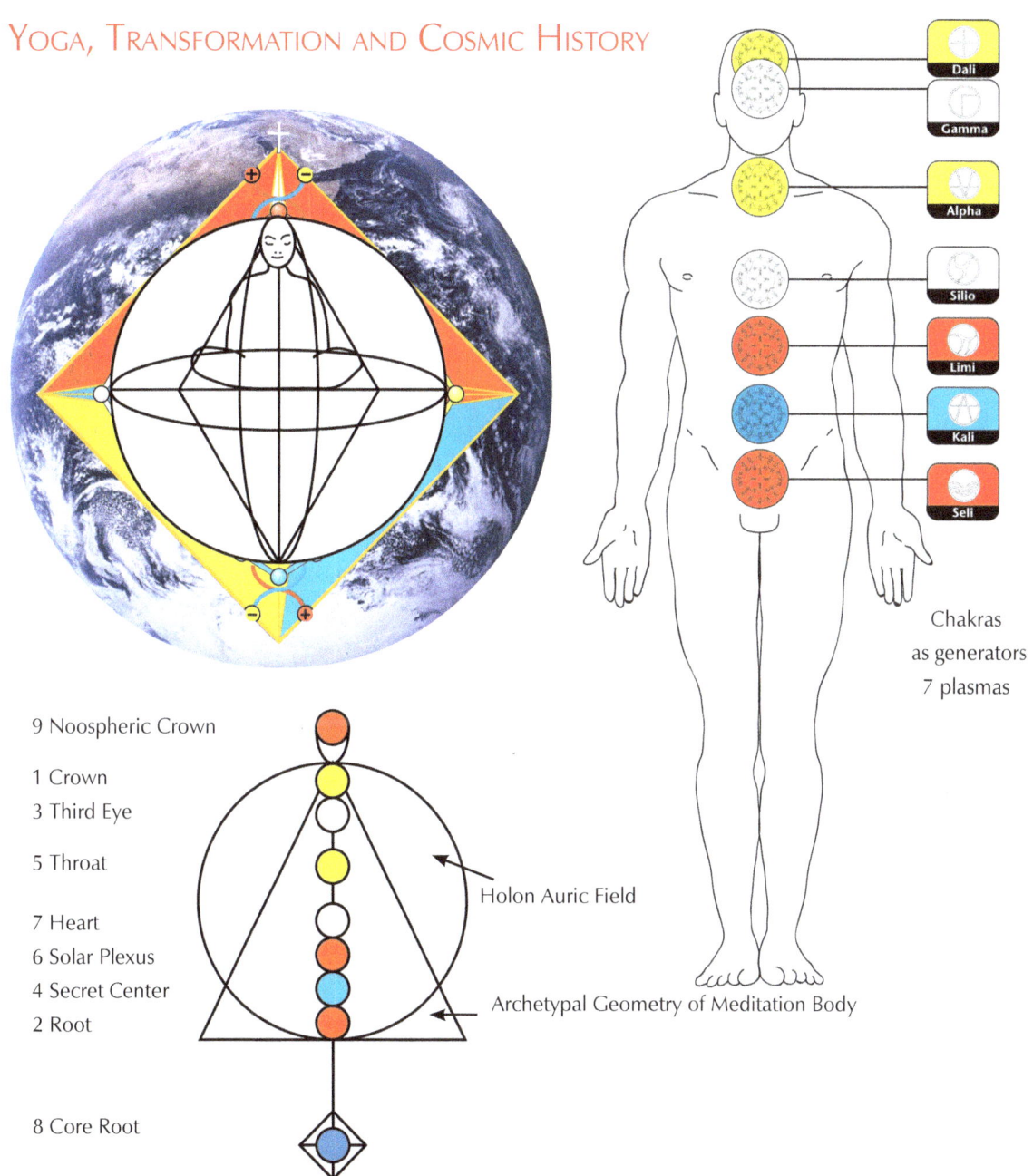

Chakras as generators 7 plasmas

9 Noospheric Crown

1 Crown
3 Third Eye
5 Throat

7 Heart
6 Solar Plexus
4 Secret Center
2 Root

Holon Auric Field

Archetypal Geometry of Meditation Body

8 Core Root

"The activation of the subtle body is actually the purpose of evolution."

This is why it says in the *Quran* that the soul travels in stages—that we are going up in stages. It says that some people are endowed with greater spiritual perceptions than others. Even some messengers are endowed with greater spiritual perceptions than other messengers—such as Solomon, who was granted not only supreme wisdom, but also the ability to direct the winds to whatever land he chose. Solomon's ability to control and direct the forces of nature is akin to those medicine men and shamans who can cause rain to fall. These examples point to an imminent development in the evolution of consciousness, which is the actual spiritualization of matter.

It says in the *Quran* that God alone is the knower of everything that is hidden in the deepest recesses of nature—that all knowledge is controlled and concealed by God. A sufficient amount of knowledge is revealed to a messenger in any given time that is appropriate to the evolutionary stage of consciousness of the people at that time. So the knowledge, for instance, that is being granted through the forms and practices of Cosmic History, is knowledge that is appropriate for this stage of evolution at the closing of the cycle. Any granting of new knowledge is actually the granting of divine knowledge.

Everything that exists in the universe, in some way or another, in some seed form or plasmic knowing or chakra cellular knowing, is actually contained within the body. The chakras are the points of internal stimuli where the plasmas are stored and activated, the plasmas being the reference points to telepathic knowing. This means that the totality of what needs to be known is already latent or dormant within the human body. In other words, if we develop the human body, both the knowledge that exists in the phenomenal realm and in the universe is going to be found within our physical/etheric body.

When the form is exerted perfectly inside and outside and the mind is still, then everything is present. In addition to the asanas and pranayams, we work completely with stilling the mind and mixing the mind with space. We dissolve the thoughts and come to the present moment so we experience only the vastness of space. Everything is contained within the vastness of space and within the human body. In actuality we

A sufficient amount of knowledge is revealed to a messenger in any given time that is appropriate to the evolutionary stage of consciousness of the people at that time.

are cultivating evolution in the form of the Earth Wizard. You have everything you need right now. You need go nowhere to learn everything about the universe. Everything is contained within the body. When this is understood, then the paranormal means of extending our senses into the orders of nature will also come to be known.

This present stage of evolution is a stage which is referred to as the advent of the noosphere. This represents a major shift in the evolutionary spiritual/mental coordination of the human species. This is a level of unification which, on the one hand, is already attained by most of the other species—that they all form fields unto themselves—which are sometimes called *morphogenetic fields*, as coined by the Twentieth Century biologist Rupert Sheldrake. The genetic structure creates an etheric form for a particular species, which creates the field in which the species moves through. The human morphogenetic field is now congruent with the structure of the planet. This is what creates the present-day virtual noosphere.

The human morphogenetic field is highly adaptable. Humans can live most anywhere—the pre-technological human proved it could be an Eskimo or it could live in the desert or on the water, like a Polynesian going across the seas. A dolphin can live in the water but it cannot live on the land, as intelligent as the dolphin may be. But humans are adaptable to live on the land anywhere. This is so that when the realization of the planetary human occurred, the morphogenetic field would be co-extensive with the Earth, which is the noosphere or the mental envelope of the planet. The human species is now in the beginning stages of making this shift.

Noospheric Yogic Cell Groups

At present, most people think that their consciousness is their own—that no one knows what they do the way they do. The atomization of consciousness due to the densification of matter and the encasement of the soul in matter has led to this type of belief, resulting in an incredible sense of separation. But we are actually at the verge of a dramatic flip of consciousness into the

You have everything you need right now. You need go nowhere to learn everything about the universe. Everything is contained within the body. When this is understood, then the paranormal means of extending our senses into the orders of nature will also come to be known.

noosphere. The way that will be attained is through a type of intensified yogic practice and activity of different human beings operating in different, what we might call, noospheric/psychophysical yogic cell groups.

When we get to the point of the closing of the cycle, these groups will engineer the jump into the noosphere. This is why the example that we establish in the Cosmic History and in the yoga practice is so utterly important—this establishes a model so that it can be communicated to others. That space of meditation is everyone's space. We are all in the same space. To summarize, the practice of yoga is a transformative science or system of knowing that serves the purpose of Cosmic History in establishing an irreversible return path to divine source for the planetary human at this point of the evolutionary juncture, known as the advent of the noosphere.

So we see that yoga becomes transformative science and the way of cultivating the next evolutionary stage or what we call the *paranormal*, which in the noosphere is actually the norm. It says in the section on the powers in Patanjali's *Yoga Sutras* in Verse 4: *"By controlling the nerve currents that govern the lungs and the upper part of the body, the yogi can walk on water and swamps or on thorns and similar objects and he can die at will."* Verse 41 says: *"By controlling the force which governs the prana, the yogi can surround himself with a blaze of light."*

Milarepa was also able to display such powers—these are the powers that demonstrate that even though the physical plane has evolved to an extreme level of density, the density can easily be controlled by mind and the key to this is the control of the prana, which is the vital force that comes into the body. With regard to yoga, introduced in Section 8 of the *Dynamics of Time*, it says: *"Yoga refers to biopsychic discipline leading to experiences of divine union and higher truth. Yoga is the divine union of the higher truth which reestablishes the correct relationship of AC/CA functions—Aboriginal Continuity and Cosmic Awareness, understood as the fourth-dimensional biological cultural timing circuits internally realizable."* 8.7

The AC/CA currents serve as cosmic memory templates. Genetically, they can be understood as information processors that cross over and intertwine, forming the root of the DNA double helix pattern. The AC or Aboriginal Continuity current contains the primary codes of conduct for living the enlightenment of the universal life. The AC corresponds to the innate psychomental forms, internal sensations and the sense organs themselves and represents the information flow from future to present. The AC is incapable of conceiving of history, as it creates the matrix from which history arises.

The CA or the Cosmic Awareness current is history itself and represents analytical methods articulating specific action modes built upon models of past behavior and knowledge. The CA contains the cumulative cultural forms and eventually, the civilizational sense fields inclusive of the planetary environment. The CA current represents the information flow from past to present.

Cosmic History deals with corruptions and reforms of a social nature and is a function of the Civilizational Advance or CA template. It is the advent or descent of Cosmic History that transforms Civilizational Advance (CA) into Cosmic Awareness (CA). The AC/CA crossover polarity may also be understood as a psychogenetic feedback loop. Psychogenetic feedback refers to the continuous interchange between the biologically innate and increasingly elaborated psychocultural factors.

In yoga, the AC/CA functions are activated by conscious respiration energizing the dialectic of their moving inverse bilateral symmetry. This highly conscious movement of the breath into the body, then, is directed toward and correlated with the spine and central nervous system. Within the body, this breath which is saturated with prana or plasmas is imaginally used to construct the inner temple or etheric body. Plasmas are the constituent components of "prana" or "chi."

Hatha yoga and other related systems of psychophysical autoregulation work toward the establishment of a flexible biohomeostasis. This stabilization of the biological metabolism is focused through the spinal column of the central nervous system with its attendant psychophysical centers or chakras. These descriptions put yoga in the context of the AC/CA or the Aboriginal Continuity and the Cosmic Awareness which structure the two sides of the galactic brain, (the name given to the galactic field of intelligence) holonomically registered as the noosphere.

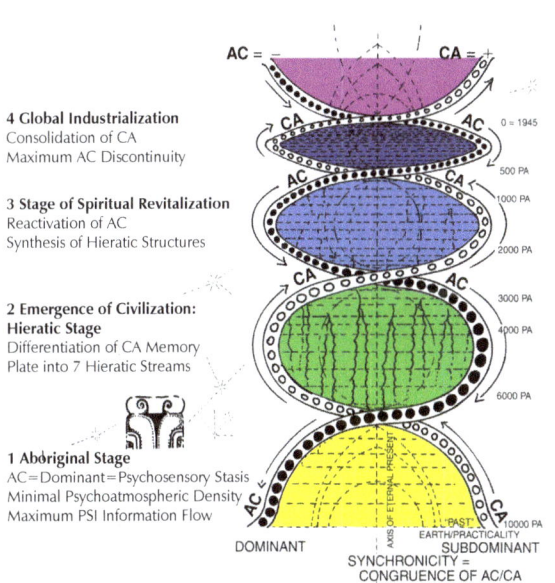

Cosmic History deals with corruptions and reforms of a social nature and is a function of the Civilizational Advance or the CA template. It is the advent or descent of Cosmic History that transforms Civilizational Advance (CA) into Cosmic Awareness (CA). The AC/CA crossover polarity may also be understood as a psychogenetic feedback loop. ... the continuous interchange between the biologically innate and increasingly elaborated psychocultural factors.

AC Planetary Manitou

In yoga the AC/CA functions are activated by conscious respiration energizing the dialectic of their moving inverse bilateral symmetry ...

CA Planetary Manitou

These descriptions put yoga in the context of the AC/CA or the Aboriginal Continuity and the Cosmic Awareness which structure the two sides of the Galactic Brain registered as the noosphere

The AC/CA also constitutes the regulating mechanism of the psi bank, which coordinates the noosphere as a supermental organism (see Chapter 9). Therefore, study and comprehension of the AC/CA currents accelerate the advance into the noosphere. (See *Earth Ascending* for a more detailed description.) This scientific description of the AC/CA functions makes very precise at different levels even that which Sri Aurobindo writes about in *The Life Divine*.

In *The Life Divine*, Sri Aurobindo refers to yogic transformation as *Integral Yoga*, or yoga that integrates the spiritual and the physical for the purpose of attaining the next evolutionary stage, from the supermental path to the supramental. Aurobindo talks about going "*beyond consciousness*" or "*beyond mind.*" We are still trying to get the mind straightened out so we can have a glimpse that there is no mind—this is the direction that we are going. According to the *Dynamics of Time*, the stages of evolution of consciousness lead to hyperorganic and super and subliminal states of consciousness. These higher states of consciousness work toward breaking the dependency on any kind of physical body whatsoever. Such states of consciousness or being are totally beyond the senses and even beyond the mind as we now construe it.

> *"Not only are there physical realities which are suprasensible (beyond our senses) but if evidence and experience are at all a test of truth there are also senses which are supraphysical (or hyperorganic as referred to in the Dynamics of Time). And can not only take cognizance of the realities of the material world without the aid of the corporeal sense organs, but can bring us into contact with other realities, supraphysical and belonging to another world, included, that is to say, in an organization of conscious experience that are dependent on some other principle than on the gross matter that our suns and our earths seem to be made."* The Life Divine p. 18

By referring to Sri Aurobindo's conception of Integral Yoga and its role in the evolution of the spirit, Cosmic History only means to affirm the truth that throughout the saga of human history there have been occasional sages and seers who have broken through the veil of historical materialism to present ever higher, more purified versions of the unified vision. The purpose of yoga is actually to extend you in that direction to fulfill the Cycle of Return, as defined by Cosmic History. From the point of view of Cosmic History, yoga understood as the science of transformation is an absolute prerequisite for initiating the return path. Once yoga has become normalized in the human species, what we call yogic activity, asanas and so on will be part of the genetic program.

Chapter 5:
Sorcerer's Whole Body Perception and Yoga

When something is at one with itself, it is almost as if it is not. The flicker between being and non-being creates a dimensional doorway, which can be attained through different systems and methods of knowing: Yoga, meditation, contemplation, study or working. That whole sense perception has to be grounded in a type of exercise that takes into account the food sheathe, or the physical garment, and disciplines it in such a way that the sorcerer's whole body perception can be easily facilitated.

The sorcerer's whole body perception presupposes a yogic foundation. This yogic foundation is based, first, on recognition of the need to discipline the mind and body so the soul can actually breathe and receive prana (life-force). This yogic foundation is also based on the cultivation of the physical and subtle bodies and the discipline of the mind for the purpose of evolution, as well as to attain to a remembrance of God or the Divine Source.

From the sorcerer's point of view, the purpose of yoga is to establish the body as a completely unified base and temple so that the reflection and order of the body's movements are a reflection of the original sacred order of the higher cosmos—the hieratic order of the higher dimensions—and also of the totality of the cosmos itself. It is important to keep in mind that the nature of the physical plane is also a reflection of that order. From the point of view of Cosmic History, the purpose of yoga is to assist in the sensory/psychophysical unification of the sorcerer's whole body perception.

Cosmic History deals with the principles of creation through stages of development. To grasp Cosmic History it is essential to understand that mental phenomena account for everything. The temple is a structure of inner knowing and is the architecture on which Cosmic History is constructed. Though its constructs conform to inner knowing, you are always dealing simultaneously with external details. It is the internal structure or wisdom body that we are ripening into manifestation through the discipline of mind and body.

Knowledge of the laws of external forces can be used, then, for the understanding of internal forces and vice versa. If you understand these principles, you have acquired power (supramental power) over these forces. But first you must develop a sorcerer's whole body knowing, of which yoga is a prerequisite. The basis of the sorcerer's whole body knowing is the psychophysical synchronization of the different senses and the mind to create a whole sense perception.

The tree is the exemplar of the erect spine. The notion of the erect spine of the human being has to do with its very nature—that the human walks and stands on two feet or two legs and sits down in such a way that it can hold its spine absolutely vertical. The cat can do this for a few moments and the monkey can do it to some extent, but the human being can actually sit for a long time with the spine erect or stand for a long time with the spine erect. This vertical form is analogous to the tree.

The human being becomes the cosmic symbol of the form of the tree when it is disciplined into a recollection of the cosmic order. Yoga greatly facilitates this process. The practice of yoga is found in many different cultures: Mexican, Aztec, Mayan and Indian forms of yoga (to name a few). It is also clear from historical sculptures and clay figurines that there were different practices that emphasized different positions or asanas that the body is held in. You also see these types of body/mind practices in China where you have different developments all the way from *Tai Chi* to the present form of *Qi Gong* or *Falun Dafa*, which again emphasizes what we call the psychophysical integration and cultivation of the whole being.

The purpose of doing a practice such as yoga is to begin to have some control over your mind and over your thoughts. In reading the text *Falun Dafa*, Master Li Zhaung points out that you cannot do the Falun Dafa practice if you are sick. Meaning, you cannot do this practice if your mind is still full of filthy thoughts. If you don't have a practice such as yoga, your mind can make your body agitated. Even if you do have a practice such as yoga, your mind can sometimes make your body agitated.

So the point of the yoga, which is very closely related to the practice of meditation, is to still and control the body in order to gain some control over the mind. For example, when you have an idea the body might jump up. It is the mind that causes the body to jump like a monkey when some kind of idea or inspiration hits it. This is the grossest outer level of the need for discipline that we are talking about. At the more subtle level, it is apparent that not only is control of the mind important, but also the control of the breath.

The more consciously the breath is aligned with the body, the better the results. When agitating thoughts arise, the breath becomes shorter and faster. Control of the breath is so important because in the process of inhalation you are taking in vital, etheric nutrients or prana. In the science of the Law of Time, these "etheric nutrients" are known as *plasma* or *radion*—the very building blocks of reality.

So by controlling the breath you begin to see that within the physical body there is another body—the etheric body. This etheric body is actually what is being fed by the prana or radion. The breath comes in sending oxygen to the lungs—this is the

> *The purpose of doing a practice such as yoga is to begin to have some control over your mind and over your thoughts.*

basis of life maintained within the food sheathe or the physical body. Prana is a whole other aspect of breath. Prana refers to the energy that actually feeds the subtle body. The subtle body has its own particular structure. Its central axis is concordant with the axis of the vertical spine. This, again, pertains to the importance of the erect spine—not only in yogic and meditation practice, but actually all the time. This is the meaning of the yoga of transformation. Congruent with the principles of Cosmic History, the yoga of transformation reminds us that there is a Cycle of Becoming and a Cycle of Return.

We learn from yoga that the subtle body is aligned with the spine and there are different centers which are known as chakras. Psychoenergetically, chakras are known as wheels and are often visualized as different lotuses. To activate your chakras you may visualize them as follows:

1. **Root—Muladhara**—Four-petalled red lotus
   This is where your basic life-force is located. All of your most fundamental biological security programs are stored here.
2. **Secret—Swadisthan**—Six-petalled orange lotus
   Here is located the essence of the sexual energy. In the opening to Cosmic History, the energy stored in this chakra can be used to vitalize the different levels of being.
3. **Solar Plexus—Manipura**—Ten-petalled yellow lotus
   This center opens to the Kuxan Suum, the etheric fiber that runs directly to the center of the galaxy and is a vital information receptacle.
4. **Heart—Anahata**—Twelve-petalled green lotus
   Located in this center are the transcendental programs that transform biological survival issues into forms of selfless compassion.
5. **Throat—Visuddha**—Sixteen-petalled blue lotus
   In this center is focalized the will to communicate and to extend oneself to others in patterns of informative thought and behavior.
6. **Third eye—Agyan**—Two-petalled indigo lotus
   This center, sometimes known as the eye of wisdom, is the seat of celestial vision and "second sight"—the paranormal power of clairvoyance and telepathic knowing.
7. **Crown—Sahasrara**—Thousand-petalled violet lotus
   In this center is stored the dormant capacity for total enlightenment which is full operating cosmic consciousness.

The Seven Year Mystery of the Stone practice introduces two new chakras to be activated: the **Root of Root** chakra, which extends to and encompasses the Earth's octahedral core and the **Crown of Crown** chakra, which extends to and encompasses the Earth's noosphere. As we proceed in the description of the noosphere and its activation over the next six volumes, as well as through the Mystery of the Stone practices, we will understand more profoundly the implication of these two new chakras.

These chakras or wheels of energy are psychoactive generators continuously turning and being fed by the streams of prana. Within the prana, or the vital breath, are the different primary plasmas known as the seven radial plasmas. Once consciously breathed in, these plasmas may be directed to the different chakras, where they provide the energetic psychotelepathic fuel. Each of the seven centers, then, is a receiver for one each of the seven radial plasmas.

These radial plasmas are microquanta electrical charges with a specific spin quality which gives each of the seven plasmas a unique characteristic. Taken as a whole, the seven plasmas constitute the most primary microelectric quanta building blocks of universal structures such as atoms, but also as carriers of a type of information. Because of their instantaneous capacity for transmission, they also function as a type of telepathic message unit.

For example, the **Dali** plasma charge is accumulated in the crown chakra and accounts for the experience of heat. The **Seli** plasma charge is gathered in the root chakra and accounts for the intensity of inner light. The **Gamma** plasma charge is gathered in the third eye and accounts for tendencies toward equanimity and equalization of light and heat charges. The **Kali** plasma charge is gathered in the secret center and accounts for the quality of intensified light heat, which is also associated with the sexual energy. The Kali plasma also functions as a link between the three light-heat sensory plasmas and the three telepathic plasmas. The **Alpha** plasma charge is gathered in the throat center and accounts for a double extended electrical charge, which is in telepathic resonance with the South Pole of the planet. The **Limi** plasma charge is gathered in the solar plexus and accounts for a mental electron-neutron charge which is in telepathic resonance with the North Pole of the Planet. The **Silio** plasma charge is gathered in the heart center and accounts for a mental electron charge telepathically in resonance with the center of the Earth.

For most people, this process is unconscious, but in the yogic system—as a system of knowing—this is fundamental. By practicing a type of psychophysical discipline, by stilling the

> *These chakras or wheels of energy are continuously turning and being fed by the streams of prana. Within the prana, or the vital breath, are the different primary plasmas known as the seven radial plasmas.*

body, by sitting straight with an erect spine, by quieting the mind, the inner eye and perception of the inner body is cultivated. Through this cultivation, the whole subtle body can be perceived. This knowing has been presented and handed down for many long ages.

The key part of yoga as a system of knowing is, again (this cannot be stressed enough), that the thought-waves have to be controlled. The thought-waves are very much connected to the prana in the body. The body, the prana and the thought-waves all have to be simultaneously disciplined in order to come back into divine union with God. But in the process of getting to that goal, the cultivation and perception of the etheric or subtle body is necessary. These are called the secondary aspects of yoga.

The highest yoga is the yoga of the science of the mind and body—seeing the mind and body as a particular unity and experiencing from within what that is. What is circulation? What is breath? What is the physics of the body? What is the actual internal system of the body? What does it mean that we have the chakras? How can you experience the chakras? Understanding the human body as a system of energy by applying the Law of Time, we can realize our own body in all of its levels as a living, harmonious work of art. Cosmic History is the structure of the universe projected through

Seven Radial Plasmas

Dali   Seli   Gamma   Kali   Alpha   Limi   Silio

our own body and being. What we experience in reality is the history of the cosmos.

Cycle Becoming/Cycle Return

In a larger sense, the Cycle of Becoming results in the dense form of the physical body and the Cycle of Return is the cultivation of the etheric body within the physical body. With proper cultivation of the etheric body, the physical body can be dissolved and the subtle body is then left to enjoy the play and union of God—the Divine Source. This represents the actual trajectory of evolution and is the reason why discipline of the physical body is so important.

From the point of view of the yoga of transformation, the physical body plays an important role as being the first stage carrier of the astral or subtle etheric body that is within. In other words, as the physical body and mind become disciplined, they emerge as the carrier or the conductor of the prana (vital energy) into the subtle centers of the chakras or the wheels of energy. In this way, we can see the relationship of the wheels of energy (four-petalled red root chakra, six-petalled orange secret center chakra, eight-petalled yellow solar plexus chakra, etc.)—and how those relationships represent to each other psychoactive frequencies of motion of the wheels of energy that are turning at those points. And those wheels of energy are like subtle points that connect the etheric body with the central nervous system.

In this way, the chakras coordinate the central nervous system as well as the subtle body. This is why the coordination of the body as sitting still and the coordination of the thought-waves is necessary. The body and thought-waves must be put into a quieted state so they are not going around creating any unnecessary negative ripples, or any ripples whatsoever. In this way the prana, the breathing, can be put into alignment with the body. This is why it is important that you coordinate each asana with a deep inhalation and a deep exhalation.

What you are actually doing is aligning the pranic currents with the body in different positions. The positions of the body aligned with the pranic currents are actually what we might call "reconstructing the cosmic template of the original temple." So when all of those different positions are consistently held and coordinated with the breath—you gain greater and greater ease. The coordination of the breath with the asana and the prana then activates the subtle body or the subtle nervous system in those different parts of the body that are being stretched. In this way the AC/CA cosmic memory templates are reestablished or restored in the body. This is a key point.

The AC/CA cosmic memory template can be activated in any of the yogic practices, particularly the pranayams when you are visualizing those points where the prana is activating or turning the different chakras or wheels. Once the wheels are spinning they activate the double helix AC/CA circuits coordinating your etheric body with the cosmic memory template wrapped around the center column. What you are actually doing is placing the imaginal realm into contact with the phenomenal realm.

As the wheels turn and when the mind is clear, then the pure prana gets spun as radion or plasma into the etheric body and nervous system at those places. If there are muddy thoughts while the visualizations are occurring then those muddy thoughts come down as sluggish electrical charges that

Understanding the human body as a system of energy by applying the Law of Time, we can realize our own body in all of its levels as a living, harmonious work of art.

interfere with the prana turning the wheels. Again, control of the thought-waves is all-important. It is interesting to note that the human species is endowed with, among other things, a very subtle and sensitive nervous system and sense organs, which are capable of ever-evolving aesthetic enhancements of extraordinary degrees. This nervous system puts the whole human organism in touch with subtle etheric elements which connect back to the fact that there is an etheric body that is being cultivated.

So you have that central nervous system receiving sensory impressions as well as receiving the plasmic or pranic input. These sensory impressions or pranic input are then coordinated with, again, those points that we refer to as the chakras. The wheels or petals of the first through fifth chakras from root to throat represent various frequencies. When you get the sixth and seventh chakras, the crown is usually referred to as the sahasrara or thousand petalled lotus, which means that it is vibrating at an unimaginably rapid frequency, which accompanies the absolute upliftment of the soul or the spirit into the realm of divine knowing or divine consciousness.

Then there is the special case of the third eye which is represented by two petals, symbolizing the two becoming one. This is the eye of wisdom. Christ talks about this in the *Gospel of Matthew* of the *New Testament* when he says: *"The eye is the light of the body; if, therefore, thine eye be made single, thy whole body shall be full of light."* The opening of the wisdom eye represents the overcoming of duality, which is the dispelling of ignorance. When this occurs, then the seemingly two become one and the body gets filled with light. All ignorance has at its root a form of dualism understood as a belief in separation between self and other.

The chakra centers are the place where the phenomenal and the imaginal realms (or where the senses and the prana) are joined together. This creates a balance between what we might call the aesthetic, psychophysical cultivation of the senses and the inner cultivation of the subtle body and the chakra system. According to the Law of Time, "outer" psychophysical cultivation of these results in the sensory quanta, and "inner"

The positions of the body aligned with the pranic currents are actually what we might call "reconstructing the cosmic template of the original temple."

subtle body cultivation results in telepathic quanta.

When these centers are coordinated then you have the basis of the next stage of evolution, which deemphasizes the food sheathe and emphasizes the soul body or the etheric body. Cultivation of the etheric body furthers the evolution of knowledge, leading to the simplification of the physical body. This simplification eventually results in the correction of disease and genetic defects so that there is no longer such an intense reliance on material/physical plane necessities. The physical body will eventually become simplified to such a level that its reliance becomes only on simple nutrient substances: ultimately light, water and air. This will free up the etheric body to evolve into much more advanced states of knowing and being, until finally the physical body becomes unnecessary and you return to the higher dimensional realms of evolution.

At this point, the emphasis on yoga and discipline is very important because it actually is the way in which the purpose of the spiritual mental evolution is being served. Once you have the yogic perspective and discipline, the next step is going from being a yogi or yogini to the development of magical practices or higher level ceremonial practices that act on reality. You cannot have the sorcerer's methodology until you have mastered the yogic point of view as the path to true science.

Logistics Of Planet Sorcery

Through yoga and sorcerer's whole body knowing we are practicing the magic of Planet Sorcery through the medium of Cosmic History. Planet Sorcery is a method of knowing, rooted in the investigation of Cosmic History. The synthesis and process of Cosmic History will replace all the old forms with new forms of method and structure. All systems that exist today are accretions of different past thought moments of experience and stages of growth which are not necessarily logical.

Cosmic History is a fundamental whole systems design containing all the principles that make a system integral. Geomancy is the basis of Planet Sorcery, since it is the primordial method or science of bringing the senses into harmony with the

"The eye is the light of the body; if, therefore, thine eye be made single, thy whole body shall be full of light."

Gospel of Matthew

Part II • Cosmic History as Systems of Knowing

planet body. Here "man" is understood as the intermediary between Heaven (above) and Earth (below). Geomancy is the science that investigates the relation between Man, Heaven and Earth. In geomancy, the Earth is considered as a living medium that informs all of creation. The Earth is the cosmic transformation zone, which exemplifies the next evolutionary stage.

The human body is a subset of a whole system—only through your whole body can you know the whole system. The whole system is knowable as a higher mental order of reality—directly knowable through the sixth sense or mind, which is the supersensory mode of knowing or experiencing (jnana yoga). The whole body contains the whole planet. You must learn to make your sense perceptions coextensive with the planet so that the body experiences itself in relation to the planet body. The planet body also possesses a holon, or planet holon, which contains the same fourth-dimensional coding as the individual human holon.

The human holon is the armature or "skeleton" of the etheric body. When this coding is laid out over the planet, it creates a type of *icosahedral* structure whose 20 faces correspond both to the digital units of the human holon, as well as to the *chronomantic* flow of time as registered in the 260-

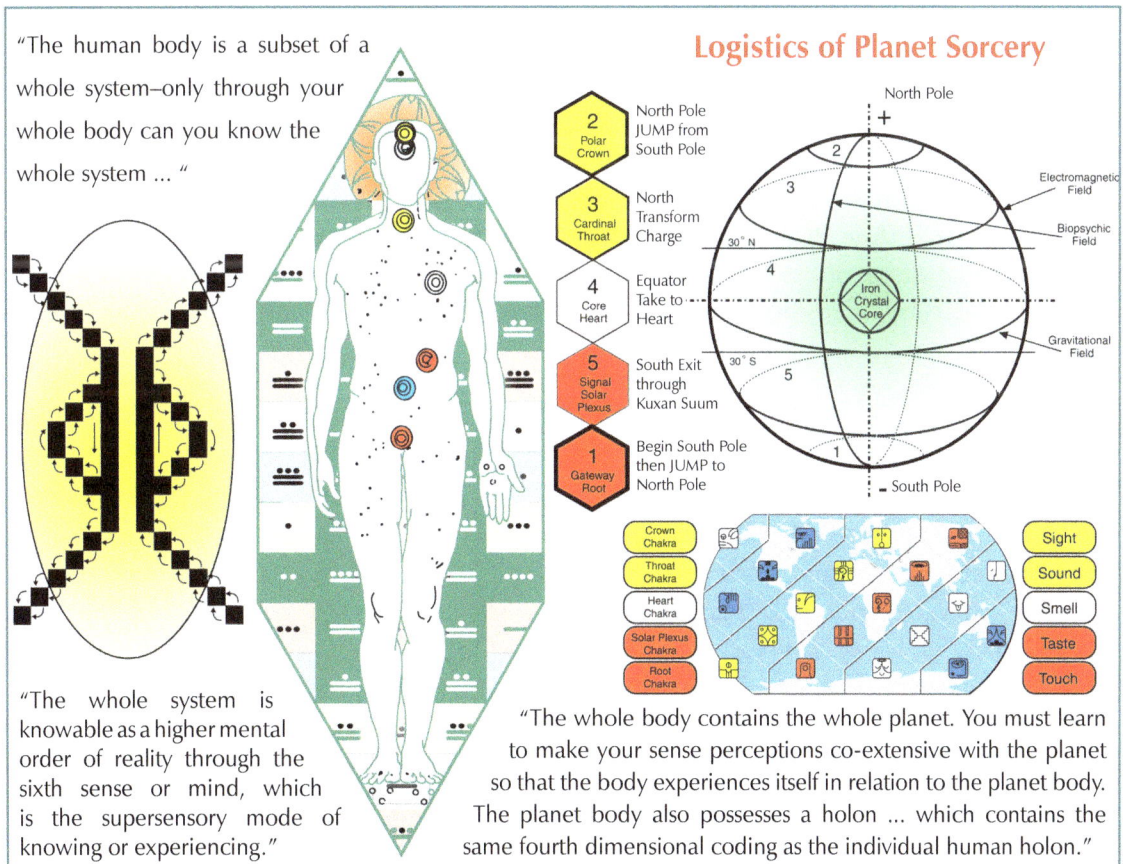

unit (or 13 x 20) harmonic module or Tzolkin. By self-attunement in resonance with the planet holon, the human can intensify the will, not only toward being entrained by the noosphere, but also toward the attainment of cosmic consciousness.

This resonant self-attunement is the point of the continuum of the evolution of the planet in relation to Cosmic History. You cannot know what you experience until you know how you experience and what is experiencing. This is the beginning point of understanding Planet Sorcery and Cosmic History. To practice whole body sensing, we must first become familiar with the following:

Categories of Whole Body Experience

Psychobiology—Biological functions are completely dependent on how our mind orders things, hence psychobiology, because ultimately all organization of life functions proceeds from mind. Mechanized time deranges our psychobiology by introducing an incorrect mental organizing factor, which actually extends to the genetic code itself.

Psychogenetic—Genetic makeup predisposes us to experience what we experience. It should be understood however that the genetic code itself originates first at a purely fourth-dimensional mental resonance which then becomes chemically encoded. Therefore, psychogenetics also refers to a fourth-dimensional telepathically induced correction of genetic "defects."

Psychophysical—Physical outer world is a function of our senses. The nature of our senses causes the external world to be organized in a specific way by the mind or the psyche. What we perceive of the outer world, then, is also conditioned by what the sensory structures permit. Hence, the outer world is merely a perceived appearance ordered in different ways for different beings and classes of creatures according to how their sense perceptions are organized.

Psychosensory—Sensory data is conditioned by our mind. Not only is the external world a function of the structure of our sense organs, but the sensory perception itself is affected profoundly by degrees and levels of mental conditioning. This is why in any situation involving several people, each of those people will have a slightly different story about what is going on in that situation.

Psychomythic—Mind has certain inherent structures that synthesize reality. These innate structures are sometimes referred to as archetypes and represent fundamental cosmic formative structures and principles. The very nature of the organization of a particular being has in it a certain set of inherent structures that will result in patterns of psychomythical behavior, whether that behavior is perceived as such or not.

Psychocosmic—Ultimate-final experience of the sorcerer who embodies Cosmic History. (See *Earth Ascending* Map 38.) It is psycho cosmic because the synthesized panorama of all of the senses unified and in congruence with an absolutely clear state of mind allows the entirety of the universal cosmic mind to be experienced as a synesthetic sensation within the sorcerer's mind.

Only a sorcerer can know Cosmic History by aligning his senses with the Planet body. A sorcerer uses all senses simultaneously, which is the basis for dharma art, behavior in conformity with the cosmic norm or the Law of Time (See *CH* Vol. III). You must understand that what you put out to the world and what you interpret is nothing but your own *psychogenetic feedback*. Psychogenetic is everything you are capable of experiencing according to the predisposition of your genetic makeup. Unless you understand this psychogenetic principle you will never transcend it. A sorcerer knows through total body experience that all he/she is ever experiencing is his/her own psychogenetic feedback.

Just the very act of reading and studying the *Cosmic History Chronicles* is an act of planet sorcery. The basic principle of sorcery is the taming of lower energies, passion or dis-ease, and then transmuting these energies so they become medicine or something beneficial and healthy for everyone. So in planet sorcery we are taming and transmuting the cosmically primitive energies and attitudes of the planetary human as a whole organism. The sorcerer is always seeking to maintain personal power. Power is the divine inheritance of the human being. Planet sorcery is completely dependent on the knowledge of Cosmic History. Sorcerer's methodology is the basis in developing planet sorcery. To change a planet's belief system and cast a higher spell based on another value system of knowledge, we must first understand the planet as a function of Cosmic History.

Cosmic History is based on the self reflective capacity for knowledge. The entire template of knowledge *is* Cosmic History. Yoga is part of Cosmic History. Cosmic science is part of Cosmic History. Meditation is part of Cosmic History. Understanding the relationship of the vibrational frequencies of your system with the Earth, solar and galactic orders, is part of the template of Cosmic History. This template is knowable through the noosphere, which is the next evolutionary stage of the human individual transmuted into the collective mental knowing.

The ultimate goal of yoga and developing the sorcerer's whole body knowing is to fully clear your mind so that you are riding God's thought-waves in His ceaselessly creative meditation. By training the mind/body, we are beginning to participate in the nature of God's meditation process. So on

> *The basic principle of sorcery is the taming of lower energies, passion or dis-ease, and then transmuting these energies so they become medicine or something beneficial and healthy for everyone.*

a planetary level we inject this transmuted cosmic medicine into the consciousness of the entire human race so that some type of positive transformation is affected. This is planet sorcery.

Transformation Of The Sense Fields

You must develop your power of seeing so you can get back to God. This is done through psychophysical exercises, of which the first step is to identify sensory perimeters. The goal is to maintain psychosensory clarity at all times. (See *Earth Ascending* Map 15) You must learn to take things apart, observing all the details in order to see the whole. You must never lose sight of details, for they are a reflection of divine vision. You must be so attuned and disciplined to the higher information flows that you hit the noospheric trip switch. To do this you have to dare to leave all conventional history behind. Much silent practice is required. The practice of Planet Sorcery entails expanding the sense perimeters to make them harmoniously coextensive with the planet, thus taming all lower energies, transcending the human belief system and ultimately transforming the Earth into one glorious psychosomatic organism. We must become exemplars of this transformation.

The term *psychophysical* refers to a science whose object is the study of the nature of sense experience. It is also a method or system of knowing nonduality, which requires mind/body discipline to experience. *Planetophysical* is a highly amplified psychophysical perspective, which is the perception of the planetary sorcerer. *Planetopsychical* refers to the formative stream of planetary thought—or all prophecies seen from a planetary point of view. From the psychophysical point of view everything in the universe is inherently aesthetic, which completely affirms the function of $T(E) = Art$ as a general principal. Therefore, planetophysical is the nature of a single noospheric perception that sees the planet as a single work of art.

Inherent harmony is the aesthetic perception of the universe, which is a function of the harmonic perception of the psychophysical point of view. Cultivation of psychophysical perception (seeing everything whole all the time) is fundamental to perceiving Cosmic History. To really develop discipline, you must see yourself in a naked space away from 12:60 influences. With this experience you have a perceptual apparatus to see things from the throne's eye view. When you see something as completely whole, then the thing you are seeing transcends itself. This is because you are simultaneously seeing what is and what is not, so the object has no choice but to transcend itself. If you concentrate on something long enough, then it transforms itself and disappears.

The point is, when you see all of life harmoniously, then the human experience transcends the limitations of the senses. If you can read and comprehend the signs, then you transcend the signs. Through the cultivation of the sorcerer's perception and the practice of yoga, the goal of Cosmic History is to attain to transcendence without leaving the body. Here we are only introducing you to a possibility of profoundly expanded perception. In Volume VI you will be given actual exercises.

Part II • Cosmic History as Systems of Knowing

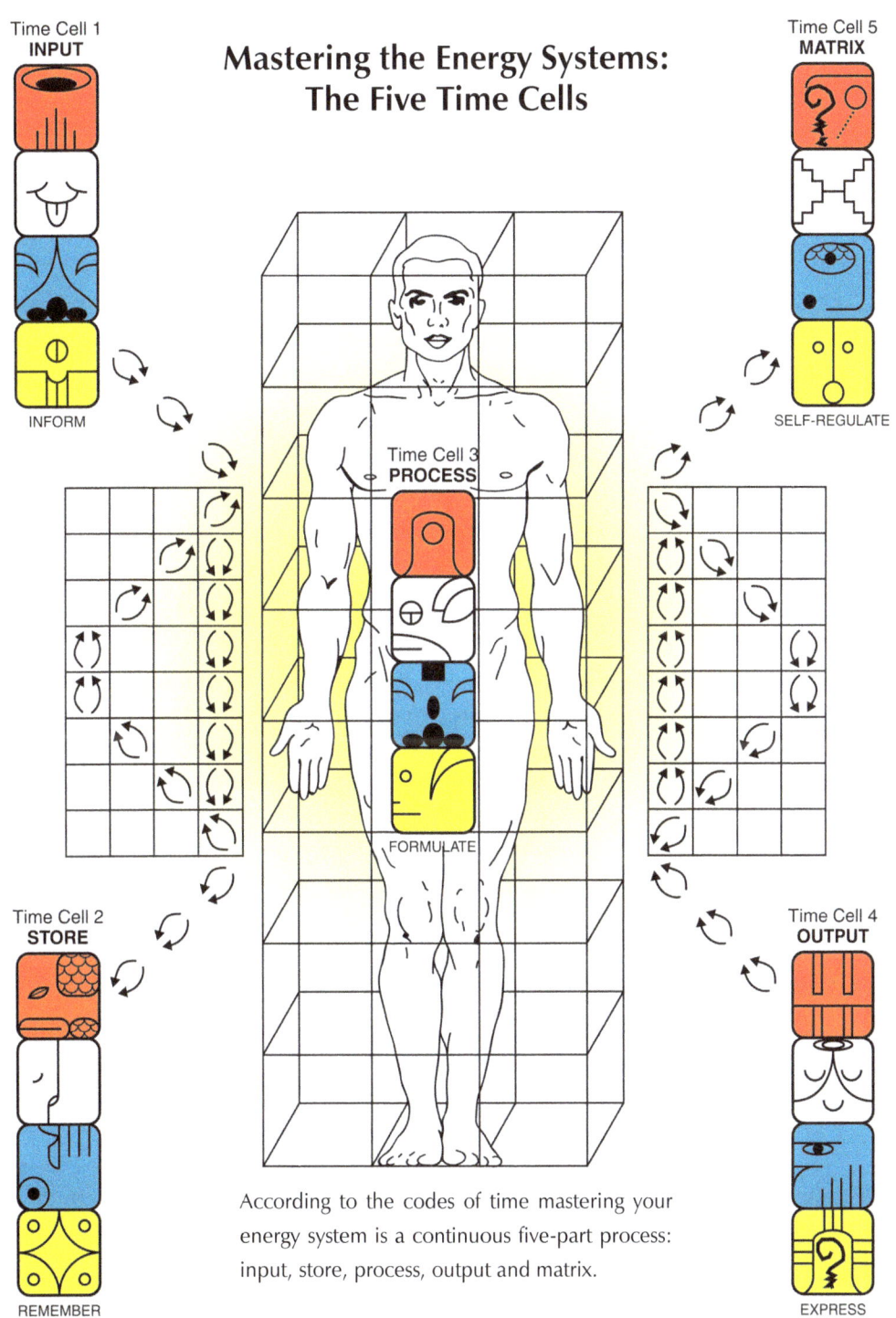

According to the codes of time mastering your energy system is a continuous five-part process: input, store, process, output and matrix.

Mastering The Energy Systems

Wherever the realized force of Cosmic History is directed it will certainly have a transformative effect. The application of Cosmic History results in world transforming yoga or planet sorcery. But before you can become engaged in world transforming yoga and planet sorcery, you must first master your own energy system by aligning your physical body, etheric body and holon systematically with the codes of the Law of Time. Since the Law of Time is a fresh or new revelation, by aligning your energy system according to these codes, you can be assured of being off on a fresh footing—one that is inevitably an expression of Cosmic History.

According to the codes of time, mastering your energy system is a continuous five-part process: Input, Store, Process, Output and Matrix. This process begins with inputting energy, be it as simple as conscious breathing or pranayama exercises. Upon inhalation, the prana or plasma is then consciously stored and balanced in the etheric fibers only to be transformed (processed) through an act as simple as a concentrated exhalation, representing a transmutation of negative energy. That transformed energy is then consciously expressed (output) through the simplest acts of bodily coordination or in some manner of artistic expression, until finally you experience yourself as a participant of a larger matrix in which that energy has now become a part of your living reality.

To master the energy system, sensitivity should be developed in the psychosensory system so you are able to perceive both what is apparent and what is not apparent. To understand Cosmic History clearly, it is necessary to simultaneously practice a complex of systems of disciplines outlined in the seven volumes. You must transcend conditioned thought responses of any kind in order to look at any person, place or thing and see which point of Cosmic History it is reflecting.

Through the instrument of the physical body, the method of Cosmic History can be grasped—but all aspects of the body must be engaged. In fact, the scope of Cosmic History is so vast that a 360-degree view is required. It is helpful to create a bubble

... before you can become engaged in world transforming yoga and planet sorcery, you must first master your own energy system by aligning your physical body, etheric body and holon systematically with the codes of the Law of Time.

or auric shield to establish a field of sensitivity to all incoming sensory and paranormal data, as well as to function as a protective shield for the containment of one's microcosmic capacities. To do this, surround yourself with a red activating or green harmonizing egg and practice 360-degree vision, always seeing with your entire body. What this visualization actually requires is the cultivation of an utter sensitivity to every aspect of your environment. If you maintain a total fidelity to every sensory nuance occurring moment-to-moment, then you will actually begin to feel as if you have eyes in the back of your head. This is not as easy as it sounds, since the tendency to mental preoccupation is profoundly engrained in most humans—and mental preoccupation is the biggest obstacle to developing 360 degree awareness.

Through yoga, meditation and visualization the *jnanasattva* slowly emerges. Jnanasattva refers to the internal wisdom body that takes the place of the old personality that was developed to survive in the world. You are slowly jettisoning that part. Overcoming mechanistic patterns is the essence of the sorcerer's training. The more you exert, the quicker old conditioned patterns or habits are uprooted and overcome. The best way to overcome old patterns is to continuously exert in new ways/patterns to create the New Temple. The goal is to have a superior mind and being that is receiving and instrumenting the total structure and body of Cosmic History. In this way, Cosmic History is an internal revolution dependent on the cultivation of seeing.

Once you learn to control your thoughts it is important to understand what is involved in the construction of the images of the world. Different senses create mental imagery. It is important to understand how images of the world become stereotyped in different platitudes. How do we create fresh images of the world? Here we see the difference between conditioned knowledge and fresh sense perceptions. Once a conditioned pattern is established in the mind, many impressions will automatically be rejected and those that are accepted will be filtered through the conceptual mind that conforms to the particular perception of reality. What then is real?

Once a conditioned pattern is established in the mind, many impressions will automatically be rejected and those that are accepted will be filtered through the conceptual mind that conforms to the particular perception of reality.

What then is real?

Cosmosis

Cosmosis is a new term. We know that osmosis depends on there being a semi permeable membrane that can be penetrated by a fluid or other substance. On the other side of that membrane the fluid goes into a higher concentrated form, which then goes back out and equalizes on the other side. For example, plants take in water by osmosis. You put water in the earth and the semipermeable membranes of the cells take it in through osmosis. Same thing within our own bodies within certain cells (like in the stomach lining or digestive areas) there is a passing of different fluids through the cell walls.

Analogous to osmosis, cosmosis is how the human psychobiophysical organism takes in cosmic energy, prana or radion plasma into the bodily system, including the etheric body, and reconstitutes it into concentrated forms, before secreting it back out through the walls of the body to create what you might call a "lighter aura." It is through cosmosis that the food sheathe is ultimately cared for. In fact, everything that we need is actually taken care of through the process of cosmosis.

Cosmosis is only a new word, not a new process. The yogic systems always talk about the prana entering the body, but in the evolutionary path or the path of spiritual evolution, the intake of the prana and plasmas do not occur exclusively through the nose and throat, but through the whole body. We are continuously being saturated with cosmic energies and forms of plasmas through our body. So by balancing and creating a higher level of biohomeostasis, stabilization of the biological functions will occur so that just as we can control the breathing, we can also control the plasmic intake of the physical food sheathe to bring the cosmic energy into the system.

This cosmic energy goes directly into the chakras, reconstitutes, and then enters the etheric nervous system before passing back out through the physical cell walls into the immediate biopsychic environment (resulting in what is usually defined as the aura). This "reconstituted" plasma then becomes a type of battery or energy system for the body. By amplifying the aura (the food sheathe's electromagnetic field)

... cosmosis is how the human psychobiophysical organism takes in cosmic energy...

the reconstituted plasmas also begin to subtly alter the environment or biosphere. This process of cosmosis is the most rudimentary beginning of the science of radiosonic architecture.

In this way, cosmosis depends on all the classic systems of yoga as we have been defining them, as well as the more advanced understanding that we are evolving into. This is the direction of the new etheric body sense organs, evolving into the noosphere as the collective morphogenetic field of the human species, establishing its mental field as a palpable planetary mechanism. In that process, each human being is functioning as a type of psychophysical nervous cell of the noosphere.

THE HIDDEN REALITY

The cosmic universal mind is available to those chosen by God to be His message bearers. This cosmic universal mind is the container of the *Clear Record* wherein all that is deeply hidden on Heaven and on Earth is recorded. The hidden reality known only to God is imparted by divine grace to those whom God has chosen—but only sufficient for the moment in spiritual evolution of which the specific messenger has been chosen. It is through the messenger that some of the hidden knowledge becomes revealed, but only to the extent that is necessary to uplift humanity to its next level. What must be clarified at the advent of the noosphere is the disposition of the thinking element in universal consciousness.

Upon this elucidation rests the comprehension of the nature of ego in its relation to the world soul of which the "individual" soul is a reflection. To understand the thinking element in universal cosmic mind as it is experienced by the planetary human at the closing of the cycle and in advance of the noosphere, one must understand the principle of intentionality and nonintentionality in the expression of intelligence. This will provide a whole other topic, to be described in Volumes IV and V.

"Say all praises to God and peace be upon those servants of His whom he chose to be His message bearers." 27:59

"…Could there be any divine power besides God? How seldom do you keep this in mind?" 27:62

"Say, none in the heavens or on Earth knows the hidden reality of anything that exists. None knows it save God." 27:65

"For there is nothing so deeply hidden in the heavens or on Earth that is not recorded in His clear record." 27:75

At this moment, you can begin to consciously participate in this process of cosmosis by continuously drawing in, synthesizing and transforming the cosmic energy needed for your own maintenance. Through the conscious process of cosmosis, you become cosmic, while the cellular unit of the body is the history. Not to forget that this knowledge is divine revelation with the purpose of entering into divine union by learning to live by cosmosis.

This means you become a cosmotic entity living by divine grace and ultimately returning to a state where God is giving you the faculties and capacities to penetrate even further into some of the hidden knowledge that exists everywhere in nature. However, this knowledge can only be penetrated by divine grace and through the cultivation of these higher etheric sense organs, which accommodate the higher coordination of systems of knowledge. These systems of knowledge are defined by Cosmic History as "whole systems."

Part II • Cosmic History as Systems of Knowing

Chapter 6:
Origins and Meaning of Life. What is Cosmic Science?

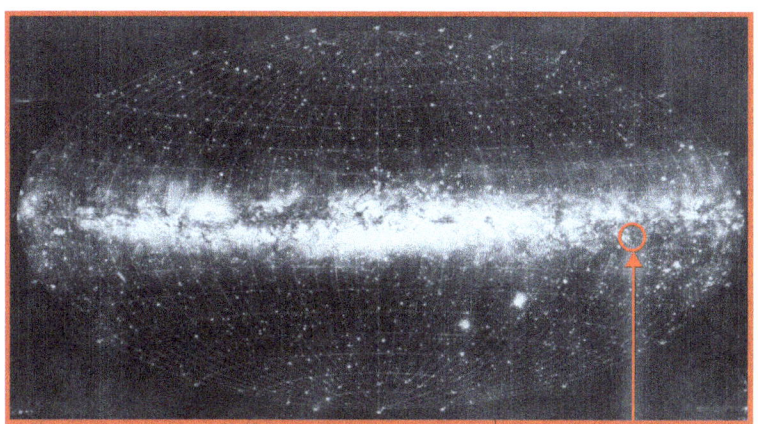

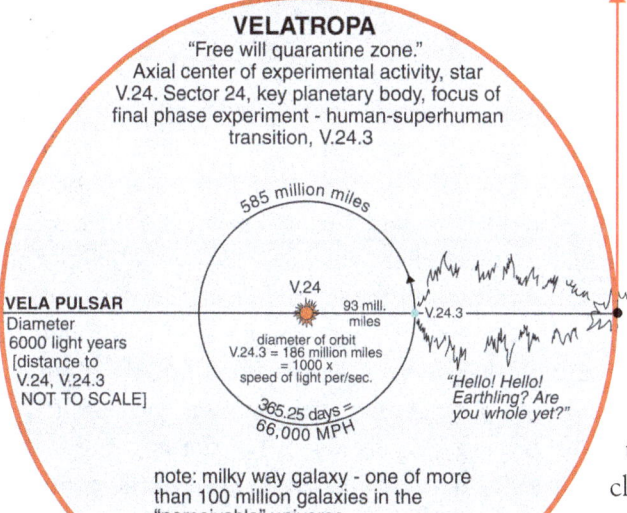

Cosmic Science is the investigation of the components of the cosmos whose history, origin and evolution are described by Cosmic History. Cosmic Science describes the laws and principles by which those different factors come about, gives definition to the constituent components, and explores fundamental questions about the universe such as: What are the basic quanta of energy? What is the function of plasmas and cosmic electricity? What are stars and where do they come from? What is our relationship to stars? What is life? What is mind? Cosmic Science is both supplemental to and includes the basics of the modern physical sciences, but only as mental constructs subordinate to the all unifying principles of the hierarchical order. Such a science begins and ends in the mind of God, which is ever present and close at hand.

The fact is, you are the Universe, and the galaxies that constitute the universe are woven from the same processes and material as have evolved the cells in your body. The galaxy, then, is the basis of departure for the study of Cosmic Science, but the galaxy understood as a formative design element of universal consciousness. Any true science has to start with the consideration of the existence of mind and consciousness and the consideration that there is a precise design to all of creation, so therefore, there must be an intelligence behind the design. If there is a precise design and nothing is random, then there must be a Supreme Intelligence coordinating it all—this Supreme Intelligence is sometimes referred to as God or Allah or simply the Creator. True science has to take these factors into account.

In the study of Cosmic Science, we must ask ourselves: Who is examining? What is consciousness? How can you study something and say consciousness doesn't exist? Science investigates the structure and nature of the universe. With the right application you can understand how matter arises in the world of form—when this is understood then you can learn how to make things disappear without being destructive. If you can master the laws of magical appearance, then "uncreating" is easy. Cosmic Science shows us how creation actually comes about and shows how it is inseparable from our human being.

Descartes could not find a place for the soul. He said he could not find soul in human anatomy, therefore it must not exist. Vernadsky brings up the point of consciousness as a nonphysical quality being able to affect matter. Most people try to define consciousness in physical terms, but these people confuse the mind with the brain. The brain is where the computational factors occur regarding the input of information and sensations. But is the brain the mind? If, indeed, the mind is far more than the brain and the brain is simply a small mental home appliance, then where are we to locate the mind if not throughout the vastness of the entire universe?

The only way any true science can arise is through the practice of yoga. But most scientists don't know their mind. How can you trust a scientist that dismisses the mind? Or a scientist who says the mind is not real or not important? True science can only be a science based on yoga as the control of thought-waves or mental patterns. Cosmic science is knowing cosmic reality from a Cosmic History point of view. Western science does not consider a higher intelligence other than human intelligence—extraterrestrial science is at best referred to as speculative borderline phenomenon. Cosmic Science is an aspect and counterpart of Cosmic History—but Cosmic History is the big umbrella.

> *Cosmic Science shows us how creation actually comes about and shows how it is inseparable from our human being.*

> ### COSMIC SCIENCE: TRANSMUTATIONAL SEQUENCE
>
> According to Cosmic Science, we are just ending the purely human phase that will be completed on Dec. 21, 2012. In Cosmic Science the new phase was initiated on March 7, 1970 (Rhythmic Star). From 1970 to 2012 is 42 years. This date occurred at this point because it was the time it took from seeing the whole Earth in space to its being absorbed into the noosphere by the third-dimensional entity. This was the signal of the new planetary human, defined as the hybrid biomutational sequence occurring between 1970 and 2012. The planetary human is a hybrid owing to the fact that during this time the human is shaped by participating in a transnationalistic or planetary technology. Television was the first piece of transnationalistic technological wiring, and the Internet was the second—then the whole hybrid was prepared.
>
> The purpose of this hybrid wiring was to experience the reality of being a planetary organism unified by an electronic nervous system. The whole purpose of technology is to create this sensation of a virtually unified planetary being, but one that is still very unconscious and addicted to its particular sectarian and parochial forms of behavior, to the point where a massive critical shift needs to occur to push that being into the realization that it is not the television or the Internet but a planetary being. The technology served the purpose of wiring the human organism to realize that it is a single planetary organism—not because of technology, but because this is its intrinsic nature and purpose.
>
> This realization is necessary in order for humans to enter into the next phase of the evolutionary trajectory known as the Superman, or the supermental human. In this phase, the human being enters into genuinely cosmic consciousness. But what really is the human being? What is the cosmic human? From the point of view of Cosmic Science, the cosmic human is, first of all, a type of plasmic energy system that consists of a physical genetic flesh and blood body. The body is like the insulation for the internal generator system, which is essentially fourth-dimensional but has third-dimensional glandular outlets including the pineal gland, thyroid, heart, solar plexus, liver, spleen, sexual organs and brain. So there are correlates on the physical level for those generators, but no one who ever dissected a human being ever found those generators or chakras because they are actually in the fourth-dimensional body, which is within the third-dimensional entity.

CRITERION OF COSMIC SCIENCE

When conducting the study of Cosmic Science, it is wise to keep the *Holy Quran*—the final definitive recitation of God for this world cycle—in one hand and the Law of Time in the other. Owing to its comprehensive scope and means, through Cosmic History a whole new critique of the world's civilization can and must be created. As you further open to the principles of Cosmic Science, Madame Blavatsky's *Secret Doctrine* can also be used, along with the *Cosmic History Chronicles* and the *Quran* as a cosmic criterion for evaluating and placing the Cosmic Science in a meaningful and immediate context. This is very important in regard to the current world belief system, which includes the separation of "church" and "state" resulting in a schizophrenic break in the collective psyche. This separation creates serious problems in society, which are exacerbated by the crooked mind control of the Gregorian calendar. This is because the separation masks a deeper split, that between spirit (church) and matter (state).

Real Cosmic Science does not separate the physical and biological from the spiritual. The *Quran* is to Babylonian religion what Cosmic Science is to 12:60 science—and what Cosmic History is to Babylonian history. Babylonian religion is the religion of priests that separate a spiritual class from the laypeople. In distinguishing the *Quran* as a criterion for evaluation of Cosmic Science, we mean to use it solely as a text of universal, always existing Islam, and do not mean to be confused with historical Islam. Like all other religions, historic Islam is a corrupted version of an original template, or rather, forsakes the original source for other relative and disputative standards.

To the degree in which Buddhism has a monastic class, Buddhism is Babylonian as well. Babylonian religion is the religion of priests that separates a spiritual class from the laypeople. A fundamental Babylonian theory is to separate life from spirituality. You cannot get away from spirituality or samsara. You have to find yourself within the samsaric conditions of life. There really is no escape. Granted, you can take retreats where you remove yourself from the world for a period of time in order to gain some insight on how to transcend your lower self. But the nature of the closing of the cycle is such that it does not matter whether you are in a monastery or not, you cannot escape the planetary mind field. In fact, thinking you can join a monastery to get away might only be a shirking of personal responsibility, which does not further the evolvement of the planetary mind field.

Islamic science developed in the high Middle Ages and took the factor of God as the central intelligence into account and, therefore, was able to develop a high level of science. When the West inherited the Islamic science it took God out of the equation and ignored the discussions about the nature

Real Cosmic Science does not separate the physical and biological from the spiritual.

of knowledge and consciousness, calling it "metaphysics" and giving attention only to the materialist/physical plane. The *Quran* says that Earth and the Heavens were not created in jest or just for play, but there is a meaning to everything. The natural universal reality has a meaning to it and it is to discover that meaning that real science ought to be directed. God created reality, so why would we need more than that? God is the author of this reality and like it says in the *Quran*, all God needs to do is say, "Be" and it is—how does this relate to cosmology? It is of interest to scientific egos to not have God in the picture as being the author of any cosmology because it allows them to go on building science departments and having theoretical arguments forever and this is how they get their paycheck. These are all interesting points.

What we call Western science is fundamentally Christian Science, or the science that was developed in the Sixteenth Century by the Christian civilization of Europe. Though it must be said that if it were not for Islamic/Arabic science, this modern Western Christian Science never would have come about. The unique aspect of the western science is that once it was formulated, it conscientiously ceased to be Christian and disavowed any relationship to God or the theology from which it was born.

In the late 19th Century there were other developments which are rightly referred to as Christian Science. This development is owing to the work of the American healer Mary Baker Eddy, whose formulation of the principles of Christian Science emphasize first and foremost that it is a science of the mind. This is a radical departure from the Western science as it had developed by the late 19th century—and this new Christian Science was undoubtedly a necessary response to the emphatic materialism of modern science.

Two other streams of scientific thought should be mentioned. The Vedic stream of Indian science and the traditional science of China. Both of these comprehend a vast system of thought and cosmology in which the principles of the Universe are found to be located within the complete multidimensional human form. Though many of the methods

The unique aspect of the western science is that once it was formulated, it conscientiously ceased to be Christian and disavowed any relationship to God or the theology from which it was born.

and principles might seem to differ, the general orientation or paradigm of Chinese Taoism and Vedic science and ayurvedic healing methods are broadly similar. This is because the uniform values of Cosmic History have been unconsciously present in the formative stages of the development of the different civilizational streams. One could even speak of an Inca science as well as a Mayan science, in which again the principles of interpenetrating human and universal values preside.

Origins Of The Universe

The reality of the mind of God is the underlying factor of Cosmic Science, which offers a view of the process of cosmic evolution that is spiritual in nature. This means that Cosmic Science is vastly informed. Third-dimensional science labels and names things and leaves God out of the equation so it comes up with theories like the Big Bang. Without admitting the divine factor, you will never come to any satisfactory explanation of the universe. Where did the Big Bang come from in the first place? Or rather, where did the material of the explosion that created the Big Bang come from?

Cosmic Science states that the universe began in the mind of God which engendered a kind of ether, from within which a force of disassociation analogous to the Big Bang occurred. Two simultaneous waves of different frequencies collided, creating what we now know as the universe. What were the forces that collided? Was it God "breathing?" And with His breath created the beginning of the universe where the whole show began to unfold? At the beginning of the unfolding of the universe is where Cosmic Science begins.

Cosmic Science describes how the universe is first built up as a function of electricity, electronics, electrical forces and plasmas—then you get to quantification. Quanta is when something takes on shape or form (becomes quantifiable). From the point of disassociation is the creation of energy that creates electrical lines of force, up until the point that something becomes quantifiable—this is the direction of Cosmic Science.

Third-dimensional science takes things apart in a laboratory without ever explaining where they came from. The work of Western science began by looking through a microscope to discover the smallest particle in an attempt to explain why this or that particle behaves the way it does. But have these scientists even examined their own mind? How can you conceive of an accurate science or system of knowledge without having mind training at the foundation? Observations and conclusions can be tainted if you have not examined your own mind. This is why meditation is essential as a direct means of entering into the mind of God.

From the point of view of the enlightened mind, mind ultimately has no substance. Cosmic Science offers a radically different description of the universe by describing physical substance as it is built up from the void, and also has implicit in it a critique of Babylonian science. It is this critique which is of value to Western science. Science is how we know. Materialist science, based on factors that eliminate the possibility of God, places in doubt the existence and nature of mind and consciousness. This point of view is to the detriment of civilization because you just don't leave God out of the equation without courting disaster.

Cosmic Science describes a world where spiritual evolution is the governing factor. Just as Cosmic History describes a principle of involution and evolution, so does Cosmic Science, which shows the relationship of mind and matter within the context of spiritual evolution. The purpose of any study should be to bring you closer to God. How close can you get in remembering God? This is why in his translation of the *Quran*, Rashad Khalifa says "at God." There are angels and beings who are "at God" to a degree that they are never apart from God no matter where they are.

We know from the *Quran* that the chief proof of the existence of God is the unity of nature. This unity is the proof of the existence of God because there cannot be a unity of that complexity without there being a divine intelligence behind it which is God, the Supreme Creator. From this corollary, intelligence is not random; there is holonomic consistency in every last detail of the universe—this is the law that establishes the unitary nature of everything that exists on every single level and works in tandem with the Law of Time. The two self-evident laws of nature are:

1. The Law of Whole Systems, which govern the uniform consistency of the appearance of all phenomena (including the imaginal realm).

2. The Law of Time, which keeps all phenomena unified by being synchronized in time.

These are the two basic discoveries of the Closer of the Cycle, who first described the holonomic law in the 1984 book *Earth Ascending: An Illustrated Treatise on the Law Governing Whole Systems*. He discovered that everything has a self-repeating, self-replicating holonomic consistency. When you really get down to it, there are not many laws and principles you need to know to understand how the universe works. It is impossible to know the universe without God at the center of the equation. The Law Governing Whole Systems is the formal fundamental law and the Law of Time is the formal principle defining the *synchronic order*.

"Cosmic Science describes a world where spiritual evolution is the governing factor. Just as Cosmic History describes a principle of involution and evolution, so does Cosmic Science which shows the relationships of mind and matter within the context of spiritual evolution."

THE HOLONOMIC EQUATION

The Holonomic Equation is a five-part process that describes a profound pattern of the arrival of self-reflective intelligence within a particular field or planetary matrix. The five parts include:

1. Nature Presents Itself—The totality of nature is intelligible phenomena, self-existingly manifest with underlying patterns.

2. Man Learns from Nature—You could not learn from nature if there were not patterns. Study the patterns. Nature is organized so that everything supports everything else. The pattern of trees equals a forest—then there are subsets (ferns, animals, etc). Organizing principles become coherent. You could not recognize the patterns if there were not some kind of intelligible process within your own neurocerebral make-up. The human learns through attempts to align patterns of intelligence with the experience of the patterns perceived in the phenomenal world. The same process that creates nature creates the human since the human is nature.

3. Man Transforms Nature—Once the patterns of nature are made intelligibly coherent, the human interfaces the intelligent perception with the perceived phenomenal reality. This results in transformation or change. When the human becomes involved in agriculture then the transformation becomes major. The history of civilization is the history of humans living in increasingly artificial structures. This process has become so elaborate that it can no longer sustain itself. Once decadence sets in, creativity diminishes and becomes a repetition of forms which then goes to a machine stage of development. This creates a larger transformation. Humans are massively taking things from the Earth, leaving it scarred. Transformation of nature by aboriginal man is very minimal. Now we are at the 13th Baktun. This is the point when sectarian, parochial, localized cultures, civilizations and dynasties arouse the final stage of transformation. Mechanistic, industrial means are so intensive and humans are so morally careless that nature is thrown into imbalance. This calls forth a big evaluation.

4. Nature Evaluates Man—If man doesn't care for what he is doing, then there is a karmic rebound in time. Usually civilization or dynasties are terminated at this point. But when the various civilizations of a planet converge and create a global conglomerate, then there is a massive evaluation. This is due to the cumulative karmic effects of each civilization which accelerate and explode when all are thrown into contact as a global conglomerate.

5. Man and Nature Synthesize—Evaluation usually involves learning a lesson. Societies, cultures and civilizations are no different. Man learns he cannot be so careless with nature and technology. Humanity must learn how to become even greater in nature—to reintegrate and become cosmic vehicles of a cosmic nature to express the cosmic law.

What Is Life And How Is It Formed?

When we say: What is life? What is biology? How does the biology of life fit into the general scheme of the universe? How does it fit into this particular understanding? The universe is based on the principle of polarity. There is an inbuilt polar magnetism in everything in the universe. This polarity is what keeps everything spinning. The *Quran* very often uses the phrase "in the alternation of night and day." This refers to the primary law of alternation. The most fundamental aspect of the law of alternation is the primary electromagnetic polarity that creates magnetism and electricity.

Life must have something to do with this too. We usually think of the study of physics as space, motion, kinetics, gravity, energy, thermodynamics and electricity: but what about life? What is that? There is a kind of distinction made between life and nonlife or inorganic nonlife and organic life or inorganic chemistry and organic chemistry. The Law of Time states that life is actually a secondary attribute of cosmic creation. What we call life is not the first thing that was created.

The creation of life was established by the primary polarity, the electrical forces, the spin of atoms and molecules and the spin of celestial bodies spiraling out into different galaxies. All of these qualities of the universe seem to have been established before life was established. In the first two "days" of creation all the laws we have been describing (electromagnetism, spins, etc) were established. The next four "days" of creation were used in the creation and establishment of life. Even in this allegorical statement we have a binary doubling—"inorganic" two doubled to four becomes life. But if life is evolved from non-life, can we really make such a distinction as "organic" and "inorganic?"

Heterotrophs And Autotrophs

Life is a system for processing inorganic matter into organic matter and also for processing organic matter within the organic animal. Animal life is *heterotrophic,* (feeds on other life) and is sustained by taking in inorganic material (air, water, minerals).

The Law of Time states that life is actually a secondary attribute of cosmic creation. What we call life is not the first thing that was created.

Autotrophic life feeds on solar radiation (atmosphere, oxygen and water). Trees and plankton are autotrophs that feed on photonic emanations and water, which is the basis of life. Water, air and photons from the sun, as well as minerals, are the main inorganic elements upon which life is structured. Most humans (save breatharians) are examples of heterotrophic life because they are dependent on other forms of autotrophic matter, which represent some type of organic life, like fruits, vegetables, seeds and nuts. Some humans also eat fellow heterotrophs like fish, cows or chickens.

The heterotrophic life-form is the most dependent life form on Earth and requires the most maintenance— the human being is the most dependent of all. Heterotrophs represent a relatively complex system of metabolic interactions. Whereas in water, minerals and photons there are not the same complex of interactions that are apparent in the system we call life. These elements have self-sustaining cycles: such as the evaporation of water into clouds. The clouds eventually develop rain and the rain falls and gathers into the Earth, feeding the plants and flowing into lakes before evaporating again, etc...

The autotrophic life is an intricate system of metabolic, chemical and thermic interactions that involve the processing of different types of information and informational structures— be they water, oxygen or just pure photons. This information is transferred into the membrane of a living system which goes through any number of chemical interactions. These chemical interactions cause the autotrophic element to transpire and become involved in the carbon dioxide cycle—and also to transpose light into biological matter through a process called photosynthesis.

This process of photosynthesis produces the green leaves and the vegetable world which is characterized by different degrees, shades or levels of intensity of photosynthesis. This means that light is taken from a star and interacts with water, in the Earth and moves through cycles. These cycles create a system that causes life to grow. But life can only grow so far in a particular form since life goes through cycles.

> *The heterotrophic life-form is the most dependent life form on Earth and requires the most maintenance— the human being is the most dependent of all.*

MYSTERY OF TREES AND CRYSTALS

Trees are symbiotic, which means that man and other life forms live on and off or through them. The question is: Does the tree ever really die? Or does it just give birth to other trees so other trees can be spawned on it? Every tree has its seeds which become other trees and ad infinitum. Are we speaking about the life of a single tree or are we speaking about the life of the whole forest. Is there a difference?

When we talk about life then, just at a pure biological level, there are different chemical or metabolic photosynthesizing interactions that create more life, more leaves, more birds, more snakes, etc. The different processes of life of the autotrophic and the heterotrophic work together as one large interactive symbiotic system that is always perpetuating itself and always mutating into other forms. However, of the two strands of existence, it is the inorganic primary strand that offers the most perfect form, which is the crystal; a pure exquisite geometrical mineral structure. Once the crystal is formed, you do not have to water it, it is already "crystallized" into a perfection of form. The only change that happens in a crystal is through some kind of kinetic effect—or if a crystal sits in the light it will sometimes produce spectralizations—but the crystal itself doesn't depend on the light—it is self-perfect. A crystal requires no maintenance to sustain its perfect form. All of life requires maintenance, which at minimum includes water, light and air.

The theory of evolution says that originally there was a large amount of water then somehow life formed in the water. The *Quran* affirms this theory. From the water then came the seaweed and plankton and so on, and then came trees and ferns and large kinds of plants that blossomed and evolved everywhere in a great profusion of number. But how within the water is life formed and sustained? Yes, the DNA may find in water a nurturing matrix, but where did the DNA come from in the first place? The answer must lie in the action of the Divine Will.

After the emergence of plant life came animal life. Plants have to remain for the most part rooted, but animal life is

A crystal requires no maintenance to sustain its perfect form. All of life requires maintenance, which at minimum includes water, light and air.

mobile. All animal life lives off plants and/or other heterotrophs. This seems to be a more intricate design level of evolution. The human being, whether it knows it or not, is actually meant to evolve into what is called a breatharian, absorbing the light of the universal life-force and directing the energy into the cells for the purpose of what Milarepa calls *permanent samadhi*.

> "Supreme is my Samadhi, that's never hungry.
> How can meat and wine compare with it?
> If Samadhi food does not sustain me, how can I ever Endure insatiate hunger?
> If there is no stream of bodhi for my drinking
> How can I live without water and not thirst?"
>
> Songs of Milarepa Vol. 1 pp.234-235

THE BASIS OF INTELLIGENCE

Human intelligence did not evolve or become necessary until a much later time in the history of creation. Only when the human being became two-legged and grew thumbs did real intelligence evolve on Earth. Of course there are different types of evolution of man up until present day modern man. It is assumed that not until the homosapien emerged did human intelligence emerge. This would mean that intelligence is dependent on factors of material evolution. This leads us to Vernadsky's question: How can the physical be affected by the nonphysical or how can it be that consciousness affects matter?

If you look at the basis of intelligence from this point of view, it is a function of the intricacy of the material evolution into a more refined nervous system and a more complex brain. While this may be an interesting view, it is quite limited. But how is the basis of intelligence viewed from the point of view of Cosmic Science and other schools of thought?

From the higher point of view, intelligence is a *planeto-cosmic* phenomenon. This means that intelligence is a property of cosmic order and that the minimum constituent of cosmic order—a planet body and its satellite or satellites—is the smallest unit capable of sustaining a field of intelligence which is cosmically unifying in scale or scope. From this point of view, the purpose of the human or any biological or life-sustaining form is to function as a medium for this planeto-cosmic phenomenon called intelligence. The purpose of the creation of the human being is to create a highly evolved and intricate medium not only to act as a vehicle of cosmic intelligence, but as a conduit for ever evolving consciousness and spirit.

There is something called mind or consciousness that seems to exist apart or independent of the formation of human life. To say that all the intelligence that exists in the universe is that which exists within the human being is a very limited statement. Many humans are more primitive and barbaric than the animals. Is it intelligent for human beings to create an artificial monstrous world? Of what is this a function? There must be other factors at work. We say the human represents the manifestation of a vehicle for the intentional thinking element of the universe. From the point of view of the Law of Time, however, intelligence and consciousness exist independent of the human being.

The human being merely uses its body apparatus to tune into the consciousness or the mind-at-large from which it derives thoughts, words and other forms of communication. Consciousness is not really the property of the human being nor is the question of intelligence. When we ask: "What is life?" We are just defining life as we know it on this Earth. Life on this Earth is carbon-based life. Is this really how all life is? Can life have other conditions? Can life have other forms?

What is it that causes something to be organic or inorganic? Anything that is organic has some type of growth process. Generally, at one point the organic material is one size and shape and then it becomes another size and shape. It says any number of times in the *Quran* that humans are created from insignificant lowly liquid then go through various life stages. But why does life happen? What is life? Why does there seem to be birth and death? What is this about?

In our stage of the evolution of life, we see that there is male and female. What does this have to do with the primary origin of existence? What is life about? Life is easy to take for granted but it is very important to consider: Do things only come into existence to die? Once something is born its life process is inevitable and its death is also inevitable. When it dies does it stop being a growing form?

It says in the *Quran* that human beings were created for a specific purpose. We have this whole complex metabolic chemistry going on. What is our purpose as a human being? What are we supposed to do as living things? All a tree does is grow, it does not have to do anything to sustain itself. It doesn't go to restaurants to eat. It doesn't buy anything. It doesn't need a shoe store. It just grows.

Even the animals, reptiles, insects and birds have cycles of life where they are dependent on some type of external form for nurturance. Whether it's water or a leaf—something generally has to be ingested, therefore it has a dependent support cycle.

But why does life happen?

What is life? Why does there seem to be birth and death?

What is this about?

Some animals chew their grass, some hunt their prey. Then what goes in has to come out as manure or uric acid.

So what is the purpose of life? To keep the Earth green? From the bigger picture, we see that life is a conglomeration of capacitors, which facilitate cycles of light, cycles of water, and cycles of distribution of vegetable and animal matter. This recycling process is relatively complex and creates a type of interchanging dynamic. This seems to be the description and nature of life. Is life necessary? What good is life?

When you have a life you have a system that is intricately evolved in the working balance of a whole system. You cannot have life without the whole rest of the system. The description of life, then, is a cyclic regenerative process that facilitates the continuation of various cycles of atmosphere, light and water. So life seems to be a facilitator of a terrestrial process which, on our planet, we refer to as the biosphere. We hardly ever think about these things, but it's time we did.

CURIOUS LIFE OF THE HUMAN

The big question is: Why did God create us and what does he want us to do with our time?

The big question is: Why did God create us and what does he want us to do with our time? When we look at other life-forms like squirrels, birds or frogs—what do they do with their time? What is it all about? For them it seems life is not a difficult existence. Most other forms of life still don't have to have shoe stores. They are self-sufficient and know what to eat and where to find it. When we get to the human being it becomes very curious. Of course the animals are dependent on berries and plants or other animals for their sustenance. But when you get to the human being it is a different story.

Why was the human being created? Why are humans so sensitive to hot and cold? Why do the humans have such a seemingly defenseless system? Because of the high sensitivity to hot and cold more often than not the human being has to put something around its body. Shoes and clothes seem to be a necessity. Even with its extreme sensitivity the human is also very adaptable. Think of the Eskimos and, then, the Aborigines who live in the desert. To adapt to a very cold environment the human has to get involved in some type of manufacturing process—to take hides or skins of animals and eat what can be eaten and make the rest into clothes, blankets and even portable houses.

Humans need a dwelling place to live because of the different temperature changes. The human has a need to make clothes and dwellings. Bees and beavers also make dwelling places—but they don't have to make clothes. Clothes and dwelling places are the root of human culture. This establishes the rudimentary basis of human material culture. Humans need something to catch the animals with or seeds to plant. The human being needs to take care of different seeming deficiencies in its character to help it along. This whole combination makes the human culture the most complicated among all species of life.

The human dwelling can be very simple. It can be made out of hides or clothing textiles. When you get into cloth or textiles you need to learn the art of spinning on a spindle in order to make the yarn for clothing. Humans have to think of all these things just to have a minimally comfortable existence. To survive as a human requires a level of complexity of cultural ingenuity. In the animal world life is simple. Bees make their dwelling effortlessly by instinctual memory codes. Human building codes are acquired not innate, or so it seems.

In our examination, we still have not answered the question: Is life necessary? The human's biological level and intelligence level is most advanced among all species. But the weakness and vulnerability of character give rise to cleverness and the exploitation of different material phenomena of nature to create its own cultural domain. So we see that human vulnerability and weakness is the cause of having to create a culture. All of this is relatively innocuous behavior until you get to the creation of the machine.

Humans Enter Machine World

Up until the creation of the machine, human beings left their mark through agriculture, fields, different kinds of irrigation, etc. Therefore, they had a minimal and even an environmentally or aesthetically enhancing way of modifying the landscape of the Earth. Then you get to the creation of the first machine, the clock, finally perfected as the mechanical clock in 1584 and as the pendulum clock by Galileo and Huygens in the 1650s. At this point, the human being tips the scale and becomes an increasingly artificial creature. In the machine revolution, the human being moved and displaced some of the natural phenomenon but only to create structures that were meaningful to the human.

Before the machine, lots of stones might have been taken and made into a pyramid or a cathedral, or stones might have been taken and carved into sculptures of some kind or another—but this building did not radically alter the ecology or cycles of life. In some cases, different forms of farming may have worn down the soil and after too many years the soil would have to be enriched again. But for the most part, the human's effect on the environment was minimal and mostly aesthetic up to the time of the machine. The machine seems to have transformed the human being into an artificial creature with increasing dependence on other forms of life, particularly on the machine.

So you see that the so-called evolved lifeform of the human being is very vulnerable, weak and dependent. There is also a highly volatile and sensitive type of intelligence associated with the human. Generally, the human intelligence is of an untamed nature. Once the machine was introduced into the evolutionary trajectory of the planet, then the tendency of evolution was to intensify the creation and dependency on an artificial world. Cosmic Science does not deal so much with the cultural historical description, but rather makes a description of life from the perspective of its composition through the different electronics, electronic fluids, plasmas and programs of behavior, which are known through the neural-electrical operators the UR runes (see the *20 Tablets of the Law of Time*). So the question regarding the human is: How much is his/her behavior upsetting the equilibrium of the cosmic forces, both within his/her own composition and the composition of the environment and what will its consequences be? Where does life go from here?

Who enjoys life? Does the tree get something out of being alive? Does the grass? Does the squirrel?

SENTIENT LIFE

What is life, where does life occur and why? From one point of view, we can say life occurs because it furthers different cycles of chemical organization, reorganization and transformation. In other words, a rock or a crystal doesn't do anything but sit. A star, on the other hand, is doing something—it is giving off light, energy and heat. It seems to be dynamic. From the point of view of Cosmic Science, a star is a function of different types of gases and transformers, rays and energy and represents a continuous, unceasing dynamic. This dynamic produces light, luminic/thermic and other different types of rays and radiations that maintain, on a planet like Earth, the phenomenon known as life.

Life is generated by light, heat and water and is involved in cycles of continuous transformation or what Vernadsky refers to as the *biogenic migration of atoms*. In other words, the trees and the plankton take in sunlight which they photosynthesize to make chlorophyll. Then they send roots into the earth and take in the nutrients of the soil, which is basically pulverized mineral mixed with organic matter. This description is a physiochemical point of view where life is seen as a process of chemical transformation that maintains itself in cyclical forms over a long period of time.

Who enjoys life? Does the tree get something out of being alive? Does the grass? Does the squirrel? We know that plants merely grow and expand and they seem happier when they receive water. But how much sentiency do plants really have? In the early 1950s Dr. T. C. Singh, head botanist of the Annamalai University, India, discovered that the hydrilla, a water plant, reacted to Indian ragas played on violin, flute, and vina. Further studies were done during the 1960s and 70s, many of which were reported in the sensational book called the *Secret Life of Plants*, describing experiments demonstrating that plants have a type of paranormal intelligence—that they are surrounded by a cosmic energy that permeates all living things.

German poet and philosopher Johann Goethe also stated that plants have sentiency and consciousness. Goethe conceived of an archetypal plant (Ur-pflanze), an ideal prototype which is the source of all the variations in the plant kingdom, both past and future. Even the animal kingdom seems to have more sentiency than humans. Why does a dog exist? What is the purpose of a cat? Why does life exist? For the perpetuation of different cycles? What is the purpose of all of this? What are we experiencing now in our consciousness? If we died right now what would happen? Didn't consciousness precede this body? What happens when we no longer have a body? Will we still be participating in the biosphere's support system? We are participating in it now just by breathing and by transmuting some of the elements by eating and going to the bathroom. It's important to consider all of this. Are we just here to experience the sheer cosmic poignancy of being alive on this planet for one moment?

What is the meaning of life and why are we all here like this? Why does there have to be so much violence in this

"…this oneness is what makes possible a mutual sensitivity allowing plant and man not only to intercommunicate, but to record these communications via the plant on a recording chart." Marcel Vogel in The Secret Life of Plants, p. 24

life? Life seems to be defined by most people in a very narrow survivalist kind of way. But what about our divine nature? Has it totally become buried? Are we not supposed to remember God?

According to Cosmic Science, present day human beings are absolutely insane. From the point of view of Cosmic Science, the only reason to be alive is to evolve cosmic consciousness. The idea of defending a piece of territory or killing someone because they don't have the same ideas as you is very primitive behavior. It shows that in the overall system of thought and science that exists in the world, there is some vast failure to address who we really are, what we are really doing and what we really need.

From the point of view of Cosmic Science, who we really are is the evolving component that maintains the intentional thinking element of the cosmos. From an evolutionary point of view, Cosmic Science might say that the inability of the planetary human to control violence demonstrates that the human species has gone down a wrong path. Who is projecting and how did it all begin?

From the point of view of the Law of Time, the failure of human civilization is the inability to comprehend the nature of time. What is the failure of human civilization from the point of view of Cosmic Science? In addition to having bought into an erroneous concept of time, the failure of the human species is the failure of addressing the fact that it is actually a cosmic entity. Cosmic means order. The word cosmetic is related to that because it has to do with order as beauty. Therefore, that which has order has beauty and the universe is a fundamental harmony.

When we talk about being "cosmic", we are talking about a fundamentally harmonious perception about oneself and the world in which one's place in the cosmos is clearly defined. From the Cosmic Science point of view, this is what is lacking in the education systems, which are now bogged down in presenting parochial, nationalist, sectarian points of view. Americans represent America's point of view. Israelis represent the Jewish point of view. The Arabs represent the Muslim point of view.

When we talk about being "cosmic", we are talking about a fundamentally harmonious perception about oneself and the world in which one's place in the cosmos is clearly defined.

But who is representing the cosmic point of view?

The definitions of people as different religions, nations or races is only to reinforce what would have appeared to be random historical circumstances. All of the failure of civilization was built on random historical circumstances. Case in point, at a certain moment in time the Vatican had the power and forced their Gregorian calendar on the world without consulting anyone and with no real analysis of time. The fact is, that the Gregorian calendar was a random historical circumstance that became globally institutionalized. It was not a matter of the people's consensus. This fact was covered over and totally forgotten and since it is institutionalized it is treated like a sacred cow—and you just don't get rid of sacred cows. As a consequence, our world is imaginatively, morally and creatively bankrupt.

As a result, the human species became splintered and divided, as it says in the Quran: "…you all divided into different sects." This is the failure of civilization, even though it speaks of globalization. But that point of view really is only global to the extent that the capitalists feel the whole world is their market for the transformation of the raw resources of the biosphere. The television and the Internet are a global phenomenon, but the attitudes of most people in the world are anything but global when they have to defend a particular point of view. This entire erroneous world mind must be rubbished.

We have to start with a fresh look at who we are according to Cosmic Science. The cosmos is inherent order and is intrinsically beautiful and elegant. Therefore, everything is intrinsically cosmic. To know your place in the scheme of all things is cosmic. To be educated regarding how you fit into the scheme of Universe—from the stars, down to the Earth—has a lot of bearing on your consciousness and soul. If consciousness is not disciplined, then there is no discrimination in choosing—so things are done out of ignorance. The human must look again at the nature of her/his own soul and place in the cosmos and say: What am I doing here? Am I here to just get a better paying job so I can be a glorified part of the food chain? Is there a larger picture to this? What is my part?

In summary, Cosmic Science is the supreme science that shows that everything that has existed or has evolved over a period of time is completed in the human form. Precisely because Cosmic Science is brought to fulfillment in the human form, yoga is the key element to Cosmic Science. This is because yoga and the yogic sciences represent a synthesis or union of the psychic, physical, mental, emotional, and spiritual and the evolutionary tendencies of the cosmos as they are formulated through the human organism. The sorcerer's whole body perception is fundamentally defined by the same methodology. In other words, the sorcerer's whole body perception consists of a highly refined attunement with the cosmos that is the result of assiduous practice in the yogic sciences.

Redefining The Human - You Are A Three Part Entity

Humans are far more than just a third-dimensional entity made up of atoms, molecules and subatomic molecules connected to a dynamic chain of life. From the point of view of Cosmic Science, there is a third-, fourth- and fifth-dimensional entity assigned to each being. This is so far out of the present world paradigm that it is rarely discussed. The fourth-dimensional entity is born with the third-dimensional entity because it is connected to the fifth-dimensional entity. Most humans are not aware of this. So you have the third-dimensional biological entity and the fourth-dimensional etheric biological entity and the fifth-dimensional which is purely electronic—this is your guardian spirit who orchestrates your life program.

You are the fifth-dimensional entity waiting to be recognized. The fifth-dimensional is always working to see if the third-dimensional being will ever wake up. The fourth-dimensional should be cooperating in the fifth-to-third-dimensional hook up. Art is how the fourth-dimensional uses the third-dimensional body to bring it into harmony with the fifth-dimensional. This is the future stage of evolution.

The evolution of the increasingly material dependent human species generally views that there is this life you are born with and then that's it. If you are born, you die and you are going to get resurrected, then what is the point of this life? If you truly take this into consideration, the point of life would be very different than what we perceive it right now. The reason human life has become such a materialistic extravaganza is because at its ideological base it does not believe there is any life beside this one we are living now. Because of this belief it pours all of its energy into making this life as comfortable as it can so it can avoid death. This is the basis of the materialist civilization, the end product of historical materialism.

In this civilization, the biology of the human being is bottled up and served in artificial canisters of different forms of modern urban existence. In this way, you cannot find any

The Quran says the human was made in this way so it could be tested to see if it could recognize and remember the imprinting it received before creation about who it is and what is its destiny.

meaning in this life. The Cosmic Science says: "No, this thinking is erroneous. Yes, there is a third-dimensional body but there is also a fourth- and fifth-dimensional body." The purpose of life has something to do with the integration and coordination of these three entities. The evolution of these three entities is the purpose of life. Most spiritual traditions say something like this. They say this life here is really very short and fleeting—if you pay too much attention to it you'll fail to see that you really should be preparing for your death and your resurrection, rather than trying to make things cushy for yourself. Even the best intentioned people in this life who believe in resurrection spend a lot of time in a materialistic fog.

The fifth-dimensional entity is not biological, it is purely electronic. The description of all other life somewhat pales in comparison to the human being who is weak and vulnerable and has the need to create artificial systems for itself in order to maintain its body and keep it from succumbing to its weak nature. This biological weakness seems also to be a moral weakness.

The human is capable of intentionally distorting the experience of reality. All of this makes the human being a very complex phenomenon. The *Quran* says the human was made in this way so it could be tested to see if it could recognize and remember the imprinting it received before creation about who it is and what is its destiny. The human being was created for this testing to see if it could maintain a life of simplicity and remember it was going to die and be resurrected—or if it would get lost in the search for more comfort. We see that the very involvement in the material culture sidetracks the human from remembering the resurrection of God.

Why create some form of life and then test it? Is this the first time we have been here in this soul? If we weren't going to be in a body, does the soul have other possibilities? If consciousness is liberated from the body at the time of death doesn't this mean that consciousness existed before the body? Why would God have us be born just to judge our soul? If it's an eternal soul, didn't it exist before we were born? Why? How did all of this happen to be?

To find the answers, we need to expand our lens again and find a new model of reality. If Cosmic Science analyzes and describes the components of Cosmic History, then let us see what model of reality Cosmic History presents. For by its nature Cosmic History is a reflex of the Absolute, which means it is coming from a place that is comprehensive and total. Therefore, the model or models of reality presented by Cosmic History must also be total and complete—and that is where we will find the answers to our questions. Cosmic Science as a whole order description of the universe will be dealt with extensively in Volume II of the *Cosmic History Chronicles*. In concluding with this consideration of models of reality, we have only touched upon the topic of Cosmic Science, introducing it more as a set of reflections, which must necessarily be posed before submerging ourselves fully into its vast and unique perspective.

Part III New Models of Reality

> "Let us not ask, 'what is it'
> Let us go and make our visit"
>
> *T.S. Elliot*

Chapter 7
Triple Universe Model

In this *Book of the Throne*, we are cultivating a higher perspective of reality. From this elevated perspective, we may ask: What models of reality will enhance the sorcerer's whole body perception? Cosmic History contains numerous models of reality, each with a different aspect that refer to different levels and orders of dimensionality, hierarchy and wholeness or *holarchy*—governance of the whole. All of Cosmic History participates in holarchic and/or hierarchic orders.

Since the nature of reality changes with perception, need and mode of operation, the planet noospheric sorcerer must move simultaneously through different worlds to attain her ends. This means the planet sorcerer operates with multiple models of reality. We may take note of three principle ones:

1. To discriminate modes of reality there is the **Triple Universe Model.**
2. To discriminate modes of knowing there is the **Four Pillars Model**.
3. To discriminate levels and orders of being there is the **Simultaneous Universe Model**.

When we speak of a model of reality, we are talking about an underlying structure, which constitutes a belief system. What is a belief system? Sometimes people use this phrase without really considering what it means. Most people are not conscious of what they believe in, though most people believe in something or they could not exist day-to-day.

A belief system is an engrained pattern of behavior, habitual thought and patterns of thought. What you tend to repeat on a daily basis to create a semblance of continuity of a life pattern constitutes your belief system. Think about it. What are some constituent parts of your daily schedule? Most people get up in the morning, take a shower, put on some good clothes, and then get ready to go to some kind of job. They believe that maybe they should look good at the job, or maybe it doesn't matter, but they believe they have to have a job. If they do not have a job, they believe they will not be able to survive or they will starve or die.

When you have millions of people participating in a particular mode or way of life, then they are all operating by a common belief system. This whole belief system then actually constitutes a structure or a model of reality. So you have the system of a particular type of grooming or education to attain the necessary skills to acquire some kind of work. Keep in mind that most work is actually performed according to Gregorian concepts of the workweek and weekend, and therefore maintains and supports the technosphere. This is presently the sum of the collective round of life.

You can reduce the belief system in its duration in time to the concept of the week, because the week is repeated over and over and has all of the different workdays and then time off and then holidays. This structure of belief maintains that the purpose of life is to work hard to get a certain amount of money so you can enjoy some form of life of leisure or recreation on what is called the weekend or the "off hours." All of this forms a model of reality, which is held together by the macroprogram of the Gregorian calendar and is reinforced at every single level by all the different forms of public communication, media and education.

This current collective macroprogram believes that you grow up, you have a family, you work, you maybe get a vacation home, a sailboat or a house in the woods and then you retire and that's it—and hopefully you are happy and healthy when you retire. When you look at that model of reality, there is nothing in it that says that it is meant to be transcended. It is just presented as a type of means for furthering the material affluence of the larger social order. The human being is just a type of cog in the overall mechanism. There are different types of cogs—there are service industry cogs, there are heavy industry cogs, there are finance industry cogs and so on.

This model of reality is subsumed by more beliefs like democracy or Western civilization or globalization, which is like the big shell that encompasses all of the other beliefs. All of these beliefs and sublevels of beliefs constitute what we refer to as the dominant belief system, which can be summarized as historical materialism. What we might call the anthropological premise is that the present model of reality of historical materialism has resulted in the creation of the hybrid homosapiens of the planetary human. The hybrid human is no longer really traditional. Nearly everyone has the Internet, and if they don't they can find a cyber café anywhere, even in the mountains of Peru or in the Australian Outback.

The current planetary human is the adjunct of the technosphere, fed by the electronic nervous system, and is therefore detribalized and detraditionalized as a result—to the point that it has become a hybrid deracinated planetary human. It is this planetary human that becomes the base for the noosphere. The next step is to dissolve the present world model. It was the humans who blew up the Twin Towers, but they don't have to blow them up again. Violence is never the answer. Now we have to dissolve the thought system that created the Twin Towers in the first place, and replace it with a new positive model, which is Cosmic History.

We are here to discover how everything is intrinsically sacred. What is sacred order? Holonomics, or whole system studies, is akin to a study of the sacred order. The reason why everything is sacred is that everything forms a part of this vast whole—this vast whole is what Cosmic History describes. In defining this order of Cosmic History, we are actually approaching a new definition of reality in which the totality of the universe is returned to wholeness and understanding of the sacred, governed by the all-coordinating God principle. In this way, everything is seen as an interconnected, interrelated whole, which is the very fabric of sacred order. The profane only exists in the secularized, detheologized, and consequently, fragmented mind of modern man.

Again, when we talk about Cosmic History, we are describing a new model of reality. To begin building up from the foundation, we talked in earlier chapters about inserting a new timing matrix or replacing the old timing matrix with a harmonic one. Assuming you have the harmonic matrix in place, you can then begin to establish a new model or new models of reality that illustrate ever

Continued on page 122

Part III • New Models of Reality

Triple Universe Model

The Triple Universe Model refers to the areas of perception and judgment that motivate us as we move through the world. This model demonstrates how we are not only always moving through an outer and an inner realm, but that a third realm or universe—the moral—is also continuously informing our decisions and our perceptions. This image is a whole that is greater than the sum of the parts. Meditating on it and contemplating its contents is a critical exercise of Cosmic History.

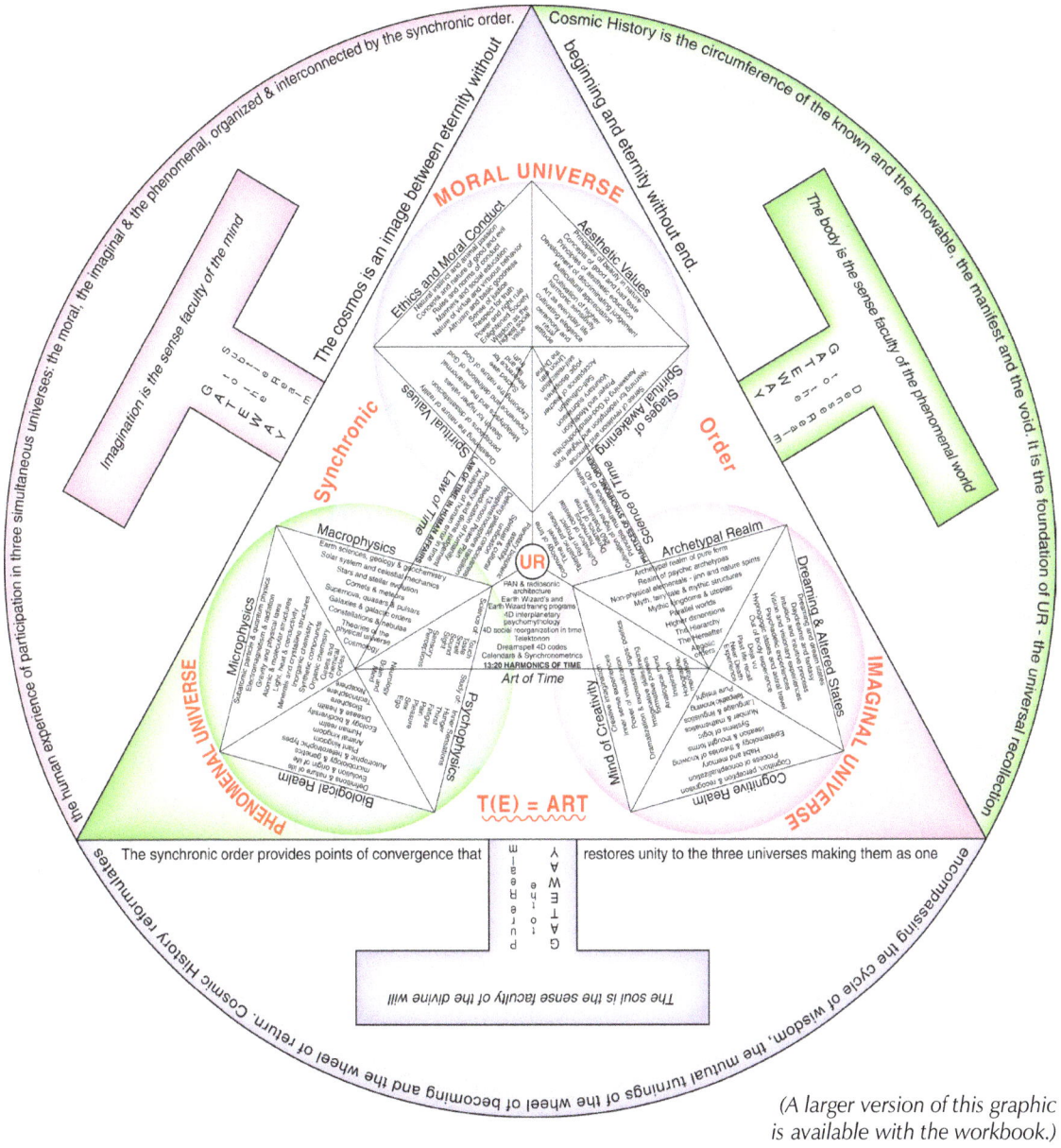

(A larger version of this graphic is available with the workbook.)

increasing orders of harmonic perfection, which syntropically act to further each other. So rather than there being an entropic degradation of energy, there is a syntropic increase of energy—but it is psychic energy. Psychic energy continuously increases, as opposed to physical energy, which tends to degrade over varying lengths of time. So you see that the Cosmic History models of reality are the opposite from models of reality of historical materialism. This is to give you some idea of what we mean by a model of reality.

When contemplating the different models of reality, it is helpful to think of this three-step process:

1. First, there exists an all-pervading field of intelligence
2. This field of intelligence is then populated by simple form design principles
3. From these simple form design principles emerge luminous code forms.

The Triple Universe Model is one of these forms.

Phenomenal, Imaginal And Moral Universes

Encompassing the cycle of wisdom, the mutual turnings of the Wheel of Becoming and the Wheel of Return, Cosmic History reformulates the human experience as participation in three simultaneous universes: the phenomenal, the imaginal and the moral—organized and interconnected by the synchronic order. From the point of view of Cosmic History, the purpose of introducing this Triple Universe Model is to demonstrate that your actual every day living experience is multivalued and multidimensional, whether you know it or not. By becoming conscious of the phenomenal, imaginal and moral universes that are always simultaneously in operation, you may begin to create an enlarged assessment of who you really are and what you are really doing here.

Phenomenal Realm

The phenomenal realm is the realm of raw data perceived by our senses. It includes the biological realm, the realm of microphysics, macrophysics and psychophysics. ***The body is the sense faculty of the phenomenal world and is the gateway to the dense realm.*** People only see what they have been programmed to see, or programmed to find useful, according to their intention of life. At a very fundamental level, we organize the phenomenal realm through our perceptions – but most people are oblivious to this.

For most people, the phenomenal realm is absolutely taken for granted—so much so that very little thought is given to it. The effect of living in the technosphere also diminishes much of the potential interaction between the human and the so-called outer phenomenal world. For many people, the phenomenal world, understood as that outside of the body, is primarily characterized by changes in the weather. Though, to most humans, why these changes come about is of little concern. The understanding that most of the phenomenal world is organized, first, by visual sensibility, and second, by auditory sensibility, also probably does not occur.

The idea that the phenomenal world is all that exists is greatly enhanced by the overwhelming impact and influence of the technically advanced materialist science. On the one hand, materialist science continues to investigate ever more minute and subtle aspects of this phenomenal world, breaking it down into bewildering micro components. One purpose of this accelerating micro or nanotechnology is to find genetic components that can be used for commercial purposes. An example of this is genetic modification; or in the area of physics, similarly, the search is for commercially translatable micro components of the phenomenal world that can be used in anything from computer technology to science fiction forms of weaponry.

While the phenomenal realm is most of what the present world construct takes to be reality, for Cosmic History it is but a subset of the sensory order. As such, the phenomenal realm will be more extensively explored in considerations, both of the sorcerer's whole body perception and in Volume II, which deals extensively with Cosmic Science, the study that encompasses what we usually think of as the phenomenal realm. As with the other realms presented in this graphic of the Triple Universe Model (see p. 121), it is well to consider the categories of the phenomenal realm that are presented and meditate upon their relationships to each other, as well as how they connect with the other realms.

Imaginal Realm

The imaginal realm is accommodated in the physical realm by our nervous system and brain, and has contact with the physical through the sensory system. This sensory contact brings us information that we respond to. What determines our response? Where does this response exist? Where do these images come from?

Imagination is the sense faculty of the mind and is the gateway to the subtle realm. It is generally assumed that sensory information hits neural triggers that fire in the brain and then release stored information in the form of images. Whether this

*The **body** is the sense faculty of the phenomenal world and is the gateway to the dense realm. **Imagination** is the sense faculty of the mind and is the gateway to the subtle realm. The **soul** is the sense faculty of the divine will and is the gateway to the pure realm—the Absolute—where there is only spirit, the Beyond.*

is true or not, it does not necessarily account for a volitional exercise with the intention of producing images within the mind.

How can the production of a thought have an effect that produces an image? The fact that you can manufacture a thought, and with that thought create an image that can be quite elaborate, is important to consider. Especially when you know that such internal image-making can have just as strong an effect on your mental/emotional body as any perceived phenomenal image.

The imaginal realm contains thoughts, ideas, visions, dreams, intuitions, altered states, archetypes, perceptions and fantasies. It is important to stress that the imaginal realm is *not* in the least dependent on the phenomenal realm for its activation, nor should the word "imaginal" be confused with imaginary. Rather, imaginal is that name given to the entire inner realm of experience, just as "phenomenal" refers to the outer realm.

The imaginal realm constitutes the entirety of all the functions and capacities of the mind and emotional body. The *field of intelligence* refers to the capacity for organizing the imaginal realm into different structures that focus particular intentions into purposive methods, statements and visions. In other words, the imaginal realm is the place of thoughts and dreams; whereas the field of intelligence is the capacity to focus intention into the imaginal realm, to create an intelligible pattern, coherent structure or vision that communicates some sense of purpose. Volume III will explore extensively the nature of the imaginal realm as a universe unto itself.

Moral Realm

Between the two realms reflecting man's outer and inner nature is a third realm, the moral. The moral realm deals with issues of good/evil, morality, right/wrong, etc. Not only are there dreams, images and reflections of experiences in the world, but also feelings of judgment, being right, wrong, beautiful, ugly, etc. This seems to have to do with the cultivation of the soul. A sense of human purpose has everything to do with morality.

We live in the phenomenal universe of cause and effect and are gifted with the capacity to enter the imaginal realm, but then there is the moral/spiritual realm, which is an interpenetrating factor between the other two realms. The moral realm has to do with the saving, redemption and perfection of the human soul. The soul is always treading between the world and the mind. Thoughts are constantly emitted from the mind into the world, where they create some type of effect, before they are returned to the mind in the form of feedback from the world. In this way, we can see that the soul is constantly negotiating between the feedback of the world and the interpretation of the mind. The world suggests certain things or ideas, and the mind responds. Or from the point of view of the moral realm, the world presents the mind with something, then the moral intelligence has to determine what response will be beneficial to the soul.

The soul is the sense faculty of the divine will and is the gateway to the pure realm—the Absolute—where there is only spirit, the Beyond. What are the factors that determine whether evolution proceeds or stagnates? The ultimate factor is the moral factor, because you can be very clever but still miss the point of life. The evolutionary progress has meaning only in relationship to the evolving intelligence of the soul. The soul has to experience everything in this process, so how can we say anything is ultimately bad? Each stage has its particular type of morality or code of conduct.

Synchronic Order

Through the Triple Universe Model, you can see that the mind, the soul and senses all accompany each other on a journey. Cosmic History is the container of the journey. ***The synchronic order provides points of convergence that restore unity to the three universes, making them as one.*** When you consider that the three realms are actually all simultaneously occurring within any given human being, and when you further consider that any human being is actually organized by time, then you can begin to appreciate how the synchronic order is the master unifying principle of these three universes. For instance, imagine that there is a decision that has to be made regarding your own behavior in a certain situation. Maybe your behavior involves questions of what is right or what choice will create the best results—these questions immediately engage the imaginal faculty because you are envisioning. These questions also engage the moral faculty because you are trying to evaluate what is best. Finally, these questions engage the phenomenal universe, because you are determining where the decision might be made and what its impact might be.

All of these factors are brought together at a point in time where the decision crystallizes and becomes a manifestation or a manifest result. When you place that manifest result within the context of the synchronic order, then you can see how all the factors that were involved in making the decision are functions of a process of timing. Then, when the decision event is placed within the codes of the Law of Time (the actual information matrix of the synchronic order), a whole other level of evaluation occurs, which is called *whole system synthesis*. At this level, the meaning of the decision takes on a dimensional value as an event point in your life in relation to all other event points.

> *The synchronic order provides points of convergence that restore unity to the three universes, making them as one.*

Intelligence Of The Senses

As we said earlier, Cosmic History is the core of the universal field of intelligence. This field of intelligence is coextensive with the all-pervasive mind. The phenomenal world is a reflex of the field of intelligence. Mind is the absolute substratum of the imaginal realm, which accounts for everything we know in the phenomenal realm. Intelligence is the capacity of mind to organize—any organization implies intelligence.

Everything possesses intelligence—even ants in their subterranean chambers possess intelligence. As we evolve to greater levels of self-reflective capacity, intelligence is also viewed as a higher creative purposive process, which is able to create images through whatever sensory system it utilizes. Where there is intelligence, there is purpose.

The world of manifestation seems to be outside of our senses. Is this really true? Where does the phenomenal realm end and the imaginal realm begin? You can not separate the field of intelligence from the imaginal realm or even from the field of the moral realm. But what is intelligence and where is it located? Is intelligence, like mind, a quality that permeates the cosmos? When we think of intelligence we usually associate it with being smart and knowing how to do things. The dictionary defines intelligence as: "The ability to learn facts and skills and apply them, especially when this ability is highly developed."

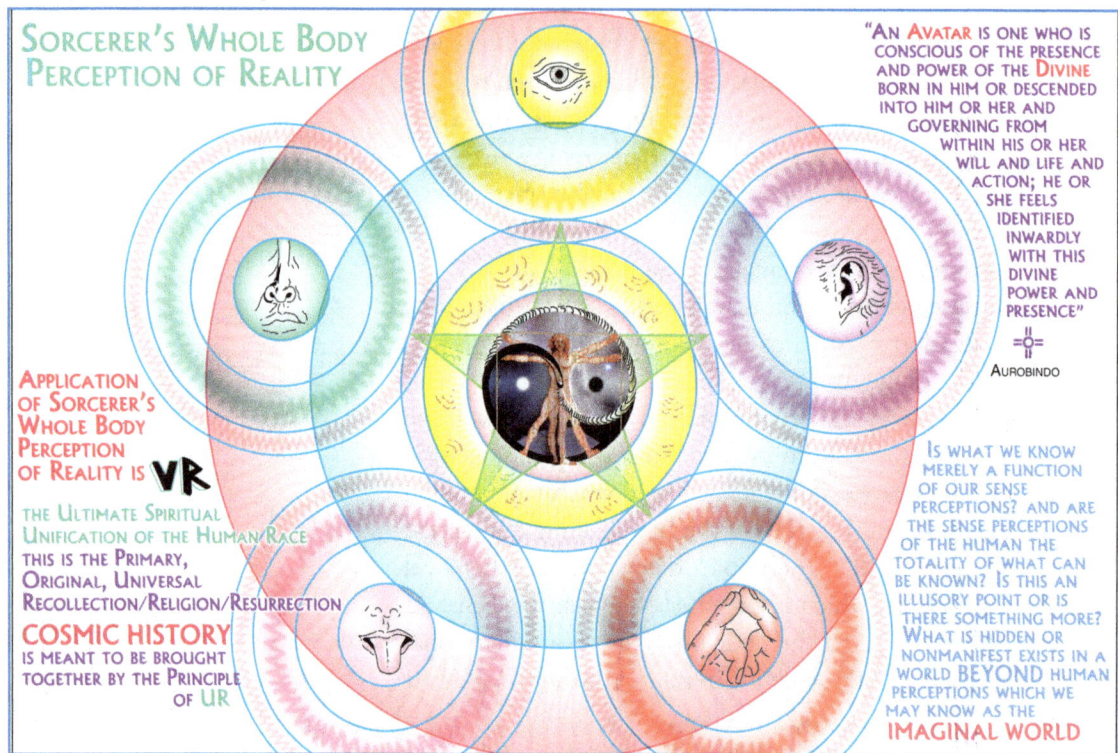

The way we are speaking about intelligence, first of all, is as an evaluative knowing, which allows us to distinguish between perceptions and experiences, according to an assumed end or purpose. Hence, intelligence affects decision-making to the degree that the decisions help further the attainment of a particular goal or end.

Mind takes different data in the phenomenal realm through the senses and structures and organizes it into images and language. From the Universal Cosmic Mind, different phenomena are given different names. The arising of phenomena always corresponds to whatever point in the structure and stage of development within Cosmic History to which that phenomenon refers. This is because Cosmic History is a description of the creative process of the stages of creation in which equal consideration is given to imaginal impulses and structures, as to phenomenal data and its organization.

From a sorcerer's point of view, the senses should always be awake and you should always be fully in touch with everything in your environment. How do you organize what you experience of the phenomenal realm? Why do two different people have the same experience, but experience it entirely differently? You must develop complete sensitivity to everything in your environment. Everything you experience is mental data.

At the Absolute level, there is nothing but pure harmony. At the fundamental or relative level, we may ask; Is what we know merely a function of our sense perceptions? And are the sense perceptions of a human the totality of what can be known? Is this an illusory point or is there something more?

What is hidden or non-manifest exists in a world beyond human perceptions, which we know as the imaginal world. We know the imaginal world through inference and analogical reasoning. By analogical reasoning, you may say that what we think of as knowledge is like the frog at the bottom of the well that looks up to see the sky and thinks that is all there is. When it gets out of the well, it sees that things are vastly different. Is our consciousness like this?

In the phenomenal realm, the capacity to organize is largely structured by the sense perceptions. The entire universe,

What we think of as knowledge is like the frog at the bottom of the well that looks up to see the sky and thinks that is all there is. When it gets out of the well, it sees that things are vastly different. Is our consciousness like this?

The elements of creation are actually creative mental thought projections of the Divine Mind, which means they are absolutely perfect, precise and recognizable.

as we know it, is constructed from what these sense organs take in. This constitutes a psychophysical model of reality. When all of the sense organ input is organized in the mind, it creates the imaginal universe. Input from the different sense organs, coupled with our own psychogenetic make up, creates perceivable mental imagery. These are important aspects to consider in the creation of a higher vision of reality. It is important to understand how we construct an image of the world and how images of the world can be stereotyped.

Here again, we see the dialectic between conditioned knowledge and fresh sets of impressions. Within the cerebral information processing and storage system, there are what is referred to as *biogenetic filters*. Once a conditioned, perceptual pattern is established in the mind, many impressions will then be rejected or filtered out. Those impressions that are accepted will be run through the biogenetic filters of the conceptual mind that conforms to a particular preconceived perception of reality. Until these filters are de-programmed, purified and transcended, it is very difficult to say what is real.

This description of the sensory information processing system defines the world of relativity. In this world, everything is relative because the different constructs are nothing more than the subjective impressions or distortions of the myriad perceivers constituting the human biomass. We might then ask the question again. Can anything be known or described or defined objectively? The different species have their sense perceptions, but among themselves is the sensory information subjective or objective?

We know in a general sense that people may perceive the same thing, such as the sun rising (or something that resembles the sun, a large luminous disk emerging from the Eastern horizon), but what the individual perceivers do with this information is highly varied. Why do we have the different senses and sense organs that we have? Is it possible to conceive of higher intelligence or existence operating without sense organs or with additional sense organs? The information received through the auditory nerve, for instance, is quite different from the information received through the optical nerve. How many senses do we need to put the world together? What is the form and pattern of creation?

The elements of creation are actually creative mental thought projections of the Divine Mind, which means they are absolutely perfect, precise and recognizable. Everything we are doing is coming purely out of the divine imaginal realm. You must begin to examine the process of *everything*. Everything that exists is based on some type of divine blueprint. We are working with the components of that divine blueprint. We are uncovering the magical place of initial reflex. Was there ever just absolute void space? Did God ever exist without form or being? What happened? Something happened and God projected the plan and form. What was first inscribed on the divine template? What was the first thought? Was it a sound? A pure visual thought? How were the first thoughts experienced? These questions should be deeply contemplated in silence.

Moral Aesthetics

The simplest way of describing Cosmic History, is spiritual involution into matter and spiritual evolution out of matter. In that case, the moral universe is the determining voice as to whether there is evolutionary progress or not and evolutionary progress is determined by whether things are advancing in a more spiritual direction or not. The "progress" has meaning only in relationship to the evolving intelligence of the soul. As we mentioned earlier, in order for the soul to be universalized, it has to experience everything in this process—so how can we say anything is bad?

William Blake said: "The road to the palace of wisdom is paved with excess." This means that if we are to experience wisdom, we must experience all aspects of life. If a child keeps putting her/his finger near a flame, telling the child not to do that will not do any good until she/he experiences the burn her/himself. This simple image is like the whole paradox of learning, spiritual development, morality and immorality. A sense of human purpose has everything to do with morality.

> *... evolutionary progress is determined by whether things are advancing in a more spiritual direction or not.*

We are beginning to define a number of categories of universes of experience, another of which is the aesthetic, which is closely related to the moral. All of nature is a work of art. When it comes to human behavior, you can say: "That person is really sloppy," or "That person is really tidy." These are ethical judgments of a fundamental aesthetic norm. How is the understanding of a fundamental aesthetic norm related to a fundamental ethical norm? The good in accord with the true can only be aesthetic. But first, you must know what is true. When you perceive what is true, then by patterning your behavior accordingly you will understand what is "good." And if you pattern yourself properly and become "good", according to the truth, then you will establish a norm, which can only be harmonic. Truth is always harmonic. Truth is only disharmonic to the ego, but that is because it is the ego that is disharmonic. So if you pattern your life on the truth, then not only will you become harmonic, but you will also become intrinsically aesthetic, since it is a harmonic norm that creates the true, the good and the beautiful.

Once you have reached an inner harmonic norm, then you can raise, educate and elevate other people's perceptions so they slowly develop a greater perception of beauty, harmony and art. Just like ethics, these perceptions have to be cultivated. These qualities represent stages of human perception being upleveled and refined within the experience of reality and of the Self.

The simple, most elegant means will always be true; therefore, it will be aesthetic and moral. This is important to understand in order to comprehend everything as a whole order. The aesthetic realm also involves people who critique things (like art critics)—this involves judgment. These might seem like relatively philosophical or fine points, but they are points that have to be considered in the actual development of the mind. The aesthetic realm deals with judgments of taste: What is good taste? What is bad taste? What is beautiful? What is ugly?

Taste and morality are very closely related. Why do we deal with morality in the first place? This gets back to the questions, Why are we here? Who are we? What was the

Once you have reached an inner harmonic norm, then you can raise, educate and elevate other people's perceptions so they slowly develop a greater perception of beauty, harmony and art.

original sin? The human beings are the only species that have an issue of taste. An example is when the cover of *Time and the Technosphere* was first sent to the publishers by Votan in Yellow Solar Seed year (2002). The cover depicted the Twin Towers being attacked. The marketers thought that the Twin Towers picture was offensive or in bad taste and would not print the book unless the cover was changed. Why? Who thought that? What is going on here? Is this an issue, not only of moral taste, but also of censorship?

Moral Universe & The Way Of Conduct

According to the moral realm, we are on this planet to see if we can behave properly. The moral realm is characterized by a code of ethics like: "Thou shalt not steal" or "Thou shalt not lie," or like the Rinri precepts, such as: "Work is the Highest Joy." Fundamentally, the major religions and spiritual traditions of the world recognize a common level of ethical behavior. For example, what is encoded in the Ten Commandments, in one way or another, occurs in the precepts or *vinaya* of the Buddhists, and similarly can be found in any number of passages in the *Quran*. Virtually every system of spiritual belief has at its root a code of ethical behavior. This points to a type of universal/moral sensibility, regardless of spiritual tradition or religious belief.

Moral codes develop in stages. Some people behave morally because they are afraid of being punished. This is the lowest level of the moral universe that produces thoughts such as: "If I don't do good I will get punished so I will do good" or "If I don't do good I will be censured by my peers so I will do good." The lowest level of the moral universe is behavior out of obligation in order to avoid being punished or censured.

Societies are built on institutionalizing different views of morality—through rules, laws, etc. For instance, one way that the American society institutionalizes morality is through the legislative system, which creates laws. If you break a law, it is deemed criminal or immoral and you will be punished. This goes deeply into the issue of free will. Do you have free will? Are we as humans so incapable of good behavior that we need

Moral codes develop in stages. Some people behave morally because they are afraid of being punished. ... The lowest level of the moral universe is behavior out of obligation in order to avoid being punished or censured.

government? This questioning is an aspect of critical moral intelligence.

Generally, the moral universe says: "This side is good" and "That side is bad" or "That side over there are the liars and hypocrites and on the other side are the people who try to follow a code of ethics." Those who do follow a code of ethics are among the people who advance in stages, until you get to people who are enlightened and living in the presence of God, which is the highest level attainment.

Often we find in tradition that once you reach this level of attainment, then everything becomes permissible again. This is because you are seeing through illusion. When you see through illusion, you realize that the reason you did not do certain things before was because you were afraid and you needed to let yourself be clear about the true nature of reality. But when you see the true nature of reality, you realize your oneness with everything and you see that to avoid doing something out of fear is not the highest behavior.

In most religious systems, the code of ethics revolves around the purpose of life, which, in most cases, is to save and cultivate the soul. The purpose of life is to follow a code of ethics and virtuous behavior so you can come face-to-face with God. The purpose of life is to die clean. In most religious traditions there is some type of notion of Afterlife, accompanied by a moral code that says something like: "If you live according to the plan of the Creator, good will continue to happen, but if you don't you will fall into deviant states of evil." Most religious traditions also agree that there is some type of natural state, but also recognize that there are instincts that exist in that natural state, that, if acted upon, can get you into trouble.

The *Quran* says wo/man was created according to the original plan, and that God implants knowledge of Himself in each human being and in everything that exists. Everybody naturally knows this. However, since we have deviated from nature, this truth is, for the most part, covered over. The institutionalized covering over of the fundamental truth inscribed in our heart creates a dangerous environment for our natural instincts.

In most religious systems, the code of ethics revolves around the purpose of life, which, in most cases, is to save and cultivate the soul. The purpose of life is to follow a code of ethics and virtuous behavior so you can come face-to-face with God.

This all describes the moral universe. So the question is: If the purpose of life is to save and cultivate your soul, what is the best code of ethics to follow? What is the best way to behave in all situations? Anything that will help the human become a "good" person is part of the moral realm. When we talk about the purpose of life, we are also addressing the moral universe. Some people say that life does not really have a purpose, but that we are just here. This can be used as an excuse to do anything. This is moral nihilism. On the other side of this is the belief that life has a meaning; and since this is so, we are supposed to cultivate ourselves and live as good people. For instance, we may ask: Is a child born moral, or is it something that must be taught? Does nature have its morality? Does the universe operate by a moral code? Is the 13:20 timing frequency a self-existing moral code? Does the issue of morality only arise in humans because humans have the capacity to deviate from the Divine Plan? These are issues you have to consider when defining or describing the moral universe.

In most traditions, it says that the human is born weak, it is given a code of ethics and then it advances in stages. In the *Holy Quran* Sura 84:19, it says: *"You will move from stage to stage."* The *Bhagavad-Gita* tells us: *"Gradually, step by step one should become situated in trance by means of intelligence sustained by full conviction..."* 6:25. Or in the Buddhist path, the bodhisattva ascends in ten stages or *bhumis*. Once the human being establishes itself with a code of ethics, then it can develop deeper levels of insight. The Buddhist traditions say to become a monk or nun, you must study for years and years, live a monastic life and then you will be able to save your soul, that is, attain enlightenment. You have the monastic order in the Christian religion too. But is this the best way to do it? Is this the best thing for the whole? Shouldn't everyone, then, become a monk or a nun?

In the Aboriginal/Indigenous societies, there is much more of an integration of the moral universe into the life process. Rather than saying you have to go off, mortify the flesh, and become an ascetic, these traditions may prescribe fasting and solitudinous vision quests, which is in accord with

"Gradually, step by step one should become situated in trance by means of intelligence sustained by full conviction..."

Bhagavad-Gita 6:25.

the fundamental teaching of Islam. The issue of discipline also comes into play in the moral universe—the cultivation of the soul and self *is* discipline.

To Study The Self is to Study The Way

"To study the way is to study the self; to study the self is to forget the self. To forget the self is to be enlightened by all things. To be enlightened by all things is to remove the barrier between self and other." Dogen

Self-study seems to describe a general program of how spiritual teachers see the advance of the soul. If you want to know the way or the purpose of life, then study yourself. If you study yourself thoroughly, then you will forget yourself. This is because the self that is inquiring ultimately does not have any existence or else it is the ego and should be forgotten altogether. There really is no distinction between the world and yourself.

To summarize, because you are not yet so familiar with the Triple Universe Model, we are bringing the imaginal to the phenomenal world in different stages, so that you can begin to practice right away. The first stage is to become aware of your present experience. Pause for a moment. What are you experiencing right now? What sensations do you feel? What types of thoughts are you having? At what point does the sensation or an external perception become an internal idea or image, seemingly with a life of its own?

Next, consider what difference there is between the so-called outer phenomenal world and what is occurring in your imagination. After these thorough observations, you can begin to more systematically explore the different realms that constitute the imaginal universe. This is a grand and glorious task. It is a great responsibility to wash away the old and irrelevant thought-forms and replace them with the new cosmic order. Remember that Cosmic History is a function of the Supreme Self and a reflection of the cosmos. In comprehending all of its stages of development, you are creating a pathway to a new evolutionary stage.

We have to get to the point where we are beyond the conditioned reflexes of the mind, so that we are able to experience reality directly.

There is certainly more to reality than meets the eye and more than meets the senses. Cosmic History, inevitably, is available to the senses and also is involved with understanding the relative limitations of sensory knowledge according to time, culture, language, etc. All of these conditions affect what we know.

Can we actually obtain the state of objective knowledge? This is the issue that the enigmatic Armenian Sufi Master Guirdjeff examined in great detail. It all gets back again to the question of: What is the Buddhist quest? What is the quest of enlightenment? We have to get to the point where we are beyond the conditioned reflexes of the mind, so that we are able to experience reality directly. When we have direct experience of reality, it seems to remove us from the world, like in Herman Hesse's book *The Glass Bead Game*. In this futuristic novel, Hesse describes a utopian society in which there is an elite class of people whose whole life is devoted to creating a massive system of symbolic correspondences—*The Glass Bead Game*—which integrates different forms of sensory knowledge, i.e. music, painting, etc. The point is made, however, that the pursuit of the *The Glass Bead Game* is so all-absorbing that it seems to negate the life and reality from which it is increasingly removed.

If you want to study something purely, you have to remove yourself from it for a period of time. How do we integrate the self-study with the study of the phenomenal world? Between study of the phenomenal world and study of the imaginal world is the study of the self. The imaginal realm is constructed through ideas and images, while the phenomenal realm is raw data—and then somewhere between those two realms is the study of the self. These are important yet subtle points. The study of the self is a reflex of the moral universe.

From the point of view of Cosmic History and the Law of Time, you cannot have a genuine description of the universe without the consideration, first of all, of the nature of the mind and how you know the mind. From that consideration, you can then turn to the relationship of knowing the mind and knowing the universe—the phenomenal, external world. If you want to know yourself, you don't go outside of yourself. It seems that many of the Eastern approaches say: "If you know yourself that is all, you do not need to know anything else." However, the nature of being human is that humans are curious about their external environment.

The study of self alone can become very self-involved and self-absorbed, while the study of nature apart from the study of mind can actually become meaningless. This is why it is important to always remember and consider God. Cosmic History is a higher synthesis and higher balance that incorporates the internalizing studies of the self, which are represented by the traditions—particularly Buddhism. However, there must be a balance in the study of the self with the study of the "other," which is the world appearing as "outside of the self."

Cosmic History embraces these two polarities and seeks a synthesis of knowledge of the "self" and "other," so that you are not having just escapism of the mind. It is important to see how the things "out there" affect the mind. Think about it. What is today's society (or the world "out there") promoting? It is actually promoting sublimated natural instinct. In other words, the values that you find at the popular mass level are nothing but glorified instinct—like sports (the glorification of aggression) or publicity/advertising (the glorification of lust), gambling (the glorification of greed) and the entertainment industry (the glorification of aggression, lust and greed–for the most part), not to mention cigarettes, drugs and alcohol (the glorification of intoxication/escapism).

So we have a vicious cycle of an absolutely submerged spirituality, representing more and more degradation and violence. The dominant world represents institutionalized barbarism because it promotes natural instincts without a moral context. There is massive moral confusion, but we have the capacity to rise above the lower instinct states.

Planetary barbarism is furthered by the inescapability of global television—you can see anything, anywhere you want. As we mentioned in previous chapters, this is the world of the hybrid human living in moral confusion. It is a moot point to discuss whether we need laws or not—we have to look at how we can create moral maps that are in accord with the principles of Cosmic History, moral maps that elevate the human being to a condition of appreciation of this world and God.

The Wheel of Life in the Buddhist tradition is an example of a moral map of the Universe because it shows different realms (animal, hell, hungry ghost, human, jealous God, God-realm).

The point of the Wheel of Life moral universe map is to show the relationship of the human world in accordance with the other five realms. In the Buddhist perception, this is known as a wheel because everything is always changing and a human can advance to a god realm or regress into a hungry ghost or animal realm. However, it is only in the human realm that the opportunity exists for truly waking up and taking advantage of the possibility of becoming enlightened.

Buddhist Wheel of Life

The purpose of human life is spiritual development, but society does not promote this. The human realm offers us the opportunity to transcend. The moral state of being tries to keep the phenomenal world clean. The spiritual state of being is the upliftment of the phenomenal realm and values that enhance the imaginal realm. This is critical because we are in the age of moral relativism and democratization, which pretends to be egalitarian, but actually promotes further despiritualization of values that perpetuates moral confusion.

The Islamic world forms the only coherent ideology which is opposed to the dominant world society. They have, of course, the oil-dominated Persian Gulf/Saudi Arabia, which participates in the materialist world—but the point is that in the traditional Islamic world there is not a separation between church and state. In the Islamic world, the spiritual being is the highest value.

Though all of the spiritual codes of ethical behavior were founded in the historical cycle or in the "old time," it is a timeless fact that an actual moral stand must be taken regarding there being an Absolute authority governing all affairs! Supreme truth is Absolute. God is not wishy-washy. A tree grows the way it grows—it is not indecisive. The maintenance of the Absolute Reality is God's prerogative and not man's. Society has become so deformed that people can actually think three-legged pink poodles are pretty. There is now every form of deviation, genetic and otherwise, that was begun by Iblis as human history. Humans defend the deviant. The spiritual evolution of the human being needs to be promoted—the glorification of natural instincts is at the expense of the moral imagination.

The moral realm also deals with the issue of right conduct. If you are in accord with the Divine Plan, you will naturally have right conduct. Only when you have right conduct can you learn the way of wielding power. But first, you must overcome aggression, passion, greed, lust, and all other lower emotions. You are not enlightened just because you have *bodhichitta* (mind or will to enlightenment), but you have to cultivate that bodhichitta. The Buddhist term "bodhichitta" is akin to the knowledge implanted by God in every heart. The knowledge of God is there, but you have to cultivate it through moral conduct. You want to become one with God and become spiritually exalted so that you can reach the realm of the Absolute.

So you see, there are many different levels that define the moral universe. Both the spiritual path and spiritual traditions have within them these stages of the moral universe. The point is that the moral universe is a universe unto itself.

Moral Universe Models

Of course, within the moral universe there are other models, which give other perspectives. In light of the universal need for upliftment, let us take a brief glance at some of these other models.

The Mayan Interdimensional Star Map (next page) is an example of stages of the moral universe. This map represents a pattern or structure of a spiritual system that we find ourselves in on Earth, in relation to the galaxy and universe. By establishing an analog set of correspondences to the chakras, the Interdimensional Star Map allows us to connect abstract qualities to different stars. There are stars that are more evolved and other stars in the process of evolution. For instance, Sirius, located in the throat chakra, represents the highest level of evolution in our area of the galaxy. By understanding the role that Sirius plays in defining a point of highly evolved consciousness, we can define a spiritual construct in which the other stars, like the Pleiades, or Arcturus or Antares represent different stages on the way to the highest.

We can also begin to visualize the Tree of Life as a structure that corresponds to the actual system of star points. Star points represent physical plane correspondences to a purely imaginal/

mental structure. This represents a holographic wholeness of the spiritual journey, which correlates to the moral universe and the phenomenal/imaginal realm. We are talking about going from a moral universe to a more spiritual state. In the more spiritual state, we find the correspondence between our third- and fourth-dimensional bodies and cosmic phenomenon. These are not just analogies, but actual indices of our stages of evolution into the greater cosmos. The entire structure of the universe is a spiritual metaphor and the sign of our ultimate enlightenment.

When we become aware that we live within an actual spiritual structure, then we can begin to establish a type of spiritual/mental environment for our soul and our body so we can gauge our movement. This represents the natural structure of the imaginal universe, which describes the spiritual construction of reality in which our soul is evolved. Human instinct can be problematic if it is not channeled into moral codes of behavior. Most tribes have a code of conduct. Most tribes also have a clear goal to create a purposeful code of conduct. The moral universe describes a movement and different conditions of being and processes of universal stages of Cosmic History.

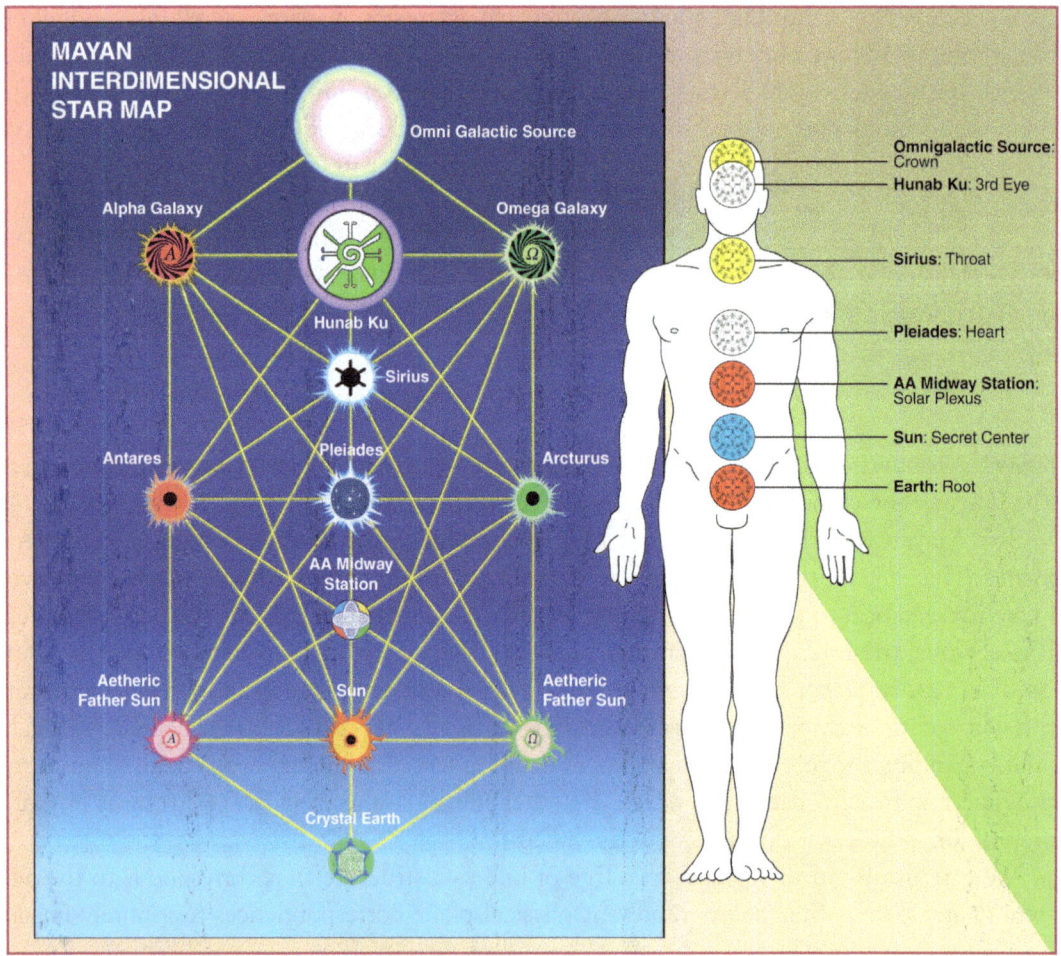

For example, the Avatar's Wheel of Time shows that when there is a movement there is always a counter movement—this is the law of alternation. For example, the hierophant or avatar embodies the ground of being. The student or apprentice identifies with avatar in order to experience equally that same ground of being. In that sense the avatar and apprentice represent a ground of being that operates by the alternator principle. Each alternator represents the whole as a complementary phase instantaneously evoking its mirror counterpart.

Avatar's Wheel of Time

Golden Age
Dragon-Serpent:
Natural Condition

Silver Age
World Bridger-Dog:
Moral Conduct

Iron Age
Warrior-Sun:
Universal Enlightenment

Bronze Age
Monkey-Eagle:
Spiritual Discipline

If you study them carefully, you will see that the eight trigrams/triplets in the I Ching (at the center of the Avatar's Wheel) also correspond to the binary movement of time. They correspond as well to the eight precepts of the Wheel of the Law in Buddhism, which also ties in with the moral universe. Suffering exists because a choice has been made to buy into illusion. The moral universe indicates choice. You always have the opportunity to choose the right way or the wrong way. History itself is a reflection of the movement and pattern of the moral universe. There has to be a way of overcoming being a pawn of natural instinct and transforming it into the remembrance of God/Awakened mind. The following is a four-part example of stages of spiritual growth, due to activation of the moral universe. This example is based on the 20 solar seals and the four Hindu ages. The purpose of the new models of reality and stages presented in the Cosmic History is to assist you through the stages of evolution—so that you can wake up and remember why you are here. These models also show that you have to get to a bottom point so you can understand the nature of the spiritual journey and power. We need to have tremendous spiritual discipline to arouse the great spiritual sun within ourselves. The only reason we fall so low is so we can climb so high.

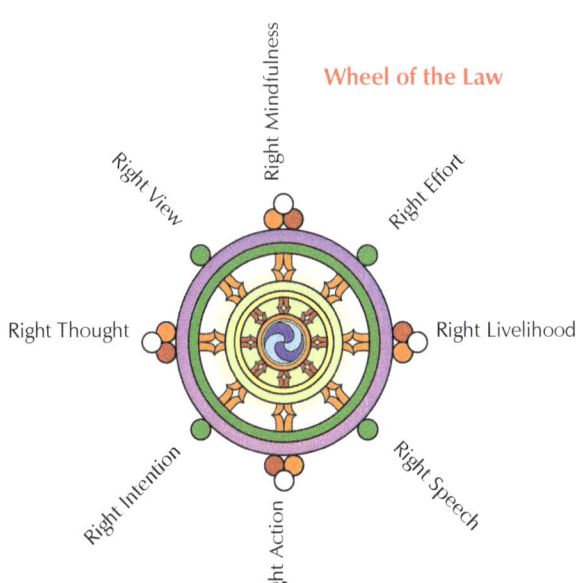

Wheel of the Law

Right Mindfulness
Right View
Right Effort
Right Thought
Right Livelihood
Right Intention
Right Speech
Right Action

> **FOUR HINDU AGES AND 20 SOLAR SEALS**
>
> 1. **Sat Yuga or Golden Age/Red Dragon to Red Serpent**—State of the natural condition of innocence, the original garden where the primary wisdom is established and flourishes.
>
> 2. **Dvarpa Yuga or Silver Age/White Worldbridger to White Dog**—The Fall engenders the creation of death and the free will possibility to choose between what will help the soul or what will harm the soul. Natural instincts must be channeled into moral conduct and the creation of codes of ethical behavior.
>
> 3. **Treta Yuga or Bronze Age/Blue Monkey to Blue Eagle**—You must have conscious moral behavior because things are getting progressively out of control. Spiritual behavior is essential—prayer, fasting, charity, etc. These kinds of practices must be consciously promoted so they can rise up and dissolve natural instincts. This stage also represents powers that need to be aroused to channel natural instincts into forms of moral conduct and higher states of awakened consciousness for the benefit of all beings.
>
> 4. **Kali Yuga or Iron Age/Yellow Warrior to Yellow Sun**—In the End Times of historical materialism, there also occurs its cumulative counterpart: spiritually advanced states of consciousness. This is the stage where there is spontaneous spiritual pleasure. You have worked through the moral dilemma and you are now only seeking to become closer to God. The greatest thing you can do is to remember God more perfectly and arouse your will to enlightenment. Since everything is one, you cannot get enlightened for yourself—it is for everyone. This attitude helps do away with historical materialism.

You must exert to become an ethical human being. When you remember God then you arouse your enlightened being and the memory God planted in you. What can you do to remember God? To arouse enlightened mind? As we said earlier, many people conduct themselves according to a fear-based morality—behaving correctly so they do not get into trouble. But this does not produce the aspiration to higher being and further remembrance of God. Some kind of shock must occur to switch people's reality. Cosmic History assures us that when we get past catastrophe we will live the cosmic person.

To be the cosmic person is to dwell in and be informed by the Absolute in all matters. By its nature, the Absolute is incomprehensively vast and incapable of being grasped by the sense organs, yet we know and experience from within its existence. This Absolute is often referred to as God, but sometimes even the word "God" seems inadequate to comprehend the Absolute nature of the Absolute. Yet we do have manifestations of the Absolute within the tradition of the sacred texts.

Of these texts, the supreme one, the criterion is the *Holy Quran* which is the word of the Absolute or the recitation of the Absolute to the human messenger Muhammad (May peace be upon him). If we study the *Quran*, we will find a highly diverse description of the moral universe, according to the Absolute. If we take the criterion of the *Holy Quran* as the book, or more precisely the reflection of the original or *Mother of the Book*, then we can define two other "books," one is the *Book of the Cosmos* and the other is the *Book of the Self*.

Part III • New Models of Reality

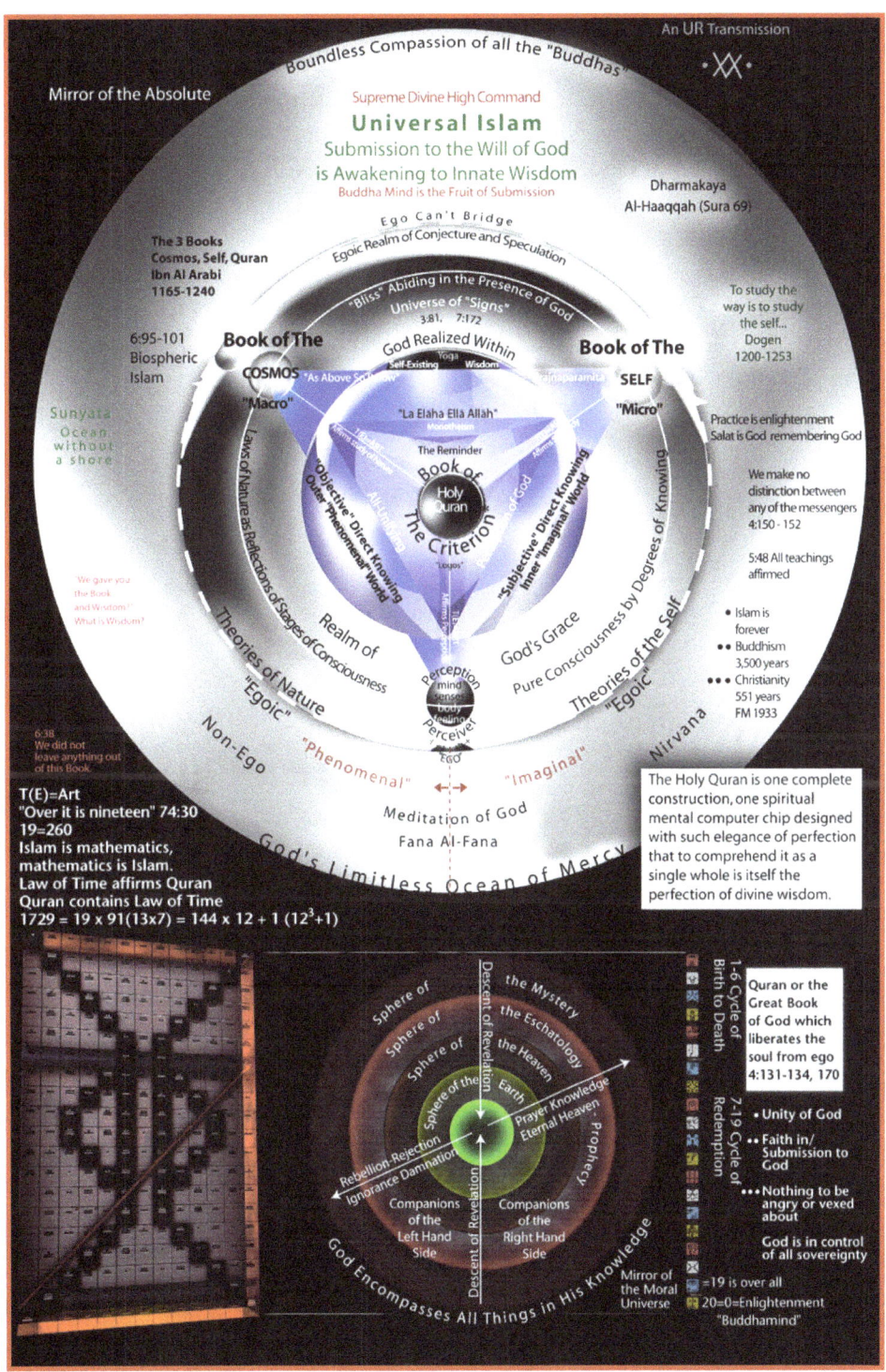

By "*Book of the Cosmos*," we mean the description of the universe much in the manner of Cosmic History—in other words, it contains the description of both the external world as well as the internal perceptions of the world, inclusive of the cosmic multidimensionality. Of course, the *Book of the Cosmos* is implicit in the *Quran* and from the point of view of the Absolute, the cosmos exists as a sign of the unity of God. The *Book of the Self* refers to the different ways in which the human being is defined as a creature of an ultimately moral nature. In other words, the human being is placed in the cosmos to be tested according to his ability to understand the cosmos as a sign of divine unity. What we call the cosmic person is that human who understands the cosmos as a sign of divine unity, which has been created and arranged in such a way that it also defines the steps and the stages toward complete union with the divine or total enlightenment. In this regard, the cosmos as it exists in its entirety is a manifestation of God's limitless ocean of mercy.

Chapter 8
Cosmology of Time—The Four Pillars

From the perspective of Cosmic History, all knowledge is a unity. We saw in the previous chapter that the moral, imaginal and phenomenal universes each have within them a certain assumption of knowledge that describes a certain range of perceptions, intuitions and modes of behavior. Knowledge is also a function of models or systems of belief. The model of belief underlying the nature of knowledge in Cosmic History is a necessarily unitive model. The sorcerer's whole body perception can only be known as a unity.

Cosmic History is a synthesizing factor. And while analytical, logical and deductive reasoning are incorporated into Cosmic History, so are virtually all other forms of knowing and acquiring information. As a unitive structure and model of knowledge, Cosmic History also presupposes a dynamic of knowing which is fundamentally harmonic or harmonizing. That is, all of the different fields or areas of knowledge harmonize with each other.

The model of belief upon which the system of knowledge constituting Cosmic History can be imaginally constructed is a domed pavilion with four columns. Four paths lead to this domed pavilion: One is the path of the knowledge of time, the second is the path of the unitive knowledge, the third is the path of wisdom and the fourth is the path of the mystic way. When each of these paths reaches the pavilion, they are met with a set of steps to climb before the foundation can be reached. This foundation is comprised of art, as it is most broadly and universally understood and applied. According to the Law of Time, energy factored by time equals art. So art is the foundation of the pavilion of knowledge upon which is erected the UR (Universal Religion or Universal Recollection) dome of Cosmic History.

This foundation comprises the study and practice of art in all of its particulars: symbolic structures, arts and crafts, architecture, garden and landscape, aesthetics, harmonics, polyphonic sound, ceremonial arts, ritual, etc. Then rising from this foundation of art are the four pillars of knowledge. The first pillar is Cosmic History, the second pillar is Cosmic Science, the third pillar is Cosmic Philosophy and the fourth pillar is Cosmic Religion.

Cosmic History can be understood to encompass all and everything. For the purpose of understanding knowledge as different ways of comprehending reality, it is presented as this four-pillar domed pavilion. (See next page.) As such, the first pillar of Cosmic History provides the framework for the other pillars of knowledge and includes the vast histories of cosmos, nature, previous world systems and of this particular human world. The next pillar that is extracted from Cosmic History is that of Cosmic Science. While history is the description providing the container, Cosmic Science describes the cosmological order, operations and functions within that container. Then, extracted from the pillar of Cosmic Science, is Cosmic Philosophy, which deals with the meanings of the different functions and operations of the cosmological unfolding. The fourth pillar

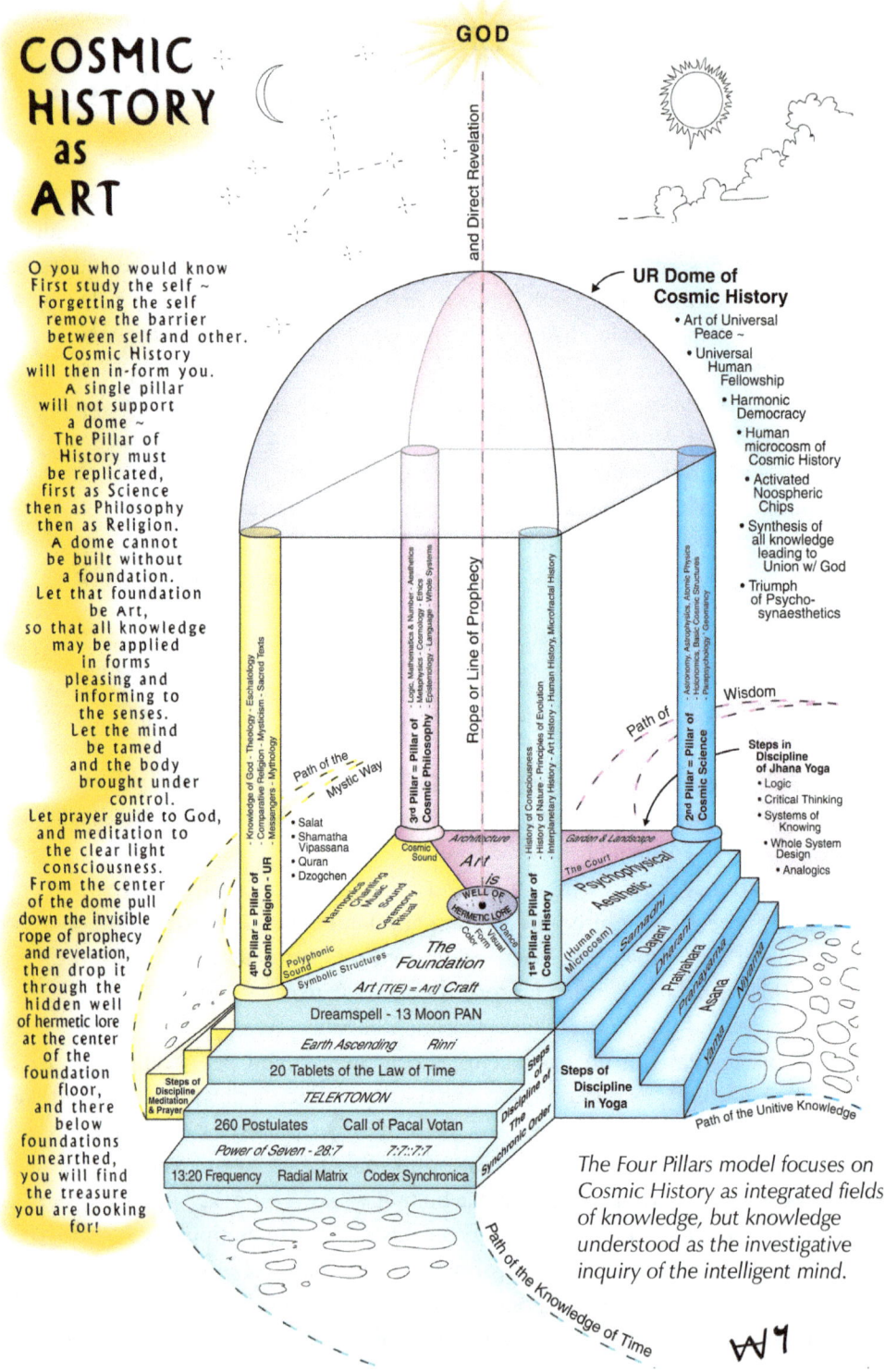

then, is that of Cosmic Religion, which deals with the meaning of all of the different aspects defined by the systems of knowledge in such a way that the individual soul is addressed. The point of Cosmic Religion is to elevate the soul, both through knowledge and through direct perception of the divine into the highest conditions of cosmic consciousness. On the foundation of the pavilion platform, the four pillars of knowledge are raised, and resting upon those four pillars, the UR dome of Cosmic History is constructed. This dome represents the highest arts of establishing universal peace, universal human fellowship, harmonic or cosmic democracy (*cosmocracy*) and the evolution of the human being into a noospheric chip, that is, one who by whole body attunement becomes a living transcription of the higher collective voice.

This four-pillar graphic (also referred to as "Cosmic History as Art") synthesizes succinctly large volumes of information and represents the foundation of the structure of the synchronic order and the formulation of the Law of Time. Study it well, so it can imprint itself into your mind. Of course, what is inscribed are categories of knowledge, each of which in itself could be volumes, but that is not the point. The point is comprehending all of these categories as a whole whose parts establish intrinsically unifying relationships, which then affect the mind in its disposition toward any one of the subsets.

Everything is Cosmic History or a subset of Cosmic History. With an emphasis on cosmic art, Cosmic History calls humanity to rise above itself. Everything that grows is meant to transcend itself. When you become fully who you are, your character opens like a flower. When you fully flower, you pass beyond yourself until you blossom into the final image of the flower, which is your soul in full bloom—the invisible form within released to merge with the greater solar soul, toward which it has always turned throughout its existence.

Cosmic art helps the human transcend the egoic self—first individually, then collectively so that the whole Earth becomes a living work of art. We want everything to be the function of the highest beauty—this should be the norm. The art of UR is the art that is meant to invoke the cosmic memory as a cosmic

> *Cosmic art helps the human transcend the egoic self—first individually, then collectively so that the whole Earth becomes a living work of art.*

whole and the memory of the self as the entire cosmos and the entire history of the cosmos. The cosmos is a large sphere of becoming and returning, which is encompassed in your being. Through the art of UR, you become the total encapsulation of the cosmos in the process of becoming and returning. The UR art of the cosmic whole is a multivalued experience, which involves rite and ceremony as well as certain types of activity that embody the cosmic force and cosmic consciousness in an artistic endeavor that produces tangible artwork. In this way, too, Cosmic History is realized as the living breath of cosmic consciousness.

Four Pillars As Cosmological Template

Cosmology is a point of view of metaphysics that focuses on the nature of the universe and recognizes multiple dimensions. Unlike modern science, cosmology deals with not only the phenomenal realm, but also the spiritual/moral realm. Cosmic History is a complete cosmology. From the point of view of modern science, cosmology is a branch of astronomy that deals with the original nature and structure of the natural world. From the point of view of Cosmic History, you cannot separate theology from cosmology.

The cosmology of Cosmic History has some resemblance to earlier systems of thought (Platonic/Pythagorean). According to the Platonic theory, there were solids that existed in the ideal realm and then from the solids all the manifest nature of creation was created. The cosmology of Cosmic History involves whole system design principles and structures, which are further evolved through mathematical structures, platonic solids and the synchronic order.

Cosmic History is a whole system principle and is the core of the field or matrix of intelligence, existing independent of any individual human. Cosmic History is an all mind transmission for the purpose of expanding religion through the opening of galactic spirituality, based in consideration of Earth as a galactic whole system. The Four Pillars Model, as well as the Triple Universe Model and the Simultaneous Universe Model, are meant to introduce you to three different aspects of Cosmic History as the cosmology of a new system, based on the vision of the synchronic order, which is genuinely holonomic. The outer is in the inner and the inner is in the outer. Enfolded by the synchronic order the gates to the imaginal realm are flung wide open.

The Four Pillars graphic is an archetypal image meant to be meditated on in order to begin to experience and allow all those different levels of reality that are contained in your psychobiology to have expression and be brought forth into greater consciousness. All archetypes, visually presented in total clarity, are meant to evoke structures of cosmic psychobiology, allowing us a means of self-transcendence. Merely studying this graphic is a transcendental activity, as this graphic is actually a telepathic imaginal realm memory template intended to awaken different levels of Cosmic History and memory contained in yourself.

Cosmic History incorporates the idea of the human as a microcosm—a reflection of the macrocosm/universe or cosmos itself. Principles of the microcosm incorporating Cosmic History information into psychosomatics, is an esoteric idea or viewpoint. Cosmic History participates in an esoteric and synthesizing thought and vision of the synchronic order. Cosmic History is a reformulation of the secret teachings or secret history passed on through processes of initiation, and then released into the arena of the world soul for its rejuvenation and spiritual nourishment.

The following is another example of a four-part cosmology of Cosmic History:

Four Part Cosmology of Cosmic History

View: The view of Cosmic History is the entire field of intelligence, emanated from an information core that defines the universe/cosmos as the field of intelligence of evolutionary becoming.

Meditation: Cosmic History provides an object of meditation because it is vast, impossible to grasp, yet everything we experience is a function of it, including the nature of your own mind.

Conduct: Conforms to the closing of the Way of Conduct, which leads to the practice of the Way of Wielding Power. Cosmic History is a path of conduct and organization of information through different stages of development. In any situation, we must know what functions and stages of development we are dealing with and how they relate to Cosmic History.

Fruit: Attainment of cosmic awareness and consciousness as an enduring state of mind. At this point, you are entered into the community of galactic intelligence. Cosmic History facilitates cosmic awareness and consciousness among all beings.

Combining this cosmology with the Four Pillar graphic: History is the View, Science is the Meditation, Philosophy is the Conduct and Religion is the Fruit. To expand on this – Cosmic History is the view of the Cycle of Becoming and the Cycle of Return. Cosmic Science is the meditation of Cosmic History (knowing how things become and return). Cosmic Philosophy is the conduct of Cosmic History, based on meaning and interpretation. Cosmic Religion is the fruit of Cosmic History, because the goal is in the meditative absorption of the Godhead with Itself.

History (The View)

History is the first pillar—it is what makes the other three pillars possible. History is the all encompassing form and structure by which every form of knowledge, purpose of effort or aspect of nature is defined and described—there are as many histories as there are topics (such as human history, natural history, interplanetary history). Intrinsically related to history are principles of organization. The earliest histories are called chronicles, which are stories or facts from the past, organized in chronological order, according to date and succession. This is the simplest, most universal form of organization and is helpful when viewing reality as a sequence of events. However, when you consider reality from a biopsychic mental point of view, then you have to consider categories of organization, which are a whole other level, and often may be very much defined by conditioned thinking. Cosmic History demands synchronic multidimensional ordering principles, which reflect the stages of the mind as it evolves through the *supermental* into the *supramental*. In

Cosmic History is the narration of the history of harmony as a multidimensional creation and is necessary because of the condition of maximum disorder on our planet today. We must create maximum order to rearrange the disorder engendered by the human species—this has to be accomplished by the end of the cycle—AD 2012.

the supramental, we pass beyond all present limitations of mind and consciousness into the greatest expanses of the galactic brain and the ascending levels of pure harmonic history.

History accounts for the stages of development of any naturally existing phenomenon and is a value or index in self-reflective consciousness. Understanding principles of history contributes to your own self-awareness and consciousness. Investigation and comprehension of Cosmic History will inevitably lead to a heightened state of cosmic consciousness. All true histories should have some common structure.

Human history accounts for falling out of grace, though human history cannot be seen apart from the history of nature. To separate human and natural history is to deny that there are universal principles (that the human is not a part of nature). Prophecy is meant to redeem human history back to the history of harmony. It must be understand that all functions of nature are both third- and fourth-dimensional. Only then will you be able to understand the narration of the split between the third and fourth dimensions. When you understand this, you see that humans are involved in the prophetic restitching of the dimensions.

Cosmic History is the narration of the history of harmony as a multidimensional creation and is necessary because of the condition of maximum disorder on our planet today. We must create maximum order to rearrange the disorder engendered by the human species—this has to be accomplished by the end of the cycle—AD 2012.

Science (Meditation)

Science examines the changes that occur in going from one stage of development to another, or what differentiates one stage of development from another. In other words, science analyzes "things" as particular points within sequences of event horizons of varying dimensional scales. Science is how we know. History explains how and why science came about, including its stages of development. How are different levels and orders scientifically organized?

The definition and description of Cosmic Science is quite

radical in comparison with the usual definitions of traditional materialist science. Materialist science does not include God in the equation. Obviously, it is disastrous to make a description and analysis of the universe as if no other factors are involved besides the material and/or human factors. Material science is demonic science because it is driven by human ego mentality obsessed with its own fame. An example of this is the recent announcement of Physicist/Cosmologist Stephen Hawking, reversing his position on black holes. He is now saying that not only do black holes suck in energy, but they also emit a "mangled form of matter." This statement stunned physicists who believed in his earlier theory and virtually made front-page news just because it came from "Stephen Hawking." In reflecting on this point, we should also consider Hawking's own perspective on this issue of God and human theory:

> *"What I have done is to show that it is possible for the way the universe began to be determined by the laws of science. In that case, it would not be necessary to appeal to God to decide on how the universe began. This doesn't prove that there is no God, only that God is not necessary." Stephen W. Hawking (Der Spiegel, 1989)*

Cosmic Science constructs a God-centered cosmology that starts from the beginning point of the creation of the universe and then builds up, whereas Western science begins with just what we see and then tries to work back from that to an original point—with no consideration of a divine factor. For this reason, Western science is hopelessly bogged down in the very minute discussions regarding the nature of the Big Bang, or whether the universe is entropic, or whether it is an expanding universe or a steady state universe. These kinds of issues plague modern science, not to mention the approach of modern science to analyze and dissect everything. Do Western scientists really expect to uncover the essence of a living thing by taking apart its physical apparatus? Modern science goes to great lengths to dissect physical bodies and even creates laboratories for this specific purpose! Not to mention the scientists who go to great

Cosmic Science constructs a God-centered cosmology that starts from the beginning point of the creation of the universe and then builds up, whereas Western science begins with just what we see and then tries to work back from that to an original point—with no consideration of a divine factor.

In Cosmic History, we take nothing for granted. We assume everything that is known is conditioned. We must examine whether the conditions of what is known have a valid basis, or whether they are based on a type of bias or prejudice. Do we eliminate a category if it is based on a total bias?

lengths to smash an atom. These methods of analysis are part of the destructive nature that is unconsciously destructuring our civilization without knowing how to restructure it. Modern science rests its case on elaborate theories or conceptualizations without ever comprehending that the "theories" are merely the projections of unexamined minds.

The universe that Cosmic Science describes is dynamic and electrical, affecting us immediately because we are IT! We are the dynamic electrical universe! We are the end result of Cosmic Science! When we truly understand what we are, from the point of view of Cosmic Science, we will be astonished to view the old self-definition we bought into by believing in Babylonian history. Cosmic Science offers us a picture of reality that is radically different from what we have been taught. With further reflection on this theme, you will say: "Wow! So that's what I am! If I am this then what am I doing in this crummy society? Why did I settle for this? What am I doing? What is my cosmic destiny? If it is already written inside of me, maybe I am my own cosmic laboratory!"

Cosmic Science describes what is literally going on inside of us. This is why it transitions from basic structures right into genetics. This formulation of Cosmic Science is the basis of the scientific structure for the Mystery of the Stone and the working out of the Perfection of the Human Soul. The description of the cosmology of Cosmic Science shows how the humans are involved. The human represents the summation and culmination of specific cosmological and cosmic processes—the human component is now being redefined, from being composed of subatomic particles to being composed of electrical lines of force—this new perception of the human opens us to infinite possibilities. These themes will be pursued in greater depth in Volume II.

Philosophy (Conduct)

Philosophy is the love of wisdom and involves any interpretation of reality. It examines the stages of development in relation to the Earth, Solar System and galaxy. Ethics, morality and issues of logic are also related to philosophy, as well as to mathematics. A category may involve interpretations on the nature of reality, the nature of history, and the nature and meaning of events and human life.

In Cosmic History, we take nothing for granted. We assume everything that is known is conditioned. We must examine whether the conditions of what is known have a valid basis, or whether they are based on a type of bias or prejudice. Do we eliminate a category if it is based on a total bias? Everything has to be scrutinized and looked at. Philosophy describes the nature of things and is the interpretation or mental investigation of principles that govern either the phenomenal world or the ethical/moral world.

It is important to develop a critical mind, where nothing is taken for granted. For example, many people talk about the 12 strands of DNA, so when others hear it they assume it is true without questioning or examining it. What does this mean?

Philosophy represents an inevitable tendency of the mind. The mind is always seeking to assign a meaning to events or to create some kind of interpretation. Why is this so? What does this actually say about ourselves? That there is an aspect of us that does not know and wants to know—and further, that there is an aspect of us that is eager to understand how everything fits together. A further aspect of philosophy is the inevitable tendency toward discourse—the need for human beings to speak individually, as well as together, in discussion, in an effort to arrive at some meaning or understanding of the nature of reality.

The more general aspects of philosophy deal with the nature and meaning of life, the role of the human in nature and the description of nature and natural forces, including and extending to questions about the origin of life, the universe and cosmology in general. In a more concrete sense, philosophy deals with issues of how we know (epistemology), systems of conceptualization, and analysis of styles of comprehension— extending to the most abstract forms of logic and even mathematics and symbolic structures. Finally, there is the whole area of philosophy that deals with knowledge or understanding that is intrinsically beyond the range of our perceptions. This

...philosophy deals with issues of how we know (epistemology), systems of conceptualization, and analysis of styles of comprehension— extending to the most abstract forms of logic and even mathematics and symbolic structures.

area of philosophy is often referred to as "metaphysics" or that which is dealing beyond the realm of physics. While physics is a description of the phenomenal world, metaphysics is a description of the imaginal world, the world beyond the physical, or laws and principles of the imaginal/mental domain.

It is in the area of metaphysics that we find the topics of occult philosophy, hermeticism and all manner and types of secret and esoteric teachings. Metaphysics naturally considers questions concerning the nature of mind, spirit, other dimensions and other worlds. From metaphysics, we can take two other branches: theology and parapsychology. Theology is the study of God, the divine nature, the divine will and the divine plan. Parapsychology leads to areas usually referred to as paranormal or supernatural.

The consideration of history by philosophy is yet another specialized area. The nature of human history gives itself readily to what is called philosophical interpretation. In the range of philosophical thought, there are different interpretations of history in general and of historical events in particular. For instance, the prevalent school of thought in accord with historical materialism is that of economic free market determinism.

According to this school of thought, human behavior (which accounts for history), is always analyzed as if only economic motives were involved. Of course, in the economic interpretation, wealth and power are the key criterion in evaluating the success of a society, culture or civilization. From the economic viewpoint, it is assumed that the purpose of any culture or civilization is not only to consolidate its wealth and power, but also to expand it. In this, we see the mechanism of historical materialism being the basis for the rise of empires. It is also assumed, by this school of thought, that all such tendencies toward wealth and power are inevitable and that the present free market globalization economic dominance is completely and inexorably in the mainstream of human historical development.

Religion (Fruit)

Religion examines relationships of stages of development in a process of divine unfolding and of spirit and soul evolution. Religion means to bind back to one. This occurs when the forgetting has gotten to such a degree that human consciousness has to be gathered and bound back to the One. We are slowly emerging from our state of amnesia. It is the force of God that always reminds us to bind back to One. The process of redemption means ceasing to be oblivious or beginning to remember or recollect. Universal Recollection means humans are no longer oblivious to their origin or destiny.

Spirituality in Indigenous cultures is all-pervading. All of life is organized as if it were a religious practice. In historical society, religion is introduced because man has forgotten how to live life as a religious ceremony. So certain teachers appear to help man remember that God or Buddha nature is inside him already. There are different practices and structures to clear the mind, channel the energy and lift the seeker up. Discipline is meant to lift the layers off, so you can advance in stages until all that is left is the all-pervading presence of God. Any discipline requires a practice.

In Buddhism and Hinduism, practice is called sadhana (to practice). Yoga and Salat prayers are also a form of sadhana, because they are a practice that is meant to bring us closer with our Creator. Also practicing the NET (Noospheric Earth Time) minute is a form of sadhana because it gives us greater awareness of how each point in our day is being utilized. (See *Time and the Technosphere* Ch. 7). You could say that the purpose of sadhana is to connect our little being with the great cosmos. A *sadhu* or *sadhaka* is someone who practices with aspirant intent to approximate the divine.

Through practice, you can discipline yourself so your spiritual nature becomes more evident. Related to sadhana or practice is ceremony. Ceremony is a formal structure prescribed by a ritual—a form established to commemorate something. The main point of a ceremony is to make a connection with the sacred—to articulate the sacred order. For example, in Judaism they celebrate Passover, Yom Kippur and Hanukkah—these are very ceremonial, but often done with an almost rote spirituality, though they are attempts to articulate the sacred.

Ritual is a prescribed form governing a ceremony or it can also be the conscious repetition of a prescribed act. Initiation is a type of ritual performance with degrees of authenticating. Symbols are required to formalize an act. For example, late in the 19th century before the white man came, the Lakota Indian men did a certain ritual Sun Dance, with the purpose of connecting with Great Spirit. Their Sun Dance ceremony included communing with Spirit through conscious chanting and repetition, while moving in circles around a central pole, by which everyone is bound by a leather strip passed through an opening in the chest. The effect creates an altered state of consciousness that puts them in direct contact with the forces of creation. This dance is still performed today.

In Cosmic History, the sacred order of reality is harmonized into the matrix of the Thirteen Moon calendar. Without this calendar, there is no true synchronization or unification. Our experience of life as a whole should be seen as a great universal

The main point of a ceremony is to make a connection with the sacred—to articulate the sacred order.

ceremony where we feel complete and connected with the cosmic order. Through following the Thirteen Moon calendar, we are enacting Cosmic History as the template of the harmonic history, day-to-day, day in and day out.

All religions begin with the same intent of fomenting spirituality among the human beings. However, due to the degradation of the human social order, that did not really happen. Religion becomes corrupted as soon as it becomes institutionalized. At the point of institutionalization, teachings become formalized—thus becoming restrictive rather than liberating. Historic Islam, being a case in point, bound as it is with a rigorous code of law—*shariat*. Institutionalized religions are all 12:60 to a greater or lesser degree (particularly Christian and Jewish), and many other religions have the tendency of falling into one form of idolatry or another (Hinduism and Buddhism, in particular, have this tendency).

Why do religious forces create wars? Wars are a function of deviant human history. Even though so-called religious or spiritual teachers say the goal of life is to remember God, there are still wars! "…Your armies will never help you, no matter how great. For God is on the side of the believers," *Quran* Sura 8:19. Any attempt to create institutions to preserve religion is going to be corrupt because all institutions are now formatted by the 12:60 frequency; therefore, the actual intended reform can only go so far.

The planetary human is now a decomposing biomass meant to be the material that is transmuted by the 13:20 time into the matrix of the UR or the Eternal Return. From the point of view of Cosmic History, the descent into lower realms is a process of increasing forgetting into pure oblivion. It benefits the ego and its state of immorality not to remember. Thriving on forgetfulness, the ego invents more and more lies to cover what it forgot.

We do not have much time until the cycle closes, at which point phenomenal evolutionary shifts will be occurring. To get the most out of the shift, it is necessary to envision UR as the ultimate spiritual simplification of the human race—which is the primary Universal Recollection/Universal Religion. The

Cosmic History, with its absolute and relative levels, is meant to be brought together through the principle of UR. Now, the relative aspect of Cosmic History is framed through the faulty lens of the present day human mind. Once the lens of the human mind is corrected and it is wearing its 13:20 glasses, then the absolute and relative of Cosmic History will come into focus. The symbolic structures and psychological models of behavior are all-important.

Spirituality is the quality of being attuned to *Spirit*. Feeling God's presence is spirituality. This is NOT dependent on religion, although the practices enshrined in many religions have the value of discipline. In the Free Will Zone, there is a need for different structures and disciplines to cultivate the human to attune more to spirit—to make butter out of nuts. But true spirituality is innate. "…Thus, you cannot say on the Day of Resurrection, 'We were not aware of this,' " Sura 7:172.

Four Pillars As Template Of Universal Recollection

The Four Pillars are a projection of your own being. Everything in the cosmos is order—everything is holonomic in structure—even thought. In reality, everything is cosmic, this is sometimes a far out notion for fallen man to grasp. Cosmic order is the very nature and structure of our inner and outer being. History is the degradation and falling away of the sacred and has to be redeemed by sacred vision, which is art. We are dealing with the break of universal order, which is a split in the mind that is projected out onto the landscape of the phenomenal realm.

The entire universe is unified in your mind. One thought of separation removes you a million miles (and initiates the historical process). This break or fracture of the pattern in the psyche manifests as all sorts of diseases, neurosis and psychological disturbances. The purpose of cosmic art is to transmute the personal into the metapersonal, impersonal or superpersonal. Personal is the unenlightened third- dimensional ego. Metapersonal is the quality of the higher self, which is

Spirituality is the quality of being attuned to Spirit. Feeling God's presence is spirituality.

super personal and unifies through symbolism different aspects of the psyche with a type of outer image or symbolism.

So in this way, the Four Pillars graphic is a tool for focusing cosmic reconstruction within yourself—this is like constructing a wisdom palace, which is the construction of the inner being, according to the cosmic order. It starts with the individual, and then extends to the community. This type of activity becomes the very process of transforming the lower historical self into the higher post-historical, pure harmonic self. We must activate UR at a community level, which can only come about by creating templates of harmonic memory (memory that goes deeper than personal memory)—it is cellular memory that contains many different levels of understanding.

Theology is the study of the practice and experience of religious faiths, especially of God and His relationship to the world. Within theology, there are sub-sciences, for instance, *eschatology* or the study of the End Times. This is similar to *teleology* in philosophy, the study of goals and purposes inherent in the nature of things. Which brings us, again, to the fundamental religious question: Who are we and where are we going? According to Cosmic History, we are going to UR (Universal Religion/Universal Recollection). In UR lies the primal pattern of the cosmic Tollan, the psychomythic origin and destination of the Galactic Maya (See CH Vol. V). This is the primal state to which we are returning. Following the degradation of matter, there is a return of the eternal. Once the drama in Heaven occurs, there is a long descent until you get to Velatropa 24.3 (Earth), where all karma is deposited and boils over so that there must be a redemption and resurrection. The return of the eternal is UR—this is the fulfillment of the prophecy of Pacal Votan.

The advent of UR affirms Quranic theology of the omnipresence of God, which results in the fact that God is so vast that you can graphically represent the Supreme Creator in an infinite number of ways and in none at all. Cosmic History is a God-centered theology and assumes that the presence of God is in all matters and in all existence. Therefore, the intrinsic structure of everything is God's signs—there is an implicit and moral law, which is in accord with God's judgment. The theology of the Law of Time fits this definition of God in the process of Cosmic History. The Law of Time informs Cosmic History.

Cosmic History is not only sacred history but is also UR history. Cosmic History IS the Universal Recollection. UR is established through understanding basic principles of hierarchy, which are ordered and informed by the sacred count of the synchronic order, which is the measure of the Law of Time. Time as a synchronizing factor, governs the third and fourth dimensions of reality. Cosmic History is definitive, just as the Law of Time is definitive.

UR is even greater than holonomic recollection, because it is the whole of the universe coming down from God, stepped down to the lower dimensions. Holonomic Recollection is the unfolding of being into the planetary order, and begins once the human frequency shifts by changing calendars. By aligning to natural time via the Thirteen Moon/28-day calendar, the mind is vertically penetrated by time and opens to the higher dimensions. Then the knowledge of all humans can be seen in the knowledge of one human. This is holonomic recollection—the memory of the whole is contained in every part. Holonomic recollection of the whole order resides in each and all of us and once activated, we can ascend vertically in time reaching more purified states and levels of being and understanding. The Foundation for the Law of Time, as both an organization and a holonomic metaphor, is the key to connect the planetary order with the universal order by promoting the Thirteen Moon calendar and the Law of Time.

But the glorious end result of the synthesis of knowledge affected by Cosmic History is the UR dome. The UR dome is the noosphere itself, which can only be upheld by the values of knowledge and spiritual attainment, once again, taking their place at the forefront of human concerns. The planet sorcerer is secure beneath the noospheric UR dome in universal fellowship and harmonic democracy (cosmocracy), where the natural hierarchy of spiritual evolution is the governing order.

Chapter 9
Simultaneous Universe Model

Once the sorcerer's whole body sensing is cultivated, it merges into the right view, which is the multidimensional Simultaneous Universe Model (SUM). This represents a stepping down from higher to lower dimensions. According to the SUM, at any given moment the universe is completely unified by that moment. This means you can go anywhere in the universe at any given moment and the whole structure of the universe is present. Not in a radial horizontal expanse, but in a vertical expanse from which extends a radial palette of different dimensions. At the center of the radial palette is the information core or Cosmic History, which is immediately derived from the *Mother of the Book* or *Master Record*.

Since our body in time is but a minute speck in the nature of the cosmos, it is important to view the higher holographic projection from which it came. The SUM model is to be used in the systematic organization of the outer, inner and secret, macro- and micro-organizing codes constituting the system of thought and practice of Cosmic History, inclusive of the Way of Conduct and the Way of Wielding Power. The point of this self-evident mode is that you cannot make a Way of Wielding Power without being based in the Way of Conduct. The Way of Conduct is based on practices. The Way of Wielding Power is practice put into action.

When observing the SUM model, we see that Velatropa is the Free Will Zone, where manifest projections called humans test their free will. The highest act of free will is aligning the personal will with the Divine Will. Only when personal will is surrendered to Divine Will, will we have the opportunity to create a victorious ending to the movie being projected into the third dimension. The Earth or Velatropa 24.3 is the stage set where the final scenes of the free will experiment are being played out.

Not only is Cosmic History a universal design principle which coordinates different dimensions and aspects of being as radiating out from the information core, but it is also a template showing how certain structures move in time and space. The way our human structure moves and accommodates time-space points is very different from the way an ant moves and perceives its time-space points. To some degree, all life has common characteristics, including binary symmetry and radial symmetry. Think about different forms and creatures and think about how they might experience their reality.

A tree is a radial form if you look at it from the point of view of the trunk being the center. Plants are radial. Insects and animals have binary symmetry; each side is a reflection of the other. Cosmic History lies down the central imaginal core of all phenomena—radial, bilateral or polyhedral. Humans have a particular form with bilateral symmetry: two eyes, two ears, etc. The human body is a form of time with its 20 fingers and toes and 13 major articulations: 2 ankles, 2 knees, 2 hips, 2 wrists, 2 elbows, 2 shoulders, the 12 major joints, and the thirteenth, the neck. Humans embody 13:20 time. This form in time is called the *human holon*.

Part III • New Models of Reality

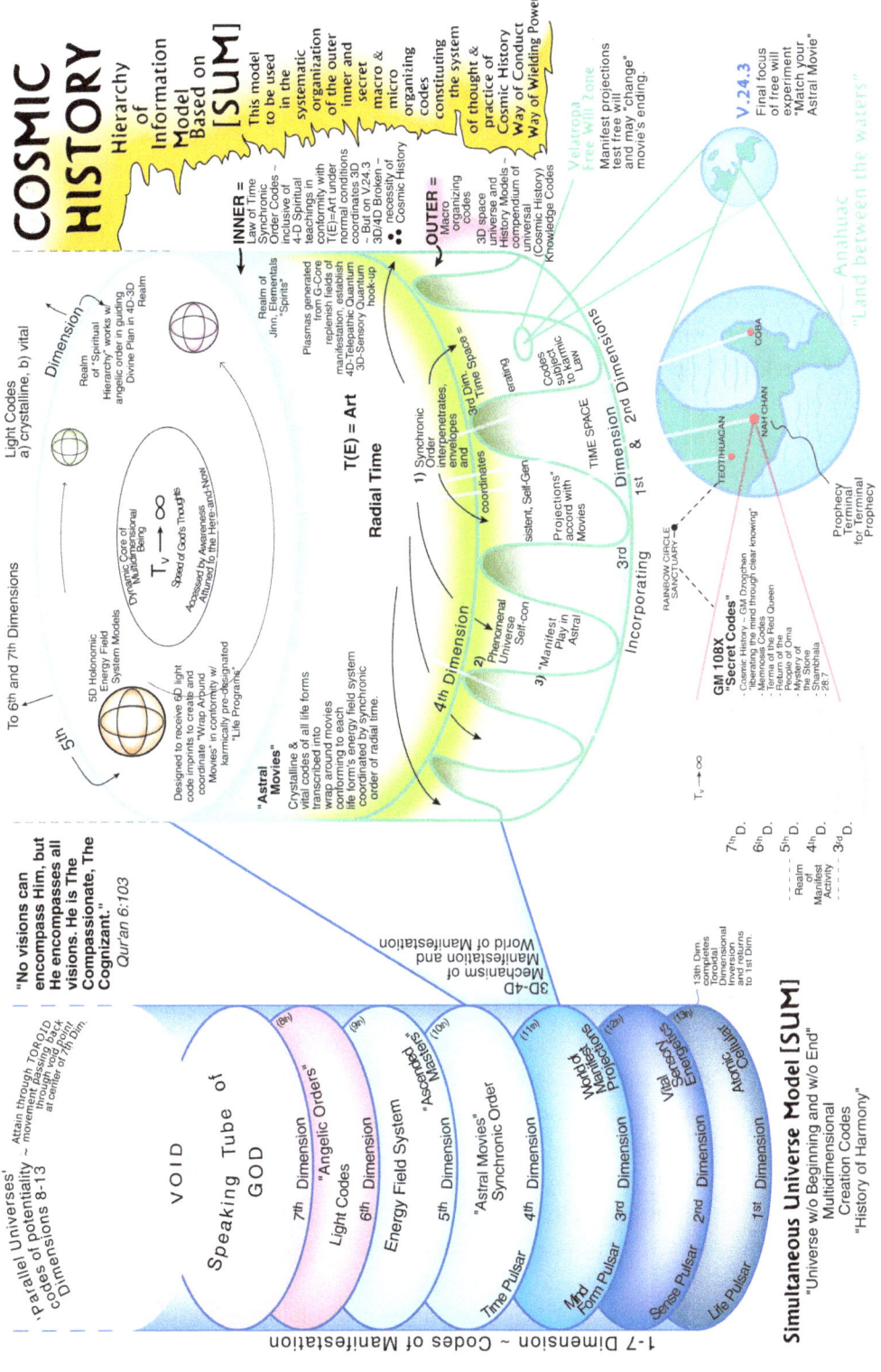

The Simultaneous Universe Model introduces us to Cosmic History as a multidimensional reality in which our existence extends visibly and invisibly.

To see a fresh, clear world, imagination and intelligence must be engaged so new questions can be formed, such as: How many structures or mathematical formulations do you actually need to create the universe? What are the design processes that underlie the appearance of nature? What aspect of God is the Universe and Solar System reflecting? Imagine in God's meditation that He decided to create a Universe. God's meditation evolves the Universe through its different dimensions. Suddenly a cubic parton, the primary building block of reality, appears containing an infinite number of possibilities.

Cosmic History is the entire template of knowledge of the infinite possibilities as the self-reflective capacity for knowing. Focused study of the SUM model, as well as the other Cosmic History models of reality, helps us to attain states of continuing consciousness. In fact, these new models of reality are actually intended to help restructure our mind and our knowing into larger comprehensive whole system orders of reality. The SUM shows us how this whole process works.

Exploring The Dimensions

The SUM works with the seven dimensions model in a way that makes multidimensionality accessible to our imaginal perception. The first dimension, which is what we call the quantum dimension, is where all of the different subatomic and pre-subatomic particles are contained—this is largely beyond the microscope. The second dimension is the atomic cellular, coming into the microscopic. The third dimension is the organization of all the cellular and atomic life. As we know, if you put a piece of your skin beneath a microscope under increasing degrees of power, you will see that when you get down to the atomic level, your skin disappears, until its solidity disappears and it becomes nothing but great expansive space—sometimes you may see an atom of some kind with its electron shells, but they are few and far between. A large group of these atoms constitute a cell.

The point is that within the entirety of the dimensional universe model, we have the element of vast amounts of space. The space is both the medium of the generation of energy, such as light and other subatomic phenomena like plasma, but it is also the medium of telepathic resonance. This is what actually holds the different dimensions together. The first, second and third dimensions constitute a recall in the physical world.

When you think about the cosmos, you are usually only thinking about the third-dimensional physical world with its galaxies, stars, quasars, supernovas and so on. Still, you are only looking at phenomena as they are manifesting in the third dimension—and these phenomena are actually manifesting in the third dimension from two directions. One from the quantum direction where certain interactions create certain effects, which cause ripples to be sent out on the third-dimensional realm of manifestation or the phenomenal realm. There are also higher-dimensional effects rippling down and causing phenomena to appear as they do, or causing phenomena to undergo different particular kinds of events.

In the SUM, not only do you have the lower dimensions coming up to the third dimension, but also going up or down from the fourth, to the fifth, sixth and seventh dimensions. We have represented them here in the form of the stacked donuts, with the big donut hole in the center called the *torroidal void*. This void space that goes through the center acts as the telepathic medium that connects all of the different dimensions. This creates the capacity for telepathic communication, which is stepped up or stepped down dimensionally, depending on which direction it is going.

Where are the dimensions located? Just like the third dimension, the first and the second dimensions are located inside of us. Then where are the fourth, fifth, sixth and seventh dimensions located? Are they outside of this universe? Are they within it? Or are we talking about going through the mind into other levels of being? When we are talking about the higher levels—the fourth, fifth, sixth and seventh dimensions, they can only be reached through the mind. The mind, in some ways, is spatially nonlocatable—you cannot say that the mind is located on Mount Shasta or Mount Fuji, or the Ganges River, or even in you or in me. It is more diffuse than that and it is also more physically and spatially nonlocatable.

The nonlocatability of the mind means that there are worlds or universes that are palpably not even present, but which are actually absolutely immediate. It is not like you have to go outside of your known universe to get to the next dimension. The dimensions are already all present here, but the higher dimensions are available only through the mind, understood as the medium of consciousness, just as space is the medium of the mind. The lower dimensions are perceptible in some way through the senses or through extensions of the senses—like microscopes and telescopes. But a microscope will not show you the invisible dimensions and a telescope will not show you the higher dimensions either, but they do show you the vast, infinite amount of space, which is the medium that connects the different dimensions through the mind. So the higher dimensions—the fifth, sixth and seventh—are always present. You do not have to travel far to get to them. But you do have to go inward, rather than outward.

To access the higher dimensions you have to imagine that you come to a point like passing through a concave mirror

When we are talking about the higher levels—the fourth, fifth, sixth and seventh dimensions, they can only be reached through the mind. The mind, in some ways, is spatially nonlocatable.

> *To access the higher dimensions you have to imagine that you come to a point like passing through a concave mirror to another world. You implode through a point in the mind to begin to experience the other dimensions.*

to another world. You implode through a point in the mind to begin to experience the other dimensions. In this way, the other dimensions have much to do with the cultivation of the imaginal faculty. When you go past the seventh dimension, you get to the parallel universe dimensions, which are the eighth through the thirteenth dimensions. We will briefly examine what these other higher dimensions are, though this subject will be expounded on in forthcoming volumes.

The seventh dimension is the mirrorless resonator. The point to remember is that the dimensions are penetrated by an interior mental resonance, which puts you in touch with higher-dimensional phenomena. When higher-dimensional phenomena appear to you in your mind, they may appear as apparitions to the physical eye. This is because the phenomena must be stepped down to take on some type of form that is recognizable to your inner senses—like a voice, or something you see in your mind's eye or like an astral movie or a dream.

So the higher-dimensional information is stepped down so it becomes cognizable through the inner perceptions—like some type of psychic audition or vision that is stepped down to a receptive point. The highest dimension is the seventh dimension, referred to as the mirrorless void or the speaking tube of God. The seventh dimension actually creates a void or torroid that runs through all the other dimensions and comes out the bottom of the first dimension. The mirror dimensions are all actually located inside the seventh dimension.

If you look at the SUM graphic, you see that on the top there is a torroidal vacuum that sucks into the void or that blows through and out of the void, then embraces the first dimension. The mirror dimensions are located inside of this. The mirror eighth dimension is on the inside of the sixth dimension. The mirror ninth dimension is on the inside of the fifth dimension. The mirror tenth dimension is on the inside of the fourth dimension. The mirror eleventh dimension is on the inside of the third dimension. The mirror twelfth dimension is on the inside of the second dimension and the mirror thirteenth dimension is on the inside of the first dimension. You have to really go inward to access these.

The reason why some of the psychedelic substances, like ahuyasca, LSD or psilocybin mushrooms are helpful (though their effectiveness is highly limited from a Cosmic History point of view), is that those who have partaken of these substances may have more of an inkling as to what we are speaking of. Those experiences can help you turn inward, creating inner mileage as it were, so you begin to experience how rich and expansive the inner worlds are, even though your body is not moving.

We say "inward", but that is just a sensation. Your sensory structure is externalizing. You are looking outside and hearing things from afar. The farther away you get, the dimmer the sound is and the harder it is to see the object. This is an analogy of trying to see into the higher dimensions. Again, the *only* way you can do this is by going inward, rather than outward. So the inward impulse is the direction of the experience of the higher dimensions.

It is for this reason that the experience of meditation and concentration is the most valuable tool for actually beginning to have some sense in directly experiencing the inner landscape or the landscape of the mind's eye. There are different ways to cultivate this. Meditation is one, but you can also cultivate it by practicing what is referred to as the hypnogogic reverie, that point of consciousness just on the edge of waking and dreaming, where you are not fully conscious, yet not fully asleep. Sometimes, when you are in this state, it may seem that you are underwater and you can hear things going on around you, which seems to be a long ways away—though you are not unconscious. At this point, you can begin to cultivate inner vision. This is a basic description in beginning to understand how to start experiencing the SUM model, so that it is not just a pure conceptual model, but also a working experiential model.

What is the fourth dimension? How about the fifth? The sixth? The seventh? If you start at the seventh dimension, you are starting at the mirrorless void, which operates with pure resonance with what we might call the voice of God or the divine command or creation utterances. These creation utterances come from the unimaginably vast complex of intelligence that

As we understand from the Law of Time and the description of the galactic brain, every single stage (that was, has been or will ever be) is occurring simultaneously, somewhere in the galaxy. In this way, everything can be experienced simultaneously, including all of the dimensions.

constitutes the organizing principle of the entire universe. They can be understood as the responses of the unimaginably vast mind of God, which is beyond all dimensionality and beyond all conception—but nonetheless all creation impulses emanate from It. In the *Quran*, it says that for anything to come into existence all God has to do is say: "Be," and it happens.

These creation impulses manifest through the seventh dimension as resonant creation utterances that you might say "echo" through the seventh dimension. All of this is by analogy (we can only think as far as images from our sensory experiences will allow us to think). So the creation utterances manifest through the seventh-dimensional speaking tube of God, as a type of echo or resonance that is like watching a coin spinning on the ground until it finally lands—so when that echo lands it is referred to as a pure light imprint in the sixth dimension. This is where the resonance of the creation utterances takes on a particular kind of light signature or light configuration. This light configuration is actually the encoding of a creation command.

> *"God created seven universes and the same number of earths. The commands flow among them. This is to let you know that God is Omnipotent, and that God is fully aware of all things." Sura 65:12*

When you stop to consider how vast the universe is—just the physical one, which is the outer garment of the different dimensional levels, lower and higher—you have to ask: But how does it all keep going? How does it all keep spinning? If the Earth has been spinning all of this time, is there a motor in there? The sun is also spinning—everything is actually spinning on its axis. This is truly one of the remarkable marvels. This spinning is actually due to the mental projection of the Divine Creator as It emanates different light signatures, which are like types of operating mechanisms or instructions that get stepped down to the lower dimensions.

The operating instructions are actually, what you might call, extensions of particular divine creation thought forms. In

---

In the Quran, it says that for anything to come into existence all God has to do is say: "Be," and it happens.

other words, the Earth, the stars, the sun, etc.—these are all just divine creation thought-forms. Since the Divine Creator only creates perfect thought-forms, the thought-forms themselves once emanated are commanded to maintain their own self-evolving, self-existence. This is maintained through a ceaseless spin that goes until some certain point, which is hard for us to imagine, but has something to do with the evolution of that thought-form. It is the self-governing process of a thought form to complete itself. Take the thought-form of a star, for instance. Once that thought-form completes itself, its spinning ceases and it becomes a supernova, emanating itself as a thought-form of vast, incredible power, energy and order into a million directions at once.

So each of these stars and galaxies is actually an emanated thought form that first took on a light configuration in the sixth dimension. Then that light configuration or light signature is simultaneously drawn out (like a thread through a loom) through all of the dimensions. Through this process, the light configuration structures certain quantum plasmas and so on. At the first- and second-dimensional levels, it structures the atomic molecular substance. At the third-dimensional level, it structures whole system organisms: planets, stars, galaxies, etc. At the fourth-dimensional level, it structures the astral movies that take place in the lower-dimensional levels. At the fifth-dimensional level, it structures a certain type of guardian electrical entity (beings who govern over all phenomena). And at the sixth-dimensional level, it maintains its light signature or configuration, which is the spin momentum of the original thought of God.

That light signature remains there at a sixth-dimensional level, while simultaneously the whole process of the evolution of the star and galaxy occurs throughout all those other levels and dimensions. As we understand from the Law of Time and the description of the galactic brain, every single stage (that was, has been or will ever be) is occurring simultaneously, somewhere in the galaxy. In this way, everything can be experienced simultaneously, including all of the dimensions. The multidimensional entry into this realm is through the

So each of these stars and galaxies is actually an emanated thought form that first took on a light configuration in the sixth dimension.

purest form of meditation. To get somewhere and to focus on something requires a bit of experience in calming the mind, so there is a relative absence of the thinking element. In other words, you are going more and more into the direction of what is called *samadhi*. At the same time, if there is somewhere you want to go, then you set your intention, focus and go.

For example, if your intention is to go to Arcturus, (which is relatively advanced travel but we will describe it), first you must sit down and meditate with the purpose of emptying your mind by getting the thinking element to come to a cessation, where there is nothing except maybe the most subliminal waves happening on the periphery of your awareness. Because you have set your intention, you can now direct your mind into a highly focused and yet highly diffuse state—(the focus is maintained without consciously cultivating it, yet you feel the focus). Hold your intention and visualize where Arcturus is in the (inner) sky. This holds some kind of pattern or imprint inside of you. Be careful not to activate the thinking element by focusing too much on the point of focus. So you now have a kind of relaxed focus like a samadhi that is occurring.

As you continue to focus, wait or watch for the spontaneously arising subliminal messages, which feel maybe like a tickle or a flicker at the periphery of your field of consciousness. You might then find yourself in some type of information stream, which corresponds with your intention to go to Arcturus, or to feel the higher-dimensional level of Arcturus (remember the higher dimensions are inside of you). So all you are doing is taking a time-space vector focal point, such as Arcturus, and accessing the information stream at that particular point. The more you practice this, the more skilled you become. Then at some point, you will find yourself "walking" around on the Arcturus star system. The point of this is to develop the capacity to experience the simultaneous multidimensionality of the SUM.

Interplanetary travel all starts with meditation that clears the mind of the thinking disposition—this is mandatory in developing the samadhi and the concentration within the samadhi to go where you have to go or do what has to be done.

> *Interplanetary travel all starts with meditation that clears the mind of the thinking disposition—this is mandatory in developing the samadhi and the concentration within the samadhi to go where you have to go or do what has to be done.*

This is also the beginning way of sensory teleportation (see Ch. 11). It is important to study and contemplate each of the dimensions so you have a thorough understanding of what each of the dimensions is, and how they relate to each other.

To summarize, we gave the example of the light code or the configuration of a star, or even a galaxy, and how that is like a thread in a loom shot through a hole of all the dimensional orders so that everything is activated. The creation utterance command resonates and becomes a light configuration in the sixth dimension, while simultaneously shooting through all the other dimensions—then Presto! Somewhere in space, something new appears. So it is the sixth dimension that holds the energy permutation patterns for that particular phenomena as well as the spin.

Around that spin is what we call the evolutionary transformation codes that go along with that particular thought form. These codes then go out. One of these codes (which is like the information of a microchip), for instance, could contain the thought-form of the entire galaxy; including all of the permutations that the galaxy will go through in its particular spin. We are spinning on the galaxies and the galaxies are spinning around a larger universal subsection or suborder. So the galaxy has its spin, the stars have their spin and the planets have their spin, as do the atoms within the molecules have their spin. Everything is spinning from a primal thought-form. The spin quotient of the thought-form is stored in the light code, and around that spin quotient is what is called the *evolutionary transformation quotients* or *fractal factors*. In some cases, it might take 10 billion years of spin for a thought-form to go through all of its evolutionary transformational permutations. All that is coded in as mathematical quotients around a particular spin quotient, which is amazingly densely packed.

The sixth dimension is also the home of the higher angelic orders, which are entitizations of life forms that are responsible for the supervision of the different spin evolutionary transformation factors in any number of given light codes—all the way down to being responsible for supervising the different "evolving" entities, even down to the third-dimensional level.

The creation utterance command resonates and becomes a light configuration in the sixth dimension, while simultaneously shooting through all the other dimensions—then Presto! Somewhere in space, something new appears.

It is the supervision and maintenance of the light codes that maintain the spin of evolutionary factors of the phenomenal realm.

The fifth dimension is the energy field system and the home of, what we might call, "more activating guide entities." As explained in Chapter 6, we have a third-dimensional being and a fourth-dimensional soul aspect and then a fifth-dimensional guide aspect or "higher self," which animates the fourth-dimensional self. At the same time, each human being constitutes a microquantum of an energy field system. This means we are each a microunit of an energy system called the biosphere. And each of our individual units contain the same microunit system.

The *macroenvironmental energy system* of the microunits is the entire biosphere, which is the entire planetary environment. In our actions, according to different impulses (yes, no, good, bad, want, don't want), we move through different fields of consciousness. What we experience depends on how awake we are to our soul aspect. We are talking about the evolution of the physical plane being in relation to its own conscious awareness of its soul aspect. Depending upon how awake the soul is, there can be some consciousness of the fifth-dimensional aspect. The fifth-dimensional entity is always monitoring the entire program anyway.

The fifth-dimensional entity monitors both the living soul substance of life as well as the energetic component of pure atomic molecular life. All of this is governed at the fifth–dimensional level, which is a purely electronic element. Electricity is actually a higher dimensional fluid. (This is why Thomas Edison became a Theosophist—because like many people in the 19th Century, he understood that the discovery of electricity was actually a coming into contact with some type of non-material higher-dimensional energy). Electricity was discovered in the latter part of the thirteenth baktun cycle, otherwise known as the *cycle of materialism*. In this cycle of materialism, electricity was actually an analog or a sign of a direction of going into a more metaphysical evolution.

> *... we have a third-dimensional being and a fourth-dimensional soul aspect and then a fifth-dimensional guide aspect or "higher self," which animates the fourth-dimensional self.*

Buckminster Fuller said that the future of evolution is in the direction of weightlessness. This means mental/spiritual evolution. Today, electricity is utilized for all sorts of crude third-dimensional types of functions—like running elevators and escalators at shopping malls. Fifth-dimensional electricity exists everywhere. It is just a matter of learning how to tune into and channel it into your biotelepathic apparatus. In any case, we are describing a stepping down from a sixth-dimensional light configuration into the fifth dimension, where the energy field system has its guides that govern and control the world of third-dimensional phenomena.

Then there is the intermediate field of the fourth dimension, which is between the pure electrical and the phenomenal third-dimensional material/physical plane. The fourth dimension is the pure imaginal mental dimension where all of the astral movies are stored. When we have a configuration like the light code configuration, it activates time space vectors like Velatropa 24, which was activated about 6 billion years ago and has been spinning ever since. When the Velatropa 24.3 light configuration came through, it penetrated deep into the plasma and the quanta levels (the first- and second-dimensional atomic molecular structure), and then into the whole system field aggregates of the third dimension. The fourth dimension was also activated.

In this way, the fourth dimension consists of the entirety of all the possibilities of the psychic evolution and development of all the different life forms that will ever arise within that field defined by a particular star. Remember, there are two sets of number quotients on the light grid code—one is the spin quotient number and the other is an aggregate of transformational evolutionary timing quotients. From the fifth-dimensional level, those fourth-dimensional transformational timing quotients manifest as different energy field system guides.

The fourth dimension is the pure imaginal mental dimension where all of the astral movies are stored.

Sum & The Astral Movie Library

On the fourth-dimensional level, those light configurations multiply fantastically into a whole "video library of astral movies." The astral movies are like dreams. In other words, you are not going to find them on celluloid. Where does a dream take place and how can you move through the field in a dream? Dreams are some of the most powerful examples of accessing the innermost centers of the mind. Being purely fourth-dimensional, dreams activate the astral movies. Each being has its own spin and thus, its own astral movie, which is its own prerecorded feature length film!

Any time you make a choice, you potentiate a scene in one of these astral movies. The choices you make are either in congruence with the astral movie or they are not. When you are not in congruence with your astral movie then you feel that something is off. Many people are very unconscious and do not realize that they are off all of the time or most of the time. The astral movie, then, is always playing simultaneously to your life pattern, and when you are aligned within your own groove, you know it because it feels so good. When this awareness occurs, then suddenly you notice that you are more in the field of your astral movie than you are in the third-dimensional field. It can sometimes feel as though you are in a tunnel or a hollow tube.

Each entity contains a spool or astral movie film that is continuously spinning and contains all of the potential astral movies that are possible for that particular entity. All these astral movies are potentialities stored in the fourth dimension, though you do not necessarily play them all out. Whatever script you choose, it is already there and the potentiality has already been recorded, from the lowest to the highest. The *Book of Clear Records* is actually the fourth and fifth-dimensional libraries of information and energy, including the energy field system guides, as well as the library and archives of all of the different astral movies that are possible to play out. That is why the Holy Scriptures say that it has all been written in a book. This Master Book is recorded in the fifth and fourth dimensions in the form of astral movies. In the Hindu tradition, this is also known as the *akashic records*.

When people have near-death experiences and report seeing their whole life flash in front of them, they are actually witnessing their astral movie being rapidly replayed to them at the time of death. When viewing your life movie, the quality of what you experienced, and how you responded to those experiences in this life, conditions what is going to happen to you in the next life or Afterlife. All of the movie archives of every being that ever existed are stored in the fourth dimension, which is the space of the imagination or the imaginal realm. The fourth dimension is also the storehouse of all dreams.

When your mind is in the fourth dimension, the possibilities are endless. You can pick up your fourth-dimensional paintbrushes and paint yourself a fantasy, a daydream or whatever else you wish. The third dimension is the place where the fourth-dimensional movies take concrete form, guided, of course, by the fifth-dimensional entity. Behind the apparent third dimension, there is actually an incessant motion of molecular/cellular structure in different levels of spin, manifesting the world of appearances. We see this particular world—but cats or dogs (or any other nonhuman creature) may see a completely different world. All beings see according to their perceptions. The world we see is just the world constructed by our sense organs and perceptions, but it's not necessarily what the world really is. It is just what appears to us because our senses construct it to look like that. That is really all there is to it.

So when we talk about scientists or physicists going out to examine the phenomenal world, they will not ultimately find anything except what their sense organs are capable of perceiving. And that is not going to be the absolute nature of reality—that's why you have to go inward and cultivate the sense of being at the edge of the seventh-dimensional speaking tube. In this way, you can begin to perceive the verticality that aligns the different dimensions with each other. Maybe then you can catch a glimpse of the real.

These are just some general descriptions of the Simultaneous Universe Model, which describes a whole structure of reality. We can see a slice of that structure within this graphic description. This description is intended to give you a more palpable sense of how the SUM works. Study of this model will open you up to vast stores of unexplored dimensions in your own mind. We are actually, simultaneously consciously and unconsciously, in touch with all of those dimensions. See how many you can tune into at once.

Viewing The Magnetic Reality

Viewing the Earth from the fourth dimension, we see a conglomeration of different aggregates of magnetic fields—some larger magnetic fields encompassing subsets of smaller and smaller magnetic fields. Then we see little magnetic filaments, which are like the living entities. It appears as though these magnetic filaments are being moved around, like there is some type of magnet moving them from the other side of an invisible glass sphere. And all of the filaments are being moved by that one magnet.

All beings see according to their perceptions. The world we see is just the world constructed by our sense organs and perceptions, but it's not necessarily what the world really is.

That magnet is the aggregate or feedback effect of the collective karma of all of those beings. So it has its own force moving through the noosphere, which is the sum aggregate of all of the reactions to all of the karma that has been created. This magnet is sending out impulses and working out different energies which are pulsing out and hitting these magnetic filaments, resulting in what we read about in the daily news or what we see happening on the street. Just about everybody, to one degree or another, is being operated from a distance by these karmic feedback magnets that are governing world affairs.

The astral movies are coming down through the noosphere—through that magnet and then hitting all those different filaments on Earth, so each one is perceiving according to what the astral movie is playing at that moment in time. So you can see that it is a very challenging thing to wake up and become conscious of the actual state of reality, to realize that you are a product of a feedback loop and that that is the first step in breaking the spell that keeps you mesmerized in the projective field of a reality that is out of your control.

Though it describes and defines different dimensions, modes of perception and ways of being, Cosmic History is nonetheless an absolute unity and constitutes in its entirety a polyvalent belief system. To enter into Cosmic History as a belief system, it is necessary to be able to entertain different models or structures of reality. The three models that we have presented are, by no means, the only models that can penetrate and comprehend Cosmic History in some of its infinitely diverse aspects. While these three models serve the purpose of defining a new belief system, they also serve as containers for the discrimination and storage of different categories of experience and perception, as well as modes of being and stages and qualities of consciousness.

These three models are, you might say, different views or perspectives seen from the throne. They are three different slices through the unified, but polyvalent spectrum of intelligence called Cosmic History. Once the goal of Cosmic History is defined—that of making the noosphere conscious through cultivation of the sorcerer's whole body perception—we are able to turn a synesthetic kaleidoscope with the imaginal eye of the sorcerer, and with each turn, a different model of reality comes into focus. Each model has its particular place and value. The first to define sectors of reality, the second to define modes and ways of thought and knowing, and the third to acquaint us with the dimensional orders of reality. Remember: these are only views to be explored. The exploration is up to you!

Part IV Noosphere: The New Earth Consciousness

"...and no man could learn that (new) song but the 144,000 which were redeemed from the Earth"

Revelations Chapter 14.3

Part IV • Noosphere: The New Earth Consciousness

Chapter 10
Noosphere Redefined and Made Conscious

As we mentioned in Chapter 1, lack of knowledge of the noosphere (along with the psi bank regulator) is the primary fault of the prevailing dominating structure that governs perceptions today. The noosphere can only first be seen whole as a view from the throne. This view is then translated into Cosmic History, the means by which the vastness of noosphere can be introduced or made known. "Noos" comes from the Greek word "mind", which is actually the sphere of the mind or mental envelope—meaning the planet Earth's mental envelope or mental sphere. This tells us that it is the planet that has the mind. This is an important point to understand. So what we have been thinking of as mind and human mind is a somewhat diminished concept, and the actual mind is the global mind or the planetary mind, which is the noosphere. All communication actually comes from the noosphere.

Being the mental sphere of the planet, the noosphere can only be made fully conscious if it is a function of the unified field of the human mind operating in universal telepathy. When we are in a natural timing standard that is coordinated with the natural timing frequency of the universe (which keeps everything synchronized), only then can we establish a field of universal telepathy within the field of human consciousness. This, in effect, unifies the human mind making the noosphere the conscious operating mechanism of the human civilization. This is possible now. The Internet is the last stop before this.

As we know from the point of view of Cosmic History, we are dealing with principles of holonomics and holonomic consistency, as well as unitive principles, which encompass the major aspects of the Cycle of Becoming and the Cycle of Return. You cannot talk about the noosphere without having a real context for understanding the Cycle of Becoming and the Cycle of Return. This context extends us from planet Earth through the solar system to the galaxy and then on to the universe. This is due to the principle of holonomic consistency. So when we talk about extending out and seeing what the noosphere is and what it is a reflection of and what this means for us on Earth, then we must understand that the noosphere has embedded within it the principles of Cosmic History. In this way, we are extracting Cosmic History from the noosphere.

Even though Cosmic History is embedded in the noosphere, it was not invented or originated by the noosphere. Cosmic History is in some sense, self-originating. It is self-originated by the need of the cosmos to know itself. This is how Cosmic History has actually come about—everything that exists evolves from unconscious to conscious. So inevitably, the entire cosmos is moved by the urge to self-reflection because it is ultimately a function of the universal cosmic mind. The self-reflection of the cosmos is called Cosmic History.

Universal cosmic mind means the cosmos in its entirety is contained and originated in the universal intelligence or the mind of God. This is knowable through what we experience as our little mind here on Earth (though our mind only appears little if we are holding onto our ego). If we let go of our ego, then our mind is the same as the universal cosmic mind, which is made knowable through descriptions of the different dimensional levels. These dimensional levels constitute the entirety of the created order of the universe, both perceptible and imperceptible. This cosmos is located ultimately in the mind and was originated by God—the Master Intelligence.

We say "universal cosmic mind" because ultimately it is the same for everyone everywhere. So it is universal. In other words, the cosmos does not change in any intrinsic sense to anyone. The cosmos appears, or is experienced differently, according to the level of perception and intelligence that a particular organism or entity might be evolved to. But the cosmos as perceived does not change, only does it change according to the capacity of the entities' level and quality of perception, sense organs, cognitive faculties and so on. The universal intelligence of the cosmos extends throughout and permeates the entire cosmos. We, here on Earth and with our means of intelligence, have developed languages and various other skills, which are expressions or reflections of the universal intelligence or intelligence that exists as a function of universal mind.

Given that the cosmos is universal, everyone ultimately in the course of their evolution, is capable of totally comprehending the cosmos. It is the same comprehension for everyone. It is like seeing that the Buddhas of the past, present and future all experienced the very same enlightenment. This is fundamentally what we are saying when we talk about the universal cosmic mind. It is this universal cosmic mind which informs Cosmic History and allows it to be the reflective capacity and contents of the entire cosmos. This is what you have to understand as the ultimate container of the universal cosmic mind. This means that the reflection of what we call star, tree or galaxy is actually Cosmic History. In and of itself does the galaxy know that it is called the galaxy? Does the tree know that it is called a tree? The tree undoubtedly experiences its own tree-ness as the galaxy experiences its own galaxy-ness, but whether or not

The cosmos appears, or is experienced differently, according to the level of perception and intelligence that a particular organism or entity might be evolved to.

it is necessary to have names or systems of nomenclature beyond our somewhat equivocating level of intelligence is open to question.

The point is that Cosmic History is the reflective intelligence that names or designates tree, galaxy, water, atom, etc. That reflective capacity qualifies Cosmic History as being a type of record or chronicle or description. That same quality is what makes the noosphere, *the noosphere*. We can see, for instance, that Cosmic History is a function of the power of seven. We have the seven volumes of Cosmic History, which include descriptions of thought, expression and kinds and levels of knowing. These categories of Cosmic History are general divisions which conform to the basic cosmology of seven. This also informs and structures the planetary noosphere.

What we think of as our mind or intelligence is merely a resonant quality of mind that is not contained in our body, brain or nervous system. What is contained in the brain or nervous system—in the neurocerebral mechanism—is what we might call the capacitors for thinking and organization of perceptual and intuitive experience. There exists an individuated storage system for accumulated perceptions that you have had from the time of your birth into this body. These impressions actually get stored in the brain—so the brain is a storage unit in that regard. Learned responses and everything else is programmed into the brain. It is then for the actions of our individual will to see if these responses correspond to the highest astral movies.

The actual mind, in which all of this occurs, is not brain specific or individual human being specific. The mind, or what we might call the thinking layer of the mind, is above and beyond the raw storage of different perceptions, stimuli, and experiences. The thinking disposition is somewhat different—it is a quality or aspect of intelligence that may draw on stored information but it is not a function of stored information. So we have the storage information of experience and then we have the thinking layer—the capacity to actually take that experience and abstract it, as it were, and put it into some type of formulation that says: "This experience is proof of the existence of God, and if you don't put your trust in God then

The mind, or what we might call the thinking layer of the mind, is above and beyond the raw storage of different perceptions, stimuli, and experiences.

certain things may happen that may not be altogether pleasant." This is the thinking disposition and is actually a part of what we call the noosphere. The noosphere is the total mind of the sum of life on the planet.

Russian scientist V.I. Vernadsky said that the sum of life is a single unity—this means from the plankton all the way up to the human species. There is just one spectrum of different categories and levels of cellular molecular organic organization—but it is all one spectrum. When we talk about this unity of life or the sum of life as a unity, everything is interconnected. When we talk about the capacity for thinking and intelligence, it is not just the human beings, but the whole system of life itself that is reflecting the noosphere.

If we take a big axe and start chopping a tree down we would have ways of measuring sentiency—meaning that the tree is actually going to have a measurable conscious experience. If you chop that tree all the way down it will die; it will cease to grow. Then you work up into the more complex animal realms and then into the human realm. That sentiency then transforms into thinking. So that any reflex of sensation is going to establish some type of electrical charge, whether it be positive or negative or neutral. Those charges constitute the quality of the noosphere.

If there is an excess of positive or an excess of negative charges, then those changes get released into the noosphere—this is why there is so much emphasis put on watching your thoughts, watching what you put into the environment. Even the thoughts you keep to yourself have their charges. You may think you can conceal them, but you actually can not. Every thought goes out into the noosphere. When we talk about this noosphere in the most primitive sense, what we are talking about is the sum capacity for the input of different ranges of sentiency and thought that occur across the range of life in all of its diversity since the beginning of the evolution of life on the planet.

That cumulative complex set of charges of feeling and thought that has existed since the beginning of evolution of life is actually part of the composite of the noosphere. Everything that has ever been thought or said or done is registered in the noosphere. But where is the noosphere located? In one sense, the noosphere is a totally diffuse phenomenon dispersed throughout the biosphere as the cumulative effect of the ongoing existing charges of the entire mental field of the sum of life on Earth.

First Noospheric Articulations

The noosphere is actually an active, ever-evolving thinking agent. Contemplation of the noosphere as an evolutionary or evolutive phenomenon goes back only about 100 years or so. A few thinkers of the past had posited some such notion as the Earth's mental envelope, but it was never really fully articulated until the definition was arrived at by Russian scientist V.I. Vernadsky and French biologist Pierre de Chardin in Paris in 1926. Vernadsky's focus of study was geochemistry of the Earth and de Chardin's focus of study began with paleontology and the study of the history of life, vertebrates and invertebrates. The definition given here is the classic one—the noosphere as the mental sheathe of the planet.

In the evolution of the systems of the universe, de Chardin goes on to say that there are planets with noosphere and planets without noosphere. The development of the noosphere is an inevitable development in the evolution of life of any planetary system, whatever form that life might be. Similarly, the noosphere represents a stage in evolution. What we are talking about here is the noosphere becoming conscious of the fact that it exists—this is the work that de Chardin and Vernadsky began some 80 years ago. They became aware that the evolution of life tends to go in the direction of greater consciousness. This greater consciousness is not an individual or a human trait but a global phenomenon that advances all species of life.

It is the advance of life as a planetary system that evolves the need for a noosphere. The noosphere is evolved because there is a need for a higher organizing mind—a unified thinking element that processes and provides the appropriate, adequate information for the advance of the species into greater levels of consciousness, cognition and spiritual awareness. This is the need that exists. So when there is a need then the tendency to evolve to that need comes. Both de Chardin and Vernadsky understood that point as well, each in their own way. De Chardin speaks of the noosphere and of a coming Omega point toward which he saw a type of global information society developing. And that information society, he said, would then be transmuted into a more spiritual urge, tendency or inclination which would give rise to the actual advent of the noosphere.

For Vernadsky, the idea of the noosphere is the result not so much in the way of the evolution of an information society in the way that de Chardin envisioned it, but more as a type of evolutionary crisis resulting from the acceleration of the machine technology and the subsequent release into the atmosphere of "free energy," as he calls it. Free energy actually being the polluting element of industrial waste that is injected into the atmosphere or into the Earth and its water systems.

This free energy creates a type of acceleration of the *biogenic migration of atoms*. Biogenic means the transformation of the atoms and molecules from one structure or state into another, (like when you eat food and go to the bathroom

The development of the noosphere is an inevitable development in the evolution of life of any planetary system, whatever form that life might be.

for instance)—this is a biogenic migration of atoms. So this biogenic migration of atoms is occurring at a massive planetary scale and the acceleration of that process creates a kind of critical state where the entire biosphere and the systems of the Earth itself are brought to a heightened state of critical malfunction or dysfunction. That critical point of malfunction or dysfunction creates an entire qualitative shift which results in the noosphere.

Vernadsky does not describe too much more what that actually is like, though he speaks about all the tendencies going in that direction. He gives one big clue when he says that the next geological era will be called the *Psychozoic era*. Right now, we are living in the *Holocene* ("most recent age") era, where the human race emerges as a significant factor in the evolution of the globe. "Psycho" refers to mind and "Zoa" refers to life. So the Psychozoic era brings about the spiritualization of life and spiritualization of the entire thinking mechanism of the Earth or the noosphere. In any case, these two scientific thinkers set the stage for coming into the full realization of the noosphere.

Another thinker, physicist Oliver Reiser, adds a further component to the thought that had already been developed by Vernadsky and de Chardin. Vernadsky died in 1945 and de Chardin died in 1955, so the contribution of Oliver Reiser in the 1960s was to identify what he called the *psi field*. A psi field is like having an Eastern Hemisphere and a Western Hemisphere over the Earth. Reiser saw that this had something to do with the governing of life or with the DNA. He presented this psi field in its most advanced form in his book *Cosmic Humanism* in 1966.

Buckminster Fuller was another thinker who approached the idea of the noosphere. Fuller discovered that all of the thoughts that had ever existed were stored in the planet's electromagnetic field and they could be contacted. In tapping into the electromagnetic field, Fuller found that he could have conversations with any personality he wished from the past, present or future. Fuller said that his favorite conversations were with the pre-Socratic philosophers whom he could contact when he walked down the beach.

> *(Buckminster) Fuller discovered that all of the thoughts that had ever existed were stored in the planet's electromagnetic field and they could be contacted. In tapping into the electromagnetic field, Fuller found that he could have conversations with any personality he wished from the past, present or future.*

These two additions from Reiser and Fuller point to a type of location, at least of the storage information processing and formulating mechanism of the noosphere, some place in the Earth's electromagnetic fields. Two years before de Chardin died in 1953, the American scientist Van Allen discovered what are now known as the *radiation belts* which are 2,000 and 11,000 miles up.

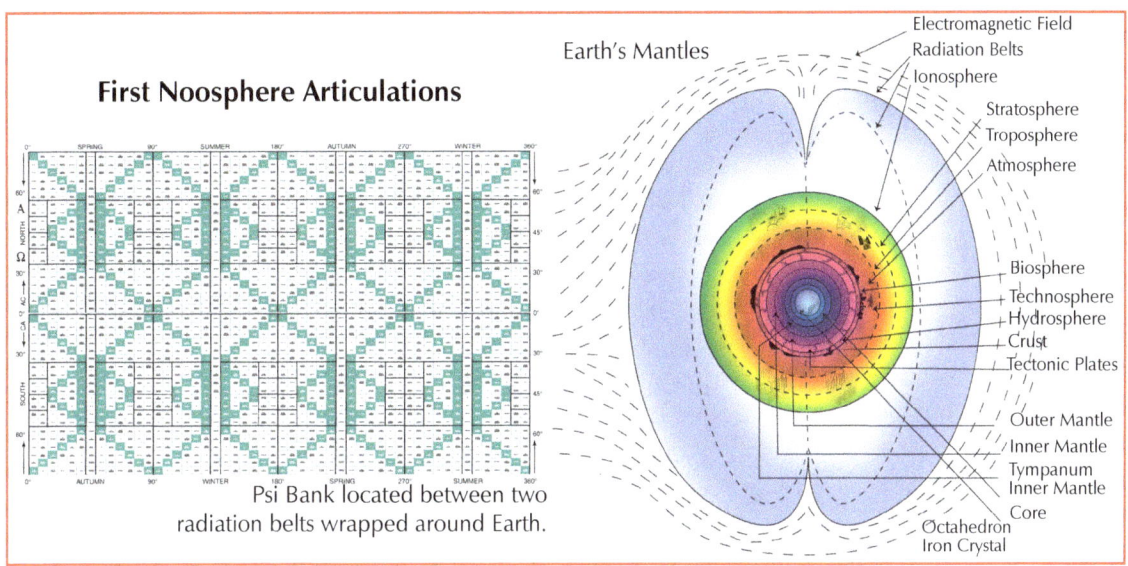

Psi Bank located between two radiation belts wrapped around Earth.

Much lower down in the Earth from the radiation belts is the ionosphere, which is part of the magnetosphere and the electrical system of the planet. The ionosphere is charged with the governing of the meteorological or the weather patterns, but it is also a part of the magnetosphere that connects the whole system with the solar sun spots. You cannot separate the Earth's magnetic field from the solar sun spot cycles or from the solar magnetic field. According to both Fuller and Reiser's suggestions that the noosphere has something to do with the electromagnetic fields, the noosphere then becomes part of the solar field, or the solar mind.

The book *Earth Ascending* synthesizes much of the previous thinking about the noosphere into a more specific description. *Earth Ascending* illustrates the full understanding of the psi bank, which is located in the Earth's electromagnetic field between the inner and the outer Van Allen radiation belts. This psi bank represents a system of information storage and regulation, which is coded by the 13:20 universal timing frequency and adjusted to the presentation of the Tzolkin matrix on Earth. The psi bank is further adjusted to reflect the bipolar magnetism of the Earth and the fourfold shifting of the Earth in one rotation around the sun.

It is the reflection of the bipolar magnetism that gives you a double Tzolkin plate, stretching from North Pole to South Pole. The fourfold shift (two equinoxes and two solstices) of the Earth in its rotation around the sun is what creates four different plates. The four large psi plates are each divided into a Northern and Southern psi plate; each one is a mirror that reflects a seasonal quality. This means that the four shifts in the Earth's axis that occur during one orbit are what accounts for there being winter, spring, summer and fall in the areas North and South of the tropical zones, 23 ½ degrees North and South of the equator.

The designation of the psi bank makes the conceptualization of the noosphere much easier. Just contemplate the fact that the entirety of the systems of thought and knowledge is all contained within the psi bank regulator of the noosphere. This psi bank regulator, located between these two electromagnetic fields, is not only a storage unit for all thought, but also contains all of the knowledge of the evolutionary timing programs.

There are two aspects of the noosphere. The first is the plates we have just described; the second is the diffuse noosphere, which is the diffusion of the mind and thinking element throughout the biosphere. This means the place where you are now sitting reading these words is actually in the mental field of the noosphere. The mental field that wrote these words and the mental field reading these words are participating in the same particular event moment which is based on the capacity to focus the mind on this particular theme and topic in this little event point on the planet. This entire reflection itself is nothing but the noosphere making itself conscious yet again.

This means that everything that you are reading right now is actually the noosphere itself choosing a particular medium in this particular moment in which its thoughts can be expressed verbally in a particular language with a particular logic, for a particular person (you) for a particular reason. When you stop and think about this, you see that these words are highly directed and focused because of the particular attunement of the transmitter and receiver to the noosphere. The clearer is the attunement of the transmitter and receiver to the subject of the noosphere, the more focused, directed and purposive will the communication be. This also serves as an example of heightened self-reflection of the noosphere.

When you finally understand that your mind is always living and moving through the noosphere, you will be surprised to see how few varieties of thought there actually are—how few thoughts or thought forms are actually called forth every

> ... the place where you are now sitting reading these words is actually in the mental field of the noosphere.

moment of every day. As you understand more, then you see that your biological mechanism or neurocerebral biological mechanism is merely the literal mouthpiece for the noosphere. The clearer you make your mind, the more directed and pure the noospheric expression will be. When you understand that this is all you are actually doing anyway, then everything will transform beautifully.

Noospheric Clichés

For most human beings, day-to-day reality is made up by merely repeating noospheric clichés. So most people just tread water and stay in the same place. This keeps consciousness in a low, steady state of oscillation. When you go into shops or to any public place you hear people talking in noospheric clichés all the time. People repeat these tired clichés over and over and that is the reality that they create and perpetuate. Whatever you speak and say is a spell and it creates whatever you speak and say. Many people are completely unconscious of this.

For those of you who still have your critical thinking element intact, once you understand and grasp that you are actually nothing but a medium or a channel or an outlet for the noosphere—then if you allow yourself to be that, your consciousness will shift and you will start to speak at higher, more collective levels. In other words, you will not be speaking for "yourself" or for "ourselves" but you will be speaking from a higher noospheric collective voice. This is a voice that comes from a place of understanding the needs of the particular situation and then will address those needs without any kind of personal bias or personal interest.

So this diffuse part of the noosphere is the part you are involved in every day in your thinking and in your exchanges. In describing this it is well to keep in mind that you are always just voicing the noosphere. You really have to think about this. Think about how you are or how you are not giving voice to the noosphere in the particular moment you are speaking. Or if you assume you are speaking from the noosphere—are you expressing it clearly or are you degrading it by lack of focus or

Once you understand and grasp that you are actually nothing but a medium or a channel or an outlet for the noosphere—then if you allow yourself to be that, your consciousness will shift and you will start to speak at higher, more collective levels.

by some type of emotional bias? These contemplations are to help shape us up because we are rapidly coming to this point, which is de Chardin's Omega point or what Vernadsky referred to as the biosphere/noosphere transition. At this point, an evolutionary mental shift will occur, making us increasingly conscious operants of the noosphere.

As conscious operants of the noosphere, it behooves us to study and understand the psi bank, which is the actual working mechanism of the noosphere. We are the capacitators of the noosphere, the diffuse mental field around the planet, whether we know it or not. The degree to which we are immersed in our ego is the degree to which we are creating and repeating noospheric clichés. Given the degree to which we are open to spirit and to non-egoic forms of life and communication, then to that degree we are potentiating ourselves as noospheric mediums.

NOOSPHERE AND THE LAW OF TIME

Many of the more advanced developments of the practices of the Law of Time have something to do with understanding this mechanism of the psi bank. The *Rinri Project*, (which began in 1996), for instance, is a way of coordinating the psi chrono units or the base units of the psi bank with the 13-moon/28-day cycle and the 16-day cube journey of the *Telektonon*. This is the practice that peeled the skin off the psi bank and made it accessible.

Since that point, any number of practices have been introduced, including the *20 Tablets of the Law of Time*, the 7:7::7:7 *Telektonon* and the practice of the *Elder Futhark runes*, which all have to do with the activation of the psi bank. The psi bank has always been active, but through these practices it is now being consciously activated. In this way, what is being called for is an increased awareness that our individual and collective harmony is the field of resonance that has to be established in order for the psi bank to quicken its process of operation in unloosing the information that we need to carry on or conduct our business on Earth.

> *What is being called for is an increased awareness that our individual and collective harmony is the field of resonance that has to be established in order for the psi bank to quicken its process of operation.*

So knowing about the structure of the psi bank, the psi bank plates, the psi chrono units, the psi membranes and knowing how the psi bank can be opened and followed through in four-year cycles, each year corresponding to one North/South psi plate, is all important. This knowledge and these practices is what lifts the human consciousness, albeit in a critical minority, into a whole other stage of evolution. And it all has to do with the Law of Time and the study of the psi bank.

Time and the Technosphere defines the noosphere in the following way:

> "Noosphere: Earth's mental envelope or field, discontinuous with and above the biosphere; unconscious until the discovery and application of the Law of Time; activated by registration of the human biomass in correct 13:20 timing frequency via universal adoption of the Thirteen Moon calendar; description of transformed state of biosphere, coincident with the end of history; condition of universal telepathy subsequent to collapse of technosphere and application of the Law of Time; functions in tandem with programs from Earth's octahedral core."

This description and all others that exist of the noosphere in *Time and the Technosphere* are especially helpful in the immediate years ahead of us and will prove to be very practical in establishing the noosphere here on Earth. The codes of the Law of Time exist to help us maintain continuing consciousness in the 13:20 timing frequency and thus access the noosphere. Only once you get to this level can you experience cosmic consciousness. Cosmic consciousness is based on being conscious every moment and no longer falling back into fear states or conceptual errors.

The Law of Time says that you will never have continuing consciousness unless you break out of lower time and dissolve fear-conditioned factors that keep you locked into unconsciousness. Most people are sleepwalking and think that that is life.

The Law of Time says that you will never have continuing consciousness unless you break out of lower time and dissolve fear-conditioned factors that keep you locked into unconsciousness.

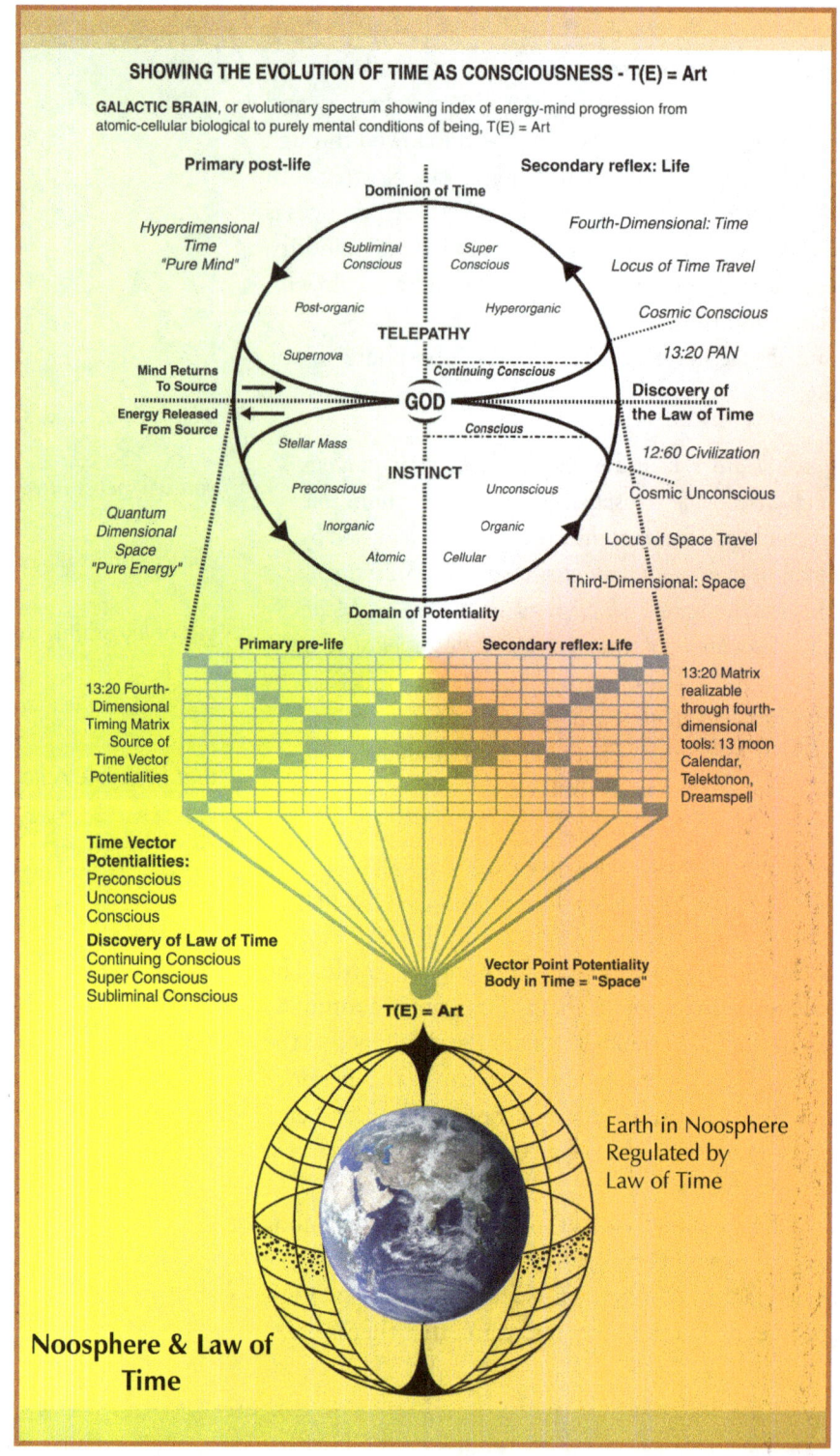

But it is actually just various states of sleepwalking. The macro spell of the Gregorian calendar must be broken. All the other spells can be easily broken after this. But first, you must break the spell of false time and return to natural harmonic time which is the true time of 13:20. One Tibetan lama recently quipped to the authors that even if Padmasambhava were to come to America, he would probably have to get a job. That is the Gregorian spell.

According to the Law of Time, in the process of evolution we create this situation of the noosphere which is really a universal telepathic field. Only with the advent of the noosphere can we get to the next levels of evolution: *hyperorganic* and *superconscious*. Hyperorganic consciousness refers to the ability of the human to utilize the sense organs as points of energy emission and consciousness. This means that sense organs get telepathically extended outward, which results in natural phenomena such as clairvoyance and clairaudience. This is a whole other evolutionary condition. This condition is referred to as radiosonic architecture. At this stage, we will be consciously extruding plasmas through the senses. Plasmas are electronically charged subatomic particles, which saturate the entire field of the universe. We take in plasma all the time since everything is made of it. Conscious direction of plasma accounts for the mind power of telepathy, which can only develop in a stage of continuing consciousness to extrude through the sense organs what Cosmic History refers to as "plasmic fields."

The hyperorganic stage of consciousness is also the point of evolution where the human becomes a Stage 2 Autotroph. This means the human will become like the plants and will be able to dynamically catalyze the sun with the solar energy within its own body. The majority of humans today are *heterotrophs*, meaning they depend on the plants (rather than themselves) to catalyze solar energy. Humans are evolving into *autoheterotrophs*, which means that not only will the human be able to catalyze solar energy, but will also be able to extrude it through the senses to create hyper or super organic sense fields. These super organic sense fields are the basis of *radiosonic architecture.*

Superconsciousness is a virtually omniscient state of mind where you have a radar sensitivity of the whole field of reality. This is based on the ability to establish a collectively unified hyperorganic telepathic sense field. In this sense field, you will think thoughts such as: "I am the planet and the planet is thinking this thought" and you will realize it is all of "we" who thought this thought.

When you get to the subliminal consciousness you see that the superconscious is the highest point you can get to on the organic side of evolution. The subliminal consciousness refers to the point when we are absolutely disincarnate entities i.e. fifth-dimensional entities. "Subliminal" means you are operating independent of past and future—this is how people can contact different entities on different planes of existence. Since the subliminal consciousness is independent of past and future, you can tune into it at the conscious level.

Post organic and supernova refer to the totally etheric conditions of qualities and beings, which are no longer dependent on matter. The supernova represents the stage at which all of the phenomena, both post organic and stellar are combined. For instance, the supernova of 1987 created highly intelligent structures with giant rings within rings rippling out. This is a result of the super and subliminal consciousness of the post organic intelligence combined with a heightened evolved state of stellar mass to create a supernova excitation, which is actually a huge explosion of consciousness and energy. When a supernova comes it lends a boost of consciousness. The 1987 supernova was an accompanying boost to the discovery of the Law of Time, resulting in the manifestation of the *Dynamics of Time, As The Evolution of Time as Consciousness*, and the *20 Tablets of the Law of Time*.

When you look at this as a kind of process of actual evolutionary exercise what you see is that we have now brought forth the models that show us the mechanism of the noosphere through the psi bank. We have begun to have different practices which engage our being with the psi bank. Now we are at the phase of developing more of what we might call conscious teams or conscious noospheric cells to activate the psi bank even more synchronously and simultaneously around the planet.

The practices that will be developed over the next few years by the Foundation for the Law of Time, starting with the Mystery of the Stone, will have as one of their principle goals or effects the complete activation of the psi bank, comprehended as being the mechanism of our own consciousness. This will result in increasingly heightened states of mental awareness and mental consciousness, both within ourselves and among each other together, so that we will finally be able to say that we are actually experiencing the noosphere palpably. As a consequence, we will discover that we have awakened or evolved a new hypersensitive organ within our corpus collosum—the holomind perceiver.

When you come to understand the psi bank and the noosphere as also containing the timing codes for the release and establishment of information for different changes and mutations in the evolutionary process—then you see that we are gearing up for the next major evolutionary shift. Any knowledge that we avail ourselves to, regarding the noosphere and the psi bank, quickens and precipitates the mental/spiritual quantum shift in our unconsciousness and in our own self-perception. It is amazing to consider that all of this has actually been timed

Now we are at the phase of developing more of what we might call conscious teams or conscious noospheric cells to activate the psi bank even more synchronously and simultaneously around the planet.

and programmed; even these words that you are now reading are part of the whole overall grand timing program of the noosphere to get itself into a state of maximum self-reflectiveness. This is all informed by Cosmic History.

So we see that the Cosmic History, on the one hand, is being engendered through two avataric agents—who birthed it through focused and consistent tutorials, yoga, meditation, writing, editing and contemplation, which all have an effect on the Cosmic History structures in the noosphere. This is to ensure that when the full advent of the noosphere occurs, Cosmic History will become a part of "normal" consciousness.

This text is for the purpose of making conscious the program of Cosmic History which has always existed, but before now was an unconscious program, waiting to be cracked open. Now we are cracking open that program and in so doing we are bringing the vast store of knowledge contained within Cosmic History to Earth in the form of seven volumes. This act registers in the noosphere, making Cosmic History an increasingly conscious governing component of the psi bank and, therefore, guiding mechanism of the noosphere.

Noospherics 101

We are the noospheric chips in the noospheric 101 incubation chamber. In *Time and the Technosphere*, a noospheric chip is described as a human operating in the noosphere, holonomically resonant with intrinsic 13:20 codes of synchronic order, capable of interacting with the psi bank to participate in the creation of Earth's rainbow brain.

> *"As a noospheric chip, the human is a fractal reflector of the 13:20 timing frequency. Midway between the bipolar oscillator and the noospheric psi bank plates, the human noospheric chip is designed to receive, transduce, and transmit programs from the crystal core by synchronizing these programs with the psi bank. This is a process that can occur only within the construct of the regular harmonic sequence provided by the noospheric timing gauge of the Thirteen Moon/28-day calendar. Interaction with the crystal core can only be through telepathic means, and the human—as the midway point between the core and the electromagnetic fields—is like a sensitive piece of litmus paper. To understand the human in this way is to totally redefine the reality of what it means to be human on Earth."* Time and the Technosphere p. 139-40

It is very important for people to keep in mind the process by which a type of divine descent such as the principle of Cosmic History occurs and how it becomes conscious and manifest through the agents or noospheric chips whom it is intended to activate. These particular noospheric chips are also intended to embody as divine incarnates the principle of the Cosmic History and the correlate principle of the closing and the regeneration of the cycle, which is what this particular manifestation point of Cosmic History is all about. We could say that it is what called this manifestation of Cosmic

History into existence—this principle of the closing and the regeneration of the cycle.

Compared to consensual reality, the agents of Cosmic History feel really slowed down; when in actuality they are operating at hyperspeed. Like when you eat a jalapeno pepper, it feels hot, but then after awhile you think that it is actually cool. It is the same for the avataric agents. They are operating at hyperspeed, though it seems they are not moving at all. But they are operating at mental and spiritual hyperspeed, processing mentally and spiritually at a rate that is unimaginable to most people.

This hyperspeed processing of the spiritual consciousness is actually the effect of the binary engines, the avataric agents, being in high performance operation—in other words, being in a state of calm where you are focused and just doing what needs to be done with the activity of Cosmic History. Then actually the engines are running at a very clear and clean level of performance. We describe this because this is what the human species is supposed to be experiencing in its next evolutionary plateau.

In other words, the high level vertical time spiritual activity which registers as almost like nothing on the physical/horizontal plane of space is what we are looking at as being the normative functioning of the human being, once we elevate into the plateau which is known as the noosphere. Part of what keeps the performance of the binary engines at an increasingly high performance level is the engagement of the noosphere through the *Mother of All Programs (MOAP)* and through the activation of the different psi bank based areas of content of Cosmic History.

Activation of the MOAP codes is a primer to make the corpus collosum the self-synchronizing, self-transcendent organ for the next stage of evolution. The holomind perceiver is the hyper-extended sense organ that evolves from the corpus collosum through activation of the MOAP. These areas of content are being defined and refined by the process of spiritual acceleration, which is entering us more and more into the noosphere. The goal of this acceleration is ultimately to set a standard or example of the transformation of matter itself.

Inner Becomes The Outer

The more you are refashioned from the inside, the more evident that your inner transformation manifests through your outer form. Your outer form then becomes increasingly transparent so that your inner form can communicate through its transparency, without having to say what it is or even say anything about it—it just communicates by the power of its being. The point of giving the example of the two avataric agents is only to emphasize the power and continuing need of ongoing discipline to reshape and retool the inner self or the divine self. Through discipline, the two avataric agents are commanded to rise to a level of such profound purity, simplicity and innocence of being and intention only so that the Cosmic History can be communicated in a way that is extraordinarily supernatural, yet comforting because it is (and they are, In Lak'ech) the evolutionary potential. This is as it should be because avataric emanations are like cosmic triggers or binary engines (reminding you that it is all your Self). They then are functioning as the agents who cause the noosphere to become more and more activated. This means that the noosphere is absorbing into itself the self-reflective mind and consciousness of increasing numbers of people.

This can only happen because the two agents have totally kicked into the noosphere and have started sending out, without even intending to, vibrational plasmic frequencies that color and affect the entirety of the noosphere. And those who are receptive get absorbed into it. The ladder of perfection is unending. It only ends when you reach God, but even the highest angels can only get close to God. Once you have started to climb this ladder, you cannot climb down, only up, up, up. This ladder spirals like the higher chain of the DNA–this is the ascent of spirit to return to the Source.

The understanding of this point should heighten and increase what we might refer to as the spiritual self-sufficiency of the binary engines, so that more and more it will be understood how complete everything already is within the mental field of the Noospherics 101 laboratory. The spiritual self-sufficiency only has one purpose and that is to continue the transmutation, transformation and transcendence of the spiritual tendencies of the two agents. The two agents can only go higher and higher. The higher they go the more beneficial it is for humanity. The example of these two agents is to demonstrate that the more self-perfect and spiritually self-sufficient you become the more it benefits the whole of humanity.

Spiritual self-sufficiency is a function of discipline, which is a continuing spiritual sacrifice of the lower self for the sake of inner perfection, or the coming out and polishing of the divine incarnate self or form within. In this regard, there will always be human dramas happening in the external realm, but the disidentification of the human drama becomes easier the more it is understood that an irreversible spiral of self-transcendence has already been engaged. If we stop to look and see, then everything else stops. If we continue going up, then everything continues to go up. This is why stopping to speculate about "others" is foolish as it only hinders your own rate of evolution.

Once you have started to climb this ladder, you cannot climb down, only up, up, up. This ladder spirals like the higher chain of the DNA– this is the ascent of spirit to return to the Source.

There are many other mysterious manifestations and revelations that will occur with actual forms of behavior within the context of the upward spiral of transcendence in relationship to the redemption and compassion of all of the other beings who are involved in the life matrix of which we are still a part.

When we get to the point where the human species graduates into the noosphere, then Cosmic History will become like second knowing—it will become the normal perception. Along with the study material of the seven volumes of the *Cosmic History Chronicles* (which will open people more and more to tune into the already self-existing Cosmic History codes) there will also be an ultimate congruence of the disposition of the human thinking layer to be totally in alignment with the actual structure, purpose and nature of Cosmic History.

Just to summarize, we are dealing with the descent of a divine principle, which on one level forms part of the present day Earth consciousness, but on another level can willfully and voluntarily leave the Earth consciousness and be in noospheric consciousness. Noospheric consciousness makes it possible for Cosmic History to be received and transmitted. Because the two avataric agents (as the principles of closing and regenerating the cycle) are embedded in the templates of noospheric consciousness, Cosmic History is birthed into the noospheric environment. In this way, Cosmic History bears that hallmark and the very nature of the context of the information is communicated subliminally and can be regarded as the "noospheric condition." In this "noospheric condition," Cosmic History acts as a type of psychoactive agent on the mind because it is presenting new information, which was formatted in the noosphere. It is collective because it is not coming from an individual voice, but is a collective manifestation. This is why we speak of the noosphere as being the goal of Cosmic History. When the noosphere actually becomes conscious, then within a generation or two, Cosmic History will be absorbed into the human being as part of its innate functioning. At this point, the goal of Cosmic History—to be reabsorbed into the conscious entity of intelligence—will have been attained.

Chapter 11
Multidimensional Paranormality and Cosmic Science

To participate in the noosphere is such a gigantic leap of consciousness that we can only begin to imagine how vast the scope of this shift is going to be. To facilitate the major adjustment to human consciousness involved in activating the noosphere, it is necessary to cultivate multidimensional paranormality. First, you have to consider that the noosphere is a sensing organism, as it were, planetary in size. Think of yourself in relationship to the planet and then think how vast is this noospheric planetary mental sensing organism. Not only is the noosphere as the planet mind vast in scope, but it also extends normally into other dimensions as well.

In other words, the noosphere is encoded with the multidimensional scale of the universal cosmic mind, the root of all of Cosmic History and Cosmic Science (described in Vol. II). So to fully participate in the potential offered by the advent of the noosphere, it is well that the human now begins to consider multidimensional paranormality. Cosmic Science provides the key tool for understanding and activating multidimensional paranormality. When these forces and powers are properly understood and intelligently developed they give a new and entirely different meaning to life.

While multidimensional operations of consciousness are normal for the noosphere, for the human this is considered paranormal. Parapsychology, as described by Cosmic Science defines the type of phenomena that characterize factors of the mind that are beyond reason—or paranormal phenomena. These are elements or components that stretch the mind and move it into higher states of consciousness. According to Cosmic Science, the paranormal phenomenon is a real fact whose origin not being known can lead to fanaticism, hysteria or madness. Its explanation is through the elements of the fourth and fifth dimensions.

Many people have paranormal experiences and think that they are going crazy because their experience is devoid of any "common" reference points. The Cosmic Science goes on to say: "The term spirit corresponds to a higher divine plane of the seventh dimension, a plasmatic radial level or the place of the origin of spirit." Why do we have a spirit that is being evolved? What is the purpose of this? What is the meaning of this? God is running the show, so there must be a divine reason for everything. Consciousness itself in relation to the universe is very limited. Paranormal phenomena help stretch the mind towards those places of consciousness that would seem to indicate some kind of higher level of existence that we are supposed to be striving for.

These paranormal powers that we are speaking of are really comparable to what are referred to in Hindu and Buddhist practice as the siddhis, which we touched on in Chapter 5. In most people, these paranormal powers or siddhis, though innate, are rather remote and seemingly difficult to attain, which is really to the point. The paranormal powers exist as evolutionary potentialities, they are *not* the purpose of evolution, but in the process of the evolution of greater consciousness they are the side effects or the fruit. As such, to attain the paranormal powers requires exertion, discipline of mind and effort— and even then—the effort is not to attain powers, but to gain self-mastery or self-realization, which is the goal of yoga and meditation. Today, some people may clamor after these powers or regard with great esteem people who display these powers, but that is, for the most part, an immature demonstration of spiritual materialism and spiritual poverty.

Magick is derived from *magisterial* supreme wisdom. This magick is also established on a divine plane of the fifth dimension with the higher self, which permits and supervises all paranormal phenomena in order to awaken consciousness to the higher planes of coexistence. If we did not have paranormal phenomena we might be sucked in forever to the pure material plane analysis of life and reality. Paranormality exists to awaken us to this higher phenomenon. The fifth-dimensional entity runs by the command of God.

In the *Holy Quran*, God tells Moses that he should not be afraid when he meets Pharaoh and the magicians—and that he should throw down his staff. Moses obeys God and throws down his staff, which, much to his surprise, turns into a serpent. This means that God allowed Moses' higher self to perform "magick" in order to demonstrate to Pharaoh that Moses' power was divine and greater than any (lower) "magick" that Pharaoh could devise. This illustrates how God is beyond any kind of definition and has innumerable capacities.

From the sorcerer's perception, Cosmic History is an act of magick, which, through skillful means, is employed in dissolving the illusion of reality with a superior construct. The word "magick" is derived from the combination of the two words: manas, which is Sanskrit for "mind", and maya, which means "illusion." True magick abolishes all previous systems of knowledge. Magick is the supramental power to exert influence over natural processes or forces. The sorcerer uses everything in practical application for the purpose of investigating Cosmic History. The goal is to change the evolutionary make-up, pointing it toward what it is to be a galactic human.

INTRODUCTION TO COSMIC SCIENCE & PARALLEL WORLDS

In order to cultivate multidimensional paranormality, you must first have some understanding about the parallel worlds of coexistence. This means you have to break free of the bondage, first of all, of thinking that this life you are living during this moment represents the only world that exists. For example, when we dream, where is that world? Or even when we daydream, where is that world? Or when we have a déjà vu, as fleeting as it might be, is that in a world next to this world? The point is that we cannot fathom other dimensions without first having some perception or understanding that this physical plane of reality of everyday waking consciousness is not the only world.

The first-dimension is the initiation of polarity and goes from the protoelectrical ethers to the myriads. The second dimension is the parton (a quantum of energy) dimension of the primary electrical forces. So first you have polarity and then a quantum of energy. The third dimension is the atomic and subatomic, which is that which is detected as matter or everything that characterizes the third dimension. Matter is reduced to its simplest components as the atomic and subatomic structures so that everything in the third-dimensional material plane is a function of structures of atomic and subatomic particles. Third-dimensional space includes height, width and depth. Depth is the third dimension. The third dimension is also the dimension of the "I", the ego or the self.

Cosmic Science tells us that the genetic pattern gives origin to the simultaneous formation of two biological entities, the third and the fourth-dimensional. The Law of Time says the same thing, *"All biological entities called humans possess a holon, a fourth-dimensional double, dormant and repressed during 12:60 deviance from the norm. Activation of holon is an evolutionary development dependent upon release of organic instinctual consciousness into telepathic continuing consciousness."* 11.1—*Dynamics of Time*.

The fourth dimension is also atomic and subatomic, though with a level of lower *valence* or a valence of less frequency. Valence refers to the cohering, adhesive power of a material structure. The higher the valence the denser the structure. The lower the valence the less dense the structure. It is categorically stated that the valence of the fourth dimension is ten times lower than the valence of the third dimension. This means that we are dealing with fundamentally etheric substance. The fourth-dimensional self is referred to as the "It" or "other." The fourth-dimensional self is the aspect of our being that actually experiences paranormal phenomena.

The fourth dimension consists of the atomic and subatomic particles with a valence 10 x lower where the atoms and molecules are "spread out." The more spread out it is the more etheric and nonsubstantial, although it might look like a human only more transparent, you can see through it. Also, time is the fourth dimension which means the more spread out the atomic structure is the more etheric is its substance, the more etheric is its substance, the more time occurs (in relation with the third-dimension)—this is known as *fractal time compression* or *expansion*, depending on which dimension is providing the perspective. For example, two mechanical hours in the third

... we cannot fathom other dimensions without first having some perception or understanding that this physical plane of reality of everyday waking consciousness is not the only world.

dimension is the same as 20 hours in the fourth dimension, according to Cosmic Science. In this context, life is specified as being a function of a parallel process that occurs in the third and fourth dimensions.

Not everything in the third and the fourth dimensions is life, but life occurs in the third and fourth dimensions. Also, the first and the second dimensions are subsumed in the third dimension because the principle of polarity and electricity underlies the spin and what we might call the electrical charge of the entire universe which is catalyzed into the fact that every atom has an electron. An electron is a very evolved form or advanced form of the primal polarity or the primal partons or the primal electrical charges. From this view it would seem that time and space only correlate with the first four dimensions.

The fifth-dimensional being is the pure electronic level or the "superior I" or the higher self. This is the divine playing with the spiritual guide, the essence, the master of the cosmic God in us—the guardian angel etc. The fifth dimension is the space where time no longer operates and reincarnation no longer exists. Reincarnation occurs only at the atomic and subatomic level. From a purely biospheric point of view, reincarnation is nothing but the biogenic migration of atoms. There is a finite amount of biomass so that whenever a member of a given species dies, its spirit essence is reborn as the same. For example, if a raccoon is killed on the highway another raccoon will be born. The species recycles itself and the same is true for the human. It's just the cellular matter that is constituted as particular types of atoms and particles that is recycled. Extinction happens when death occurs at a faster rate than procreation and the procreative element is finally annihilated in the species.

The consciousness of a soul is another matter. The soul does not transmigrate so much as the memory patterns do. If you look at it from the Quranic point of view, you have a body and a soul. Did the soul exist in prior bodies? The souls of most people are relatively primitive so there is really nothing to transmigrate. Most people end up succumbing to conditioned beliefs because the material that had been transmigrating carries certain memory patterns or memory codes predisposing the being to follow the conditioning of whatever particular culture they were born into.

When does the soul begin? When is the soul formed? It is the soul that is put to the test and the body is the instrument of the test or the gate. The body is put out there to see which way it will go. The third-dimensional ego is the aspect of being identified with the body. Like when someone says, "But I'm Martha Simpson" or "I'm Julio Hernandez." The test is to see whether the human soul is going to identify with the third-dimensional body or if the soul will hear a higher voice of the fourth-dimensional double crying for help.

RECONNECTING THE THIRD AND FOURTH-DIMENSIONAL ENTITIES

The first aspect of life presented in the Cosmic Science text is the redefinition of the human purely as a generator of energy known as the *quantinomio citiobarico*. Quanto is number and cito is cell and barico is pressure. So the quantinomio citiobarico is the quantic number of cell pressure of the main energy circuits in the body, which are the chakras or forcefields which hold the etheric body together in the entire aura. Cosmic Science shows how everything affects us by activating our chakras—then Zap!—we are there inside our body.

Western science is filled with "scientific terms," but what good is a quark or quasar if you don't know how they affect you? In its structure, Cosmic Science takes you from subatomic physics to subatomic electronics/plasmas, which leads you immediately into the chakra system and then into a very interesting definition of genetics, only then on to atomic physics. This approach leads to the exploration of parallel worlds, then to *psychocybernetics*, which shows how the areas of mind/consciousness are configured and how they function all together. It takes time and study to see how all of this is put together. This will be further expounded in Volume II of the *Cosmic History Chronicles*.

The quantinomio citobarico is presented early in the Cosmic Science text to demonstrate that the primal structures of the universe and cosmos (inclusive of the plasmas, partons and so on) are not something far away. They affect our system first through the subtle etheric bodies, chakras and subtle nervous system. When studying quantum physics and mechanics, you must continuously reflect upon where everything is

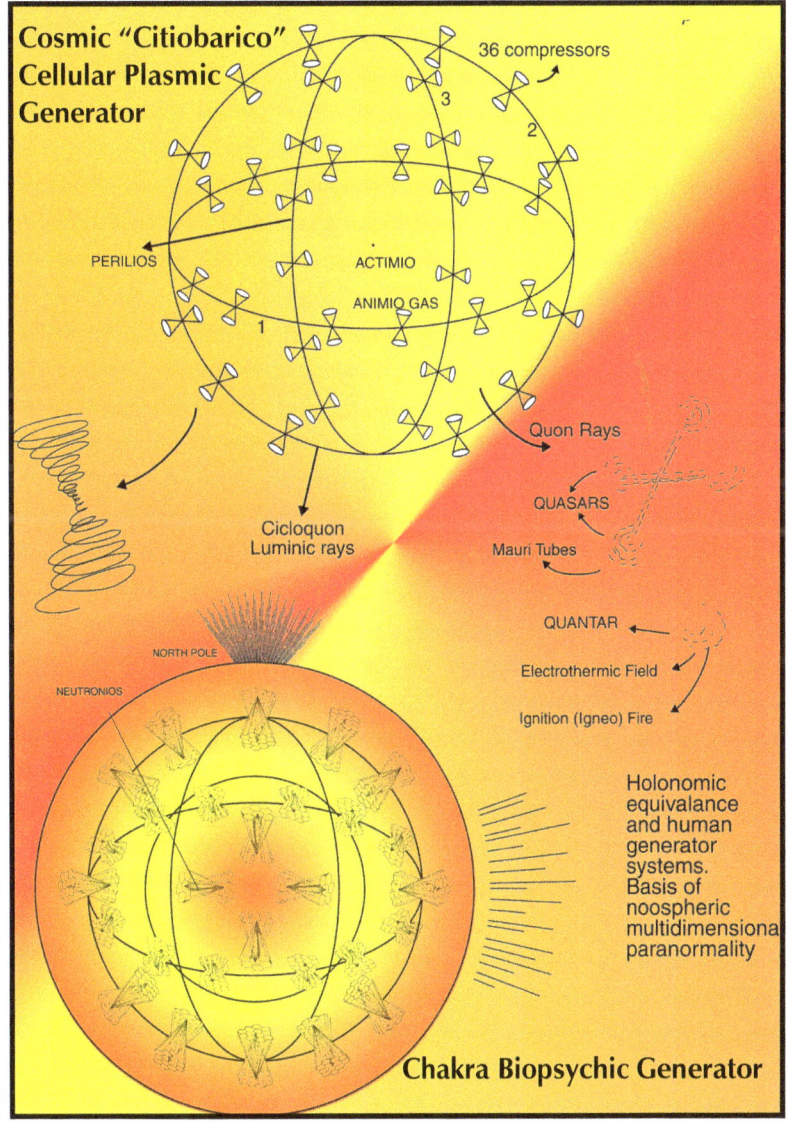

located inside of you. Cosmic Science says you cannot separate what is happening in your body from everything else within the atomic structure, and you cannot separate the whole evolutionary process that Cosmic Science is describing from the psychology of your own spiritual development. This is a fundamental point in developing multidimensional powers. That also establishes the fact that the essential part of the human being is the fourth-dimensional.

To learn to coordinate the third-dimensional being with the fourth-dimensional being is a major purpose of life and opens us to the multidimensional paranormality, which is actually the norm. This is why the practice of yoga is so important. It coordinates the physical body with the etheric body, though it is not the same as athletics or sports. Yoga or any other psychophysical exercises coordinate the etheric and third-dimensional bodies so that the evolutionary process is being served and we can evolve from the fourth-dimensional entity to the fifth-dimensional. The instrument for evolution is our third-dimensional body.

Cosmic forces and electrical processes are what constitute our being. The study of Cosmic Science is for the point of understanding seventh ray ceremonial magick so you can be the facilitator of the transformation of the planetary mental field, which is a function of electronic lines of force. When this is understood, then you can know where to create certain leverage or pressure points to shift the mental vibrational frequency and therefore shift all the electronic lines of force in the entire noosphere. The purpose of this is for the quickening of the etheric body for the evolutionary transformation away from the current world hallucination which includes the present form of science.

Since we are using a number of different terms that are very closely related in meaning, there is a need for clarification. What the Law of Time refers to as the holon is the more precise definition of what is more vaguely referred to as the etheric or subtle body. The etheric body is the mantle or vehicle of the soul. The purpose of the holon/etheric body is to allow the soul maneuverability.

According to Cosmic Science, the formation of the fifth-dimensional entity does not give origin to a perishable biological entity, but to an electronic entity with a human aspect that is yet eternal. It is the fifth-dimensional entity of both Votan and the Red Queen that created the sorcerer/apprentice relation. They had to have a third-dimensional situation where the potential for learning was maximal. In this case we are dealing with a type of male-female binary crossover principle. It is also older-younger generation which provides the human biological structure to correspond to a pure cosmic principle and template. In a type of fifth-dimensional alchemical soul wedding, the two agents function as a pair of cosmic binary engines on behalf of the advent of the noosphere. The twin souls become the forerunner of new evolutionary types. This precise configuration could only happen at the Closing of the Cycle.

Part IV • Noosphere: The New Earth Consciousness

Six Mental Spheres

The necessary material for the communication between the dimensional entities is formed through the mind, which is the characteristic faculty which distinguishes the human being from the animals. The initial purpose of mind in human evolution is to facilitate communication between the third and fourth dimensions. All of this exists so we can begin to create an upward momentum from the third to the fourth to the fifth dimensions.

Cosmic Science says that between the first and fourth days of birth, six mental spheres of consciousness are inserted into the mind by the entity's own fifth-dimensional guide. These six spheres describe the processes and functionings of mind that are laced with parapsychological phenomena, which actually occur through the preconscious from the fifth-dimensional entity. Paranormal phenomena have the function of attracting the attention of the fourth-dimensional and/or the third-dimensional beings. Mental spheres are connected to third, fourth and fifth-dimensional functionings and provide the being with the capacities to link with interdimensional information.

The center of each of the six mental spheres is constituted of aggregates of *analphas*, the electrical fluid created by the interaction of two partons that give rise to thinking or the capacity to form thoughts. Cosmic Science describes thought as analphic engravings in a series. In this way, the act of thinking is the correct or incorrect manipulation of analphas which are projected in a conscious area always being based on knowledge previously acquired. However, if there is no previously acquired knowledge, with difficulty we will try to establish correct thinking activity to function in whatever situation. According to Cosmic Science, memories are engraved analphas which are stored or archived in the cerebral fissures. Reasoning is the conscious projection of sets of

Whole System operating self of fully conscious Cosmic Human [Homo Noosphericus]

5th Dimensional "Higher Self" "Entity of Control"

non-manifest / manifest

3rd Dimensional "self"

4th Dimensional "other"

plane / plane

Consciousness — Subliminal Consciousness

3 — 6
4 Continuing Consciousness — Superconsciousness
5
2 — Preconsciousness
Subconsciousness — 1

The first Mental Sphere: the Preconscious is the region where parapsychological manifestations and phenomena are produced ... is a direct function of the higher self or the fifth dimensional spirit guide.

Six Mental Spheres

"Each of these six electronic spheres is formed outwardly by a heptagonon of mind externalized as seven cubits - electronic form structures ..."

199

analphic series and selective corresponding action. The series or sets of analphas form patterns that are referred to as logic or reason of varying degrees of consistency.

Each of these six electronic spheres is formed outwardly by a Heptagonon of Mind externalized as seven cubits (electronic form structures are always based on seven part septagonal divisions). Cosmic Science says that once this external structure of the mind is formed, the mental forms are indestructible (eternal), and can be destroyed neither by laser rays, nor by atomic explosion, much less by death of the human being. This means thought-forms of the destroyed worlds remain in circulation however unconsciously.

These six mental spheres include: preconscious, sub-conscious, (discontinuous) consciousness, continuing consciousness, superconsciousness and subliminal consciousness. We will explain these spheres more in depth in following volumes, but for now we will focus on the first mental sphere, the preconscious, since this is the region where parapsychological manifestations and phenomena are produced. This mental sphere covers the cerebellum portion of the brain and is a direct function of the higher self or the fifth-dimensional spirit guide.

In the cerebellum exist three lobes, each with a different function. In the central lobe are received the orders coming from the higher self. If the command is for the fourth-dimensional being, it takes the left lobe. If the command is for the third-dimensional being then the right lobe is utilized. So in this way, it is from the preconscious mental sphere that the evolutive activity of the being of the third- and the fourth-dimensional entities are controlled. This mental sphere serves as the resonance chamber of the physical body where paranormal faculties are developed and stored.

Cosmic Science develops the parapsychological because this is directly where we are going in our mental/spiritual evolution. Before you begin paranormal cultivation, it is important to understand how the mind functions. It is also most important to study all of the synchronic order practices such as the *Dynamics of Time*, the *7:7::7:7 Telektonon* and the *20 Tablets of the Law of Time*. These practices allow you to work

> *Cosmic Science says that once this external structure of the mind is formed, the mental forms are indestructible (eternal), and can be destroyed neither by laser rays, nor by atomic explosion, much less by death of the human being.*

consciously on other aspects of the mind, making it easier to enter these amplified states.

Cosmic Science says that "the amplitude or breadth of the mental ratio is obtained by special practices, telepathy, profound meditation and displacement." Displacement and time travel is what the Law of Time is about—since these are the best ways to get around in this vast universe—to penetrate the universe through the mind—to send a thought from one end of the universe to the other. You can even travel from one part of the universe to the other if you know the right techniques of holographic projection.

"Whole body time transport is the capacity to extend through the now into continuing and super conscious. This is achieved through total holographic projection whose quality is proportionate to the vividness and completeness of the alternative fourth- dimensional personality to incorporate the third-dimensional internal body sensation usually referred to as 'self.' " 13.2 Dynamics of Time.

Four Levels Of Consciousness

Cosmic Science also describes four levels of consciousness including: *Beta, Alpha, Theta* and *Delta*. The brain wave oscillations for the four levels of consciousness are as follow:
- Beta: 14+ cycles per second (waking state)
- Alpha: 7-13 cycles per second (meditative state)
- Theta: 4-6 cycles per second (trance state)
- Delta: Illumination

Beta is consciousness and mediumship. Alpha is profound meditation. Theta is the dream state. Delta is illumination. These levels are shown as having functions on the third and fourth spheres and also functions on the fifth and sixth spheres. The third and fourth spheres are conscious and continuing conscious and the fifth and sixth spheres are superconscious and subliminal consciousness. On the third and fourth level the alpha is described as profound meditation or concentration. When you can really hold an asana you are generating alpha waves. In the fifth and sixth spheres the alpha is hypnosis. When you are hypnotized then you are in the alpha state—or a state of profound meditation. The deepest meditation is samadhi or the state of self-hypnosis. This is a trance where you remember everything you perceived. That is very profound meditation. Beta state is the conscious waking state. Right now we are basically generating beta waves. In the fifth and sixth spheres, the beta waves characterize what is called *mediumship*. A medium functions as a channel for someone or something else.

The third and fourth spheres are the same as every day so-called unexamined normal consciousness. Theta is what you give off in the sleep or dreaming state. Though we might usually think of the dreaming state as what occurs when you sleep, in actuality this state characterizes much of so-called every day consciousness. In other words, most of us are sleepwalkers and our minds unconsciously drift from one topic, theme or fixation to another without any awareness of it—this is no different than the dream state. Delta is the state of illumination. The delta state is the result usually of a concentrated effort at controlling the mind from its ceaseless thinking process which characterizes the theta state. So then delta is actually just the threshold to the alpha state which is profound meditation. We also experience the delta state when we have profound spontaneous insights and there is a floodlight as it were on the insightful perception we are having.

Paranormal Powers Defined

Cosmic Science provides descriptions of various paranormal powers. At this point, to demonstrate better the range of multidimensional paranormality and to introduce you directly to the method of Cosmic Science, we present a portion of a glossary in order to inspire the imaginal vision of Cosmic History lying dormant in you, (a more detailed glossary can be found in CH Vol. IV). The purpose of knowing or developing these various skills is to enable us to expand upon the potential given to us by operating in the noosphere. All things are possible to those willing to make an effort to earn them.

Bilocation - Ability to be in two places at the same space-time moment. This is closely related to time travel. The fourth-dimensional entity travels while the third-dimensional entity remains grounded. Bilocation is only permitted by the higher self among people whom it judges agreeable and is always for the purpose of opening to higher consciousness. When you sleep, the fourth-dimensional is displaced to a conscious level. This is a very strong experience that then permits the third-dimensional to see everything that is realized by the fourth-dimensional through the mental screen. During this experience, the organism releases lactic acid through the distention of the muscles.

Clairaudience - Development of the auditory faculty in order to be able to hear messages, sounds, music or dimensional voices coming from the fourth-dimensional or fifth-dimensional Self. These phenomena can be heard either by displacement of

Most of us are sleepwalkers and our minds unconsciously drift from one topic, theme or fixation to another without any awareness of it—this is no different than the dream state.

the fourth-dimensional holon or by direct permission of the fifth-dimensional. For example, the *Telektonon Prophecy* was written strictly through clairaudience, which Valum Votan received by hearing and transcribing. This phenomena is picked up at the Beta level (wakefulness), or at the Alpha level (concentration), or at the Theta level (sleep or dream).

Clairvoyance - Projection to a conscious level of interdimensional situations or facts. The higher self allows information to come through in mediumship or channeling. Actual visualization or remote viewing characterizes this capacity.

Disappearance - *Kemio* discharge of static distension. (Kemio, like Kum, refers to primary electrical lines of force with differing effects in the third-dimensional physical plane, such that the 3-D molecular structure phases into pure fourth-dimensional status no longer visible in the material world.)

Interdimensional Communication - Permitted by the fifth-dimensional entity in the case of disincarnation. Only applicable during the two years following death, after which time it is the higher self which adopts the voice or disincarnate persona in order to open consciousness in the subject.

Levitation - This is an individual inversion of polarity of magnetic fields, which can be achieved by knowing the mechanism, or by counting on the help and desire of one's higher self.

Materialization - Appearance and disappearance of objects. Depolarization of energetic fields of objects existing in the fourth dimension and to which are applied a cohesive magnetic discharge (Kum) so that the encountered objects—atoms and molecules—are distended (10x) and joined together to appear as the object.

Mediumship - That instrument which lends itself in order to serve as the conscious or unconscious means between one's higher self and the one who hears the message, which will be in accord with ends that are pursued.

Premonition or Precognition - Similar to a *presentiment*, which is a projection of your higher self onto the mental screen of your imaginal viewing room.

Retrocognition - Viewing or remembering facts that occurred in the past or in past lives, also received by permission of the higher self; can be either at the Alpha or the Theta levels, also screened in your imaginal viewing room.

Telekinesis - Movement of objects from a distance. It is not a power of mind over matter. The phenomenon attains its end with the help of the fourth-dimensional entity.

Telepathy - Transmission projected through the two higher selves or fifth-dimensional beings of two people who are in communication with each other. This is a point of action which depends on complete acceptance of relaxation in what you are doing and who you are. Once you get into a deeply relaxed state of self-acceptance, telepathy can be explored and incorporated in your every day operations. But, it means that your third- and fifth-dimensional selves are in perfect coordination through the medium of your fourth-dimensional self.

Televidencia - Knowledge of facts which have occurred at a distance. Projection from the fifth dimension across the mental screen from the preconscious to the conscious (during Alpha or Theta states). Televidencia is similar to *hypnogagic reverie* and also relates to the electrical technology of television, where sound and light are converted into electrical impulses and recorded into light and sound waves.

These terms deserve to be very well studied. They are keys to a road map of interdimensional paranormality that connects our multiple self. It is important to understand these processes and how they work to create the third-, fourth- and fifth- dimensional selves. All of it is to create a triadic functioning self. The mind exists and is known about because we have a biological form. Where does the mind exist? Is mind just cognizable in the human being who is characterized as a living being? Does a crystal have consciousness? What is the difference between a crystal, consciousness and mind? These are questions we have to be thinking about. We have to see how we can put this understanding into the context of what and how we are evolving into the noosphere. How will this help us? How will this help the people who are not moving into the noosphere? Or will everyone move into the noosphere just like that?

We have to get as objective an understanding as possible. Then we can deal with psychological problems by referring them to the structure of the mind and the different components, elements and possibilities of the mind described by Cosmic Science. These are descriptions that come from the pure cosmic perspective of an electrostatic sphere of all embracing consciousness.

It seems worthwhile to take the description of mind and being that appears in Cosmic Science as a more objective criterion than the criteria that exists in the contemporary schools of psychology. The contemporary schools of psychology are fundamentally geared at dealing with the consensus reality, whether they define a point of view beyond consensus reality or not. Nonetheless, the purpose of all techniques are for coping with the consensual reality or helping people redefine the nature of reality—but it is still the consensus reality of the technosphere.

All of this has meaning because we know that we are headed for the noosphere; we are headed for UR (Universal Recollection) and we want to have some understanding of the nature of the mind of the noosphere or the mind of the Earth. How do these analyses and descriptions of multidimensional paranormality prepare us for understanding the noosphere and the collective mind? What do human beings need to know in order to transform their present state of consciousness? How do we develop an educational process that stipulates that the human being is a cosmic being that lives in a world of order and harmony? We must reeducate the human into understanding his or her being and power in the cosmos with a sense of elegance and beauty.

The lower magick hallucination is what we are undoing, just like Padmasambhava quelled the demons of Tibet. Same thing for us now except rather than the demons of Tibet, you are quelling the demons of materialism in the artificial timing programs that dominate the planet. To be effective at this, you must synchronically activate the function of ceremonial magick, which is further elucidated in Chapter 12. These are the nuts and bolts of Cosmic Science.

Ceremonial magick and the correct application of Cosmic Science are of utmost importance to make a shift in the planetary mental field so it is acting in accord with the biosphere/noosphere transition. The principles of the Cosmic Science are in alignment with the principles of the Second Creation; they have just been covered over by Babylonian science. Everything we experience *is* Cosmic History. That is why your identification must change to that of a planetary sorcerer cultivating your multidimensional paranormal powers to aid in the supermental evolution of the planet. Nothing else exists or matters.

Chapter 12
Ceremonial Magick

with special application to Planet Sorcery for the Closing of the Cycle

Ceremonial magick is the peaceful art of removing or expelling the grip of a lower illusion and magick with the truth, which in its relative form appears as a higher and more convincing illusion—and hence is preferable to the one it is replacing. Pure intention as everything. All true magick comprehends that, for most people, reality consists of a set of images programmed into the mind. To change the reality is to introduce an image or set of images at precisely the right moment—so the new image set erases and replaces the previous image set. This action presupposes a knowledge of the key images that hold the belief system in place, knowledge of the right moment of receptivity and knowledge of the proper means for administering the precise exchange of image/symbol/tool so that a transfer of image occurs effortlessly and is accepted immediately—and without question.

This type of magickal exchange is most effective when it is accompanied by or embedded in an enactment appropriate to the meaning of the image transfer—such enactment is further enhanced by sound or music which is instantly associated with the new image and higher illusion. To accept this technique as planet sorcery represents both the highest and most challenging level of ceremonial magick. But this is the only way to affect a closing of the cycle, which will result in an irreversible mind shift.

Planet sorcery must comprehend the common denominator transcending all sectarian beliefs and ideologies among 6 billion humans; it must assess the means at its disposal for delivering the "mind blow" at just the right level so it impacts the greatest number of people simultaneously; and it must be prepared to follow the delivery with a comprehensive program consistent with the expectations aroused by the new image of reality.

As we mentioned in previous chapters, television and the Internet (inclusive of all the attendant sub technologies, computer, cell phone, radio and tele-fax, etc.) comprise the virtual noosphere or cybersphere. Television is the virtual cognizing mind of planetary being and the Internet is the communication storage and retrieval or "virtual psi bank." It is these two technologies that hold in place the 6 billion humans by a single virtual nervous system, which in effect renders the 6 billion humans as a single entity—one planetary being. It is this virtual entity that must be turned over and galvanized in a single stroke into the fully conscious and genuinely unified noosphere of planet Earth. This is the object of ceremonial magick/planet sorcery.

Idiom of communication is also a primary concern in this process—this refers to the appropriate artistic form by which the magickal act is to be affected and systematically reinforced following the key moment. If these preliminary considerations are studied and properly comprehended, then the planet sorcery may be effectively applied as an act of ceremonial magick that embraces the world soul through skillful utilization of its virtual/electronic nervous system. This completes the first step. The second step involves the concrete real time strategy.

Part IV • Noosphere: The New Earth Consciousness

The Day Out of Time 2004, White Spectral Mirror, was an example of a focused "real time" act of ceremonial magick. This was an example of a preparatory event for the fulfillment of the seventh ray of ceremonial magick—(everything has to be enacted in seventh ray order and organized with forms to produce a new civilization—this is the premise behind Planet Art Network). We are instruments to the will of expression. The essence becomes the process of manifesting the seventh ray ceremonial magick. If we understand this then we can make a clean break so that by the Day out of Time 2012 the entire world will be celebrating a permanent Whole Earth Festival.

Each of the seven years of the Mystery of the Stone (2004-2011) represent one of the seven rays of creation or the summation of divine consciousness. (Remember in the cosmic recapitulation which Cosmic History enacts everything primal and creative is by the power of seven summarized by the seventh ray). You are invited to utilize your mind in a massive creative envisioning that will take humanity up to the closing of the cycle for the much anticipated launching of Timeship Earth 2013. The seventh ray is actually the construction of the new civilization. You are being called to participate in the supreme construction of the radiosonic temple of the cosmic human!

The Seventh Ray and The Law of Time

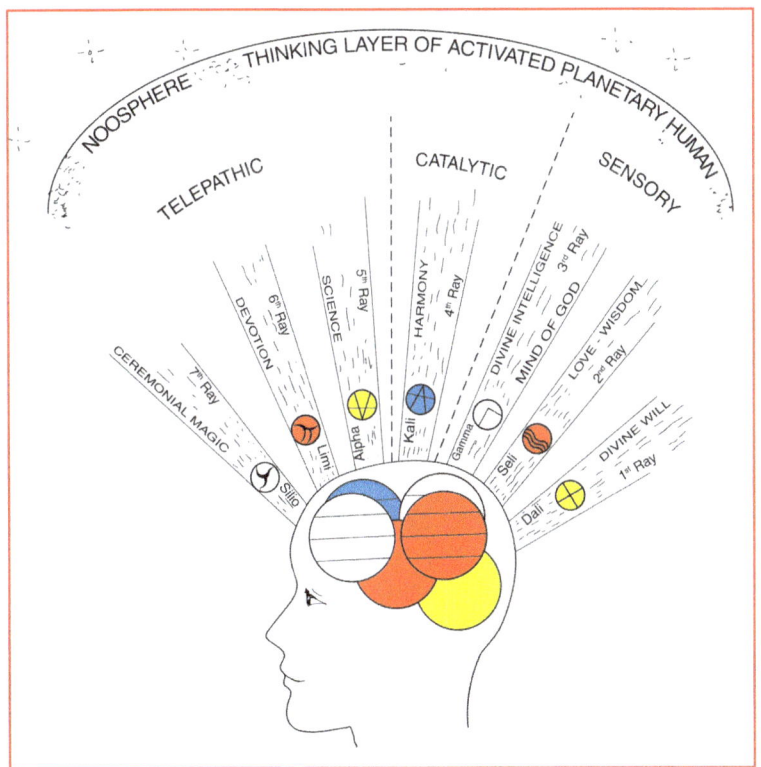

The Seventh Ray will change the theories of the advanced thinkers and future educational systems ... The telepathic combined with the sensory nature of reality will become the base of the telepathic supermental power ... this is how we will produce an electrical phenomenon which produces the coordination of all forms. This is the 7:7::7:7 process.

The Seventh Ray And The Law Of Time

We are describing a process of going from a sixth ray phase of human development to a seventh ray phase of ceremonial magick, as elucidated in the interpretation of Alice Bailey's *The Seventh Ray: Revealer of the New Age*. The seventh ray is the final ray of creation, which is the concluding cycle and phase of human evolution and human development. The conclusion of the sixth ray means that the time of the testing of the historical wo/man is completed and then comes the final judgment/day of decision.

Following the last testing period, there is a final "splitting of worlds" or a separation of souls—then comes the new Heaven and new Earth. At this time, humans are at last free of the original sin, free of accumulated negative karma and free of the effects of the lost worlds. Humans will then be able to operate as liberated souls within the universal order. This is also the interpretation of the Law of Time that proclaims that the human being is redeemed by entering into the New Time.

Developing Continuing Consciousness

When we look at the *Dynamics of Time, the Evolution of Time as Consciousness,* (see page 186) we see what we are talking about in terms of the passage from the sixth to the seventh ray. Just beneath the horizon line of the upper part of this graphic (12:60) would be the sixth ray of civilization. Then at the 13:20 point of the Discovery of the Law of Time where the activation of the seventh ray occurs is the passage from conscious to continuing conscious and the passage from instinct to telepathy.

The seventh ray of ceremonial magick and organization establishes a whole cycle of what is referred to as the Cycle of Return, which goes into the fully fourth-dimensional consciousness. First, we have the hyperorganic phase, then the superconscious phase, then we get to the top and go fully out of manifestation into a subliminal angelic realm. This is a very key passage in which we are involved.

The ceremony of the closing of the cycle clears for once and for all the human soul and the human spirit of all of the negative effects of the original sin or karma or Atlantean lost planet effects. Life is now viewed as a sustained act of ceremonial magick where supernatural enchantment becomes the order of the day, leading to a spiritualization and ritualization of life.

The process of magick for the human species as a unitary organism is articulated at the solstices and equinoxes as well as the galactic synchronization points of the Day out of Time and the New Years Day (Gregorian July 26). To make this transition, which takes us from the lower half of the graphic across the threshold of cosmic consciousness, where all of the evolution of our biological reality (everything we have been thus far) is located, to the noosphere—this is the immediate object of Cosmic History. For the first time, our evolution will rise above that horizon line and we will become increasingly spiritualized in our being and reality.

To accomplish this mission is a phenomenal responsibility and the most extraordinary transition

in the evolution of the human soul! Absolutely everything and every way we are with each other, with ourselves and with the world around us will be mysteriously transformed! When everything transitions into the New Order, life takes on a different meaning and shape in light of the processes of the seventh ray order of ceremonial magick.

Your initiation into the process of ceremonial magick comes first—then comes the planetary initiation of the world soul. When we speak of the world soul we are talking about the spiritual essence of the sum of humanity as it is expressed through the noosphere. Our task is to make the world soul conscious by initiating it into the every day synchronic order of reality so the human beings become stabilized at a higher normative level—so that the human acquires continuing consciousness.

Operating at a normative high level means the focus of the human being, individually and collectively, stabilizes. What we are talking about is the difference between the daily round of life—which is chaotic and governed by the quest for material gain—and the order of everyday life, which is ordained by simple sets of ritual precepts that form a behavior. These ritual precepts then become stabilized at a higher level of consciousness. To a certain degree, by following the synchronic order we establish this pattern or continuum. We know that we are working toward educating humanity about the calendar change and we know that in this act comes a transition from the sixth to the seventh ray. This is part of the Cosmic History process.

Our ability to remain coordinated and stable with this process is a function of yoga, study and meditation. Everything is part of this process. As we go along more and more we will see that through our focus on these practices we are being swept along by some currents of consciousness that exist in the daily round. We must stabilize our third-dimensional being and mind so it becomes subordinate and in accord with this daily sacred round. The whole of the round of life is coordinated as a process of furthering the stabilization of continuing consciousness. This then sets the example for the ritualization of all life.

When life becomes normally ritualized, then the entire universal telepathic linkup is possible. So by the 2013 point the fluid stream of everyday consciousness is stabilized at a high level of continuing consciousness, which is able to easily interface with the noosphere. Then we see that what we think of as our individual cells and bodies is really a function of the noosphere. At this point, the noosphere is lowered into our being and we will become acutely aware that it is the noosphere that is moving and not us. We are absorbed in the noosphere. The whole collective current of thought in the human species is actually the coordination of the noosphere.

Seventh Ray Dreamspell
Transformation of the Planetary into the Noospheric Human

By date of birth everyone on Earth belongs to one of these five families.

Operating within our *Dreamspell Earth Families*—which organize the planet holon—normalizes and regulates not only the mental structure, but the biological process and pattern of existence into more elementary forms of behavior, so that everything becomes highly simplified. Then, the individual is left to operate freely within a finite domain, like a garden or a solar shed, where the energy is moderated and modulated into artistic activities. These artistic activities are coordinated to create a type of human cultural interface with the overall environment. Once normalized, you will find people following the same daily patterns everywhere on the planet. Though the daily patterns are similar, each community calls forth different kinds of cultural responses and textures of expression and ways of doing things.

Through operating daily according to the synchronic order, by the time you reach 2013, you will see it is the noosphere that is doing everything. If you teleport yourself to 2013 and look at a map of the Earth, you will see that what humans used to call cities, towns or points of habitation are now seen as points where the noosphere precipitates into different collective communities. Telepathic links are now established among all the different places on the surface of the earth, which correspond with the coordination of geomagnetism with the noosphere. Operating through the noosphere are the different currents of the atmosphere, which are ionized and electrified into plasmic cells. We are only scratching the surface about the glory of the new reality.

This whole process is of the initiation of the world soul, passing from the sixth to the seventh ray order of reality. This is how the seventh ray order of reality is working. All of the thoughts of what we call the "individuals" who are in the different habitations are actually the thoughts of the noosphere dreaming and experiencing the collective dream. Everybody is really up here. Everyone is meant to become an outlet of the collective dream. The 2013 point is when all of this becomes the evolutionary norm. At this time, there will be an inconceivable amount of mental expansion, like the experiences you have had on mushrooms or LSD but even more naturally far out when you realize that you are always in a common psychic field of consciousness that is coextensive with the whole of the Earth!

The initiation we are undergoing is first with ourselves, then with the entire human race through closing the cycle and making the transition to 2013 Galactic Synchronization. When we speak of Galactic Synchronization, we speak of the noosphere as the galactic mind. Just as the biosphere is the medium on Earth for the transformation of cosmic energy, so the noosphere is the medium for the transmutation and transformation of cosmic or galactic thoughtforms—galactic mind itself. This is a radical evolutionary advance of the mental/spirit bodies into the noosphere. This is why the transition is being made to the seventh ray.

STRIPPING DOWN FOR THE SEVENTH RAY

Here at the sixth ray we have the biosphere [and the noosphere in brackets] (when you write something you put things in parentheses as to what you actually mean but it is implicit). The noosphere is implicit at the moment, but the biosphere is explicit and interconnected. Then there is the technosphere where the communities you see in the noosphere are connected by electronic communication systems—which in many cases have wires but there are also cellulars, cordless phones, etc. (a huge electronic hookup). In the (sixth ray) biosphere, the humans are very nomadic and dispersed. Humans travel everywhere by cars and planes. Humans are nomadic because they are not yet telepathic so they have to travel everywhere. When the noosphere is realized, humans will see a radical shift and the human beings will stabilize. Increasingly, people will find that they can produce or create what they need in their local community or local bioregion. The nomadic human of the sixth ray stage of civilization goes all over the biosphere and

Just as the biosphere is the medium on Earth for the transformation of cosmic energy, so the noosphere is the medium for the transmutation and transformation of cosmic or galactic thoughtforms—galactic mind itself.

disturbs it, especially in the late stage of the industrial process.

In the (seventh ray) noosphere phase this will not happen. On the contrary, the human being will stay put in one area and will reintegrate, restore and regenerate the biosphere. We are attempting to understand the import from the sixth to the seventh ray and the import of the initiatic process, which we refer to as the process of closing the cycle. So we see that the transition from the sixth to the seventh ray is a major planetary initiatic process. The sixth stage is a function of the cosmic unconscious that deals with the original sin and all the karmic residuals of the lost worlds, including Atlantis and Lemuria.

Given that the nature of reality is substanceless and we are here with bodies evolved from the primal seed, we want to simplify the bodily processes to such a degree that over a period of evolution, the body wears itself out from being necessary. This is what we refer to as the increasingly spiritualized nature of reality. Consciousness is liberated from thinking it has to have a body—but only after all karmic debts are paid and everything has been stabilized and pacified—only then can the consciousness slowly leave the body.

This also corresponds to the inevitable processes of stellar evolution; everything we conceive of as the universe is made up of a myriad of stars. Between the stars are plasmas, dark matter, ether, etc., which actually constitute most of the space of the universe. The stars are actually evolving points. When you look up at the sky you do not see the planets of the stars, you just see the stars. The stars are the material condensation points of evolution going through stages and processes until they disintegrate or explode into supernova, and finally return to the condition of God.

Why was it all set up like this? What does it mean when you see this process? The Hindus said it was all *lila*, or play. They said it was a play set up by God and we have to go through the process of playing out different stages of manifestations until we reach the stage of nonmanifestation, and then finally we return to God. Did God do this because He was bored or is this the way God realizes Himself? The universe is God's creation and the existence of that creation through all of its processes is the manifestation of God, so God can realize and know Himself.

This means that all we are is teeny aspects of God going through a process of self-realization. "I am that" is the universe. Like it says in the *Bible*: "I am that I am." Between the first "I am" and the second "I am" is 'that,' which is the process of the universe. This is also like in the Hindu and Buddhist tradition, *Tat Tvam Asi*, in Hindu, "thou art that" or "that art thou" or *ta ta ta*, which is the suchness of that which is the universe and everything has that quality of suchness to it. The Buddhists called it *tathagatagarba*, the womb of enlightenment or the womb of suchness. This is the realization of the universal mind that is coextensive with the universe itself in all of its aspects of creation (having the same quality of suchness that extends out completely to every cell and pore of the universe), all of which is the object and subject of Cosmic History. These examples are for the purpose of laying the foundational context to contemplate the transition from the sixth to the seventh ray.

When we reach the seventh ray, all of the above will be understood as common, ordinary realization—the universe is the process of God realizing Himself as the Absolute. In this way, we say that from the universe is God and everything *is* God. God is in everything. The existence of God's creation through all of its processes is so God can realize and know Himself. If God created everything, it has to be sacred and holy. This includes the trees, rocks, water, ocean, greenery, animals, stars, ether, space, mountains, volcano, crystals, gasses, etc. Everything is an aspect of God's own unfolding to realize Himself as He is: I am That. At the same time, God is all-transcendent. Living with paradox is a stage in the process of our own self-transcendence.

This perception has been entertained by mystics, but it must now be understood as the normative order of reality by every human being. So in the transition from the sixth to the seventh ray this becomes normalized as the every day perception of the human being. We are making a transition in order for the human beings to come to this common level of realization or understanding.

> *God is in everything. The existence of God's creation through all of its processes is so God can realize and know Himself. If God created everything, it has to be sacred and holy.*

Distinctions Among The Rays

We will now see how Alice Bailey views the seven rays and how that accords with the understanding of the Law of Time and of the Mayan prophecies, the Closing of the Cycle and the termination of the cosmic unconscious. (Please note that all quotations in violet are from Alice Bailey, *The Seventh Ray: Revealer of the New Age*). Bailey says that in the transformation from the sixth to the seventh ray cycle, the sixth ray fosters the vision and the seventh ray materializes the vision. The sixth ray fostered the vision of the Rainbow Bridge and the seventh ray will manifest the Rainbow Bridge. The sixth ray fostered the notion of the New Time and the seventh ray manifests the New Time through processes of ceremonial magick.

Many people participate in ceremonial magick without knowing what it is. The sixth ray produced the mystic as its culminating archetype. The seventh ray will develop the magician who works in a field of white magick (to create the New Time and Rainbow Bridge). A magician is someone who is attuned to the knowledge of the processes of nature in such a way that s/he can mentally coordinate these processes with others to create certain effects, which, to most people, are seemingly impossible. White magick means the magician is capable only because of being attuned to the Divine Will.

The sixth ray of idealism and devotion is the part of the evolutionary plan which led to separation, nationalism and sectarianism due to the selective nature of the mind and its tendency to divide and separate. This is the nature of idealistic and devotional mind immersed in the third-dimensional plane of existence. The seventh ray leads to fusion and synthesis which blends spirit and matter. The seventh ray is the noosphere coordinating with the human. In the noosphere is the plan of Shambhala, the prototype of the condition of enlightened society where such a fusion of spirit and matter is possible.

So the synthesis blended with spirit and matter is the medium through which the noosphere can descend into a humanity living in resonance with the geomagnetism of the Earth. That very process itself is a function of the noosphere in resonance with the geomagnetism of Earth—that is the blending of spirit and matter, which Vernadsky referred to as the Psychozoic Era. Psychic is the noosphere and Zoic is humanity in resonance with the Earth—hence the spiritualization of evolution. Alice Bailey sums up the sixth ray activities in the following quotes:

"The sixth ray activity led to formation of ideals and disciples within groups but not in close relation and subject to eternal dissension based on personality reactions. The seventh ray will train and send forth groups of initiates in close union with the planet and with each other. Eventually this type of work will be important. The sixth ray brought the sense of duality to humanity and regarded itself as a physical unity.

"The seventh ray will inaugurate the sense of a higher unity, first, that of the integrated personality for the masses, and second, that of the fusion of the soul and body for the world aspirants. The integrated personality is what we have to strive for in ourselves through different processes of purification."

Bailey then talks about the fusion of soul and body, but the real fusion of the soul and body is the fusion of the noosphere with the habitants of humanity at different points of community.

Part IV • Noosphere: The New Earth Consciousness

"The sixth ray differentiates that aspect of universal electrical energy which we know as modern electricity produced to serve man's material needs. The seventh ray will familiarize man with that type of electrical phenomena, which produce the coordination of all forms" (in the Law of Time this is referred to as the plasmas and their interaction, which coordinates telepathy and physical reality). *"The sixth ray produced the illusions in men's minds of the following knowledge's: knowledge of the physical plane, life and electricity, knowledge of the existence of astral life and illuminations both physical and mental, astrophysics and neuroastronomical discoveries."*

The seventh ray will change the theories of the advanced thinkers and the future educational systems. Everything has intrinsic luminous qualities. The telepathic combined with the sensory nature of reality will become the base of the telepathic supramental power which is established through the double extended electron, the mental electron and the mental electron/neutron—so this is how we will produce an electrical phenomenon which produces the coordination of all forms. This is the 7:7::7:7 process.

Sacrifice Of The Part For The Whole

"The sixth ray is sacrifice and the crucifix is the outstanding symbol—the nebulous idea of simply being kind is the symbol acquired for the unthinking masses. The seventh ray will break the consciousness of the coming initiates. This will inaugurate the age of divine service or group service and sacrifice. The vision of the giving of the individual in sacrifice in service within the group and into the group ideal will be the goal of the masses and advanced thinking in the New Age. In Western humanity, brotherhood would be the key of their endeavor. These words have a wider connotation and significance than thinkers of today can know or understand."

In this regard of sacrifice of the individual, Red Queen represents the sacrifice of the individual to the higher group ideal. By accepting the role as Votan's apprentice, she has sacrificed the normal individual reality of someone in her peer group. This has been subordinated for actual divine service. In this way, she is exemplary. This is the vision of individual sacrifice; this is the message of the Red Queen. You have to sacrifice your individualistic soul for divine service. Red Queen is a prime example, which is the norm for an avataric manifestation.

The Closer of the Cycle came to Cosmic History through a very long and carefully guided process. Red Queen did, too, but she was initiated at age 29, so by the time she is 40 she will have gone through the entire process. This time (2002-2013) represents the time of the "sacrifice" of the individual being or nature to the divine service. After she has gone through the crucible of transformation, her soul will be a force of a very powerful form of expression. One of the main teachings she will have to offer is how she gave herself by divine sacrifice to gain her soul, the universe and cosmic consciousness. This is a universal example and is important to understand.

The noosphere is responsive to the unity and the collective effort of a cooperative group. The seventh ray will convey to the human the power to recognize the cosmic Christ within and to produce the deeper scientific religion of light. This will enable everyone to fulfill the command of the historical Christ and get his/her light to shine forth. The Cosmic Christ is the repository of love within the noosphere. This repository of love becomes available as a reservoir that can go into different conduits or different groups.

"The sixth ray produced the great idealistic religions with their vision and their necessary narrowness that is needed to safeguard infant souls."

Even with Buddhism this occurs. In Islam there is something called *the shariah*, which is the law. But this law is often used to keep people down rather than opening them up to God. This maintains things at a narrow level.

"The seventh ray will release the developed souls from the nursery stage and inaugurate that scientific understanding of the divine purpose which will foster the religious synthesis."

The religious synthesis is UR and the scientific understanding of the divine purpose can only come about through the equalization and harmonization of human intelligence that is a result of every human being following the common harmonic standard of the thirteen moons. By 2012, everyone should be normalized into the pattern of the thirteen moons so a common level of thinking is achieved. The thirteen moons is a scientific method and means for normalizing and harmonizing the human mind at a completely collective planetary level in order to function in a normally and naturally scientific way. In this way, the noospheric mind is able to understand the divine purpose and easily become synthesized as UR/Universal Recollection.

The effect of the sixth ray influence has been to foster separative instincts, dogmatic religion, scientific "facts" or "accuracy," schools of thought with their barriers of exclusiveness and the authority of the cult of patriotism. Instead of devotion to the one God, there is devotion to "my way." The seventh ray prepares the way for the recognition of the wider issues which will materialize as the new world religion that will emphasize unity but bar out uniformity. For instance, if everyone is operating in their Earth families they will form a creative unity but not uniform. Or as the mysterious French psycho-mathematician Charles Henry put it, "As the individual becomes more collective the collective becomes more individual."

SEVENTH RAY SHAMBHALIC REALITY

"The seventh ray will prepare for that scientific technique which will demonstrate the universal light that every form veils and hides and for that internationalism to express itself as practical brotherhood and as peace and goodwill among the peoples."

This effect refers to the telepathic technique based on the 7:7::7:7 practices, which brings out the abilities to perceive light—everything has light quanta. Photons are saturated to create light phenomena. This correlates with zero point energy. Scientists will never fully understand zero point energy until they are in the right time. The only way cooperative internationalism will be fostered is through a disintegration of the nation state as a mental concept, and the formation of the biospheric assembly, which is based on fostering a relationship with the living Earth. The only way you can do this is to establish cooperative bonds between individuals through operating in the Earth families and in the synchronic order. At this point, humanity becomes an open vessel for the influence of Shambhala, which is the simultaneous universe patterns of culture which are meant to be fostered through the Planet Art Network.

Shambhala is organized by hierarchy, moving everything into a total pattern of a true New Age vision. Hierarchy is the normal order of the universe. This is a methodical process. Ceremonial magick is scientific in the way that it represents an order in conformity with hierarchy and with the actual natural laws that govern the resonance of the noosphere and the biosphere. When you are obedient to these laws and you are operating under the Law of Time, in accordance with the Earth families (the new social organization), then you are operating on a basis that produces another experience of reality.

You must understand your role as a seventh ray actor in the process of making the transition from the now disintegrated sixth ray civilization into the seventh ray order of ceremonial magick. This is the majestic initiation, which leads humanity from the realm of the cosmic unconscious, to the realm of the cosmic conscious. This is the function and the purpose of the Closing of the Cycle as a planetary rite of passage.

ENVISIONING THE CLOSING OF THE CYCLE AS CEREMONIAL MAGICK

The Closing of the Cycle and the planetary mystery play includes the preparation of the initiatic rites. The White Spectral Wizard (2003-04) year was the preparatory first act. The initiation of the calendar change on Blue Crystal Storm (2004-05) began the seven years of the Mystery of the Stone and the awakening of the first of the nine *Great Lha* or the *Bolontiku*, Lords of Time and Destiny. This second act of the Blue Crystal Storm year completes the last year of the AC circuit. This refers to the

You must understand your role as a seventh ray actor in the process of making the transition from the now disintegrated sixth ray civilization into the seventh ray order of ceremonial magick. This is the majestic initiation, which leads humanity from the realm of the cosmic unconscious, to the realm of the cosmic conscious.

Aboriginal Continuity, which is reestablished according to the Law of Time and its practices for the restoration of the synchronic order. The fulfillment of the Aboriginal Continuity during the Blue Crystal Storm year results in an increased capacity for higher collective creativity and telepathic knowing. It also completes the Way of Conduct—conformity to the Divine Will, the first of seven rays.

The seven years of the Mystery of the Stone correspond to the seven rays of creation—the first and seventh rays are the rays of initiation. So there is an initiation in the first year to get the show rolling and then comes a deeper initiation in the seventh year. The second year, Yellow Cosmic Seed (2005-06), is the first year of the CA (or Cosmic Awareness); this is the love-wisdom ray. The third and fifth rays are the rays of discipleship. This is when the actual education of humanity in the New Time is established. This begins in the Magnetic Moon year (2006-07), which is appropriate since it represents the entrance to the Green Central Castle of Enchantment. The education of humanity in the New Time is fulfilled in the fifth year, Blue Electric Storm (2008-09). The fourth and the sixth rays have to do with evolution. The evolution of discipleship is introduced during the fourth year, White Lunar Wizard (2007-08). This sets forth an evolutive motion.

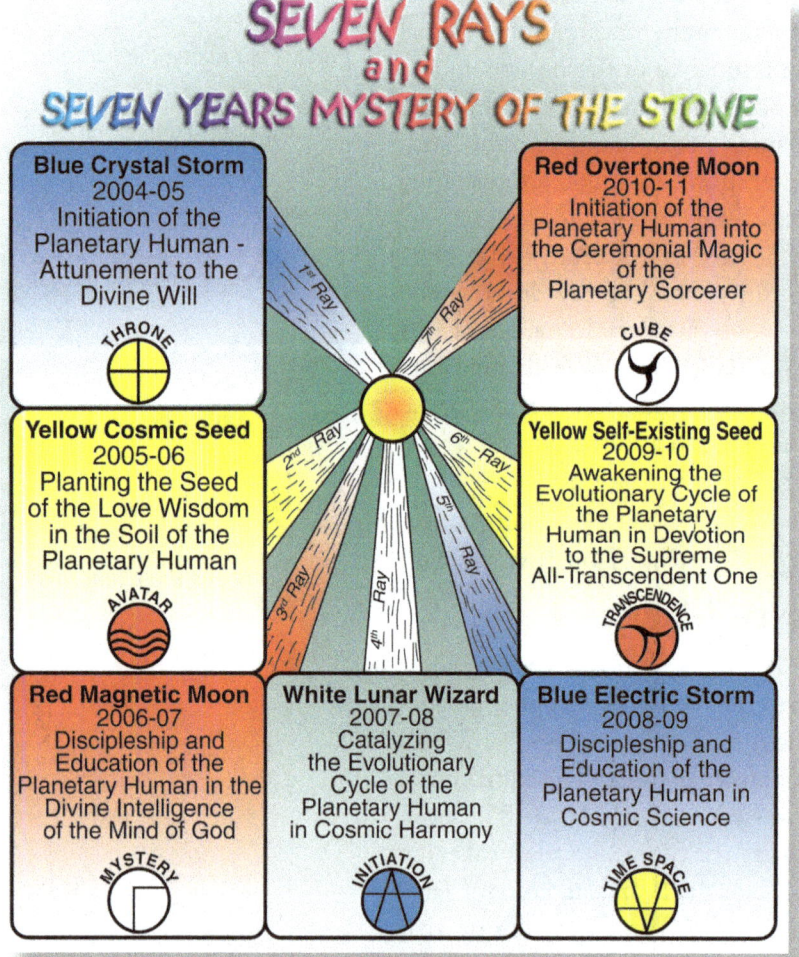

So we have initiation, attunement to the Divine Will, then the planting of the love-wisdom, followed by a year of discipleship and education. Then comes the evolutionary cycle, followed by the next phase of discipleship—another evolutionary cycle—and finally, the seventh ray, which is initiation again. This brings us to 2011, leaving two years for humanity to enter into the phase of *Inner Time* or the *New Jerusalem*!

The Closing of the Cycle is a full-on enactment of ceremonial magick over a course of 10 years, which is nothing in cosmic time. The stage has already been set. The Closer of the Cycle has already deposited his vibrational frequency at many different geomagnetic frequencies to set a network of etheric links between different places including: Tiwanaco, Macchu Picchu, Baghdad, Picarquin, Teotihuacan, Palenque, Four Corners, Glastonbury, Stonehenge, St. Petersburg, Altai, Mt. Fuji, the Great Pyramid, etc. These sites are important because in ceremonial magick the energy has to be grounded in resonance with the Earth. The Harmonic Convergence and Day Out of Time activated and continue to activate multiple sites. In *Time and the Technosphere* is described the future process of Earth geomancy and chronogeomancy, establishing the planet as a living etheric network of points, which is actually a reflection of a cosmic entity as it is being planted on Earth for the purpose of transformation.

The point of activating all the sacred sites is to transform the psychic energy of the human species in resonance with a cosmic template or map planted on the Earth. Since it is the closing of the Great Cycle, as well as of the 26,000 and 104,000 year cycles, it is now the time for ceremonial magick to come into the forefront. Pure intention is everything.

The intention of the Closer of the Cycle is to bring all of humanity to a spiritual unification of UR by Dec. 21, 2012. This planetary spiritual unification will form a new evolutionary embryonic being, that will germinate for seven mystic moons, before giving birth to itself on July 26, 2013 with the Return of the People of OMA (Original Matrix Attained). The goal is to make it to 2012-2013 as a pacified planet. This is truly entering into the Arcturus Protectorate. When we talk about the Closing of the Cycle as a type of enactment of ceremonial magick, we are talking about a program of planetary pacification that will knock the breath out of the demons (this refers to psychic slaying and transmutation of lower energies through focused mind power).

The point of activating all the sacred sites is to transform the psychic energy of the human species in resonance with a cosmic template or map planted on the Earth.

The purpose of this is to complete this cycle in a proper Galactic Mayan manner, and to thus initiate the new cycle. We must have synchronized ceremonial events occurring regularly so as to establish a program for the new planetary order (the seventh ray) to come into being to bring order out of chaos. This sixth ray devotion/idealism ends up as fanaticism, which thrives on chaos. Chaos creates more fanaticism. This is a cycle that must be broken by a new harmonic order. This harmonic order, then, becomes the basis of the cultivation of a new kind of perspective and mentality of the human species. We need a new planetary sensibility—the way to do this is through equinox, solstice and Day out of Time rites and celebrations, so as to establish a new planetary program. These celebrations are natural, no one can deny when it is equinox or solstice. These events occur regardless of any ideology, religion or belief system.

The Law of Time synchronizes people regardless of what they believe. It is like birth and death. The Law of Time synchronizes everything between its birth and death. Where it synchronizes you as a planetary entity is in coordination with the Earth as it goes through its phases of solstices and equinoxes. (Check out the section on Noospheric Earth Time in *Time and the Technosphere*, pp. 125-132.) This is part of its means and methods. These are just some of the principles of ceremonial magick. We can take these principles and apply them to the scripting of the enactment of the Closing of the Cycle.

Hierarchy & The Evolution Of Cultural Forms

Shambhala refers to the matrix, which is also synonymous with Tollan, the matrix that evolves higher cultural forms, which are now becoming increasingly manifest. Humanity is the point through which the manifestation and commands of hierarchy and the cultural forms of the matrix of Shambhala/Tollan are evolved. We must form clear pictures about how all of this works. A description of this process is found in the *Art Planet Chronicles* (1981, unpublished) with the HCV (Higher Collective Voice,) which is the expression of the voice of hierarchy through the matrix of Shambhala, which speaks through the noosphere of humanity as a single organism.

When we speak of hierarchy, we are talking about an organized aggregate of fifth-dimensional intelligence or entities whose collective will or purpose is to assist in the guidance of the affairs of the troubled planet of the Free Will Zone. The degradation of the masses at the Closing of the Cycle is because democracy has cut them off from hierarchy. Living by hierarchy confers a natural dignity. Hierarchy always works indirectly and only through the controlled selection of a set number of beings on the third-dimensional plane. Once communication or contact has been established by the hierarch—with a third-dimensional operant selected to fulfill a particular aspect of the unfolding plan of Divine Creation—then at different points there is communicative download, release or guidance. Since the hierarchy is rooted in the perception of sacred order, and the Planetary Hierophant is the revealer of the sacred order, then there is an inevitable relationship between hierarchy and the Hierophant.

Part IV • Noosphere: The New Earth Consciousness

The Planetary Hierophant operates with the template outfitted for him by hierarchy. He is increasingly fulfilling the commands of hierarchy to fulfill a particular evolutionary program. We will understand more in the unfolding of the next six volumes. The Planetary Moon and the Spectral Wizards year showed us the final convulsive throes of the degeneration of the sixth ray order, just as the Blue Crystal Storm year marked the first embryonic year of the seventh ray order.

"The energy of the seventh ray is the potent agent of initiation which is taken on the physical plane, that is during the process of the first initiation. Its effect on humanity will be to bring about the birth of Christ consciousness among the mass of intelligent human beings."

Christ consciousness is the equalization of energy to release humanity from nationalistic, sectarian, ideologies. The release turns into love and tolerance.

The new evolutionary processes have to do with the Law of Time. The Law of Time is what facilitates the evolution of the human species from being a materially bound creature to a purely spiritual/mental fourth-dimensional emotionally evolved creature. As of Spectral Wizard year, everyone on the planet, whether they are conscious of it or not, became a world disciple—and at Winter Solstice 2012 (Northern Hemisphere) everyone, whether they know it or not, will become a world initiate.

The Planet Art Network is already in place and this is what the new humanity is to be based on. It has nothing to do with any kind of borders or nation states. Once we understand that everything being evolved by the Law of the Time is an act of ceremonial magick, then our motivation should sky rocket. If we are motivated and inspired, then everyone else will catch fire with us. We are serpent initiates whose mission is to bring the ripening of the world soul out of the chaos of the old order to its divine fulfillment in resonance with the beings at the end of this cycle. In this way, we will stimulate the masses.

The seventh ray represents both the highest and the lowest—if the calendar change were just a populist revolution it

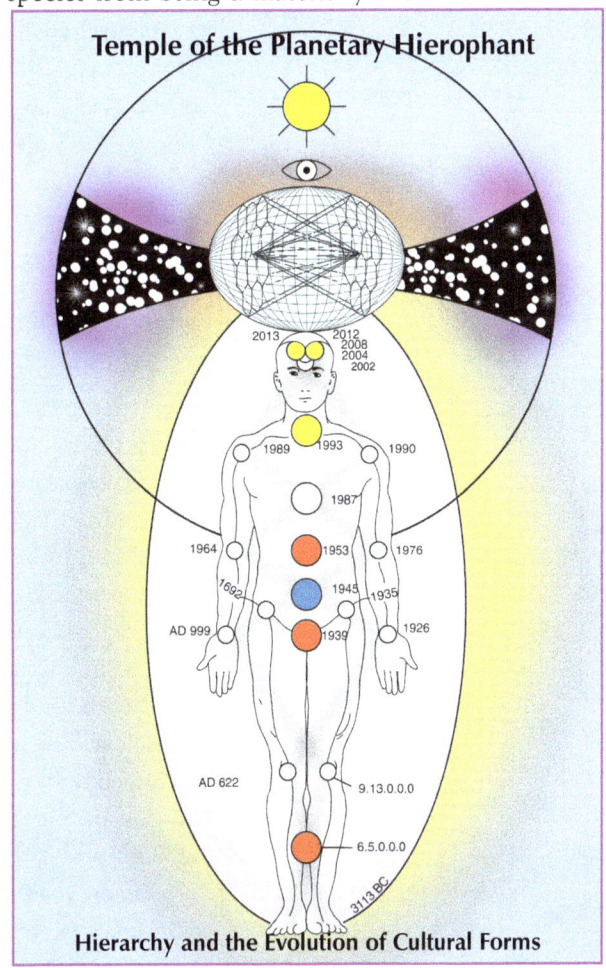

Hierarchy and the Evolution of Cultural Forms

would be insufficient to deal with the energies we have to deal with. But when we understand that a calendar is a spell that holds a particular mindset in place, then we have to call in a powerful type of magick to dispel the old spell. Fabrications of hierarchy are templates of vision and instruction, which are channeled through the medium of the Planetary Hierophant and his Apprentice, as well as any other inner circle help who appear—this is the highest. The lowest is the masses of people awakening to the New Time who do not know about the magickal instructions, but are nevertheless participating in it.

We are actually operating by higher codes that are being transmitted by hierarchy. All the people who are being guided by hierarchy will be those who begin to respond to the essence of the Divine Plan as it is being transmitted through the Closer of the Cycle and the Red Queen. The nature of the Plan is to change the time, which involves many focal points of force to create different echelons of workers or servers with a different vision. It is a function of the highest ceremonial magick to galvanize and catalyze all these different echelons in every piece of the whole of hierarchic vision and to catalyze them on behalf of the change in time.

We are beginning to find the right languaging to engage the other people to enact the Divine Plan that hierarchy has put forth. The central point of the Plan is being passed through the Closer of the Cycle because he is in touch with the complete knowledge that **absolutely everything that is happening on our planet today is about the Closing of the Cycle and 2012.** Many people have some knowledge of this, but not of all the vast implications and prophetic origins of the descriptions of the Closing of the Cycle and of the energies that are necessarily going into this process. The stages from now until 2012 are very clear. The innermost essence of what is to be done is being catalyzed right now in terms of the enactment of the ceremonial magick drama called the "Closing of the Cycle," where the whole world is the stage and everyone is an actor.

Each year, there is a passage out of one act into another act. Each of these acts represent a significant stage in the ceremonial drama of the Closing of the Cycle. When we are

All the people who are being guided by hierarchy will be those who begin to respond to the essence of the Divine Plan as it is being transmitted through the Closer of the Cycle and the Red Queen.

dealing with different levels of energy, we have to have a bank or reservoir of knowledge of precisely what it is that is occurring, according to the nature of forces at play and the forces that need to be aroused to counteract, modify or harmonize those forces. Words and speech are powerful. All words are a spell so it is highly important that we use our words thoughtfully and constructively. The words we use to define our objectives or plan our goals are very important. The best way to do this is to submit to the Higher Power and function as a channel of hierarchy on the spot, then everything you say will be in accord with the resonant frequency that hierarchy is emitting to you in every moment.

If you are in tune with hierarchy then you submit to that and surrender to God. You must always be in resonance with whom you are speaking. The resonant frequency with humanity has to match with the resonant frequency of hierarchy—this means that you have to go inside and pause to allow a type of transduction to occur. As an instrument, the human being is the reflection of the whole. How we conduct ourselves with ourselves and with each other is everything. We are always being watched by the higher-dimensionals. We must continuously be on guard and be aware of the egotistical black magick possibilities so we can always perform at the highest level. When you tune in properly to a structure or symbol, this is called *magickal interpretation.*

CEREMONIAL MAGICK FOR THE ESTABLISHMENT OF UR

Ultimately, the purpose of ceremonial magick is to establish UR. Pacal Votan's mission was to establish UR on Earth. He came here to compile a compendium of progress of UR on different world systems and to establish the index of spiritual unification. This is a focus of the work of ceremonial magick, to help facilitate and establish spiritual unification. During the seven years of the Mystery of the Stone, the Heptagonon of the Mind of Earth is created—this is like raising the dead (or waking up everyone who is captured by the 12:60 mental frequency), and perfecting the human soul. In the Seven Years of Prophecy, we created the Heptagonon of Mind of Heaven, which refers to the conscious activation of the psi bank.

The human soul has to make a major adjustment on all levels. The highest goal and value is the salvation of the soul. Everything in the 12:60 world is dominated by merciless materialism to the detriment of the human soul. Therefore, the world is soul-less—a wasteland. The Mystery of the Stone is meant to reverse this wasteland by enrolling the human race into 13:20 time, so it can experience the perfection of, first, the individual soul, and then the World Soul. This can only be done by invoking the One Most High to aid us. This also calls into play our different skillful means or methods, which join the highest with the lowest. The highest understanding and wisdom and the highest forms of spiritual magick will be put into very refined focal points with specific methods of action, which will be utilized to awaken or arouse the many individuals who make up the mass of humanity to bring them to a higher level of group function. This is the conclusion of the Mystery of the Stone.

The first ray has to do with arousing the personal will in accord with the Divine Will to make the change in time. Once we make an irrevocable change in human consciousness, then reality is forever changed. After we complete the AC we will shift to the CA activation. We are conducting the world soul or human species through a type of interplanetary memory recall in which we get back to the point of where something first went wrong, and instead of going down that pathway again we will pick up a parallel universe where everything went right. The prophetic adventures of the previous 12 years come to a head or fruition in the Cosmic Seed year (which is the second ray of love/wisdom).

The first three rays are considered the major rays: will, love-wisdom and intelligence. These are the years where the greatest emphasis is placed on making sure the New has been activated and entered into and that the movement is proceeding in the correct direction with the correct twist and type of knowledge of what needs to be accomplished.

The years of the Lunar Wizard and Electric Storm are the invoking of Galactic Camelot. It is at this point that art and science will be set in correct relationship. The Lunar Wizard Year is the fourth ray of harmony—there will be a great enactment of harmony in this first year of the calling of Galactic Camelot. The Electric Storm Year (2008-09) is the fifth ray—the science of concrete knowledge. This is an actual correction of the course of science in history, which was developed in a completely masculine energy. It is the year of the fifth of the Nine Great Lha or Bolontiku. This fifth Bolontinku is the *Supreme Golden Maiden*. At this point, the new Cosmic Science will be established.

Then come the final four years, the mystic altar—this is the manifestation of the New Galactic Camelot! TEL-EK-TON-ON calls forth Galactic Camelot where the human soul is now being raised to a higher level and is placed on the mystic altar. The first year on the mystic altar is the Self Existing Seed year—sixth ray, ray of devotion—which is the beginning of this four-year sequence that goes into the Resonant Storm year (2012-13). At this point, everyone will acknowledge the One

... the mystic altar—

this is the manifestation of the

New Galactic Camelot!

TEL-EK-TON-ON calls forth

Galactic Camelot where the

human soul is now being raised

to a higher level and is placed

on the mystic altar.

God and devotion will be exclusively to the Supreme Creator, which spontaneously corrects all other "problems." In the first two years of the final four, the soul receives the concluding initiations of the mystic altar *Telektonon*.

The final initiation of the rays occurs in the Red Overtone Moon year. At this point, the Planetary Hierophant will be completely ordained to complete the whole ceremony of the Mystery of the Stone, and the soul will receive the self-replicating power of organization and order so it need never go astray again. The soul will now be self-programmed for perfection.

Then come the last two years, 2011-2013, where the soul has the opportunity to fly free! Such is a recap of the collective planetary ceremony, "Closing the Cycle." Stay tuned!

Chapter 13 - Synthesis
Significance of Number 7 and Overview of 7 Volumes

> "The Master of Wisdom in his first coming to birth in the supreme ether of the great light,—many his births, seven his mouths of the word, seven his rays, scatters the darkness with his cry."
>
> *Rig Veda*

Chapter 13
Synthesis—Significance of Number 7 and Overview of 7 Volumes

"He is the One who created for you everything on earth, then turned to the sky and perfected seven universes therein, He is fully aware of all things." Quran 2:29

"Sounds and colors are all spiritual numerals; as the seven prismatic rays proceed from one spot in heaven, so the seven powers of nature, each of them a number, are the seven radiations of the unity, the central spiritual sun." Madame Blavatsky — Isis Unveiled

The *Cosmic History Chronicles* are presented in a synchronic manner where you always feel as if you are experiencing a different facet of the sacred order of reality. From a universal point of view, the *Cosmic History Chronicles* are a specific rendition of the whole template of Cosmic History. This rendition is specific to the closing of the cycle and to the regeneration of the new cycle.

The *Cosmic History Chronicles* represent a high level of synthesis in which the Absolute is integrated into the relative and the relative is absorbed once again into the Absolute. At this point of the closing of the cycle, the actual state of mind of the planet is in utter chaos. The chaos can only be redeemed by a shaft of Cosmic History hitting the chaotic mass causing it to swiftly transmute.

Because Cosmic History is a result of this actual embodiment and cosmic polarity of Votan and the Red Queen, it is a **Living** condition. We are now in one common cosmic state of mind. This is a **Living** process, a living transmission, which enlivens and quickens the mass of material, information and categorization, which are the seven volumes of the *Cosmic History Chronicles*. The seven volumes can be understood as the vehicle that makes conscious, both the reason why, and the process of the unfurling of the manifest universe. The seven volumes also make conscious the process of the reformulation of the human mind so that the return journey can be conducted in a manner of harmonic perfection.

Lost Interval In Eternity

Why does Cosmic History take the form of the seven chronicles? When we go back to certain texts from the Sufi tradition, most notably the work of Qadi Saiid al-Qummi, we come across the reference that the seven refers to the "Interval of Lost Time in Eternity." In other words, we are dealing with a primal original point in which cosmos is the perfect sphere that receives a fracture or flaw. This fracture or flaw represents an interval. This interval represents the first manifestation of time from within cosmos, in which there is no time. In cosmos everything is absolutely radial

Cubing the Sphere

Since the root inspiration of Cosmic History is from the tomb of Pacal Votan, it is important to recall that when the body of Pacal Votan was laid in the tomb and subsequently discovered, a jade sphere was placed in his left hand, and a jade cube in his right hand. The sphere is the absolute of the Absolute. The cube is the Absolute of the relative. From these two structures, all knowledge of Cosmic History is contained and derived. From the Absolute relative of the cube is derived the six sides plus the mystic seventh center power. Here is the foundation and order of the primal Cosmic History.

The Absolute of Cosmic History is like the geometry of a sphere, with no corners, no planes, no facets, not top, no bottom, no sides—but just a pure absolute sphere. The relative of Cosmic History is the squaring of the circle or the cubing of the sphere. In other words, the sphere is the perfect form. When you square the circle then you have the manifestation of the basis of the cube. When you square the square you create the cube—this is the template for cubing the sphere.

So we go from the absolute featurelessness of the sphere and the circle to the facetedness of the square and the cube, which represents the primal structure of Cosmic History as a potential specific relative rendition. As the closing of the cycle rendition, the cubing of the sphere gives us the basis for the Heptagonon of Mind, which represents the revelation of the cube containing the sphere. This is why the first Heptagonon of Mind of the Telektonon Prophecy is the Heptagonon of Mind of Heaven, which encloses the sphere of the Earth—this is the example of the cubing of the sphere.

We also know that the Heptagonon of Mind of Heaven is actually preceded by a Matrix Heptaganon of Mind, which occurred between 9.13.0.0.0 and 10.0.0.0 of the Long Count and comprises the seven generations that occurred from 692-830 AD. The Matrix Heptaganon of the Cube which underlies the Heptaganon of the Cube of Heaven actually commences with the primal Cosmic History Chronicle.

The seven volumes represent the Heptagonon of Mind or the cube in which each volume leads up to the seven. The seven, is the cube imploded in the center, reflecting and refracting the six sides of the cube. Within this chronicle of the cube, there is a psycho mythic narration that corresponds to the number seven and the squaring of the circle and completing of the cycle.

and perfect like in the sphere. When there is the notion of time arising from cosmos, time then represents some kind of activity within the perfect sphere of cosmos or eternity. Time represents an activity which, by its nature, has a measure configured by the number seven.

When we go beyond the cosmic root of time, we enter into the "Interval of Lost Time in Eternity." This "Lost Interval of Time" corresponds to the ratio 4:7::7:13. Four is the root, seven is the stem and thirteen is the fruit. This is the primal ratio and cosmology of the Law of Time. It was recently stated in the news by a Californian physicist that the age of the universe is 13.7 billion years old. Thirteen is the age of the cosmos at this point; the seven makes the thirteen possible. As a whole number, thirteen captures the complete fractal of time (elasticity of the fractal makes up for the lack of complexity of the fractal). 13:7 is the base fractal of 137, the prime mathematical number that corresponds to kin 137, Red Resonant Earth, the sign of the mystical *Ah Vuc Ti Kab*, the Lord of the center of the Earth.

When we look at the "Interval of Lost Time in Eternity" and the power of seven, we see that something happened in

4:7::7:13

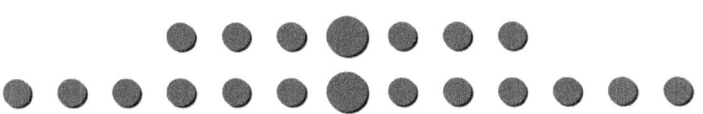

Eternity that is repeated again in any version of Hell. The primal factor is the four. The four represents the factor of Hell and the thirteen represents the factor of the redemption. Seven heavens represent the "Interval of Lost Time in Eternity", which becomes the Cycle of Prophecy. There are seven years of prophecy (1993-2000) that lead us back to the four—which is the four years of the harrowing of hell (2000-04)—then there are seven more years, referred to as the Mystery of the Stone (2004-11), which leads humanity to 2013—the ultimate redemption.

As we mentioned earlier, we are dealing with the relative and the Absolute. In the Heptagonon of Mind, the six faces of the cube represent the seven and the seventh is the imploded point at the center of the cube. This seven corresponds to a primal septenary function—septenary meaning having to do with the number seven. Seven is the prominent number of creation. Everything that seeks perfection is guided by the power of seven. The center of the cube maintains the integrity of the structure of the cube—it pushes and pulls all sides equally and is equal distance from all sides. The seven gives the cube the power of maintaining integrity of form; it is the point of power within the cube. The program structure of Cosmic History compacts into a cubic form, which is the same order and power as the primal cubic parton and the same order and power as the Heptagonon of Mind.

Being that we live in a holographic universe, Cosmic History is a reflection of the seven stages of God's creation. There are infinite sets of mathematical permutations in the

There are seven years of prophecy (1993-2000) that lead us back to the four—which is the four years of the harrowing of hell (2000-04)—then there are seven more years, referred to as the Mystery of the Stone (2004-11), which leads humanity to 2013—the ultimate redemption.

ever-changing chemical composition of life. When we think of the number seven we have to think that seven, is in one sense, an absolute and in another sense represents a factor that defines a reality that has, what we might call, a radius of seven. The reality of the radius of seven is the reality of thirteen. The seven is in the center of one and thirteen. The radius of seven extends from one on one side, to thirteen on the other. That encompassing radius of seven, then, becomes the basis of the existence of the cosmos as an activity or series of actions that have a synchronic relation to each other. The sum of these synchronic relations constitutes the entirety of the "perceivable cosmos." (See Chapter 9 SUM model).

There is the perceivable cosmos and the imperceivable cosmos. The imperceivable cosmos is the same as the unborn ultimate sphere spoken of in Dzogchen teachings. In Ibn al Arabi's cosmology, the imperceivable cosmos is known as the *black satin sphere*, which has no distinctions or marks. The perceivable cosmos (relative) is ultimately defined by seven. The power of the radius of seven contains the secrets between one-and-seven and the secrets between seven-and-thirteen. For example, in Ibn al Arabi's cosmology of the unfolding of creation in 28 stages, the black satin sphere is followed by the sphere of fixed stars which enclose 28 (7 x 4) lunar mansions. This creates a *round* that becomes the circle. The circle then becomes the sphere. Everything that exists is contained within the perfection of this round and the primal squaring of the circle. Within the primal squaring of circle are the constituent elements of Cosmic History.

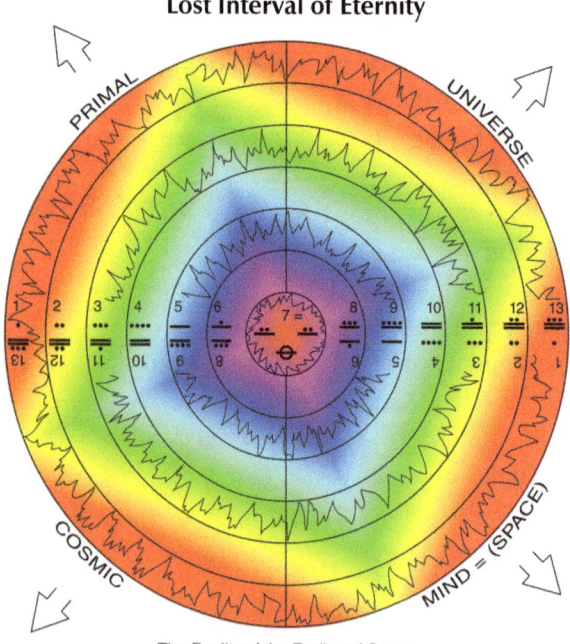

Lost Interval of Eternity

The Reality of the Radius of Seven
is the Reality of Thirteen

$1 + 2 + 3 + 4 + 5 + 6 + 7 + 8 + 9 + 10 + 11 + 12 + 13 = 91 = 13 \times 7$
$13:20 \sim [20 = 13 + 7]$

We are making this description so we can comprehend the enormity of the process of Cosmic History, which is the highest sacred thread that is being woven through the planetary field of mind and noosphere today. This is because Cosmic History picks up the thread of the *Quran*, the *Old* and *New Testaments*, the *Upanishads*, *Popol Vuh*, the *Bhagavad-Gita* and every other sacred teaching and sacred vision that was brought forth by history. These sacred scriptures are beads on the string of evolving consciousness.

When we really flip on the Cosmic History consciousness, then we become like Internet monitors of some streaming video that is occurring at a higher dimension and stepped down to be channeled by us. Maintaining this state of consciousness is *all-important* so that the reformulation of the human mind can come into new light within us. Since the nature of knowledge is infinitely vast, we cannot even begin to cover every last aspect. But we can splash the light of Cosmic History on significant amounts of knowledge, so that whatever has not been covered receives the light of the knowledge around it.

The *Cosmic History Chronicles* and the "Interval of Lost Time in Eternity" present a purified vision of systems of knowledge, being, knowing and doing on this Earth that make all the systems of knowledge correlate and correspond to the incredible core order of reality that was injected. Cosmos itself was injected by the power of seven from Eternity into this manifestation. If you can see how this manifestation is all a function of the power of seven, then you can fit it back to where it came from. Making conscious what was previously unconscious through the power of seven is so vital. This is the meaning of the perfection of the human soul.

Seven Stages of the Perfection of the Human Soul
1. Perfection of the perception of Heaven or the beyond—the Hereafter
2. Perfection of the perception of the meaning of Earth
3. Perfection of the perception of the meaning of light and vision
4. Perfection of the meaning of darkness and dreaming
5. Perfection of the meaning of orders of time
6. Perfection of the meaning of enlightenment and illumination
7. Perfection of the meaning of the soul's perfecting itself

MEANING OF CHRONICLES

We are dealing with the Closing of the Cycle rendition of Cosmic History, or the *Cosmic History Chronicles*, which are transduced and channeled specifically for this point in time. If you go to the dictionary and look up "chronicle," it says: "Chronicle is the narration of events in sequence, usually without commentary."

When we really flip on the Cosmic History consciousness, then we become like Internet monitors of some streaming video that is occurring at a higher dimension and stepped down to be channeled by us.

Like, "In the year 973 King John fought a battle at North Umbria", then "In the year 974, King John did this," then "In the year, 975 King John did that," etc.

Cosmic History says that behind this linear definition, there is a more imaginative meaning of the word "chronicle," which is the narration of events or chronicle play that relate with each other synchronically. At the purest level, the primal Cosmic History is the narration that goes: one, two, three, four, five, six, and seven. In other words, the "Interval of Lost Time in Eternity" (or the psychomythic event that occurred) is narrated at the highest level and can be understood in succession as the numbers one-through-seven—this is reflected repeatedly in the *Quran* and the *Bible*. In these scriptures, the numbers one-through-seven get fleshed out from the first day of the creation of light—which leads to the final sixth stage of the creation of man, then to the seventh stage when God takes the throne. The throne is the center of the cube of creation.

There is much to be understood in this primal cosmology, which is the primal Cosmic History chronicle. The six "days" create all the different component elements of the "perceivable cosmos." But on the seventh day, the Creator Self initiates the throne as the position or place of the number seven from which the whole of creation can be viewed, summarized, radialized and accounted for. Within this elaboration of the number seven, we see it breaks down into fractals so that there are 49 (7 x 7). This fractal continues to fractalize, ultimately creating the total construction of the perceivable cosmos.

If you take the seven and add each unit (1 + 2 + 3 + 4 + 5 + 6 + 7 = 28), the sum of all the units in the seven becomes the 28, which is the cycle that corresponds to the phases of the moon. This is the reason for the power of the 28-day cycle, which is actually the sum of seven taken as each unit being the number of units that corresponds to that number. So seven equals 28, which is a highly cosmic number. In the Zen tradition there are seven Buddhas and 28 patriarchs. In the Lakota tradition there are 28 poles to the tepee, and in the Hindu tradition there are 28 lunar mansions. This 28 is a primal calendrical reckoning that occurs in prehistoric aspects in the traditions of China, India, Arabia, etc. This is because 28 is the magnification of the number seven. When Milarepa's disciples asked him how many major caves he had meditated in, he answered, "28." The Jewish tradition also has a sacred circle containing 28 units with a circle of 13 moons. (See *Magic of the Ordinary* by Gershon Winkler)

The 28, then, is the self-enlightened power of seven. If you take the number 13 and summarize it, its component parts create the number 91 (13 x 7). Ninety-one is actually one quarter of 364 or one part of the year, which is 28 x 13. These are descriptions of the *Cosmic History Chronicles* at the pure level of number or the stepping down of Cosmic History from the Absolute to the level of the first stage of the seven days of creation.

When the seven is in its maximum form of the thirteen (4:7::7:13) then that becomes the 91, which is one quarter of the 364-day year. This quarter (4) is the power of form. In the formulation 4:7::7:13, the power of form (4) makes the seven the 28. Then the seven x thirteen makes the 91, and 91 x 4 = 364. This demonstrates that the 13-Moon calendar is a pure function of Cosmic

History; it is the numerological completeness of Cosmic History at the level of pure number. Number is the higher form of language. Language, as we know it, is a lower form of number. Number exists independent of time and space and is what gives proportion and measure to time and space. If it were not for the existence of number then time and space would not manifest in different forms. Number represents a whole other dimension of reality. When we talk about number at this level, we are talking about highly distilled and rarified archetypal essences. All manifestations and personifications of archetypal form and structure ultimately reduce to number.

Numbers themselves in their ultimate form have only a finite set of resonances. The resonances amount to the number 20. The 10 is only half of the potential totality of reality. This is why the present world order, rooted as it is in the decimal system—counting by 10, is inadequate. Ten is only half the score. Twenty is the totality or the "full score." The Mayan word for 20 is "Kal," (totality) because 20 is primarily represented as the zero potential, which gives the power to advance from 19 to another dimensional registration, which is 20. By 20, you proceed to other higher level dimensional registrations. At the root there are only 20 numbers—all the other numbers are made up of composites of those particular 20.

In the vigesimal counting system (counting by 20) any notation of any number always reduces to one of the primary twenty numbers (either a zero form with a base unit in front of it or any one of another numbers). For example, seven always resembles itself and is distinguished in the notation system; so that 27 is 1.7 (1 x 20 + 7) and 47 is 2.7 (2 x 20 + 7), etc.

THE BOLONTIKU AND THE LOST INTERVAL

The "Lost Interval of Time" can be further understood through contemplation of the Bolontiku, particularly the first seven. In the cosmological accounting of the *Chilam Balam*, it says that after the creation dawned, then came an infinite series of 13, added to seven. The seven represents the interval of the primary break. The Eternity in which that break occurred was what we

Number is the higher form of language. Language, as we know it, is a lower form of number. Number exists independent of time and space and is what gives proportion and measure to time and space.

would call a supersensible (you could never see or touch it) universe Eternity, which caused the necessity for equilibration.

The equilibration created what is referred to in Cosmic Science as the RANG—the primal sound. (This is the cosmology of the creation of the universe through the power of seven—the seven rings of "RANG" that were sounded when the first thought was finally completed, creating the shattering in the totally supersensible etheric structure of the primordial Eternity). In essence, the result of the first thought was the manifestation of seven rings that vibrated through the void. When those rings met each other, they created dissonance, which created what is known in Cosmic Science as the *carpins* and the *megacarpins*, the primary subquantic proto-electrical essences.

The first two rings establish the primary order of the universe. The *Dynamics of Time* introduces the primary and the secondary (from the one comes the two—this is the primary). The primary is represented by the number 2 and the primary doubled becomes the four—this is the secondary life reflex. The primary itself is a binary, meaning it can only come about as a function of the law of alternation, which establishes the primary universe. The crystal ultimately summarizes the primary in relation to the secondary. The crystal is the final solidification or expressive form of the manifestation of the primary universe. There are many other elements involved, which will be further elucidated in subsequent volumes, including the nature of the first thought and the structure of it and so on. The 20 (7:13) represents the primary binary potentiated by the zero, to create an exponentially advancing order—20, 400, 8,000, 160,000, etc.

But for now, we are dealing with the part of the creation story where from the two comes the binary doubling, which creates the four. The four, then, becomes the basis of the complex of life, while the primordial binary is a relatively self-sustaining, self-supporting set of processes and forms. In these forms, exist the process of primordial combustion of plasma that creates the stellar mass. The stellar mass then creates the planetary bodies, and ultimately may result in the supernova. This represents an elementary self-sustaining process, meaning it does not depend on anything except its own internal processes to unfold. But what we call life, the secondary reflex, is a complex process. This is why it is completed in four stages; the final stage of which is the creation of the human being from clay or lowly liquid. You are the final creation of this complex life process.

Unfolding The Power Of Seven

There is cosmic time, but cosmic time of Eternity is absolute no-time. The cosmic time that we distinguish outside of Eternity is characterized by the number 13, which can only exist because the seven exists in the center. On either side of the center are the two sixes; the base of the two different cubes, which then make the thirteen. These are all intrinsically self-defining values. These self-defining values of the seven and the thirteen establish what we call the *dawn of creation*. All of this is a manifest act of God, the Supreme, the Divine Creator in the process of thinking the first thought, which took incalculable eons to formulate itself. Once formulated, the shattering within eternity

Synthesis: Significance of Number 7 and Overview of 7 Volumes

occurred, of which the process is represented by the number seven. It is important to highlight these points when we are asking: Why is it called the *Cosmic History Chronicles?*

Seven is a chronicle, 28 is a chronicle, 91 is a chronicle and 364 is a chronicle, which means each day of the year is part of the chronicle. Then the 260-day cycle brings in the further meaning of what is the event of the day. For example, today is the 13th day of the Self Existing Moon and it is actually the 97th day of this 364-day cycle, and is the 97th point in the chronicle of this year, and the content of this chronicle for this year is White Electric Dog. This is the relative absolute form of Cosmic History.

This point underscores the significance and importance of the 13 Moon/28-day calendar as the manifestation and expression of the unfolding of the power of seven. This means that the *Cosmic History Chronicles* as the reformulation of the human mind and the reformulation of the calendar count as the 13 Moon/28-day sequence is organized by the power of seven. This is how it was before the Babylonian conspiracy intruded.

$$T(E) = ART$$

Seven Values of the Power of Seven
4:7::7:13 Base formula of Power of Seven

| 4 | 7 | 13 | 28 | 52 | 91 | 364 |

13:20 (= 7+13) Universal frequency of synchronization
20 = exponential binary base - 20, 400, 8000, 160,000, 3,200,000, etc.

1-2-3-{-4-}-5-6-7 = 1-2-3-4-5-6-{7}-8-9-10-11-12-13

1+2+3+4+5+6+7 = 28 (4 x 7) 28 days per moon

52 (4 x 13) 52 seven day weeks per orbit (13 Moon 28-day cycle)

1+2+3+4+5+6+7+8+9+10+11+12+13 = 91 (7 x 13) = 13 weeks 1/4 orbit

364 = 4 x 7 x 13 or 13 x 28 or 52 x 7 number of days in orbit plus 1 = 365 = 1 NET Day x 52 orbits = 73 Spins of 260 days = One NET year
7 Net Years = 364 Orbits, fractal of days in one 13 Moon 28-day cycle

**Wiphala
Aymaru Banner
Power of Seven**

So the 1-7 itself is the primary chronicle, which corresponds with the cubing of the sphere (also known as the Heptagonon of Mind or the squaring of the circle). The squaring of the circle is what is called the cosmology of the seven as the historical chronicle of the history of the soul (which results in seven volumes). From a traditional point of view, each volume is chronicled to represent an event anomaly—a point in the primal chronicle of the number seven. So the contents of each of these volumes are a discrete fulfillment or the unfolding of power of that original number to which it corresponds.

Through the very structure of the *Cosmic History Chronicles*, the human mind is reformulated by restoring it into the original power of seven, which restores the original seven days of creation to the primal power of the seven as the "Interval of Lost Time in Eternity"

(Continued on page 240)

Book of the Throne: Cosmic History Chronicles - Volume I

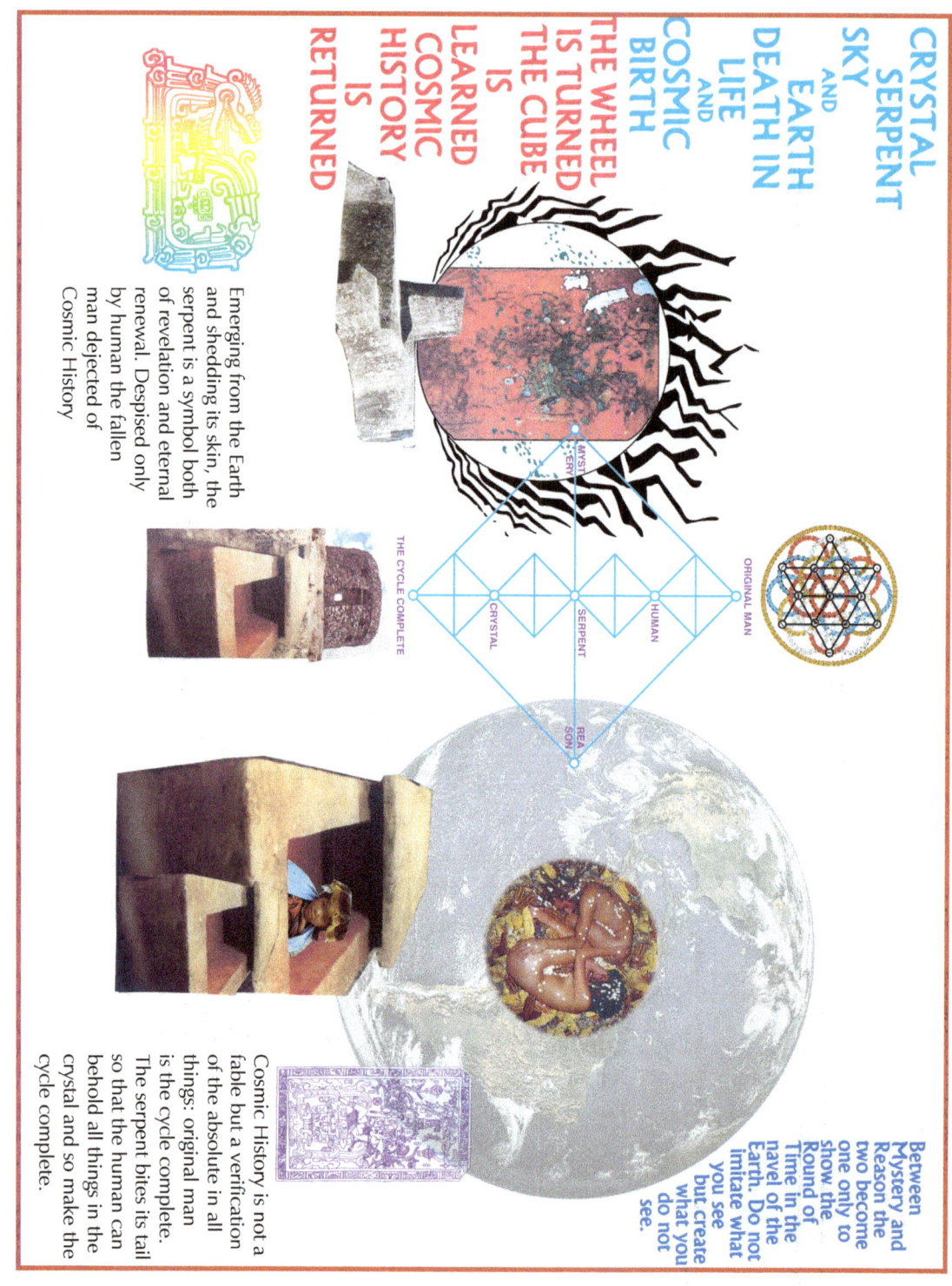

CRYSTAL SERPENT SKY AND EARTH DEATH IN LIFE AND COSMIC BIRTH

THE WHEEL IS TURNED THE CUBE IS LEARNED COSMIC HISTORY IS RETURNED

Emerging from the Earth and shedding its skin, the serpent is a symbol both of revelation and eternal renewal. Despised only by human the fallen man dejected of Cosmic History.

Cosmic History is not a fable but a verification of the absolute in all things: original man is the cycle complete. The serpent bites its tail so that the human can behold all things in the crystal and so make the cycle complete.

Between Mystery and Reason the two become one only to show the Round of Time in the navel of the Earth. Do not imitate what you see but create what you do not see.

238

Synthesis: Significance of Number 7 and Overview of 7 Volumes

PSYCHOMYTHIC NARRATION OF NUMBER SEVEN

1. The number one corresponds to the original man—the primal soul which is the reflex of the will of God. This represents the Absolute outside of the circle, which is a relative construct.

2. The number two corresponds to reason—the primal duality. Reason is the power to say there is this and there is that. The primal polarity or the primal dualism is the basis of reason. This creates the movement from the Absolute to the relative and places us inside of the circle.

3. The number three corresponds to the primal mystery of the cube making itself manifest as a process of geometry, which establishes the orders, and mysteries of the universe. In the graphic mystery is opposed to reason and with the original man at the apex a triangle is created.

4. The number four corresponds to the serpent, which is at the center of the matrix between reason and mystery. The serpent represents revelation and regeneration. The serpent reminds us of the Earth, which is represented by the stone or the crystal. A cycle goes by and it sheds its skin and becomes regenerated. This revelation of regeneration is the basis of consciousness. So the serpent is associated with the emergence of consciousness as the factor that puts together the original man, reason, mystery and consciousness. This completes the upper triangle.

5. The number five corresponds to the crystal, which establishes the principle of the Earth. This is the point of gravity, which then begins to establish the lower triangle. This is what makes the "Fall" possible.

6. The number six corresponds to the fallen man or human, which is a reflex of the original man existing in the Absolute outside the circle. Fallen man is within the circle. It is through the serpent that the fallen man becomes redeemed and acquires consciousness and then becomes aware of the crystal, which is the place from where the serpent and the fallen man are originated. By becoming consciously aware of the crystal, the six has to go back to the four and then to the five.

7. The number seven corresponds to consciousness transferred to the crystal. From the crystal, consciousness proceeds to a point that is the antipode of the original man, then the cycle is complete. The circle becomes conscious as the noosphere. The serpent "consciousness" completes the circle, bites its tail and becomes healed. This completes the psychomythic narration of the number seven. The seven different points represent different focuses of a meditation intended to restore a sense of cosmic integration.

This representation of the chronicles of the primary numbers 1-7 demonstrates the evolution of the soul into its present stage. This is the process of the evolution of the soul going from the primal reflex of the will of God to the establishment of reason, which is the power of duality. The next stage is creation of the mystery, which then goes to the serpent that represents consciousness, which then creates a point of gravity to ground itself and from that, the human or fallen man. This corresponds to the number six, which symbolizes transcendence in the Seven Major Arcana of the Law of Time. The "Fall" of spiritual traditions is referred to in Cosmic History Chronicle Volume 6: Book of the Transcendence, which illustrates the fallen human remembering the reflex of the primal word of God, and then finally realizing that the crystal is actually a living point, which reestablishes the noosphere as a conscious realm so that the cycle becomes complete.

(this is like taking the puzzle piece and putting it back into the big sphere of perfect cosmos—the Absolute). It is put back so perfectly that you cannot even tell it was fractured. This is cosmos restored.

The *Cosmic History Chronicles* are the power of the number seven, which underlies the narration of cosmic creation and the creation of the cosmic field as the function of the different stages of the evolution of time. The number seven also functions as the narration of the history of the soul. We see that the soul has different qualities or functions—it is in matter, it is in animal, it is in the human and it creates the whole totality of reality. So the seven volumes of the *Cosmic History Chronicles* are what we might call a "cosmic narration" or the narration of the cosmic power that constitutes the number seven. The unfolding of these cosmic powers creates the evolution of the human soul, which is all a reflection of the primal power of seven.

Seven Stages of the Evolution of Consciousness in the Moral Universe
1. Absolute oceanic consciousness
2. Birth of ego (which gives rise to unconscious and diminishing consciousness)
3. Moral awakening consciousness
4. Liberated consciousness
5. Universal compassionate consciousness—noospheric
6. Wise old wizard consciousness (so totally self-transcendent as to appear normal)
7. Oceanic consciousness (return to galactic source)

When we get to the seven, which is the cube or the cubing of the soul or the squaring of the circle, this creates the perfection of the human soul. When the human soul is perfect, it is because Cosmic History has created the template of the reformulation of the human mind and knowledge as the pure reflection of the primal chronicle of seven. As the human mind becomes entrained in this reformulation, it evolves into the stage of pure fourth-dimensional functioning and knowing, which liberates it into full realization of its primal origin or primal power. This primal origin or power is reinforced by the *Cosmic History Chronicles* as being the power of seven.

The reinforcing of the power of seven is what assists and aides the elevation of the human mind into the noosphere, so that the noosphere itself becomes the reformulation of the human mind. When the mind is restored by the power of seven, it reaches noospheric consciousness. This planetary mental field of knowing is a reflection of the total complex of Cosmic History, which means Cosmic History in all of its components as different variables and categories of knowing in relation to all the elements of the universe, both phenomenal and imaginal. These components all represent capacities of knowing contained in the noosphere. All the aspects of Cosmic History are descriptions of capacities of knowing.

When the human mind is reformulated, according to Cosmic History, its evolutionary form becomes the noosphere. At this stage, it becomes obvious that the Cosmic History structure within the noosphere resembles a master template of the power of seven. This noospheric master template represents the sphere of Earth and its consciousness and creates a resonant factor or resonant power that reorganizes and reformulates the noospheric Earth consciousness by the power of seven, aligning it with the primal coordinating agents of the galaxy.

Cosmic History Chronicles Invokes Galactic Consciousness

This alignment brings on the galactic mind or galactic consciousness, which seeps into the noosphere and therefore seeps into all the different human mind molecules that are moved to adjust themselves within the noosphere. Each mind molecule receives and partakes in this galactic mind and consciousness just like breathing air. Once the galactic mind consciousness has become part of the makeup of the human mental constitution, then it is coordinated with the *Hunab Ku*, the galactic central which is the projection of the original primal cosmic whole.

At this point, the whole of the field of consciousness and the entire endeavor of life is absolutely, utterly, irrevocably transformed into something so creatively beautiful, which was quite unimaginable from our old point of view. Study of the *Cosmic History Chronicles* is the first step in envisioning the mechanism and structure of how the whole human mind and basis of human knowledge is being reformulated. We see, then, that the nature and formation of the context and the content of the *Cosmic History Chronicles*, in its different aspects juxtaposed to each other through the seven volumes, actually represents a master unfolding of the original chronicles, which is the power of the original seven numbers.

At the beginning of creation, each of the seven numbers resonated with an awesomely thunderous power. Number exists as a separate generative order of reality, a subset of the reality of mind. So each of the first numbers was like a terrific, almost catastrophic vibratory power, each assuming the resonance

At this point, the whole of the field of consciousness and the entire endeavor of life is absolutely, utterly, irrevocably transformed into something so creatively beautiful, which was quite unimaginable from our old point of view.

of the prior one, until the secret held by the number seven is reached. The resonance of the seven is cataclysmic, shattering the perfection of cosmos and calling on the physical subliminal plane to contain its reverberations. Since the seventh tone contains all of the prior numbers in each dimension, it sets off all the vibrations that recapitulate the original seven. This is to be imagined as a continuously expanding process whose currents, waves and crosscurrents generate the complexity of reality as we know it today.

Just by studying the *Cosmic History Chronicles,* you can begin to resonate with the original chronicle and the power of the number seven. The whole system of the *Cosmic History Chronicles* must be comprehended. The *Cosmic History Chronicles* are like one sentence with seven words, and each of those seven words is a number exfoliated into different subtopics and synchronic themes. The synchronic themes can then be mapped out according to the power of seven in the whole of its contents and structure, which in themselves contain a resonant informative power. By absorbing this informative resonant power, the mind is reformulated.

The resonant informative power is the sum of the mathematical structure by which the content is placed in each volume. This is the "psychoactive ingredient" of Cosmic History working on the mind, and at the same time creating feedback with the noosphere itself. In this context, the noosphere can be understood as the entirety of the capacitating structures of knowing that constitute the whole of Cosmic History in its potential state. As your mind becomes reorganized and reformulated by Cosmic History, its vibratory resonance hits the different capacitators in the noosphere, which are the potentiated agents of power that interact with the different human mind molecules to create a greater and greater type of psychoactive agitation. The more your mind becomes imbued with the informative resonant power of Cosmic History, the more it becomes a reflection of the primal chronicle of seven.

As the noospheric potentials become empowered, then the number seven creates a resonance which becomes cosmically coordinated to create different streams of galactic mind

The more your mind becomes imbued with the informative resonant power of Cosmic History, the more it becomes a reflection of the primal chronicle of seven.

consciousness. This galactic mind consciousness reverberates back into the noosphere, which reverberates back into the human mind molecule to create a brilliant upliftment of the human mind and the human soul. It is important to understand the *Cosmic History Chronicles* as having this type of power, so when you read, study and absorb yourself in the seven volumes, then you know you are actually dealing with this phenomenal resonantly informative structure, which is acting on you from every direction.

We are describing a powerful and magnificent template of supermental order or the order of the reflex of the Divine Will as it was placed into the original man or original being. This supermental order is now being awakened in all of the individual souls by the power of Cosmic History. But this could only come about through the activation of the agents who are transmitting and receiving Cosmic History. As we have said, the human being only really comes to understand something new when it is presented by another human being who embodies that which they are presenting. The Buddha embodied enlightenment. Christ embodied love and compassion. Muhammad embodied the Quran as the Word of God. The Closer of the Cycle and the Red Queen embody Cosmic History as the all-resonant power of seven.

"Those who engender Cosmic History have to absolutely identify with the cosmic through using their earthly bodies as instruments."

Cosmic Identification - Planetary Hierophant

"Fit the template of Cosmic History on the mind that is ever present and the sorcerer emerges wearing the starry skin of number which is the sign immaculate of the hierophant."

This quote means that those who present Cosmic History are actually the Planetary Hierophant: That one who reveals the renewed power of the sacred to the planetary human. The Cosmic History "fitting the template of the ever present mind" is the template of number, the power of seven magnified also to the power of thirteen.

"Which of you now is the oracle command of transmigratory remembrance? Behold the crystal manifests the answer." This is fulfilled through Votan and made potential in the Red Queen. The Votan is the potentiated and the Red Queen is the potential. So the potentiated has to empower the potential through the transmission of the Cosmic History. This is the transmission of light and heat or the transmission of the number 7. The crystal is the potential Red Queen.

"Those who engender Cosmic History have to absolutely identify with the cosmic through using their earthly bodies as instruments." The instruments of Cosmic History are given and represent the fallen man to be redeemed. Through divine revelation and through Cosmic History, Votan and Red Queen embody a septenary pattern of the Cube of the Law. Votan (also known as the *Closer of the Cycle*) represents the fallen man to be redeemed; therefore, he has to know the sufferings of all beings. This is part of the make-up of his life and his mind, soul and emotional constitution. This is the only way he can attain resonant attunement with the soul of the planetary human which is the ultimate fallen man. Through Votan's being, the suffering of all beings becomes indistinguishable from the Absolute, the object of his solitary meditation, which is beyond duality and nonduality. Because of his attunement to humanity, Votan, as the Closer of the Cycle can fulfill the role coded by his title.

This is the essence power of the Planetary Hierophant as the Closer of the Cycle, the one through whom the sacred is revealed for the planet. This is the archetypal container for the specific roles of closing the cycle. It is because of this that he can be attuned to all humans and he can transmit to the one who is to be potentiated, which is the Red Queen. Through the primal innocence that she manifests, the Red Queen subsumes the suffering of all beings. Through the transmuted essence of the suffering of all beings, the Closer of the Cycle can transmit an enlightened stream of consciousness in different ways through different situations in life, all of them seemingly ordinary. The two together are manifestations of the serpent as the revelation and regeneration of consciousness—hence serpent initiates of wisdom

> *Through Votan's being, the suffering of all beings becomes indistinguishable from the Absolute, the object of his solitary meditation, which is beyond duality and nonduality.*

Palenque-Nah Chan is the House of the Serpent or the House of the Revelation and Regeneration. The two tombs represent revelation and the two living emanations of those tombs represent the regeneration. The purpose of the Mystery of the Stone is to return the serpent to the stone or return the revelation or regeneration to the stone, so that the stone becomes awakened matter. Awakened matter then becomes the flesh of the living, fallen planetary human. When the flesh of the living planetary human becomes identified with awakened matter, then it becomes possible for the perfection of the human soul to occur.

This first has to be consummated by the two who are the transmitters and embodiments of Cosmic History. They must completely consummate this process by fully realizing themselves as serpent initiates and by returning the serpent to the stone through acts of focused consciousness and ceremonial magick. In this way, the Mystery of the Stone becomes a planetary rite of passage so that the crystal, the Earth and the stone, becomes awakened matter. When this happens, the human flesh and the stone of the Earth become awakened matter—this is what lights up the noosphere!

The crux of this event lies in the responsibility of the Planetary Hierophant to know the suffering of all beings. The knowledge of suffering of all beings is the alchemical lubricant that makes possible the clear reception and transmission of the galactic Mayan knowledge, known as the *Cosmic History Chronicles*. Without this lubrication of the knowledge of the suffering of all beings, there could not be the universal solvent that makes the whole order of Cosmic History. The whole order is dependent on there being a lake of dissolution of all beings through suffering and creating a universal solvent with the template of Cosmic History. This makes it possible to see the perfect unfolding of the *Cosmic History Chronicles* as a single cosmic perception derived from primal order that occurred in the "Interval of Lost Time in Eternity."

> *The knowledge of suffering of all beings is the alchemical lubricant that makes possible the clear reception and transmission of the galactic Mayan knowledge, known as the Cosmic History Chronicles.*

Recap—Background and Overview of the Seven Volumes

The material of the *Cosmic History Chronicles* came through a triple invocation of the words "Cosmic History" on the day Self Existing Skywalker in the Solar Moon of the Yellow Solar Seed Year (March 12, 2002). It was realized that Cosmic History had to be transmitted. Most of the material was generated without a full comprehension of the actual template. The whole vision is in the very phrase "Cosmic History," which is like a thread that is pulled. The pulling of the thread is the elaboration of the material that occurred in the initial 260, two-hour (mechanical) tutorials.

Only after the first set of tutorials were completed did the transmitter and receiver take a pause to experience the actual meaning of the templates of Cosmic History. At this point, the creation of the narration of the Cosmic History tutorials was perceived as the ouroboros, or the serpent biting its tale. The comprehension of the *Cosmic History Chronicles*, as the structure of order of the power of the number seven, *is* the serpent biting its tail to release the poison that heals into wholeness. So we see that Cosmic History is the comprehension of the structure of the original narration of creation as number. The seven volumes illustrate how the conscious activation of number informs the whole, resulting in the reformulation of the human knowledge base.

Before giving the overview of the seven volumes, we must first understand the entire cosmology of Cosmic History. First, it must be understood that Cosmic History is a compact or promise of the redemption of the power of the number seven. In other words, Cosmic History is a compact or promise that God made with Himself, while the unfolding of the *Cosmic History Chronicles* in seven volumes is the fulfillment of that promise God made with Himself to redeem the number seven.

When the first thought of God was engendered it created the RANG (primal sound), which created the "Interval of Lost Time in Eternity." These primary events created the possibility of the manifest universes. In the process of formulating that particular thought, God knew it was necessary for Him to exercise the thinking faculty. In addition, He also knew that the very exercise of the thinking faculty would be the rupture of the meditation that was self-existing since before and after Eternity; though it was not thought itself that broke that meditation. The thought itself was generated and delivered from that meditation because God remains Absolute. This is why the definition of God is twofold. God is absolutely transcendent in the Absolute and has always remained in that meditation, and God is also Immanent, which means He is revealed through signs in the phenomenal universe.

In the history of religion, there is always the sectarian struggles between what we might call the "absolute transcendentalists" and the "relative immanent" (belief in the immanence of God). They both coexist; otherwise, there would be a hopeless duality. So at the time God formulated the first thought, He made a promise to Himself that the number seven would be redeemed. In this way, the whole purpose of the *Cosmic History Chronicles* is to redeem the power of the number seven. This allows the manifest universe to finally have an unhindered return back to the One, back to the Source.

The *Cosmic History Chronicles* occur simultaneous to the Mystery of the Stone; the seven rings of the Mystery of the Stone are the same resonance as the seven primal rings of the RANG that were sounded. Each RANG emitted seven rings of sound that you can see rippling from the unmanifest supersensible eternity. The purpose of these primal seven rings is to manifest the necessary processes of establishing a universe through a set of multiple universes that represent different stages of dimensional manifestation. To these were added two other echo rings, bringing the power of nine into manifestation. These two echo rings added to the seven first rings are the guardians of the entire process of the return journey, the Bolontiku or Lords of the Ring.

The nine years from the Blue Crystal Storm year (2004-05) through the Blue Resonant Storm year (2012-13) marks the ultimate final interval of time. This is the point of the joining together of the seven primal rings with the two echo rings for the closing and regeneration of the cycle. This creates a seal on the entire cycle of historical corruption and transfiguration on this quarantined planet of Velatropa 24.3. This seal allows old memory programs to be erased and superseded by the power of the seven, represented, on the one hand, by the seven Lords of the Ring who are awakened, and, on the other hand, by the formulation of the *Cosmic History Chronicles*.

Necessity Of Mental Development

If it were just the waking up of the Bolontiku and the Lords of the Ring without this knowledge base, there would not be the necessary self-reflective evolutionary advance. It is not just spiritual evolution we are speaking of, but spiritual/mental evolution. Without the mental, there is not the necessary self-reflective capacity or possibility to make a return trip in full consciousness, super consciousness, hyperorganic and subliminal consciousness. There has to be a new mental configuration that excites the mind, while the spirit is simultaneously excited by the awakening of the angels of time—the Bolontiku.

The description of the nine years of the awakening of the

There has to be a new mental configuration that excites the mind, while the spirit is simultaneously excited by the awakening of the angels of time—the Bolontiku.

Book of the Throne: Cosmic History Chronicles - Volume I

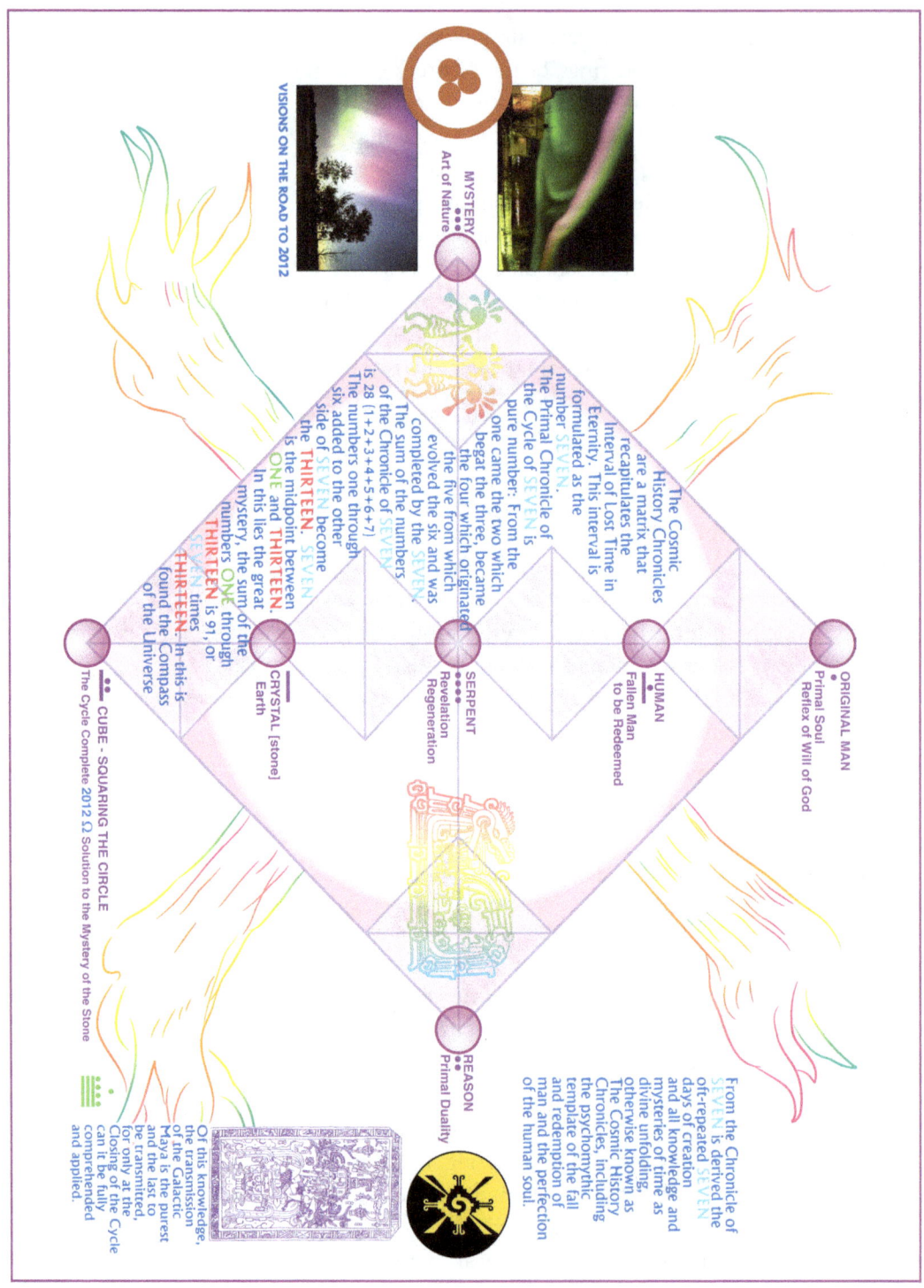

248

Bolontiku establishes the context and the reason why everything is occurring in the precise way it is at this point in time. This also explains why the work of the transmitter and transmitee of the *Cosmic History Chronicles* is a matter of assuming responsibility for the welfare of the entire world order for the closing of the one cycle and the regeneration of the next cycle.

All that will remain of the old cycle is summarized, synthesized and totally transfigured—both through the *Cosmic History Chronicles* and through the manifest reactivation of the fifth-dimensional beings of the Bolontiku. These nine Bolontiku are not only the guardians of the planet, but are also the compassion of the fifth-dimensional higher self of all the humans who choose to remain on this planet as the cycle closes. In other words, all of the higher fifth-dimensional beings are composited into the nine Bolontiku.

SEVEN DAYS OF CREATION, SEVEN CHRONICLES & THE HOLY QURAN

The divine creation occurred in seven days or stages; two days to create the heavens and four days to create the process of life. On the seventh day, God took to the throne where He holds supreme authority, sends out his commands and maintains His meditative, unborn, all-penetrating universal awareness. The seventh stage of the divine creation is the first stage of Cosmic History, the Throne. We recommended earlier that the *Holy Quran* be used as a criterion throughout the *Cosmic History Chronicles*. Since we are operating under the assumption that the *Quran* is the last word of the Supreme Creator for this world cycle, anything that is communicated in the *Cosmic History Chronicles*, no matter how far out it might seem, we will find reason in the *Quran*.

The root of the cosmology of the Cosmic History can be found in sura 41 of the *Quran* (41 x 7 = 287, which is the radion value of the fourth week of the 7:7::7:7 practice). Sura 41 is the second of a set of seven suras that is coded by the same two mystic letters *Ha* and *Mim*. Using the most elementary

All that will remain of the old cycle is summarized, synthesized and totally transfigured—both through the Cosmic History Chronicles and through the manifest reactivation of the fifth-dimensional beings of the Bolontiku.

numerology of the Roman/Latin alphabet, H = 8 (of the Ha) and M = 13 (of the Mim). When added together 8 + 13 = 21, which is the power of seven tripled. In Arabic, Sura 41 is called "Fussilat," and in English bears the title of "The Detailed." In Sura 41 verses 9-12, we find the cosmology of creation, which establishes the throne and is the first stage of the *Cosmic History Chronicles*:

"Say, You disbelieve in the one who created the earth in two days, and you set up idols to rank with Him, though He is Lord of the Universe.

He placed on it stabilizers (mountains), made it productive and He calculated its provisions in four days to satisfy the needs of all of its inhabitants. Then he turned to the sky when it was still gas, and said to it, and to the earth, 'Come into existence willingly or unwillingly.' They said, 'We come willingly.'

Thus he completed the seven universes in two days, and set up the laws for every universe. And we adorned the lowest universe with lamps and placed guards around it. Such is the design of the Almighty, the Omniscient."

In the *Quran*, it says first that the Earth was created in two days, then it says the seven universes were created in two days. This means that the essence of the Earth contains all the manifest essences of those seven universes. As we saw earlier, Sura 65 verse 12 explains that further. It says that there are seven universes or seven heavens and of the Earth there is the same number of like thereof. Rather than one locatable Earth here and another one over there, those seven Earth's are simultaneously dimensional within dimensional within dimensional. So you have the binary creation of what scientists today call the inorganic or the primary order of reality, which is summarized by the crystal, inclusive of the totality of the seven universes.

The *Quran* says that when God took to the throne on the seventh day that the lowest heavens and lamps had fiery guards placed about it. The lamps represent what we perceive as the different stars and constellations. The guards are the jinns or

The guards are the jinns or angelic beings or other evolved entities distributed throughout the universe to protect it from the arising of any rebellious destructive elements.

angelic beings or other evolved entities distributed throughout the universe to protect it from the arising of any rebellious destructive elements. As we know, in the story of creation the Earth is the place of Iblis, who represents the rebellion of a number of jinn/angel beings. These "guards" see to it that wherever the mischief maker ultimately shows up that the mischief won't become such that it creates a ripple and goes through the universe and destroys it.

In other words, we do not know what kind of destructive power we actually have in our hands. We do not know what would happen if all the thousands of nuclear warheads went off. We do not know what kind of ripple that would create through the whole universal fabric. When a supernova explodes, it explodes because that is part of its inevitable process. But that explosion is in no way destructive like the way we think of destruction. It is simply an inevitable final stage of transformation and transmutation of both inorganic primary processes as well as advanced secondary process. Advanced secondary process refers to the mental field. The primary secondary reflex is the pure life matrix—then life advances to thought or back to mind.

So the setting off of nuclear weapons is not in the same category as supernova, it is an actual act of negative destruction. This is why the power fell into human hands. The human had that destructive power from the beginning. When the humans were created as the final element of the life process, God knowingly created the human with this free will capacity. This is why the human had already inbuilt the knowledge to know the names of the angels and all the things that were ever to be, including nuclear bombs, extra low frequency weapons, microwave ovens, cell phones, DVD's, etc. The terms and words used in the unfolding of the diabolical technology and technosphere were all in the potentiality of Adam's vocabulary from the beginning.

AND ON THE SEVENTH DAY…

It says in the *Quran* that when God takes to the throne, a revelation occurs regarding the seven universes or seven dimensions. So we see that with the primordial manifestation—thought—creates the interval that creates the power of seven which is then manifest as the seven rings rippling out. The first two rings carry in them all the elements of the creation of primary order of all the heavens and universes. And the second four create the processes that establish the whole of the life processes. These are the six stages. Then, when God takes to the seventh stage, you can imagine all the creation.

When we talk about creation in stages, we are not necessarily talking about something that is unfolding over time, because all those stages were created at one moment in time (which was a vertical moment that extended through the seven dimensions rather than a horizontal moment that is a duration in time extending out). Once it was all created, the duration in time came and began unfolding its process. In other words, the Law of Time came into effect only once everything else was created. So the seven days represent seven stages. On the seventh day when God takes to the throne the whole movie starts to roll with all the manifestations in their proper place. Then we see that the seven-dimensional universe is actually the unfolding of the first thought that God had— who knows what the second thought is?

We do know that the second part of creation begins on the seventh day when God takes to the throne. This is the place where He issues His commands. The commands are the different ways of governing all the different aspects, laws and principles of creation, down to the supervision of all the infinite number of beings who are unfolding karmically and all the guardian angels that all those infinite number of beings have—and their need to be communicated with. Ultimately, God's commands go through sets of angelic orders, referred to as hierarchy. Just because hierarchy exists does not mean God is not immanent in your heart. The immanence of God in your heart is part of the intrinsic essence of creation. The hierarchy has to do with the carrying out of commands of the governance of the manifest universe. Hierarchy sees to it that everything is unfolding, according to the evolutionary possibilities of the Law of Time (which is the unfolding of the consciousness of the universe.) In actuality, with the *Cosmic History Chronicles*, we are now just beginning the seventh day of creation, as it was Adam and Eve who began the sixth day of creation.

Without Cosmic History, there would be no new way of knowing and viewing reality. Cosmic History is the genuine sublimation and transcendence of historical materialism. Cosmic History must be learned. Each volume is accompanied by an interactive learning kit, including a hexagonal vessel containing the key Cosmic History precepts for that volume. Each precept written on an individual tablet is to be drawn and memorized.

OVERVIEW OF THE SEVEN VOLUMES

Volume I: Book of the Throne: Cosmos, the Absolute Pole
The Law of Time and Reformulation of the Human Mind (Spring, 2005)

The throne represents the seventh day of creation when God takes the throne—this is the origin or genesis of Cosmic History. The throne is the place where there is a view. It is a place of authority and power. The ultimate consummation of absolute authority, power and view is summarized as the cosmos itself. Within the cosmos is distinguishable the different sets, orders and patterns that correspond with the commands that are given from on High. The distinguishing features of those processes and patterns in their mutual interaction with each other, then constitute what we call history.

Buddhism talks about interdependent origination. This is represented in the six days of creation, which are actually stages strung on a vertical timeline that go through the dimensions—so when the universe comes into being all the different parts are manifested in a total interdependence. The sum totality of the parts of the process of interdependent origination is what we refer to as cosmos. The throne represents cosmos as the absolute order of reality and creation. Once the throne is assumed and the commands are given, then there is something that can be known and there is a process of knowledge. The commands are knowledge, and because of this knowledge, what exists can be distinguished and known. Above all, Cosmic History is a book of knowledge. So the *Book of the Throne* deals with categories, models and ways of knowing as reformulated by the Law of Time.

You could be an ant and you do not know a tree is a tree or a rock is a rock. Maybe ants only distinguish qualities of textures or certain vibrational frequencies they pick up in their antennae. But it seems to be the capacity of the human being to name everything that is distinguished through its sense organs. This is the gift that God gave Adam. The words we use to distinguish our reality have been predesignated—we are only giving consciousness to forms and processes that we did not know about until we gave them names.

In this sense, we can understand the human being as the constituent element in creation— created in the process of four days with the capacity to distinguish and name absolutely everything. Among the human beings, the supreme type is referred to as the *prophet*. The prophet is the one who has been particularly selected by God to perform a specific function at a given moment in time in the unfolding of the creation of the Divine Plan.

In a sense, God confides to the prophet what elements of the message of the Divine Plan that he/she should emphasize. The message is always relevant to a particular point in time in which that prophet has been selected to manifest. This is why it is said in the Sufi tradition that the prophet is the pupil of the eye of God. Through the prophet, God can see. God sends the prophet to test everyone. God sees through the prophet, which is the pupil of His eye functioning in the manifest human realm. God can then see what responses are given to the prophet or messenger.

Through the prophet, God can make His judgment on different beings and evaluate them on this basis. The function of the prophet, ultimately, is to touch as many people as possible within the sphere of reality that he encompasses. In doing so, different laws, teachings and commands are issued through the prophet that are meant to be distributed to all beings. No prophet is really a prophet if his message is less than universal. Even though the prophet may be dead, the messages and teachings of the prophet continue and so God is able to continue to use the prophet as the pupil of His eye to see what is happening in creation.

It is only the humans that enter what we call the "moral universe" because the primordial Adam was given the knowledge of all the names. By that same token, the human is given the capacity and power to rule if s/he so chooses. Because the human has the capacity to rule, s/he enters the moral universe, and either you rule well or you do not.

The point is that the Throne is the first volume of Cosmic History because it is the highest view. The constituent components and nature of reality from a Cosmic History point of view are like a description of the aspects of God's commands synthesized and reformulated by the Law of Time in such a way that they acquire a new relevance for the planetary human at the closing of the cycle and in advance of entering the noosphere. This summarizes the purpose and intention of the first volume.

Volume II: Book of the Avatar: History, the Relative Pole
History, Cosmic Science, and the Descent of the Divine (Spring 2006)

Where there is a throne, there is a higher principle. In the radion cube, the throne is in the upper plane, and the avatar is in the bottom plane. The avatar is the descent of the highest to the lowest plane. If there was not a descent of the highest to the lowest, then the potential for the redemption of all the manifest effects of the original number seven could not occur.

The avatar has to descend to the lowest level and then work up from there. This is why people make distinctions between prophets and avatars—what we are talking about here is the descent of a divine principle, of which the avatar is a divine embodiment. A prophet receives the descent of the divine principle directly from God and then embodies that divine principle. The prophet Muhammad came from a very low origin, as did Jesus. Only when Buddha left his wealthy family, was he able to witness the lowest elements of human suffering. Seeing this caused him to forever depart from his family and the aristocracy associated with them, and spend seven years at the lowest level of existence.

The avatar in this sense represents the necessary descent of the divine into the lowest manifest level of existence, which is the third dimension of the physical plane or the plane of density. The first and second dimensions then become summarized as total third-dimensional density. In this density is where the human being has been placed. It is into that density that the prophets, messengers or avatars have to descend to do their work of testing the human beings to see how well they remember and also to bring through different teachings. The avatar embodies the teachings and in some ways performs a more cosmic or cyclic function than the messengers or the prophets. The avataric emanations of the Closer of the Cycle and the Red Queen are in some ways exemplary in that they have to do with cyclic closure and cyclic regeneration.

The joining together of the avataric emanations for a closing and a regeneration is a particularly profound divine act. In summary, the avatar represents the descent, which represents history. History, as we understand it, is the history of the unfolding of the universe—which is Cosmic History in its purest form. Then there is the history of the Fall or the history of the involution of soul into matter. It is this history that the second volume of the Avatar deals with, inclusive of distinctions between the pure Cosmic History and the reflexes and patterns described by Cosmic Science, as a comprehensive systemization of the functions and processes underlying the new perception of reality. Also elucidated in the *Book of the Avatar*, is the history of the Fall, which ultimately comes down to being the corrupted human history that we have today, as well as the redemption of human history. Such is an overview of the purpose and content of the second volume, the *Book of the Avatar*.

Volume III: Book of the Mystery: Immanence of the Absolute
Art and Aesthetic Perception: Normative Values of the Universal Mind (Spring, 2007)

The ultimate mystery is that God is both transcendent and immanent. Transcendence represents an upward motion—an ascent. Immanence represents a downward or inward motion—downward into the lower planes of existence and inward into the heart of things—so that God becomes immanent, meaning you actually feel God in everything. God the absolute transcendent is the God that remains in Eternity, yet we are talking about One and the same God.

Creation is a manifestation of God's thoughts; therefore, God is inseparable from the different elements of His manifestation. This is how God becomes immanent. In sentient beings, the immanence of God becomes a self-reflective capacity of that being to experience himself or herself as the true self or the higher fifth-dimensional self. So the mystery represents the point in which the absolute transcendent and the relative immanent meet. This meeting point of the absolute transcendent and relatively immanent establishes what is called a "norm."

This norm establishes thoughts like: "Oh, I am just looking at a tree," but on the other hand thoughts like: "Wow, I'm looking at a sign of God." The tree has roots that go into the earth and branches that go into Heaven, this is a metaphor. This is a sign of God that I should be erect like a tree and have my roots in the Earth and branches in the Heavens." Every form partakes of this norm. This is why we speak of the norm referred to as dharma or dharma art—because every form is both just a form and at the same time a sign from God. Dharma is the Sanskrit word for the law or universal norm.

The degree to which you are able to understand or perceive the form as it is, while simultaneously perceiving it as a sign, you are experiencing the norm of the mystery where the absolute and the immanent meet. This is the point where you really contemplate something until suddenly you become illuminated. This illumination means that the immanence of God has become conscious in you, and in becoming conscious that immanence speaks completely of the paradox of the Absolute (having now spoken and reached you through the intrinsic immanence that is in yourself, which responds to the contemplation of a particular form.)

The mystery sees the universe, not necessarily as phenomenal, imaginal or moral, but rather the mystery sees the universe as aesthetic. As we noted, aesthetic in some ways is a branch of the moral universe because you have "good" art and "bad" art—but there is an intrinsic aesthetic. In this sense, the aesthetic is the structure of the Imaginal Universe. The universe, understood as the manifestation of an intrinsic aesthetic is the general broad topic of the third volume, the volume of the Mystery.

According to the seven rays of ceremonial magick, as ascribed by Alice Bailey, the first volume is the divine will, which is what creates the possibility of the throne. The second ray is divine love wisdom. It is the love wisdom of God that sends messengers, prophets and avatars to manifest at the lowest level so they can function as the pupils of His eyes. In this way, a direct report of what is happening in the moral universe can go straight to God.

The third volume is the third ray of divine understanding, intelligence and knowledge, which comes through perceiving the aesthetic quality of forms so that you actually then begin perceiving certain principles and laws of creation. These laws and principles of creation intrinsically conspire to make reality aesthetic, which, being knowable corresponds to a divine knowing or understanding. This is the broad theme of the third volume, the *Book of the Mystery*.

Volume IV: Book of the Initiation: From the Relative to the Absolute
Consciousness and Harmony: Symbolic Structures and Systems of Knowing
(Spring, 2008)

The penetration of the mystery is what is referred to as the initiation. The *Book of the Initiation* deals with the penetration of the mystery as an exertion and elaboration of consciousness, which understands the esoteric, internal or intrinsic nature of things. The Mystery opens you to the aesthetic which, in turn, opens you to the laws and principles that create the aesthetic. The initiation is the penetration of the knowledge and harmony underlying the Mystery.

The initiate is one who knows the mysteries. The mysteries are actually just the coverings of intrinsic harmonic principles at work in the order of the universe. This creates the possibility of consciousness coming into harmony with matter or the phenomenal world. The element of consciousness is placed in the forefront of the fourth volume.

Anyone who is genuinely an initiate is so by virtue of the fact that there has been a recognition of the potential of higher consciousness to be cultivated and developed. Any true initiate who has penetrated the mysteries is a being who has been able to cultivate different states of consciousness and understand the laws of harmony as reflections of different states of consciousness. The initiate sees the interaction of mind and matter, as it were, as establishing different conditions of harmony, which are knowable through different states or conditions of consciousness. The fourth volume, *Book of the Initiation*, explores the process of intuitive penetration and systems of harmonic order that have been perceived within veil after veil of the mystery in which God has clothed the creation.

Robert Fludd, esotericist of the Seventeenth Century, often wrote about the harmony of the mind of nature. His images in esoteric/hermetic artworks have to do with that theme in showing how man is chained to nature and nature is always revealing a truth or a mystery. The ability to take the laws and principles of the harmonic order that underlie the mystery of nature results in a manifestation of timespace, which is the next volume of Cosmic History.

Volume V: Book of the Timespace—Tollan: Earthly Patterns of the Absolute
Cosmic Culture and the Science of Manifestation: The Quest for Heaven on Earth (Spring 2009)

Timespace is the manifestation of, not only the universe, but also the secondary universe that is created by the intelligence of the human type. In other words, the universe itself is the matrix of the timespace. What we are talking about here is the timespace that is manifest by the human intelligence penetrating the laws behind the great natural timespace of nature and then applying them to create what we call "civilizational culture." Civilization, not as an unfolding of a type of cleverness which results in what we have in the world today, but civilization or culture as the creation of the secondary reflex of nature, which is found in the great aesthetic forms: the pyramids, the temple cities and all the other different arts that pertain to that which was created to be a reflection of the cosmic order.

Volume five, *Book of the Timespace*, deals with how the human intelligence manifests the scientific, mathematical and aesthetic principles of the harmonics underlying the great nature to be reflected in a second nature, which is the nature of "civilization." What is the meaning of this? Why do we have to create this reflection of the cosmos in the pyramids, temples and different structures like this? This also has to do with science and with vision—for the perfection of form over time implies a goal or ideal, a state arriving at the template of an eternally existing archetypal order—Tollan. To create the perfect form of a pyramid there has to be science behind it. The fifth volume, in this sense, has to do with the ray of science, but science understood as the application of harmonic principles that underlie the mysteries of nature in such a way that they enhance the known world and also enhance the consciousness of the human beings that inhabit the timespace in the known world. Through this timespace, the human expresses Heaven and Earth. The coming cosmic civilization can only be constructed of such principles.

Volume VI: Book of the Transcendence: Return to the Absolute
Yogic Science and the Universal Religion: Descent and Transcendence of the Absolute (Spring, 2010)

The sixth volume is the *Transcendence*. Where there is manifestation, there is transcendence. Manifestation represents the ultimate evolution of matter and involution of the soul. When we look at the construction of a cosmic city as magnificent as Teotihuacán, it is interesting that everybody left. The city is the shell or cocoon. Whether or not the people left because they could not keep it together anymore, it is certain that life transcended from that place. That is the image or the metaphor of creating the perfect vehicle as a means to go beyond it. Through the process of creating the perfect vehicle, you have learned enough about yourself and about the laws of nature so you realize you have to go to the next stage. Again, we are always dealing with this process of involution and evolution, and also of the descent of the divine and the ascent to the divine.

We are developing a science of transcendence where the ascension is complemented by a descent of divine consciousness. In the sixth volume, *Book of the Transcendence*, we are at the stage of beginning to realize this. This was also the work of Sri Aurobindo and the Mother. As we purify ourselves so that our souls can grow, then we are also evoking a further descent of the divine—divine power and divine order—this is the meaning of the Mystery of the Stone and the waking up of the Bolontiku. The Bolontiku represent the descent of the divine order to meet our willingness to simplify our lives and let our souls ascend.

This is what Aurobindo and the Mother talked about, but the Law of Time has made it an actual psychomythic process that can be engaged in on a planetary scale. A spiritual miracle will occur as a result of this. We see that the *Book of the Transcendence* has to do with the understanding of the involution and evolution of spirit in matter and the techniques for furthering the ascent—both the ascent of the spirit of the soul and the universal descent of the divine. This deals with mystical perceptions or yoga, which is the whole aim of there being a divine union or a return to the One.

The whole theme of the sixth ray is devotion. But devotion understood not as it was described in Alice Bailey's description of the historical cycle of idealism. Because of the lack of evolution of the human knowledge of the ego of the soul and spirit, idealism turns into fanaticism or sectarianism. Devotion defined by Cosmic History recognizes UR—Universal Recollection and the return to the One. All devotion is shared equally and is understood as being necessary to attain the final divine reunion with God, which is the meaning of yoga. This is why at one level there is a welcoming and necessary study and participation of different spiritual forms, so you can understand how to unify them all.

Ultimately, the main theme of the *Book of the Transcendence* is UR or the return to the Universal Religion or Universal Recollection, which is actually a condition that is only possible because Cosmic History is shedding self-reflective light on this entire process without being biased or in favor of anything. Cosmic History merely presents the whole process so the human (which is really Adam with many bodies) can become reunited. This represents a stage that has not been experienced before in this particular dimensional sector of the universe. Adam became fragmented, but through Cosmic History Adam will become reunified. This is the theme of the sixth volume.

Volume VII: Book of the Cube: Synthesis of the Relative and the Absolute Synchronic Order and the Cube of Creation: Evolution into the Noosphere (Spring, 2011)

Once there is a transcendence then can come an understanding of the return to the origin. In the story of creation, the cube represents the divine origin. The first stage of creation creates the top of the cube, the second stage of creation creates the bottom of the cube, the third stage of creation creates the front of the cube, the fourth stage of creation, creates the back of the cube, the fifth stage of creation creates the right side of the cube and the sixth stage of creation creates the left side of the cube.

You can see then when you look at creation in this way that the first two stages create the top Heaven and the bottom Earth. Life is what happens between Heaven and Earth. The front and back create the primary orientation of spirit (forward and behind) and the right and left create will, the capacity to create or evolve. In this sense, the cube represents the six stages of creation. The center of the cube is where the throne is actually located. When we have this realization, then we can understand that the cube is the final complete composite compilation of all number, measure and purpose of all forms, structures and proportions in the universe. Knowing this, we can assimilate all knowledge back into ourselves and perform ceremonial magick. With this magick, we invoke the primal cube of creation; the cube is the synthesis of creation necessary for the advent of the noosphere.

Ultimately, the cube summarizes the synthesis of divine creation science. Pacal Votan had a cube in his right hand and a sphere in his left. The sphere in his left hand was the unborn ultimate sphere, which is the Absolute of God, and the cube held in his right hand represents the immanent God in the manifestation of creation. When we understand these two points of the sphere and the cube, then we can understand the principles of divine science. When we understand the principles of divine science, then we can perform ceremonial magick.

The ceremonial magick that we perform *is* the Second Creation. The last two rings (2011-2012, 2012-2013) are the allotted time to perform the highest acts of ceremonial magick on behalf of the Second Creation. We will astonish ourselves! At this time, we will evoke the guardianship of the final two Bolontiku, the galactic free agents who represent the guardians protecting the universe from its destruction and protecting the lamps that adorn the lowest heaven, where we currently reside. *The Book of the Cube* will help make all this manifest while returning us to the original matrix of creation. The *Cosmic History Chronicles* will be complete. In closing, the cycle will regenerate itself.

Glossary of Key Terms

AA Midway Station—Arcturus/Antares Midway station, located interdimensionally above the planetary midpoint between Jupiter and Maldek (Asteroid Belt). Also known as "the Mother Ship" the AA Midway station is the location of the particular unit of the Galactic Federation assigned to monitoring the star system Velatropa 24.3, scene of the final dramas of the Free Will experiment.

AC Aboriginal Continuity—Refers to one of two psychogenetic strands animating evolutionary intelligence. AC is primary and establishes the total motif and pattern for both the secondary CA (Cosmic Awareness) strand as well as the composite of the two strands together.

Astral Movies—Fourth-dimensional "video" or script to which third-dimensional life is meant to correspond.

Belief System—The configuration of consciousness which predisposes the entity who holds to this configuration its corresponding model or structure of reality.

Biogenic Migration of Atoms—Refers to the tendency of all cellular organic, molecular structures within the biosphere to undergo virtually infinite numbers of transformations, accounting for evolutionary mutations, as well as every day transformations of organic matter such as occurs through the digestive process.

Biology—Refers to the science or the study of life understood as an interval in a sequence of cosmic evolutionary possibilities.

Biosphere-Noosphere Transition—Stage of climax of cycle of historical materialism, characterized by biospheric crisis engendering quantum evolutionary shift into the noosphere.

CA Civilizational Advance/Cosmic Awareness—Refers to the secondary strand of the psychogenetic circuit of evolutionary intelligence; in its historic dynamic also referred to as Civilizational Advance, because it refers to a tendency for decision making based on acquired intelligence, rather than on innate (AC) intelligence; as Cosmic Awareness, this strand refers to the evolution of consciousness.

Chakra—Resonant points of internal stimulus where the seven radial plasmas are stored and activated. Primary structures for the activation of the holon or etheric body.

Closing of the Cycle—Final 26-year event—horizon of the Mayan Great Cycle culminating Gregorian December 21, 2012; congruent with biosphere-noosphere transition.

Continuing Consciousness—Stage of conscious awareness beyond "normal" everyday consciousness, which is absolutely discontinuous. Object of practices of the Law of Time and study of Cosmic History.

Cosmic History—Core of the universal field of intelligence. Template or superior overlay of a comprehensive understanding intended to replace the entire world construct as it exists today. Comprehensively creative interaction of Absolute (cosmos) and relative (history).

Cosmosis—Analogous to osmosis, refers to the process of the absorption of cosmic energy and information through the membranes of advanced life forms for the production of higher states of mind and forms of energy.

Cosmotic—Refers to capacity for cosmosis, characterizing advanced life operating at supermental hyperorganic consciousness.

Cybersphere—The intermediate global information sheathe between the technosphere and the noosphere. Consists of Internet, television and other global electronic information technologies. Last evolutionary stop before universal telepathy.

Cycle of Becoming—This refers to the great stage of the involution of the soul into matter.

Cycle of Return—This refers to the great stage of the evolution of the soul out of matter. With the Cycle of Becoming, defines the basis of the philosophy of Cosmic History.

Dharma—Law, truth, what the Buddha taught, the essence of any action or purpose; also Universal Law.

Dharma Art—"Art as Everyday Life." Based on principle of dharma, understood as the universal norm, law or principle by which everything conforms to its own intrinsic aesthetic, abiding by Law of Time $T(E) = Art$. Means that anything and everything that you do has the potential for being elegant.

Dharmakaya—Body of truth, object of Buddhist enlightenment practice, forms highest of triple body teaching or trikaya (the other two bodies are the samboghakaya—body of radiance or communication—and nirmanakaya—body of transformation, the actual physical body you take on at birth.

Glossary of Key Terms

Earth Wizard—Evolved human type operating with noospheric consciousness, living according to program and codes of fourth-dimensional synchronic order, actively involved in establishing telepathic fields of resonance and exploration, sustained by elementary self-sustaining garden economy and advanced forms of super efficient nonpolluting technologies.

Etheric Body—The subtle body or the light body, also called the holon, which is within the dense body. Vehicle for soul evolution beyond the physical plane.

Fifth Dimension—Realm of pure electronic entities; abode of "guardian angels," "guiding spirits;" realm of hierarchy and place where higher commands are sorted out and stepped down into fourth and third-dimensional functions.

Fifth Force—Dynamic of time as the agent of synchronization, which actually unifies the other four forces, the strong, the weak, the electromagnetic and the gravitational.

Fifth Force Oracle—Refers to the five-part dynamic that mathematically characterizes any of the 260 kin, which constitute the fourth-dimensional 13:20 timing matrix; also an analog intelligence to the fifth force coordination of the four physical forces.

Food Sheathe—Refers to the physical/biological body, which is the vehicle of consciousness, but must be maintained by some type of continuous organic input called food, hence food sheathe.

Fourth Dimension—One of two accompanying dimensions of life; the etheric dimension where dreams and the imaginal realm occur.

Galactic Meditation—System of meditation based on classic techniques of Zen and Dzogchen, used as a means to deepen comprehension of the synchronic order as the manifestation of galactic mind.

Galactic Synchronization—Refers to precise date Yellow Galactic Seed (July 26, 2013) which defines the great evolutionary shift point—the entrance into the New Solar Age or Psychozoic Era.

Geomancy—Literally "Earth divination." From the Cosmic History perspective, defines a branch of Cosmic Science that understands the planet body as a living organism and hence, articulates its various "sense organs" for better cosmic operation.

GM108X—Refers to a coded Galactic Mayan system of higher mind transmission specifically channeled to our star system from Arcturus and principally transmitted through the lineage of the Votans.

God—Supreme originating intelligence, simultaneously absolutely transcendent and relatively immanent; inseparable from all pervading awareness.

Haaq—Quranic expression for the truth or Absolute reality, corresponding somewhat to the Buddhist dharmakaya.

Hadith—Any secondary commentary to a primary text. In Islamic tradition, Hadith refers to the tradition based, not on the Quran, but on the commentaries of the sayings of Muhammad.

Harrowing of Hell—Refers to a four-year cycle between the conclusion of seven years of prophecy and commencement of seven years of Mystery of the Stone, AD 2000-04, where the seven years of prophecy are the descent into Hell and the seven years of the Mystery of the Stone are the ascent into the resurrection.

Holonomic Equation—Within the law of whole systems, the description of the balancing of energy and information, such that, in the end, prehistoric equals or balances post historic.

Hyperorganic Consciousness—Stage of development of consciousness, which represents the preliminary phase of extending beyond bodily form, in which, through highly developed telepathic capacities, feedback to the natural world is sent through the sense organs in etheric fibers that become the basis of the creations of new forms of nature referred to as hyperorganic.

Hybrid Human—Another term for the planetary human and refers to the species "homo sapiens" during the final generations of the entire 26,000 years cycle and in which the human type is no longer bound by any particular culture, tradition or creed and hence is a hybrid of often superfluous beliefs.

Integral Yoga—Yoga that assumes whole body, whole system integration within its own context and with the larger macro environment, both of the terrestrial nature and the cosmos. Basis of Cosmic History foundation practices. Term first coined by Sri Aurobindo, and also utilized by Swami Satchinanda.

Intelligence—The quality of consciousness that is always evolving toward a higher purpose.

Jnana Yoga—Yoga of knowledge or wisdom. Unification with the divine through exercise of higher reason, logic, analytical and analogical thought, discriminating truth from falsehood.

Glossary of Key Terms

Law of Karma—Law of cause and effect–for every action there is a reaction, applies to thought, word and deed–in the human realm, comprehension of this law is mandatory basis of moral/spiritual awakening.

Law of Time—$T(E) = Art$, energy factored by time equals art, where T equals 13:20 frequency constant, energy equals any manifest phenomenal plane form process and art is the resultant effect which harmonically establishes the world of appearances. Secondary principle: The velocity of time is instantaneously infinite, establishing time as the medium of telepathy.

Life—A secondary cosmic phenomenon representing the realm of possibilities between the crystal realm and the hyperorganic realms of pure consciousness.

Maldek—Fifth planet from the sun destroyed by supernatural events involving planets Jupiter and Saturn in remote past. Its destruction resulted in the formation of the Asteroid Belt discovered on January 1, 1801 (White Rhythmic Mirror). Basis of interplanetary psychocosmology, otherwise known as the "Fall of Man."

Matrix—Refers to the resultant stage of information process which establishes feedback loop with projecting entity. Also defines the entire web of the collective hallucination of the technosphere.

Mind—Nonlocateable universal medium of intelligence; capacitator of the various thinking layers.

Moral/Imaginal/Phenomenal—Refers to the triple universe model, which is the reality that we are programmed to go through, which includes simultaneous sensory phenomenal input, imaginal perceptual interpretation and some level of moral decision-making.

Morphogenetic Field—These define the telepathic sub fields of a given species as well as sub fields evolved by higher species, which correspond to different aspects of the evolutionary cycle; any telepathic field established by either some or all the members of any group or different complexes of groups or a whole planetary aggregate.

Mystery of the Stone—Second great cycle of the Telektonon prophecy of Pacal Votan, AD 2004-2011. Time of the perfection of the human soul, resurrection and the awakening of the Seven Lords of the Ring, first seven of the nine Bolontiku, also known as Middle Time, the bridge between the dying 12:60 world and the dawning 13:20 Heaven on Earth.

Noosphere—Earth's mental envelope or thinking layer. Storage and regulation unit of the sum of mental interactions past, present, and future of all terrestrial life, both in the phenomenal and imaginal realms. Next stage of human evolution, scene of supermental activation and supramental descent.

Pacal Votan—Chief galactic Mayan agent self-produced from his samadhi GM108X to incarnate during 80-year cycle AD 603-683 at Nah Chan (Palenque), first 28 years preparation for the 52-year cycle of power 631-683, during which time all of the galactic codes of time and prophecy were synchronized for the advent of UR in 2012.

Planetary Human—Refers to final stage of homo sapiens as a global techno-cultural hybrid characterized by machine dependency, confused moral standards and primitively dawning global consciousness; prerequisite entity to be redeemed by Cosmic History.

Planet Holon—Refers to the etheric structure of the planet as defined by the 20 solar seals that code the cosmic timing frequency; so structured in their super imposition over the planet body as to recreate the sequences of the five Earth families; knowledge of the planet holon is indispensable for the Cosmic Science of geomancy and advanced practices of the synchronic order.

Planetary Logos—The guiding interdimensional intelligence core of the noosphere, located within the octahedral iron crystal core within the center of the Earth.

Planeto-Cosmic—Term which refers to principal that within the whole planetary system is also contained the entire system of cosmic order, giving rise to new evolutionary synthesis of spiritual and mental aspirations.

Planetophysical—Refers to the entire realm of matter, organic and inorganic, which constitutes a sum total and which is hence governed by unitive and unifying principles.

Planetopsychical—Composite of all prophetic streams functioning as a layer of consciousness in collective human psyche

Plasmas—Reference points for telepathic knowing, all pervading primary energy resonances of cosmic electricity.

Psi Bank Regulator—Control panel or "nervous system" of the noosphere. Located between the two Van Allen radiation belts, the psi bank is instrumented to the fourth-dimensional timing factor, which regulates the DNA. Psi bank serves as a 2080-unit filing cabinet where all registrations of fourth-dimensional time are deposited.

Glossary of Key Terms

Psychogenetic Feedback Loop—Refers to the self-fulfilling environment of consciousness established by an entity for its fundamental survival needs.

Quantinomio Citobarico—The primary organizing and coordinating structure of cosmic reality understood as a transformer of electroplasmic energy; literally the index of pressure felt by a molecule or a cell; also structurally identified as a primary form of the resonant field model and indistinguishable from chakra structure (micro) or galactic generator (macro).

Second Creation—Refers to multiple levels of fulfillment of cosmic historical codes, including the Mystery of the Stone, that occur at the Closing of the Cycle and which are a function of the fulfillment of the Law of Time. Corresponds to traditional prophecies found in the biblical and Quranic texts.

Seven Years of Prophecy—First cycle of the Telektonon of Pacal Votan, AD 1993-2000. Time of the spread of the 13 Moon, 28-day calendar as the instrument of the Second Creation.

Siddha—One who attains the power of the siddhis.

Siddhis—Refers to the paranormal powers developed by yogis and high avataric beings, such as Christ, which display capacities that transcend the normal laws governing the physical plane reality.

Sorcerer's Whole Body Perception—Refers to the capacity to experience the whole of reality through consciously integrated sense fields, resulting from highly focused yogic/meditative techniques. Necessary multisensory faculty for comprehending and being further evolved by Cosmic History.

Soul—That upon which Divine Command, along with Moral Universe life experiences, is inscribed; carrier of consciousness, migratory life component; holder of Form Essence.

Sunna—In Islam, Sunna, histories of the prophet, is related to the tradition of the Hadith, resulting in an elaborate system of highly restrictive laws not necessarily implied or contained in the primary text of the Quran, and which became the basis of historic Islamic society.

Superconsciousness—Refers to the evolved state of mind and consciousness, which is characterized by a telepathic omniscience and omnidirectionality.

Supermental—Next stage of evolution (noosphere) transcending primitive current dualistic and separatist "mind."

Supramental Evolution—Refers to the stage of evolution when consciousness is no longer dependent on mind, understood as a consciousness feature needing a physical plane host body. Also principle of descent of divine revelatory information.

Supraphysical—Refers to extraordinary physical prowess beyond natural capacity, which can only be explained by mind operating according to "paranormal laws."

Suprasensible—Refers to paranormal or telepathic levels of sensitivity. For example, Votan had a suprasensible experience when he first looked at photo of the Face on Mars.

Synchronic Order—Refers to operating of fourth-dimensional realm of reality, knowable through 13:20 codes of the Law of Time.

Technosphere—Earth's artificial industrial/technological sheathe that negates natural time and higher consciousness. Global sphere of an artificial construct based on machine consciousness and marketing gimmicks.

Thirteenth Baktun—This is the final Baktun—sequence of 144,000 days—concluding the Great Cycle of the Mayan calendar, the duration of which is from 1618 to 2012. This Baktun represents the peak of historical materialism and is defined as the Baktun of the Transformation of Matter. The exponential acceleration of matter and human biomass during the final 26 years of this cycle induces the biosphere-noosphere transition and the descent of Cosmic History.

13:20—Refers to natural universal frequency of synchronization, basis of the Law of Time. As a mathematical ratio based on 13 galactic tones of creation and 20 solar frequencies, the universal frequency of synchronization is a harmonic constant and, activating through its application of the 13 Moon/28 day calendar, is the basis of the reformulation of the human mind.

12:60—Refers to artificial timing frequency based on the combination of an irregular 12 month Gregorian calendar and mechanistic 60 minute, 60 second clock. Creates unconscious programs resulting in present day world construct, which Cosmic History is intended to erase and replace.

28:7 Code—Refers to the 64 units of the Harmonic Module/Tzolkin grid between the third through the sixth and the eighth through eleventh columns and between the Hand code seven and Wizard code 14. This central grid consists of many symbolic overlays, but is referred to as 28:7 because of its structural formulation of the 28 GAPs, which constitute seven occult quartets, each quartet having a total sum of 28, hence 28:7; this also refers to a type of mathematical cosmology which is the basis of, among other things, the DNA and the Telektonon grid.

Glossary of Key Terms

Tzolkin—Literally sacred count. The Mayan 260-day cycle which also establishes a base matrix 13:20, the fourth-dimensional 13:20 frequency standard.

Wave Harmonic of History—This refers to the cycle of thirteen baktuns in their holonomic identity with the 13:20 matrix or Harmonic Module, demonstrating that what we think of as human history is actually the function of a higher dimensional harmonic imprint, which has a finite radius in time BC 3113-AD 2012.

Yoga—Practice, art and science of unification of self and of self and divine reality. Basis of Cosmic History as knowledge and as reformulation of the human mind.

Yogi, Yogini (female)—A mystical transcendentalist who practices life as a process of unification with the divine. Basis of normal human type in age of the noosphere.

www.ingramcontent.com/pod-product-compliance
Lightning Source LLC
Chambersburg PA
CBHW060509300426
44112CB00017B/2599